Accidental Pluralism

American Beginnings, 1500–1900

A Series Edited by Edward Gray, Emma Hart, Stephen Mihm, and Mark Peterson

ALSO IN THE SERIES:

The Province of Affliction: Illness and the Making of Early New England
BY BEN MUTSCHLER

Puritan Spirits in the Abolitionist Imagination
BY KENYON GRADERT

Trading Spaces: The Colonial Marketplace and the Foundations of American Capitalism
BY EMMA HART

Urban Dreams, Rural Commonwealth: The Rise of Plantation Society in the Chesapeake
BY PAUL MUSSELWHITE

Building a Revolutionary State: The Legal Transformation of New York, 1776–1783
BY HOWARD PASHMAN

Sovereign of the Market: The Money Question in Early America
BY JEFFREY SKLANSKY

National Duties: Custom Houses and the Making of the American State
BY GAUTHAM RAO

Series titles continue following the index

Accidental Pluralism

AMERICA AND THE RELIGIOUS POLITICS OF ENGLISH EXPANSION, 1497–1662

Evan Haefeli

THE UNIVERSITY OF CHICAGO PRESS
CHICAGO AND LONDON

The University of Chicago Press, Chicago 60637
The University of Chicago Press, Ltd., London

Published 2021
Printed in the United States of America

30 29 28 27 26 25 24 23 22 21   1 2 3 4 5

ISBN-13: 978-0-226-74261-8 (cloth)
ISBN-13: 978-0-226-74275-5 (e-book)
DOI: https://doi.org/10.7208/chicago/9780226742755.001.0001

Library of Congress Cataloging-in-Publication Data

Names: Haefeli, Evan, 1969– author.
Title: Accidental pluralism : America and the religious politics of English expansion, 1497–1662 / Evan Haefeli.
Other titles: American beginnings, 1500–1900.
Description: Chicago : The University of Chicago Press, 2021. | Series: American beginnings, 1500–1900 | Includes bibliographical references and index.
Identifiers: LCCN 2020024371 | ISBN 9780226742618 (cloth) | ISBN 9780226742755 (ebook)
Subjects: LCSH: Religious pluralism—United States—History. | Religious tolerance—United States—History. | United States—Religion—History. | Great Britain—Colonies—America—Religion—History. | United States—History—Colonial period, ca. 1600–1775.
Classification: LCC BL2525 .H335 2020 | DDC 323.44/2097309032—dc23
LC record available at https://lccn.loc.gov/2020024371

♾ This paper meets the requirements of ANSI/NISO Z39.48-1992 Permanence of Paper).

Für Eva Lanz
die mir gezeigt hat,
wie man einen Gipfel erklimmt

Contents

Introduction · 1

PART 1
Tudor-Stuart Foundations, 1497–ca. 1607

1. Colonization: Religion, Expansion, Guiana, and Slavery · 17

2. Conformity: Religious Change, Obedience, and Virginia · 38

3. Jurisdiction: Ireland, Scotland, and the Limits of Authority · 60

4. Dissent: English Papists, Puritans, and Others · 77

PART 2
Jacobean Balance, ca. 1607–1625

5. Balance: Virginia, Bermuda, Newfoundland, ca. 1607–1618 · 99

6. Polarization: Plymouth, Avalon, Nova Scotia, New England, 1618–1625 · 117

PART 3
Caroline Transformation, 1625–1638

7. Favorites: Saint Christopher, Barbados, Maryland, 1624–1632 · 141

8. Puritans: New England, Providence Island, the Leewards, 1629–1638 · 161

9. Catholics: Montserrat, New Albion, Maryland, 1632–1638 · 180

PART 4
Civil Wars, 1638–1649

10. Fragmentation: Rhode Island, Madras, Trinidad, 1638–1643 · 201

11. Toleration: New England, Bermuda, Madagascar, 1643–1646 · 221

12. Revolution: New England, the Bahamas, Barbados, the Leewards, 1647–1649 · 242

PART 5
Commonwealth, 1649–1660

13. Republic: New England, the Caribbean, Acadia, 1649–1654 · 265

14. Empire: Surinam, Barbados, Jamaica, Dunkirk, 1654–1660 · 284

Conclusion · 304

Acknowledgments · 313 *Abbreviations* · 317

Note on Transcriptions, Dates, Sources, and Terminology · 321

Notes · 323 *Index* · 367

INTRODUCTION

American religious freedom—that peculiar mix of pluralism, tolerance, and liberty—is widely deemed to be an essential characteristic of its nationhood, one of the valuable treasures the United States of America can export to the world. Unfortunately, the question of how it emerged in the first place is rarely asked. Nor has it been effectively answered. Religious freedom is so closely identified with the existence of the United States that Americans have difficulty seeing it as anything other than inevitable. Treating it more as an accomplishment to be celebrated than as a problem in need of explanation, as something intrinsic to the American experience that sets it apart from Europe, is a habit that dates back to the outbreak of the American Revolution. Thomas Paine, in the midst of his electrifying argument for independence, *Common Sense*, gave it a providential gloss by pointing out that the "reformation was preceded by the discovery of America as if the Almighty graciously meant to open a sanctuary to the persecuted in future years, when home should afford neither friendship nor safety." This recent English immigrant's sense of America's religious destiny has proven irresistible.[1]

Ever since, the idea that the colonies began as a religious haven has served as a cornerstone of American national identity. Seven years later, as the Peace of Paris that secured the independence of the United States was being signed, Ezra Stiles, a Congregational minister and president of Yale College, celebrated "American ideas of toleration and religious liberty" in a sermon praising the new nation. He predicted its ideals "will become the fashionable system of Europe very soon." America's special religious arrangements were deliberate, the manifestation of "wisdom and enlightened politics." Looking to the future, Stiles anticipated that the

"United States will embosom all the religious sects and denominations in Christendom." Of course, Stiles only welcomed this pluralism because he was certain that Protestants like him would dominate it, as they did for the next two centuries thanks in part to the efforts of Yale graduates who, soon after Stiles gave his sermon, began fanning out as missionaries across the new nation.[2]

Lately, scholars working on the more modern manifestations of American religious freedom have become less celebratory. They point out that within the United States and abroad, American ideals of pluralism and religious liberty have generally served to strengthen Protestant hegemony in a world becoming ever less Protestant. The current insistence that America began as a "Christian Nation" is only the latest effort to shore up that hegemony. These debates remind us that religious freedom has always had a political dimension. Never a neutral category, it has always been tied to a particular religious context that tends to favor some groups over others. To treat it as the natural or ineluctable culmination of colonial American history grossly oversimplifies a far more interesting story and undercuts our ability to explain it.[3]

The tendency of early American historians to emphasize the end result of religious freedom over the uncertain path that led there impedes our understanding of this crucial aspect of American society. The botanical metaphors of growth they habitually deploy effectively marginalize conflicts and contradictory trends like conformity, unity, and establishment. Those were not only the original religious goals of English colonization; they remain issues that can help address some of the concerns raised by scholars of modern American religion and politics. While there are a number of good accounts of religious conditions on the ground in the various colonies that eventually became the United States, we still do not have a good account of the bigger picture. We remain trapped in the religious nationalism of the revolutionary generation, approaching colonial American religious history through the anachronistic framework of the future United States. This is not an effective framework for historical analysis: it only encourages us to trace the evolution of religious pluralism from a seventeenth-century seed to a revolutionary era blossoming as if it were an almost natural process. Reading back the nation into the colonies just sets us up to anticipate what will come. Obscuring the early modern English origins of our religious arrangements deprives us of the ability to critically account for them.[4]

As anyone who has ever taught early American history can confirm, Americans *expect* their country to be pluralistic. Historians bear some responsibility for creating this expectation by regarding it as a foregone conclusion. Instead of wondering how or why religious freedom was possible, they have engaged in a competition for pride of place, arguing over when or where it first appeared. They point to the influence of a special colonist, like Roger Williams; to a particular denomination, like the Baptists; to a specific colony, like Maryland. One has even claimed that America's "*cradle of religious liberty was first rocked upon the barren shores of Newfoundland in 1627*" (his emphasis), because of the Avalon colony founded there by Lord Baltimore before he founded Maryland. This fight to be the true seed of American religious freedom ignores the fact that there were many different seeds, not all of them designed to produce the same plant—and none of them destined to be the sole source of what was, in the end, a jumbled, unintended hodgepodge.[5]

The examples of individual colonies are an important part of the origin story of American religious freedom. However, no single colony can explain the whole. The emergence of religious pluralism, toleration, and liberty in early America cannot be traced to any single actor or idea. It was the fraught result of a contested political process. The story of each colony has constitutional significance because they became the states that became the building blocks of the constitutional order of the United States. Ultimately, the variety of different religious arrangements within the thirteen colonies that declared independence in 1776 ensured the United States would not—could not—have a national religious establishment. Explaining the origins and character of the religious arrangements in the various colonies is thus crucial to American religious as well as constitutional history. It is, indeed, the primary purpose of this book, regarding the colonies created before 1660.

However, we need to do more than recount a series of local histories. Scholarship on early America is hampered by the habit of thinking about religion in small pieces. We have studies of individual religious groups, like Quakers, or a single region, like New England, but we lack a bigger account of how those pieces fit together. As Carla Pestana has pointed out in her survey of religion in the British Atlantic, it is a "story that has not been told except in fragments." British historians are as much to blame for this as American historians, for they have yet to develop a religious history of the first British Empire that we could draw on. Confusing the religious history of their empire with the Anglican Church, or assuming imperial religion is about missionary efforts to non-British peoples rather than the religious lives of the people inhabiting the empire, they generally skip over the complex period before 1660 and marginalize the role of the many non-Anglican groups that also played an active role in colonial expansion. These so-called Dissenters are treated more as annoyances to imperial religious life than partners in its creation. This approach is worse than anachronistic. It is partisan, for it adopts the polemical arguments of eighteenth-century Anglicans as historical analysis. Especially in the era of the American Revolution, those Anglicans insisted that they alone were the true imperial religion. Wittingly or not, this attitude preemptively writes the religious diversity of the thirteen North American colonies out of the British Imperial picture—just as Thomas Paine did.[6]

Alas, colonial America cannot take credit for its religious pluralism alone. It was, in fact, very much the legacy of its membership within that emerging empire, as the story that follows demonstrates. However, to see the bigger picture, to tell an overarching narrative, to devise an interpretive framework capable of accounting for the whole and not just some of its parts, we need to step out of the realms of both colonial American and imperial history and return to early America's primarily (but never exclusively) English origins. It is there, not within the boundaries of the future United States, that we can find not only the fundamental context but also the key causes of the peculiar religious arrangements in the colonies. This approach is especially relevant for the years before 1660, when the majority of adult colonists had been born and raised in England. Although resident in New England or the Chesapeake, England remained their primary frame of reference and crucial point of contact. Crossing the seas created physical distance, but not a separate identity or even a distinct history. Far from isolated, colonists remained in close contact with English developments. Regular voyages across the Atlantic kept them in touch with a time lag of a few months at most. Trips from England to the Americas varied from the approximately five weeks it took to get to Newfoundland, to the seven and a half weeks to New England, the eight weeks to the Caribbean, and the eleven and a half weeks to the Chesapeake, but, with trips back to England generally taking even less time, any colonist could participate in multiple round trip voyages in a year.[7]

Understanding the complex web of early modern England's connection to colonial America is essential, but it is not enough. We need to situate the origins of American religious pluralism within an even wider context: the English world. I use the term as convenient shorthand for the jumble of different jurisdictions stretching from the Low Countries to America and India that shared a common political subordination to the government seated on the banks of the Thames River at Westminster. In the early seventeenth century, that world included the three kingdoms of England,

Ireland, and Scotland; their dependencies, such as the Isle of Man and the Channel Islands; and a growing number of overseas conquests and colonies. English people made up a majority of its population, but it also contained Welsh, Irish, Scots, French-speaking Channel Islanders, the occasional Huguenot and other European immigrants and, by the mid-seventeenth century, a growing number of Native Americans, Indians, Africans, and Jews. "English world" is not meant to diminish this diversity or exalt a particular ethnic affiliation or outcome. It simply highlights their common political and religious ties. England was dominant, but it was never the sole nor the exclusive reference point for those who lived under its authority.

I have turned to this framework of an English world after several decades of sorting through the historiographical trends of early American and early modern European history. At both ends, the tendency has been to push England and colonial America further and further apart. On the English side, the writing of early modern history has been buffeted since the 1970s by a dizzying series of historiographical transformations from revisionism to postrevisionism and beyond that have rendered it increasingly difficult to connect English history to the colonial context, partly because the historical analysis has gotten so complex, but mostly because these scholars have largely neglected the periphery to focus on the English core. Imperial history pays more attention to the colonies, but tends to treat them as a distinct sphere of action—socially, culturally, and politically distinct from the English center. As such it has little to offer the period before the eighteenth century, when the connection between the colonies and the center was often quite direct and intimate. The new endeavors of "British" and "Archipelagic history" have rightly corrected the revisionist tendency to focus on England alone by drawing attention to the relations between the "three kingdoms" of England, Ireland, and Scotland. Other historians have with equal justice emphasized the importance of connections to Europe. Still, these trends also marginalize the colonies.

The priority on the European side has been to resituate England within European history. Colonial historians have returned the favor by developing historical models rooted in various American geographies that marginalize Europe: the Atlantic world, North America, or #VastEarlyAmerica. Privileging inter-American entanglements, they emphasize connections across and between the empires, colonies, and peoples of the Americas while neglecting their European context. There are a few exceptions, chiefly in scholarship on puritanism or Roman Catholicism in Maryland, which are closely attuned to their transatlantic English context. However, these are self-consciously partial histories working within individual strands of scholarship. They suggest paths for reconnecting colonial America to its English context but only within the segmented structure of early American historiography. Concentrating primarily on one religious group or one region, they do not challenge the traditional model of the colonies as religious refuges from England but rather encourage it by focusing on the exceptional cases.

My approach defies the underlying tendency of these historiographical trends to take in a bigger picture that sees the Anglo-American colonies not as alternatives or exceptions to the religious dynamics of the English world but merely variants along the broad spectrum within it. The emergence of colonial religious pluralism was not a distinctively American process but rather symptomatic of the colonies' participation in the religious struggles of the English world. Although they rarely touch on the colonies, the rich early modern English historiographies on religious change and state building offer an effective new path forward. This study has benefitted from the combination of work on high politics and local context. Usually, these topics are treated separately, but especially in the early colonial context both are essential. Revisionist historians of high court politics have portrayed the central government as weak, ineffectual, and overwhelmed by the challenge of balancing the many different jurisdictions—especially the three kingdoms of England, Scotland, and Ireland. Meanwhile, scholars working at the community level have shown that the enforcement of social and religious norms could be remarkably severe and effective. The formation of the early modern English state now looks like both a top-down and bottom-up process. It is a model into which the colonies can easily be included. Colonial American community studies support the findings of English local studies about the tremendous power of local elites, but those elites only had that power thanks to the colonial grants bestowed on them by the central government (in these years usually, but not always, the monarchy). The patronage of that central authority was crucial in determining who got to be in charge of colonies, even if the whims of local elites largely determined how that authority was carried out. Far from exceptional, the colonies are a quintessential manifestation of this dynamic of early modern English state building.[8]

The unstable outcome of that state building process has great significance for early American history, for in the end American religious pluralism owes more to the decline of religious unity within England than to the rise of religious tolerance in the colonies. Since it is difficult to avoid using terms like tolerance and toleration when discussing the coexistence of different religions in the early modern English world, some clarity about my use of these terms is in order. Scholars often seek to distinguish between personal attitudes and official policies by characterizing personal attitudes in terms of "tolerance" (or horizontal tolerance) and official policies in terms of "toleration" (or vertical tolerance). At both these levels, tolerance can be directed at those with whom one disagrees but who nevertheless share the same religion and/or church membership; or it can be directed at those who do not share one's religion and/or church membership. Historically these have been treated as distinct spheres of action. Early modern Europeans labeled the tolerance of one's fellow worshippers *concordia*. Scholars sometimes refer to it as ecclesiastical tolerance—that which happens within a single church or religious community. The tolerance of outsiders, what scholars sometimes call civil tolerance, early modern Europeans labeled *tolerantia*. *Concordia* and *tolerantia* generally precluded each other. The more latitude granted to individuals within one's group, the less patience for people to remain outside of it. Correspondingly, stricter criteria for internal membership often facilitated the acceptance of differences outside the community. In practice, it could and can be difficult to keep these distinctions clear. They overlapped, intersected, and coexisted. More importantly, even for the most indulgent early modern European humanists, tolerance was almost always seen as a recipe for an eventual religious unity. Few people imagined or advocated it as a permanent or desirable condition, never mind a universal value that should be applied equally to all.[9]

Closer attention to these contemporary attitudes demonstrates that religious freedom was not originally part of the plan for America. Instead, colonies were granted with the express purpose of extending the religious establishment of England overseas, not least by converting the Indigenous peoples who came under their authority. Religious unity was the proclaimed goal and the law. Virtually no colonial entrepreneur before the upheavals of the 1640s endorsed religious diversity, which was almost always discussed in the negative. That religious unity was not, in the end, colonial America's fate is the story recounted in this book. It demonstrates the many ways domestic English religious politics intruded into colonization by tracing all of the colonies established, attempted, or even contemplated between 1497, when England first made formal contact with the Americas, and 1662, when the foundations of the modern Anglican Church were established. There was, it turns out, no single, decisive, moment, idea, place, or person. Instead, several often competing and contradictory influences produced a result that was unforeseen and unwanted by most contemporaries. The "accidental" in this book title is the most concise way I have found to convey this complex dynamic.

As for pluralism, I use it here as shorthand to describe situations where more than one religion coexisted within the same political space, albeit often on unequal terms. My use of pluralism does not mean to imply it was or is an ideal, although I recognize that the word has of late taken on that quality for many, who consider it something one does, "a commitment to recognize and understand others across perceived or claimed lines of religious difference." As such, pluralism has long been held up as a solution to the challenges of religious diversity in the United States. Such an ideal did not exist during the early modern period covered here. Much of the pluralism, be it Roman Catholics living under a Protestant regime, the increasing numbers of Protestant alternatives to the established Church of England, or the non-Christian beliefs and practices of Indigenous or African peoples, was illegal and neither officially recognized nor formally tolerated. Nevertheless, it happened. Rather than remain within one official church, people gathered in separate spaces—churches, huts, synagogues, domestic spaces, and so on to worship in ways that deviated from the religion holding the legal monopoly on official, public, religious space. The resulting disjuncture between ideal and reality fed much of the contemporary theorizing and advocacy of religious toleration, which still fell short of the modern ideal often associated with the word pluralism. As scholars of religion have recently come to recognize, even as an ideal, pluralism contains its own dilemmas, raising questions like who wants to overcome what diversity? How? To what end? In what follows, similar questions guide my account of the often resented and resisted, but ineradicable (for all sorts of political reasons), pluralism of the English world.[10]

Religious diversity is another term I have had to rely on in the following account. I use it to conjure up something different from pluralism. Where pluralism suggests a variety of religious spaces owing different spiritual allegiances, diversity is more about the range of views and opinions within a single religion—in this case, usually, the Church of England. Indeed, that diversity, which included puritans, avant-garde conformists, and even Roman Catholics who occasionally conformed, is the main motor of the story that follows. Pluralism was its end result, but the ideal for almost all facets of this religious diversity remained unity. They wanted to retain a single church, but their failure to agree on what version of Christianity to unite around opened the door to pluralism. The subsequent challenge of fitting all the many different inhabitants of the

English world, from the Irish to Native Americans, within a church whose character was so contested gave pluralism a permanent home in a world that, officially, continued to reject it.

Overall, this book rests on the recognition that the colonies were not refuges *from* England but *extensions* of it overseas. To only tell the story of the colonies that were successfully planted within the borders of what later became the United States would misrepresent the broader context that produced them. The process of establishing colonies is central to my analysis. Key factors and steps include the individuals who aspired to create a colony (or just drew up proposals for colonization), the administrators willing to grant them a patent or charter to establish a colony, the individuals who actually planted the colonies overseas, and the laws regulating religion within each colony. Finally, there is the problem of enforcing those laws at the local level. As studies from around the English world demonstrate, the official religion could be accepted, resisted, or circumvented depending on who was in charge, who they were in charge of, and how they related to each other. Only by examining this extended process—and not just one portion of it, like the ideas—can we see the relationship between the religious and political developments at the center of the English-dominated world and the religious possibilities emerging in the colonies.

The conditions affecting this process changed significantly between 1497 and 1662, hence chronology is a key part of my analysis. Breaking the geographical habits that shape so many studies of the colonies has been one of the greatest challenges of writing this book. Yet favoring chronology over regionalism not only clarifies the connections between the individual colonies and metropolitan developments, it also reveals new links and comparisons between them. This book takes into consideration all the colonial enterprises I could find. By including not just the colonies that flourished, but also those that were attempted and failed, as well as those that were simply proposed or imagined, we can trace the relationship between religion and overseas expansion and properly assess to what degree the colonies ever were seen or imagined to be a refuge from Europe. The colonies that eventually became part of the United States were part of a bigger, global, process of which, it turns out, they were almost always the more conservative and less religiously diverse manifestation.

The book's five parts are designed to highlight the relationship between major turning points at the center and colonial religious developments. Each of these subperiods had a distinct set of religious possibilities. England first sank its claws into America in 1607, but it had been grasping at it for over a hundred years, and the first two sections are divided by the years around 1607 to capture the connection between the century of exploration and failed colonies and the era of permanent colonization. The founding of Jamestown laid a permanent foundation for English colonization, making 1607 a traditional starting point of American history. However, its survival remained uncertain for years. Indeed, it is impossible to claim 1607 as anything more than one lucky moment in a process dating back to 1497. By starting in 1607, histories of America leave out so much that was crucial to the entire relationship between English religion, expansion, and pluralism. By beginning at the earlier date, even though it left no permanent trace on North American soil, we can recuperate that essential context and see how things could have been different had one of the earlier colonial enterprises been able to survive.

The first part thus surveys the connections between Renaissance English religious history and the explorations and colonizing expeditions between 1497 and 1607. The key factors of this era for colonial religious life included first and foremost the ambition to expand Christendom. This ideal justified all colonial enterprises. Accompanying it was the expectation that the colonies would be included within the official Church of England, not separate from it. Second was the role of conformity in securing obedience to the established church. How conformity was defined, changed, and enforced altered significantly over these years, with major consequences for the colonies. Third is the wide variety of jurisdictions, from the Channel Islands to Ireland, through which conformity had to be implemented. Understanding the diverse outcomes of that history in Europe helps understand the diverse outcomes in the colonies, which were merely new jurisdictions created within this ongoing dynamic. Everywhere, local context and authorities impinged on the demands issuing from the center of the English religious world. Fourth were the varieties of dissent that arose in the sixteenth century in defiance of, or dissatisfaction with, conformity. Roman Catholics refused to become Protestants; puritans did not think official conformity was Protestant enough; avant-garde conformists elevated what puritans criticized into a revised ideal of conformity; radical Protestants rejected the ideal of a national church in favor of more individual approaches to spiritual purity. Traces of all these elements can be found in colonial efforts preceding 1607 and the tensions between them determined colonial religious politics thereafter.

While chronology matters more than geography in this analysis, a purely chronological approach would be incoherent. Within each subsequent part, chapters are divided into microperiods of roughly three to ten years organized around a crucial interpretive theme. Specific colonies are discussed as they emerge and in relation to the most relevant theme for their religious politics. This structure aims to break the long-standing habit of thinking vertically through time in a particular space, like Massachusetts. Instead, this approach reads colonial religious history horizontally across the Atlantic, to see, for example, how Massachusetts or Barbados fit into what was happening elsewhere in the English world at a particular time, like the 1630s. Although, in the end, not all of these colonies is equally relevant for what becomes American religious history, it is essential to understand the whole to appreciate the most significant parts. Massachusetts is the subject of the great majority of studies of religion in seventeenth-century America for a number of reasons, not least because it is unusually well documented, but before 1660 it was just one, often quite exceptional, part of a bigger story. Bringing in the religious histories of the many other colonies, or colonial attempts, was not easy. In many cases, the available sources are scanty and scattered at best. In these poorly documented instances, sometimes one can do little more than suggest the likely religious environment. In these cases understanding the wider transatlantic context is especially helpful.

For the first three parts of the book, the variety of themes and colonies do not fit perfectly within sharp chronological bounds, but the correspondences are surprisingly close. By the time the English revolution takes over in part 4, it becomes increasingly easy to tell a coherent narrative. Nevertheless, there is almost always some small exception. This combination of prevailing trends and persistent exceptions is, really, the heart of our story and an instrumental aspect of early American religious pluralism. Only the comprehensive approach undertaken here can capture that. Otherwise one runs the risk of turning an exception—like Massachusetts—into the rule. Nevertheless, as the final part argues, one can see the possibility of a new religious unity for the English world emerging in the 1650s—only to be cut off as the wheel of revolution turned once again.

In the course of writing this book, I have found the rich scholarship on early modern British and Irish religious politics to be helpful but also challenging. One of the most important trends in recent years has been to break down the neat categories American historians have long relied on like Anglican, Puritan, Catholic, Independent, Presbyterian, or Separatist. Drawing attention to the ways individuals and groups actually related to each other, scholars have shown that these categories do not refer to fixed, discreet groups. Instead, they are the products of contemporary religious polemics and struggles. Puritans, for example, were defined as such by their enemies. Far from unanimous in purpose, they existed on a spectrum from radicals who barely sustained a connection to the church to moderates who did all they could to remain within it. While religious leaders certainly wanted clear and separate distinctions between different groups, for many individuals the dividing lines were not so distinct or stable. Spiritual journeys moved between different religious positions. Many began within the church, then slid through a number of religious positions while still remaining within its ambit. Others fell out of it but then returned. Others began or remained outside of the church, denying its monopoly over their religious lives. These individual experiences need to be kept in mind in what follows, where the colonial evidence only occasionally allows us to glimpse these processes.[11]

The dividing line of 1662 is designed to highlight a major turning point in the religious politics of the English world before and after that year. Before 1662, Anglicanism as such did not exist. The character of England's church was still up for grabs. The roots of modern Anglicanism were present, but they competed with alternative possibilities, especially those associated with so-called puritans. To pit Puritans against Anglicans before 1662 is to preemptively award the victory to one of several contenders and write puritans out of the history of the church they had struggled to control. Instead the key term here is conformity. The recent scholarship on conformity helps recapture the complex, contested, and changing meaning of what it meant to be Protestant within the established church and the issues raised by that scholarship—how conformity was defined, what it meant, how (or if) it was enforced, how it was resisted, how it changed—figured in the early colonies as well. Conformity had its limits, but it was a crucial manifestation of the ideal of religious unity, something that persisted even after the episcopal Church of England was abolished during the revolutionary 1640s and 1650s.

Puritanism is without a doubt the single most important factor in the story that follows, but we need to remember it was a force *within* the Church of England, not separate from it. Puritans were neither intrinsically antiestablishment nor a separate religion, although their Jesuit enemies portrayed them as such. They also were not intrinsically Presbyterian, Congregationalist, Baptist, or Quaker, although all of those churches emerged out of the puritan movement. Instead, before 1640 they are best understood as awkwardly unhappy members of the church representing, as Peter Lake describes it, "the areas of tension and disagreement" accompanying "the Protestant impulse" as it "worked its way through the national Church and English society in the decades after the Elizabethan Settlement." Massachusetts represented just one of the possible outcomes. Puritans in power, as in New England after 1629 or across the English world in the 1650s, are better described as Reformed Protestants rather than Puritans. For this reason, scholars have taken to using the lowercase "puritans" instead of "Puritans," to both suggest the fluid character of the category and to reject the idea that they were a distinct religion apart from the official Protestantism of England. For much of the period discussed here, being Calvinist did not put one at odds with the national church. It was, rather, integral to the conformity of many English Protestants. How and why that then changed is a key aspect of the story that follows.[12]

Since the story that follows is primarily about the relationship between different religions, or what were perceived to be different religious ideas, attitudes, or positions, it does not go into much depth on their internal workings or theology. Key points of difference are highlighted, but otherwise such issues are better addressed elsewhere, as in the two magisterial accounts of early American puritanism that appeared just as the final touches were being put on this book.[13] Here, the focus is on the relationship between this evident pluralism and diversity, the efforts to incorporate it into a single, official, church system, and the connection between that dynamic and the creation of overseas colonies. By culminating with the 1650s, this book also hopes to drive home the idea that puritans were not intrinsically dissenters. They aspired to dominate the religious life of the English world, and for a brief period they did, however imperfectly. In this picture, New England is more of an advanced imperial beachhead than a religious refuge.

Ultimately, my primary aim has been constructive. I have striven to create a narrative order out of a mess of disconnected and, especially in the Caribbean, poorly known histories. It is hoped that, at the least, the end result lays a solid foundation for future work on early America and the early modern English world, both separately and in relation to their many connections. It is also hoped that by demonstrating just how unusual, contingent, and generally undesired the emergence of American religious pluralism was, Americans will take it a little less for granted. Perhaps then we can also be more modest in demanding others imitate what was, in the end, an accident.

PART 1

Tudor-Stuart Foundations, 1497–ca. 1607

ONE

Colonization: Religion, Expansion, Guiana, and Slavery

English America was supposed to have the same church as England. Had matters not changed within England after 1530, it would have been the Roman Catholic Church. Landing on what is now Newfoundland, Canada, in June 1497, the Venetian navigator John Cabot staked England's claim to American territory by planting a crucifix, then raising three different banners representing what Anglo-America's religious and political loyalties should have been. The arms of the pope represented the spiritual jurisdiction of the Roman Catholic Church. Those of King Henry VII, in whose service Cabot sailed, represented England's secular ruler. Those of Saint Mark, patron saint of Cabot's native Venice, gave a personal touch.[1]

Religion was as fundamental to England's efforts to colonize America as it was for the other Europeans powers. An essential cultural and institutional bond linking the different corners of the English world, religion also justified colonization by promising to incorporate non-Christian peoples into Christianity through conversion. Nevertheless, historians have paid little attention to the religious dimensions of early English exploration and colonization. Instead, they emphasize the practical aspects.[2] Even studies of law and ideology say little about religion and much more about Renaissance humanist thought, Roman law, or the civic ideology of classical republicanism.[3] This neglect is both a shame and a sign of how skewed our approach to colonial American religion is. By associating it almost exclusively with puritan New England, we are not only missing out on the religious aspects of the many other English colonial enterprises that surrounded and preceded New England; we are also misconstruing the basic relationship between religion and empire building. Religion was not exceptional or even oppositional to colonization, but rather integral to it.

Of course, religion was never the sole purpose of colonization. The quest for wealth and resources is what drove most investors and colonists to engage in overseas enterprises. Those ambitions also occupy the bulk of the surviving evidence, especially before the formation of the Massachusetts Bay colony. Still, the desire to get rich was never seen as incompatible with or even subverting the religious purpose of empire. On the contrary, conventional belief held that the two worked in tandem, reinforcing each other to the benefit of Christian colonizers. Of course, England's failure to fulfill its proclaimed goal of converting non-Christians suggests that the alliance of trade and religion did not work as expected. The quest for profits from the land and labor of others posed one unanticipated obstacle. Resistance and resilience on the part of the non-Christian communities formed another. Together, they allowed a sizeable non-Christian community to develop within what was supposed to be simply an extension of English Christianity overseas.

*

It is important to remember that Protestantism was not England's only religious influence on America. The first attempts at colonies took place at a time when England, like the rest of western Europe, was still Roman Catholic. English Catholics never forgot this early connection with America and would remain active leaders of colonial efforts into the 1640s. In the fifteenth and early sixteenth century, the English could draw on an international network of Roman Catholic merchants and churchmen for support. The Venetian John Cabot is just the most famous example. Recently discovered scraps of evidence suggest that he took advantage of his Italian connections to actually establish a mission at what is now Saint John's, Newfoundland. The few Italian Augustinians who apparently went there did not stay for more than a couple of years, but their mission is the likely origin of the place's Christian name. The island's climate was harsh. It would disrupt many subsequent colonial efforts as well. Other important connections led to Spain where, from Seville, the recently established community of English merchants sent back information about the Americas, whetting appetites for a new world of opportunities.[4]

From the beginning, religion accompanied trade to America. Cabot had likely followed a route pioneered by fishermen from Bristol and the West Country. Already in March 1498 a "prest" had prepared to go "towardes the

FIGURE 1. English Americas before 1630

new Ilande." In 1501 Henry VII granted a patent to a group of merchants "to find, recover, discover and search out whatsoever islands, countries, regions or provinces of heathens and infidels, in whatever part of the world they may lie, which before this time were and at present are unknown to all Christians." Another priest accompanied fishing boats "to the new Ilande" in 1504. By the 1520s, the trickle of fishermen from Bristol and the West Country had grown big enough to be called a fleet. A plan was drawn up to sail over the Arctic to Asia. In 1530 and 1532, William Hawkins, patriarch of a merchant family from Plymouth, sent ships to trade between Africa and Brazil. Similar voyages followed.[5]

On the eve of the Reformation, Catholic Englishmen were roaming across the Atlantic world. These years also saw the first vision of a pluralistic overseas empire, in Sir Thomas More's 1516 book *Utopia*. This humanist and royal minister was not advocating pluralism. He clearly believed it was a source of weakness. Indeed, *Utopia* describes how a man named Utopus conquered and ruled a distant island because its inhabitants were too religiously divided to unite against him. Once in power, Utopus realized that maintaining pluralism would serve his reign better than an imposed religious unity, so he tolerated all existing religions and passed laws against "fighting and rioting" between those who sought to force their views on others. Religious coercion was not necessary, for if "one religion is really true and the rest false," it would eventually "prevail by its own natural strength" through reason and moderation. However, Utopus refused to tolerate "impiety" or atheists. Atheists were untrustworthy, but not even they were forced to convert. Instead, they were drawn into debates with "the priests and other important persons, in private." Admittedly, Utopia's toleration was facilitated by the fact that all the Utopian sects agreed "that there is one supreme power" in religion. This shared fundamental belief resembled what Catholic theorists called the "natural religion" shared by all humans. In More's words it was a common "worship of the divine nature," albeit undertaken in slightly different ways. Utopians had "various particular doctrines" attached to diverse objects: the sun, the moon, a planet, a hero. For the majority, it was "a single power, unknown, eternal, infinite, inexplicable . . . diffused through the universe." Significantly, this shared religious affinity allowed Christians to easily make converts among the Utopians. Notwithstanding its talk of toleration, *Utopia* was, at root, a Roman Catholic vision of colonization, missionization, and religious unity.[6]

Sir Thomas More's attitude to religious diversity was shared by his famous friend, the influential humanist Erasmus of Rotterdam (1466–1536). Both were convinced of the truth of Roman Catholicism but preferred to indulge differences of opinion rather than force people's consciences. Erasmus's life represented, in one historian's words, "a commitment to work for concord between Christians who agreed on fundamentals but disagreed on secondary matters." However, his rather condescending tolerance toward erring Christians was not accompanied by a similar indulgence of non-Christians. In 1516, while More was publishing *Utopia*, Erasmus was praising France as the "purest blossom of Christianity, since she alone is uninfested with heretics, Bohemian schismatics, with Jews and with half-Jewish marranos." Other English Catholics shared this attitude, most importantly Cardinal Reginald Pole, who, under Queen Mary, would become the last Roman Catholic archbishop of Canterbury. Though praised by the great Protestant martyrologist John Foxe as not one of the "bloody and cruel sort of papists," Pole, like other Catholic humanists, ultimately felt that heretics could be coerced if they obstinately refused to renounce their errors.[7]

English Catholic colonizers expected America to adopt their religion while they harvested America's wealth. As Richard Eden, who authored the first book in English about America, insisted, through overseas expansion "not only worldly ryches are obtayned, but also God is glorified, & the Christian fayth enlarged." This observation appears in his *Treatyse of the Newe India*, a 1553 discussion of the Iberian discoveries in Asia. It was based on Eden's translation of *Cosmographia*, an encyclopedic description of the world by the German Protestant Sebastien Münster. In it, Eden goaded his countrymen to imitate the Iberians, "to the glorye of God & commoditie of our country" rather than die "in soft beddes at home." If they had had more courage in the reign of Henry VIII (1509–47), America might now be English. Instead, the Spaniards commanded the "infinite riches" of Peru, Hispaniola, Cuba, and "other Islandes there aboute." In his first book dedicated to America, the *Decades of the newe worlde or West India*, a 1555 translation of portions of two major Spanish histories, Eden anticipated "how farre owre posteritie shall see the Christian religion enlarged" by colonization. It was, he reiterated, both "goddes cause" and "owre owne commoditie." If the English missed this opportunity, they would "doo nothynge worrthy memorie amonge men or thankes before god, who maye herein worrthely accuse us for the slacknesse of ower dewtie towarde hym." That duty included having Native Americans "embrase . . . owre religion." Eden dedicated the book to his queen, Henry VIII's Roman Catholic daughter Mary, and her husband, King Philip II of Spain. He continued to translate travel accounts and scientific works after he and England became Protestant several years later, including the first manual of navigation to be published in English.[8]

Protestant advocates of overseas expansion saw no more contradiction between religious and commercial expansion than Roman Catholics. Under Queen Elizabeth, major trading companies like the Levant Company (1581) trading with the Ottoman Empire and the East India Company (1600) trading with Asia required their servants to carry out "the dayly invocacon & religious wo[rshi]p: & service of God," and employed chaplains to lead them. A legal official investing in the early Virginia Company voyages prayed that "god blesse them and guide them to his glory and our goode." A London merchant captain promoting investment in the Newfoundland Company insisted it was for God's "glorie and the good of our Commonwealth," denouncing those spreading "malicious and scandelous speeches" (probably about the island's frigid weather) as "malign persons" acting "out of envy to God and good Actions (instructed by their father the Devill)." Soon thereafter, people in the west of England were encouraged to support the colonization of New England "for the advancement of Christian religion and a good addicon to trade and profitt to our kingdomes and people." These and many other examples show the proprietors of early Maine were not alone when they claimed that they had established their colony "for the Honour of God, good of the Nation, and propagating the gospel, with hope of improvement for the future."[9]

Men of the church agreed that religion, trade, and colonization reinforced one another. Describing his motives for serving as chaplain on Martin Frobisher's third voyage in search of gold and the Northwest Passage in 1578, Robert Wolfall, the first English Protestant minister to visit the Americas, declared that "the only care he had [was] to save souls, and to reform those infidels if it were possible to Christianity." Though noted for his ability to preach "a godly sermon," he had no chance to make any American converts. The expedition proved as fruitless as Frobisher's previous two. Still, the professed desire to spread England's religion remained a standard part of overseas expeditions to America, Africa, and Asia.[10]

Like their Catholic predecessors, Protestant colonizers also assumed that the colonies would belong to England's official church. As the 1584 parliamentary bill confirming Sir Walter Ralegh's patent for the Roanoke colony made clear, colonization was linked to the suppression of false and bad religion in the name of religious unity and purity. In Parliament's words, Queen Elizabeth's desire that "the knowledge of god and trewe religion might by her heighnes Labors be propagatyd Amongeste foreign Nacions" equaled her wish "that the gospell of our saviour Iesus Christ might be trewlye and syncerlie sett forth, And Ignoraunce error and superstición Abolished within her Maiesties Domynions." Roanoke, the first English outpost established within the future borders of the United States of America, showed some promise of fulfilling this mission. It witnessed the first baptism of an English person born in the Americas (Virginia

Dare) as well as the first baptism of an Indigenous person (Manteo). A ship's chaplain probably performed these baptisms as the colony never had a resident minister.[11]

The principal change with the shift to Protestant colonization was the anti-Catholic ambitions professed by most colonial promoters. This is clear in the narratives of England's early explorations that began to be collected and published, first in Richard Hakluyt's 1582 *Divers Voyages touching the Discovery of America*, then in Samuel Purchas's 1625 *Hakluytus Posthumus or Purchas his Pilgrimes*. Hakluyt and Purchas, both clergymen, presented colonization as a staunchly Protestant endeavor, part of the broader global struggle against Roman Catholic hegemony. For Hakluyt, colonization had three basic purposes: "1 to plant Christian religion 2 To trafficke 3 To conquer." These were all part of the greater goal of "the inlarging of the dominons of the Queens most excellent Maiestie, and consequently of her honour, revenues, and of her power by this enterprise." While trade and "conquest" (i.e., governing) occupied twenty-nine of the thirty-one "inducements to the liking of the voyage intended towards Virginia" that Hakluyt drew up in 1585, the first two inducements were religious: the "glory of God by planting of religion among those infidels" and the "increase of the force of the Christians." These goals, along with a proposal from the 1590s written by Edward Hayes, a veteran of the Roanoke colony, "to plant Christian people and religion upon the Northwest countries of America, in places temperat and well agreeing with our constitution," were reprinted in an account of a 1602 expedition to New England. Insisting that the English would be better than the Spanish, Hayes clarified that their "intent" was not "to provoke" the Native Americans as the Spanish did, but "to cherish and win them unto Christianitie by faire meanes."[12]

This religious reasoning figures in the 1606 patent for Virginia. The Virginia Company was ordered to see that the "true word, and service of God and Christian faith be preached, planted, and used, not only within every of the said colonies, and plantations, but also as much as they may amongst the salvage people which doe or shall adjoine unto them, or border upon them." This injunction was not a recipe for religious diversity. Only Christianity "according to the doctrine, rights, and religion now professed and established within our realme of England" was permitted in the colony.[13]

Colonial entrepreneurs extended these religious ambitions to the South Atlantic. After his failure at Roanoke, Walter Ralegh had sent three expeditions to South America in hopes of discovering El Dorado and perhaps some Amazonian warrior women. After the first, in 1595, he wrote about his discoveries in an effort to raise funds. A second expedition, in 1596, came no closer to finding El Dorado. The third discovered that Ralegh's publicity campaign had inspired other Englishmen to profit from the region's trade in tobacco, dyes, and hardwoods. One was John Ley, who had accompanied Frobisher on two of his voyages. Like other Elizabethan explorers and colonizers, Ley had previously fought in the Low Countries against the Spanish and in Ireland against rebellious Irish Catholics. Sailing on three voyages to Guiana between 1597 and 1602, Ley became the first Englishman to explore the Amazon but died in 1604, before he could establish a colony. We know little about the religious tenor of these colonial expeditions, but can surmise they reflected the ethos of Roanoke and early Virginia.[14]

The English involvement in Guiana was vital to the success of other English colonies, for Guiana was the source of Virginia's profitable Orinoco tobacco. Yet religious tolerance was no more in evidence in Guiana than anywhere else in the English world. Indeed, several of the merchants drawn to the region had outspoken religious ambitions. Charles Leigh, a London merchant and sea captain, had connections to England's radical Protestant fringe. He took up where John Ley had left off, exploring the coast of Guiana in 1602 and returning in March 1604 with forty-six men and boys and a Native guide named William. William had lived for a time in England and helped the English establish an outpost on the Wiapoco. In July, Leigh reported his conviction that "God hath a wonderful work in this simple-hearted people," but then he and many of his men fell ill with fever. Leigh died. The survivors returned home in March 1605. His less radical brother, Sir Oliph Leigh, sent out a relief expedition in April. Missing Guiana, it attempted to colonize the island of Saint Lucia but abandoned the effort in the face of starvation and attacks from local Kalinago (or Caribs).[15]

These deaths and failures did not discourage English hopes for Guiana. Between 1609 and 1612, Robert Harcourt established a profitable trading post on the Wiapoco River, working with the Anglo-Irish merchant Philip Purcell, who developed a separate Irish outpost near the mouth of the Amazon. Estimating that he had earned £10,000 in tobacco sales in 1610 alone, Harcourt stressed his desire "to plant that contry with his Majestie's subjectes, to the greate benefitt of this Kingdome, by the increase of trade and reduceinge of that people to civility of life and Christianity" in his 1613 petition for a colonial patent. He received the patent but lacked the resources to develop a colony.[16]

Harcourt was the first Englishman to articulate at length a religious vision for Guiana. However, it reflected a somewhat different perspective than that of Charles Leigh. A gentleman from Oxfordshire, Harcourt had been a Roman Catholic before conforming and marrying into the staunchly Protestant Vere family. This experience may explain why he spoke about religion in general terms and was not as anti-Catholic as others. The "glory of God," Harcourt wrote, came from "the prosperous grouth and happy increase of his Church" through the conversion of "heathen and barbarous Nations . . . to the profession and practise of Christianity." Like Richard Eden, he hoped the English would follow the "memorable examples" of the Spanish where the "wonderfull workes of God" had "reduced" the Americans "from their abhominable life and cruell manners, to the knowledge of God." Harcourt's outpost lacked a minister, but he and his men observed a regular "time of prayer" and even baptized the children of their Indigenous neighbors. Believing a "Schollar in divine learning" could "worthily labour the conversion of infinite numbers of unbeleeving people," Harcourt offered a special award of "worthy shares" in the colony to "Divine Preachers that will imitate the glorious examples of the Apostles (who ceased not to travell amongst all sorts of Heathen and savage people for the plantation of the holy Gospel)." Dedicating his account to Prince Charles, the Prince of Wales, Harcourt reminded him that the Welsh prince Madoc had discovered America back in 1170. Wishing Charles, "the dominion of many rich and mighty Kingdomes in this world, and in the worlde to come, a Crowne of Glorie, in his eternall Kingdome," Harcourt also repeated his hope to reduce Guiana's "unknowne and barbarous people (void of all knowledge of God, and civill governement) to Christianity and the subjection and obedience of our Soveraigne."[17]

In the meantime, Sir Walter Ralegh had not given up on his dreams for Guiana—even though he was now imprisoned in the Tower of London for suspected treason. In 1610 he gained the approval of Prince Henry and minister Robert Cecil to sponsor an expedition to Guiana led by Sir Thomas Roe, a London merchant and investor in the Virginia Company. Although Roe failed to find El Dorado, he did establish an outpost on the Amazon, where his men grew tobacco and traded with the Indigenous people. This fledging colony included a number of Irish men recruited through Harcourt's associate Philip Purcell. We know almost nothing about life in the colony, but we do know that the English and Irish (who were not necessarily Catholic, though at least some likely were) managed to hang on for over a decade as other expeditions arrived and failed, including one led by Ralegh in 1617 that attacked a Spanish town instead of establishing a colony. For this illegal act of war in time of peace, he was executed upon his return. In 1619, a group of anti-Spanish merchants headed by the militantly Protestant Earl of Warwick received a charter for a new Guiana or Amazon Company, but King James revoked it after the Spanish ambassador complained. Besieged by the Spanish, Portuguese, and their indigenous allies, a few of the remaining Irish and English colonists managed to hold out (with Dutch assistance) until 1627, when a new Guiana Company was created. Led by Robert Harcourt and Robert Hayman, who had earlier governed a colony in Newfoundland, this effort ended in 1631 with both Hayman and Harcourt dead of disease. Spanish and Portuguese forces destroyed whatever remained, and the English and Irish survivors fled north to the Caribbean.[18]

Guiana was a graveyard of colonies, but it continued to attract English "adventurers," a term referring to those who ventured their capital as much as their persons on the overseas voyages. In 1632, it was the turn of Thomas Howard, Earl of Berkshire, son of the eponymous first Earl of Suffolk and husband of a niece of Robert Cecil (son of Richard Eden's patron William Cecil). The pamphlet promoting his colony invoked religion at length, evidently hoping to take advantage of the current exodus to New England. Explicitly directed at "all faithful, and well-affected Christians," it pointed out that the opportunities for profit were much greater in Guiana than New England. Comparing colonization to the migrations of Abraham and "the Children of the Prophets," Berkshire's pamphlet argued that the English could lawfully coexist with the indigenous people as long as they were "willing that Gods people shall inhabit with them." Guiana "may proove profitable to the Church of God" as a place where "the word of the Lord might bee fulfilled in those Heathen through Gods infinite goodnes & mercy." Rather than "live heere like plants," those interested in "the propagating of Gods truth" could take advantage of the more "fruitfull" soil of Guiana. Berkshire wanted to do better than other colonies where idle, "desperate," and "lawlesse" people caused "the heathen" to think the Christian "God as evil as their owne." By sending over "plantes of grace," or people who "feare God," the "Americans" could be converted "to the Christian faith." Filled "with the fruits of righteousnesse," the "pure conversation" of the colonists would persuade "the Heathen" to embrace "the knowledge and love of God our Father, and the Lord Jesus Christ." The colonists, "like fruitfull trees" (botanical metaphors abound here), would then make Guiana like "a Vineyard which the right hand of the Lord hath planted, and may growe up before him in the wildernesse." Displaying no more interest in religious refuge or pluralism than any other colonial entrepreneur, Berkshire aimed to create a "unity of faith" with the Guianans who would "agree to worship" God "in sincerity of heart."[19]

These assumptions about the religious purpose of colonization were shared by colonial entrepreneurs across the English world. In 1614, Sir William Alexander, the Scottish poet and courtier, waxed lyrical about the religious purpose of European expansion: "In this last age, Time doth new worlds bewray [reveal], / That Christ a Church, over all the Earth may have." When he received a royal patent for Nova Scotia, he promoted it in his 1624 tract *An encouragement to colonies* as a land of opportunity provided by God out of "pitie of the Christian who for purposes of small importance did prodigally prostitute" their lives in bloody European wars forgetting how "precious a ransome" Jesus Christ had paid for them. Alexander's vision was not pluralistic, as his discussion of the failures of the sixteenth-century Huguenot colonies indicates. French Brazil, containing both Catholics and Protestants, had been "crossed . . . by the difference of Religion." The resulting "disputations" had "distracted" the colony "with severall opinions," weakening it until the Portuguese captured it. As Sir Thomas More had argued a century earlier, religious pluralism made a society vulnerable to conquest. Religious unity was strength.[20]

When another Scot, Sir Robert Gordon, received a patent to build the colony of New Galloway on Cape Breton Island, he claimed the religious motive came before "private and particular gaine" or serving his "Prince, and native Countrie." His 1625 *Encouragements* appealed to investors by proclaiming his desire to advance "the glorie of my great and mightie God," the service of "my dread Soveraigne, and my native Countrie," and profit for himself and "such as shall bee generouslie disposed adventurers with mee." Insisting that "the chiefe and primarie end of mans creation is the Worshippe of God," Gordon also claimed that colonization was "the dutie of Christianitie in us, to behold the imprinted footsteppes of GODS glorie in everie Region under Heaven." In fact, it was "the policie universall, from the creation of the World unto this time, of all civile States" from the time of Adam and Eve, through Noah, the Greeks, Goths, and Romans, up to the recent efforts led by figures like Christopher Columbus and Sir Walter Ralegh, to replenish "the World with Colonies of their owne Subjects." Still, the conversion of the Americans was to "bee the first aime of our hopes." As the Gospel enjoined, his colonists would trade "the pearles of Heaven" in exchange for "the pearles of the Earth," advancing God's "Glorie" and propagating "the Gospell of Jesus Christ"

FIGURE 2. Illustration from Sir Robert Gordon, *Encouragements* (Edinburgh, 1625), RB 17927, Huntington Library, San Marino, California

among America's "Heathen people" who knew not "the worshippe of the true GOD." Gordon wanted to "cast downe the Altars of Devills, and to raise up the Altar of Christ: to forbidde the Sacrifice of men, that they may offer up the Sacrifices of contrite Spirites." To illustrate this point, his title page contained a dramatic image of two wild men. Covered only by a modest kilt of leaves, they carried clubs and stood under the boldly printed injunction "DREAD GOD."[21]

A 1623 proposal from Ireland professed similar aspirations. The Englishman Henry Cary, Viscount Falkland, serving as the lord deputy governing Ireland on behalf of England's monarch, advertised his colony of South Falkland in Newfoundland by emphasizing the economic benefits. Ireland's mercantile wealth would increase through the fishery, fur trade, and attendant domestic industries. South Falkland would also serve as an outlet for the country's population, which had "encreased to such excessive numbers, as the land seemes alreadie to groane under the multitude of the inhabitants." By the "disburthening of them at home," the colony would permit "the multiplying of them abroade." Emigration would serve a religious purpose. The "Christian inhabitants" would reduce "to Civility and Religion" the "Savages who live in the adjoining continent of America." This "worthie undertaking" would thus bring profit to Ireland, enlarge the king's dominions, augment his customs and revenues, and serve "God in propagating of Religion" in a place that "hath onely served as a den for wilde beasts."[22]

In the meantime, with the tobacco trade booming in Virginia, John Donne, a poet, dean of Saint Paul's, and a convert from Catholicism, held the colony up as proof of how "profit . . . and Religion may well consist together." In a sermon arguing that Virginia's economic success by no means undermined its religious credentials, he claimed the people "of our Profession that goe" to Virginia, as well as those "who send them" over "doe all an Apostolicall Function." Through the example of their civility and their religious teachings to the indigenous inhabitants, they added "persons to this Kingdome, and to the Kingdome of Heaven." Virginia's success had a partisan religious dimension as well: "Papists" (i.e., Roman Catholics) were "sorrie we have" Virginia, whose prosperity vexed Roman Catholics more than "Lectures in matters of [religious] Controversie." Meanwhile, the wealth was not to be shared with "odious" Protestant "Heretiques and Schismatiques."[23]

Even Maryland's Catholics proclaimed the same basic religious purpose. Their "first and chief object" was to "carry the light of the gospel and of truth" into Maryland "and the neighboring places . . . where it has been found out that hitherto no knowledge of the true God has shone." Cecil Calvert, Lord Baltimore, the Roman Catholic proprietor of the colony, included this statement of purpose in a manuscript circulated to recruit colonists for the first voyage to the colony. The "rescue and salvation of souls" was "a glorious work, for it is a work to the glory of Christ our King" and would extend "the empire of the realm" while earning "profits and honor"—which was important. After all, "most men regard rather pleasures, honors, and wealth, as if in love with them." Fortunately, in Maryland profit and piety would easily coincide for, as if by "some unseen power, or rather by the manifest remarkable wisdom of the Deity," chances for profit abounded. The resources were plentiful: fertile land, the fur trade, the chance to discover gold, and "other advantages, both numerous and lucrative." Hearkening back to English Christianity's early medieval roots, Calvert praised the "design" of planting "religion and piety" in Maryland as "truly worthy of Christians, worthy of angels, worthy of the Angles," the Germanic ancestors of the English. This referred to a remark by Pope Gregory I who, on seeing some enslaved Angles in Rome, allegedly had blurted out, "They ought not to be called Angles, but Angels." Soon thereafter he sent the monk Augustine to convert the English, beginning with the conversion of the Anglo-Saxon Kingdom of Kent.[24]

Christianity first took root in Britain and Ireland at specific places thanks to the efforts of specific men. Augustine's work in Canterbury, capital of the Kingdom of Kent, is commemorated in the archbishopric of Canterbury's position as head of England's church. In Wales, the most prestigious bishopric is Saint David's, where the missionary Saint David had his monastic settlement. In Ireland, the primary archdiocese was Armagh, where Saint Patrick, credited with the conversion of the Irish, served as bishop. The small town of Saint Andrews became head of Scotland's church after the relics of Saint Andrew were brought there, giving it more spiritual power than any other place in the kingdom.

Would Virginia be the American equivalent of Canterbury? In 1610 the Virginia Company proclaimed the "*Principall* and *Maine Ends*" of the colony to be the conversion of its native inhabitants "by propagation of that *Gospell*, to recover out of the armes of the Divell, a number of poore and miserable soules, wrapt upp unto death, in almost invincible ignorance." William Strachey extended this evangelical ambition to Africans and Muslims (both commonly known as Moors) in his 1612 dedicatory poem to the published volume of Virginia's *Laws Divine, Morall and Martiall*. Strachey urged Virginia's council to "imitate your maker in his will, / to have his truth in blackest nations shine. . . . And where white Christians turn in maners Mores / You wash Mores white with sacred Christian bloud." People in England made private donations "for bringing up the children of infidels in the true religion," while in 1623 King James drafted a letter to the archbishops of York and Canterbury soliciting their help to propagate "the Gospell amongst infidells: wherein there is good progresse made, and hope of further increase." To help with "the erecting of some churches and schooles for the education of the children of those Barbarians," they should have their bishops order "the ministers & other zelous men of their dioceses" to solicit donations "in all the particular parishes foure severall times" over the next two years.[25]

The collection was never taken up. The outbreak of the Powhatan War in 1622 almost destroyed the colony and caused English missionary efforts to collapse. In Newfoundland, colonists never even managed to establish relations with the indigenous Beothuks, who rigorously avoided contact with Europeans. In the Caribbean, colonists were more likely to massacre or expel their indigenous neighbors than preach the Gospel to them. Even in New England, missionary endeavors were sporadic and ineffective before the 1640s. Only in Maryland, where Jesuits successfully converted the neighboring Piscataways, was much progress made.[26]

Maryland, the first colony to successfully expand British Christianity to an Indigenous nation, seemed most likely to become America's Canterbury until its Jesuit mission was quashed by a Protestant revolt in 1644. Then Massachusetts began to take up the mantel. Five sachems placed themselves under its authority in 1644. In 1646, the General Court urged ministers to begin evangelizing the sachems' people by passing a law to encourage missionary work. It ordered "yt ye necessary & holesome lawes wch may be made to reduce ym [the Massachusett nation] to civility of life shalbe once in ye yeare (if ye times be safe) made knowne to ym" by selected ministers assisted by an interpreter. After all, "one end in planting these prts was to propagate ye true religion unto ye Indians." Now that "divers of ym are become subiects to ye English, & have engaged themselves to be willing & ready to undrstand ye law of God," it behooved the colony "to bring ym to ye knowledge of ye truth, & their conversion to Jesus Christ."[27]

Later that same year, John Eliot, minister of the church at Roxbury, began his famous mission to the Massachusett. After learning enough of their language to make some converts, Eliot established a mission village at Natick in 1650. More so-called Praying Towns for converts and proselytes followed, supported by funds from the Society for the Propagation of the Gospel in New England, a corporation founded in England in 1649 with the help of the Plymouth colonist Edward Winslow. This financial assistance allowed New England to become the most successful Protestant missionary zone in the English colonies. No individual colony, even within New England, had the resources necessary to fund a missionary enterprise on its own. For most, the conversion of the Americans remained little more than an aspiration. For Roger Williams, on the other hand, there was no point in trying to convert the Narragansetts on whose lands he had settled. He worked closely enough with them to learn their language and regularly berated them for their religious failings. However, he believed they had to come to Christianity through the workings of their own conscience, not the coercive environment of a mission. For that reason he supported the Narragansetts' 1651 petition to Parliament "that they might not be forced from their Religion." Their Indigenous Massachusett neighbors were trying to get them to convert to Christianity, telling them that, "if they would not pray they should be destrouyed by war."[28]

Roger Williams's willingness to tolerate Indigenous beliefs was exceptional. No other colony did so. More typical was Williams's belief that the Narragansetts' lack of Christianity was wrong and that they *should* convert, notwithstanding his willingness to tolerate their errors in the meantime. Unlike Utopus, English colonists did not see toleration and pluralism as useful tools of empire. Where Indigenous religion survived in the colonies, it was because colonists lacked the ability to suppress it. Indeed, one New England colonist explicitly justified the expropriation of Native Americans as better than tolerating their non-Christian rites. Writing to John Winthrop in 1645, his brother-in-law and governor of Massachusetts, Emmanuel Downing Sr., referring to the Narragansett in Rhode Island, mused, "I doubt whither yt be not synne in us having power in our hands to suffer them to maynteyne the wo[rshi]p of the devill, which their Paw wawes [powwows; spiritual leaders] often doe." Anticipating a war, Downing noted that if it were "a Just warre" and "the lord should deliver them into our hands, wee might easily have men woemen and Children enough to exchange for Moores," meaning Africans. The potential bounty from the war captives, "wilbe more gaynefull pilladge for us then wee conceive," he argued. Indeed, he could "not see how wee can thrive untill wee gett into a stock of slaves suffitient to doe all our busines." The English had sold some Pequot prisoners of war into slavery after their war against them in 1637. Others they held as servants. While they left their Narragansett allies in peace, Downing worried that New England was such a large country that "our Childrens Children will hardly see this great Continent filled with people." Until then, "our servants will still desire fredome to plant for them selves, and not stay but for verie great wages. And I suppose you know verie well how wee shall maynteyne 20 Moores cheaper then one Englishe servant."[29]

Downing had nothing to say about the religious fate of the Africans he wanted to enslave, but it quickly became evident that the growing reliance on enslaved labor was creating a tension between the religious and economic priorities of colonization. The directors of the Providence

Island colony in the Caribbean—no less puritan than the men colonizing Massachusetts—initially wanted to bring Indigenous men into the colony, "but no Indian women," in hopes "that by wise carriage and religious conversation those poor creatures may be won to the love of religion." In the meantime, they would serve as a source of cheap labor. The colony's directors refused to tolerate Indigenous religion: if the Americans insisted on worshipping after their traditional manner, they would be sent off the island, "so there may be no mixture of paganism with the pure religion of the Almighty God." However, when the colonists failed to acquire Native American servants and turned instead to enslaved Africans, these Christian imperatives quickly dwindled away. The Africans' enslavement was justified by their "strangeness from Christianity," discouraging efforts to convert them. Only one colonist publicly denounced this apparent contradiction of the island's godly purpose. By 1641, Providence Island had become the most intensive enslaved society in the English world. Barbados would not see anything comparable until the 1660s; the Chesapeake only several decades after that.[30]

The turn to slavery took place with surprisingly little debate. While slavery had ceased to be practiced within England long ago, its persistence elsewhere suggested it was acceptable for geographically and culturally distant people like Africans and Native Americans. Early English antislavery sentiment protested the enslavement of English people by North African Muslims but did not question the legitimacy or righteousness of the institution. Rare was the man like Maine's governor Thomas Gorges who, speculating in 1642 about using "slaves out of Ginney" ("if theyr bodyes can agree with the coldness of the country they would be excellent"), mused, "I believe I could frame an argument against the lawfulness of taking them from theyr own country & soe have them & theyrs." Sadly, he never did.[31]

It is striking how few colonists gave any thought to the religious consequences of slavery. After all, they were importing African beliefs along with the Africans. Contemporaries recognized that enslavers' indifference to the spiritual fate of those they enslaved was effectively a form of toleration. A French Catholic priest on Barbados in the 1650s remarked that, since the "masters never think of their slaves' souls," they let them indulge in "wonderful jumping and dancing" on Sundays. Sometimes they even gave them "a flagon of brandy." With no one to "speak to them about any religion or religious exercises," the enslaved people "content themselves by baptising their children in the house." Some, who had a "tinge of the Catholic religion, which they received among the Portuguese," preserved it "the best they can, doing their prayers and worshipping God in their hearts." Those without it "do not have any knowledge of religion." They lived "like beasts . . . in just as deplorable a state as savages, except when regenerated by baptism."[32]

Other scattered sources confirm that African religious life persisted within the limited domestic realm allowed by slavery. Around 1651, one observer on Barbados noted "that after their day labour is ended, they will not goe to their Sports, which usually they have every night, till they have in their Cottages mumbled over some prayers." As for "what they are, or to whom directed I cannot tell." He "could never yet come to know what Religion they are of," but clearly saw something religious going on. A 1667 account of Surinam describes enslaved people working all week "till Saturday afternoon, when, they are allowed to dress their own Gardens or Plantations, having nothing but what they can produce from thence to live upon." Although the author claimed they "practice no Religion there," he found that "many of them are Circumcis'd" (a physical mutilation of religious significance to Christians) and describes some of their beliefs, such as "the Ancient Pythagorean Errour of the Soul's Transmigration out of one body into another." The Africans believed "that when they dye, they shall return to their own Countries and be Regenerated," thereby living "in the World by a Constant Revolution." This "Conceit," as the Englishman called it, "makes many of them over-fondly wooe their Deaths, not otherwise hoping to be freed from that indeed un-equall'd Slavery." A missionary working in early eighteenth-century South Carolina reported how enslaved people were "allow'd by their Masters to have Sundays at their own disposal and to work for themselves, or to play and dance together in what manner they pleas'd." If the enslaved people "were Baptized," he pointed out, "they should be debarr'd of this only freedom belonging to them."[33]

A rare inside account of the sort of power enslavers had suggests how little room they allowed for Christian evangelization—as well as how important religious difference was in justifying the slavery. A number of royalists prisoners transported to Barbados managed to submit a petition to Parliament protesting their obligation to work alongside servants and enslaved people who were made "miserable, beyond expression or Christian imagination." The royalists suffered under "the unlimited power" of their enslavers, who bought and sold them at will. They could be "whipped at the whipping posts as rogues for their master's pleasure." They slept "in sties worse than hogs in England," and worked "grinding at the mills and attending to the furnaces, or digging in this scorching island, having nought to feed on (notwithstanding their hard labour) but potato roots, nor to drink but water with such roots mashed in it." In "the heathenish Indies," Barbados had become "the Protestants Purgatory." Even "the cruell Turks" would not "sell and enslave these of their own Countrey and Religion."[34]

In the Roman Catholic Iberian colonies, enslaved people were baptized and given at least some rudimentary introduction to Christianity. By contrast, in the Protestant colonies, preserving religious difference had come to serve the purpose of distinguishing between those who deserved freedom (Christians) and those who could be enslaved (heathens, pagans). The more colonists exploited Africans and Native Americans, the more they drew these distinctions. In the early 1620s, Guiana was described as a place were "Christians" lived easily while "the Indians both house them, worke for them, bringe them victualls, and theire commodities for a small reward and price." In 1627, Henry Winthrop reported that Barbados had a population of "but 3 score christyanes and fortye slaves of negeres and Indyenes." These religio-ethnic distinctions were made on both sides of the Atlantic. For example, when a Scottish aristocrat compiled a list of the population of various parts of America in the mid-seventeenth century, he divided it into "souls" (i.e., Europeans), "negroes," and "indians." The idea that Europeans were "white" and Africans "black" can be found on Barbados as early as the 1640s, but religion remained the primary marker of European difference until the 1680s. Virginia's 1660 act regulating servitude said no servants "of what christian nation soever, shall serve longer than those of our own country, of the like age." Barbados's 1661 slave code, like others that followed, drew a distinction between "Christian servants" and "heathen Negros."[35]

Since Christians could not be enslaved, Protestant enslavers insisted that the enslaved should not, or maybe even could not, become Christian. The few exceptions only highlight this rule. One of the first recorded baptisms of an African in English America was on Barbados in 1651. A smattering of other converted Africans then appear in other colonial records, including in Virginia. Generally something set these individuals apart from the rest of their fellow Africans: a position of authority or trust or some intimate connection to their enslaver. Most seem to have either been emancipated or at least granted a special status. One historian claims seventeenth-century Virginians developed the idea of "hereditary heathenism," that a predisposition for heathenism passed from one generation to another like their status as enslaved persons. No one phrased it as such at the time, but it was not until the late eighteenth century that the idea that enslaved people could become Christian and still remain enslaved gained widespread acceptance.[36]

By the 1660s, then, non-Christian religion was being unofficially tolerated in some form or other across the English colonies. This tolerance occupies an uncomfortable, and largely unexplored, position in the broader history of religious toleration, which tends to focus on Europe and Europeans. There, religious differences existed among people who were more or less social and ethnic peers. Students of American enslaved societies, on the other hand, generally assume that toleration means the great social gulf separating the enslaved from their enslavers should somehow be overcome through a shared religion. As one scholar describes it, planters "tolerated African worship practices on their plantations" even though they disdained and feared them, because they "feared Christianity among their slaves even more." He considers the "'toleration' of African religions" an inferior sort of tolerance, "much more a de facto accommodation to the spiritual needs of the enslaved workforce than a de jure recognition of dissenters' right to free worship." Nevertheless, it was an integral part of colonial life up through the era of the American Revolution.[37]

*

As ever more Native Americans, Africans, and others fell under English authority, the exclusively Christian future imagined in 1497 became clouded in unanticipated ways. England's official Christianity was supposed to accompany the quest for trade and profits overseas. Every early colonial charter and promotional pamphlet saw colonization as a way to both spread true religion and acquire new sources of wealth. No colony proposed the toleration of non-Christian religion, but that is how matters turned out in various colonies, with the emergence of sizeable communities of non-Christian Africans and Native Americans. Missionary aspirations were thwarted by a variety of factors. There was Indigenous resistance, such as the Powhatan Uprising that destroyed the budding mission in Virginia. In Maryland, it was Protestant rivals who destroyed the promising Jesuit mission. New England's small missionary effort proved more effective, but it too faced challenges from both Indigenous people and Europeans like Emmanuel Downing Sr., who preferred to expel or enslave the Indigenous Americans.

More jarring, because even less anticipated, was the religious pluralism that developed under slavery. Some Indigenous people were enslaved, but most of the enslaved people toiling on English plantations were originally from Africa. The religious repercussions of this transformation of colonial English society were not thought through. Despite some platitudes to the contrary, very little was done to Christianize Africans in the colonies before the eighteenth century. Instead, religion served as the initial marker of difference between enslavers and enslaved. Ironically, this system allowed Africans in English America to preserve something of the beliefs and practices they had been raised with. Indeed, forcing them to remain non-Christian was essential to legitimating their enslavement.

Altogether, this rapidly growing population of non-Christians put the lie to the visions of Christian expansion that had justified colonization in the first place. However, it was not the most important factor in undermining the religious unity of English America. Much more significant were the official changes in England's religion that began in the 1530s. Over the next century, they unsettled the religious unity of the English world, pitting Europeans against each other and pushing the question of evangelizing non-Christians to the sidelines. Those changes did not mean that Anglo-America was inevitably destined for pluralism. However, by adding the challenge of enforcing conformity to an established church whose religion kept shifting during the initial phase of colonization, the English opened up dangerous cracks in their religious unity overseas as well as at home.

TWO

Conformity: Religious Change, Obedience, and Virginia

In the summer of 1583, Sir Humphrey Gilbert claimed America for Protestant England. Standing at Saint John's, Newfoundland, before an international crowd of fishermen and sailors from England, Spain, France, and Portugal, he announced Queen Elizabeth's "right and possession of those territories," then ordered "that Religion publiquely exercised, should be such and none other than is used in the Church of England." The laws of the colony were to be in accordance with the "true Christian faythe or relegion nowe professed in the Church of England" and "as nere as convenyently may be agreable to the forme of the lawes and pollicie of England." Gilbert even had a sensible plan for building up the Church of England in America. By dividing his colony into parishes of a manageable size, "neither more nor lesse then juste three Englishe myles square," churches could be built conveniently "in the Middeste thereof," while parish ministers would be provided with three hundred acres of good land conveniently near the church for their glebe—the farmland that was one of the prerogatives of being a parish minister. Further grants of land were foreseen for bishops and archbishops, all to be held by the church in perpetuity. Such a solid material base would have given the Church of England in America a far stronger foundation than it ultimately received.[1]

Gilbert's establishment of the Church of England has not gone down in American history because Gilbert went down in a shipwreck on the voyage home. His investors, deeply in debt, abandoned Newfoundland to the fishermen. Nevertheless, the episode reveals Elizabethan England's ambition to have the colonies conform to the established church. The Church of England governed the public religion of the nation, not through an Inquisition-like insistence on individual theological orthodoxy, but by laws—laws that could, and did, change. Laws passed by colonial proprietors like Gilbert planted English religion in the colonies, where they were commanded to attend church and other religious exercises, just as in England. Of course parish life in the early colonies could not completely replicate the English experience, but governors in conforming colonies like Virginia were regularly ordered to sustain "an uniformity to the doctrines and discipline of the church of England" and to maintain "the true worship and service of God" by "havinge the Gospell preched, frequent prayers and the sacraments often administred" in accordance with "the constitucions of the Church of England in all fundamentall pointes." They were also expected to uphold conformity by "punishinge of all atheisme, prophanisme, popery and schisme." When Virginia established an assembly in 1619, the General Assembly, one of the first acts was to insist on religious uniformity with England. Subsequent acts ordered that "there be an uniformity in our church as neere as may be to the canons in England; both in substance and circumstance, and that all persons yeild readie obedience unto them under paine of censure." In 1621, Governor Sir Francis Wyatt was reminded to "keep up the religion of the church of England as near as may be."[2]

More than anything, it was the challenge of maintaining conformity at home and overseas that fed the growth of early American pluralism. Legally and politically, the Church of England was the church of all English subjects, and conformity was the mechanism through which their religious allegiance and belief was enforced and sustained. Since subjects' religious and political allegiances were supposed to be the same, this was a political as well as legal and religious process. On the surface, conformity was not about belief but about behavior. Protestant reformers knew they could not suddenly force several millions of people into a massive religious conversion. They could, however, enforce external religious observations, like attending parish church services where the new religion would be preached. The demands for conformity fell more heavily on the church's ministers, who had to organize their worship services according to a prescribed formula and, often, restrict themselves to officially approved sermons when they preached. In theory, by compelling the minister and their congregants to behave in a uniform, officially approved manner, all would eventually become not just Protestants, but exactly the sorts of Protestants that the government wanted them to be.

In most cases, conformity worked. Had England's monarchs been consistent, the story of North American religion could have resembled that of Latin America. However, because the Protestant Reformation placed the monarch at the head of England's church, changes of monarch produced changes in religion, however minor. In the century from the 1530s to the 1630s, England's monarchs altered the official religion more than half a dozen times—sometimes quite drastically. Under the sixteenth-century Tudor monarchs, England went from Catholic to Protestant to Catholic to Protestant again. Under the seventeenth-century Stuarts, official Protestantism was gently nudged away from its Calvinist roots and toward what scholars now call avant-garde conformity, a generally anti-Calvinist approach to religion that imbued the external manifestations of conformity with a new spiritual significance. On paper, the Church of England in the 1630s was essentially the same as what Gilbert attempted to establish in the 1580s. Practically and spiritually, however, its character was noticeably different. Understanding this peculiar ability of conformity to be both the same and yet change is essential to understanding early American religious history, where so much evolved from the religious changes taking place within the heart of the church.

*

The religious foundations of both colonial America and the British Empire look very different depending upon where one starts. If one begins in the 1580s, as many do, colonization seems to have begun as a militant Protestant and anti-Spanish phenomenon. If we start earlier, however, we find a more complex story. Going back to the initial contact made with America in 1497, we have a very different story of England insisting on religious conformity, but exactly what the official religion was changed—more than once. Those changes fed a political struggle for control over the character of the church that was not settled until 1662. Before then, dissenters were never only religious dissidents. They were contestants for the power to decide what sort of church their countrymen should conform to.

Efforts to enforce religious unity overshadowed England's connection to America from the beginning. Just eight months before Cabot landed at Newfoundland, four Lollards stood at Saint Paul's Cross, the outdoor pulpit on the grounds of the cathedral of London: the most public religious space in the country. Listening to a sermon chastising their beliefs while their religious works were burned in front of them, they made a public penance and knew they were lucky. So-called Lollards had been around since the 1380s, when the Oxford theologian John Wycliffe first inspired people with his Bible-based criticisms of Roman Catholic worship. Since then, dozens of Lollards had been burned alive as heretics. Lollardy would survive into the Reformation era, but by 1497 it had been so effectively marginalized that no Lollards thought to seek refuge in the colonies nor did they have any special influence on the Reformation. The Roman Catholic campaign against heresies old and new continued throughout the first decades of England's encounter with America. In 1516, Bishop Richard Foxe founded the influential Oxford College of Corpus Christi to promote "the extirpation of heresy and error, and the augmentation of the orthodox faith." In 1522, King Henry VIII denounced the "sacrilegeous opinions" of Martin Luther. His book *Defense of the Seven Sacraments* earned him praise from the pope as a defender of the faith.[3]

Had Henry stuck to his guns, English America could have been solidly Roman Catholic, for, ever since it expelled the Jews in the 1290s, England led one of Europe's most ruthless and effective campaigns against religious dissent. This campaign against religious difference drew on a theological tradition dating back to the fourth-century alliance Christians forged with the Roman emperor Constantine. Christianity suddenly went from being a minor, persecuted faith to the faith of the emperor. Now religious and political loyalty combined into an entity known as "Christendom"—a concept both territorial and religious. Soon Saint Augustine made the case for state coercion as a spiritual good. After all, if magistrates refused to impose the true faith, was that not an utter disregard for peoples' salvation? Did not tolerating religious difference effectively condemn the tolerated to hell? In the thirteenth century, churchmen like Thomas Aquinas began describing heresy as a disease to justify even harsher treatments of religious dissidents. Killing heretics was like cutting off an infected part of the body to prevent the spread of an illness. Similar attitudes persisted into the 1660s, when, in response to complaints from Dissenters, a royalist apologist declared, "That which you call Persecution, I translate Uniformity."[4]

Religious conformity was thus as much about maintaining social and political order as it was religious faith. Rejecting the official religion could be considered an act of treason. The English did not pioneer the burning of heretics, but they became enthusiastic practitioners after burning a few Cathars in 1210. Where most of Europe experienced a lull in religious executions between the end of Cathar heresy trials in the mid-fifteenth century and the advent of Lutheranism in the 1520s, the English continued apace, trying hundreds of accused heretics, mostly Lollards. They burned about fifty after passing the statute *de haeretico comburendo* (on the burning of heretics) in 1401. About another fifty people, both Protestant and Catholic, were executed in the last years of Henry VIII's reign (r. 1509–47):

one notable July day in 1540 witnessed the burning of three Protestants for heresy and the beheading of three Catholics for treason. Two Protestants were executed for heresy under the Protestant Edward VI (r. 1547–53); at least 280 under the Catholic Queen Mary (r. 1553–58); six under the Protestant Queen Elizabeth (r. 1558–1603); and two more under James I (r. 1603–25). In addition, several hundred individuals were executed because their religious choices were deemed treasonous: mostly Roman Catholics but also a few Separatist Protestants whose denial of the monarch's role as head of the true church had political as well as religious consequences. The last victims burned for heresy were in 1612, but English magistrates and ministers continued to advocate burning as a punishment for Protestant heretics until Parliament abolished the death penalty for ecclesiastical affairs in 1677. Scotland, which had its own Parliament until 1707, performed the last British execution for heresy in 1697.[5]

Following the break with Rome initiated by King Henry VIII and his Parliament in 1533, Protestant Reformers drew on this tradition of coercion to craft the framework of conformity. First came the Statute of Restraint of Appeals, which made it illegal for English subjects to appeal religious or other decisions to the pope: the pope no longer had any authority within King Henry's lands. Then, in 1534, the Act of Supremacy vested supreme religious and political sovereignty within "the realm of England" in the Crown. King Henry owed allegiance to none but God. The following year, the monasteries were dissolved, instigating a massive property transfer from the church to royal and private hands. Henry VIII was a religious conservative, not a committed Protestant reformer. His church was antipapal, but less than fully Protestant, as its main statement on doctrine, the six basic articles of faith included in the 1539 "Act Abolishing Diversity in Opinions," indicates. Several Catholic elements remained in his church: auricular confession, a prohibition of clerical marriage, and an endorsement of those who pledged their chastity to God.[6]

The shift to Protestantism interwove England's political and religious constitutions more tightly than ever. The church was part of the monarchy (bishops sat in Parliament's House of Lords), and the monarchy part of the church (the king appointed the bishops and archbishops who ran the church). The Church of England was now the church "as by law established," with a "mixed" constitution combining religious and political loyalty. Those who refused to recognize the monarch as the head of the church could be executed for treason, as Sir Thomas More was in 1535. Roman Catholics regarded him and many other similar victims as martyrs, but Protestants insisted such executions were about politics, not religion. They prided themselves on being different from Roman Catholics who, through institutions like the Inquisition, punished people for their interior beliefs as well as their external behaviors. Conformity only demanded an outward adherence to the legally prescribed forms of worship, not doctrinal belief. Of course, it was hoped that correct belief would eventually be inculcated through church attendance, but no mechanism was set up to police individuals' inner thoughts. As one historian has pointed out, "even the most hardline advocates of religious coercion" in the establishments of both England and Scotland "insisted that they had no intention of persecuting people simply for erroneous or heretical *opinions*." Only "if they revealed their gross heresies" through public acts, such as refusing to attend church, circulating their views in writing, or holding alternate worship services, would they be punished, especially if, in addition to actively propagating their views, they "stubbornly refused to recant" when confronted about their errors.[7]

Conformity thus sought to create religious change on a national scale by insisting on external obedience to the legally established church. While many early reformers were strongly influenced by the Reformed Protestant ideas coming out of Switzerland, including Calvinism, it was conformity more than any specific theology that defined what it meant to belong to the church. Indeed, beyond conformity, it could sometimes be difficult to describe exactly what the church stood for. The Henrician Reformation did away with the Roman Catholic system of monks, nuns, and religious orders, but it preserved much of rest of its hierarchical ecclesiastical system, merely replacing the pope with the monarch at the head of the church. The church continued to be governed in an episcopal fashion with, at the top, its two archbishops, York, overseeing England north of the river Trent including the Isle of Man, and Canterbury, overseeing the rest of the country and its overseas outposts. These archdioceses were subdivided into bishoprics, where bishops took the lead in managing religious affairs, not least through their power to ordain new ministers and thus perpetuate the church. At the local level, episcopal authority was primarily experienced through the church courts, which had jurisdiction over a variety of aspects of civil law, from sexual and social transgressions, like fornication and drunkenness, to family law and inheritance, especially the proving of wills. Additionally, from the 1530s to 1641, there was a royal Court of High Commission, which had the authority to discipline ministers and laymen from across the country for failing to respect the rules and regulations of the church. If convicted, ministers could be deprived of their post; laymen could be physically mutilated.[8]

FIGURE 3. English World: Europe

The American colonies' connection to England's church hierarchy ran through the bishopric of London. The city's leading role in overseas trade and exploration meant its bishop generally had oversight over overseas outposts. Like every other diocese, London was divided into dozens of parishes, each centered on a single parish church. Everyone resident and born within the parish was automatically a member of the Church of England. Around 1600 England was divided into roughly nine thousand parishes that varied in size, population, terrain, and wealth. London had 111 parishes crammed into its narrow confines, some as small as four acres square. In thinly populated parts of the countryside, on the other hand, parishes were much larger. Some extended for so many miles that it was difficult for all the parishioners to attend services regularly in their parish church. In these cases, small chapels were built. If not staffed by a regularly appointed chaplain, they were served by occasional visits from the parish minister or his curate. Early colonial parishes, especially in Virginia, tended to resemble these large, poorer rural parishes. The parish was the basic unit of worship and the communal center of religious life. It was also the level at which, for most commoners, including early

FIGURE 4. Archdiocese of Canterbury

colonists, religious politics was experienced. On Sundays and other special occasions, everyone within a parish was required by law to resort to their parish church. Repeated absences could be punished, either by parish officials or the bishop's church courts. Virginia began as a single parish, the parish of Jamestown. Placed under the jurisdiction of the bishop of London, its first rector (or senior minister) was Richard Hakluyt, the Elizabethan propagandist of empire. Like many rectors, especially in rural areas, Hakluyt never took up his post in person. Instead, as was also customary for wealthier rectors who held more than one position, he hired a curate to fulfill his parish obligations. Hakluyt's curate, Robert Hunt, became Virginia's first minister. Every English resident of Jamestown parish was considered to be a member of the Church of England and expected to act as such.[9]

Pressure for religious conformity could be applied in different ways at the various levels of spiritual jurisdiction. First came the individual body, which housed the conscience governing each individual soul. Protestants debated endlessly over exactly who had a conscience, how it was acquired, how it worked, and how much liberty it should have. Well into the eighteenth century, the tendency was to give more respect to the workings of the consciences of privileged individuals, especially free, European adult men, than to those of poorer, subordinate people, like women, children, servants, non-Christians, and non-Europeans. Ideally, as mediator of an individual's relationship to, and understanding of, divine truth, the conscience would agree with the commands of religious and secular authorities. However, as Martin Luther demonstrated, it could defy them as well. When charged with heresy, Luther responded that he could not "retract anything; for it cannot be right for a Christian to speak against his conscience." When his accusers pointed to the disorder that could ensue if everyone had liberty to follow their conscience instead of respecting church authority, Luther responded that he was not speaking of the "freedom to follow one's subjective ethical convictions" but rather the "freedom from false doctrines and authorities" (i.e., those of the Roman Catholic Church) that was necessary for the conscience to find its true freedom in proper subjection to God. Nevertheless, Luther's respect for conscience was not incompatible with conformity. On the contrary, he argued that, although a secular government could not coerce its inhabitants' consciences into believing the religion that was preached, it could force them to outwardly conform (to the true religion) and suppress manifestations of (false) religious alternatives. Extended through John Calvin and Ulrich Zwingli, this line of argument justified the enforcement of religious conformity throughout the English world.[10]

The enforcement of conformity became an increasingly vexed issue as the Tudor monarchs died and were succeeded by a new monarch with rather different ideas about how to organize the national religion. In January 1547, the conservative Henrician church ended with Henry's death and burial in traditional Catholic style. Before he died, he had assigned a group of councilors, or Protectors, to help his nine-year-old son and heir, Edward VI, rule until he attained the age of maturity. These Protectors had ambitious plans for church reform. Rejecting the Protestant extremes of theologically conservative Lutheranism and radical Anabaptism, they favored the Reformed Protestantism gaining ground in Switzerland, France, and parts of the Holy Roman Empire. To move England's church in that direction, the Protectors oversaw the passage of a new series of laws that, among other things, allowed priests to marry, opposed the use of images in worship, and replaced the celebration of Mass at the altar with sermons explicating Scripture from a pulpit. Especially influential was Archbishop of Canterbury Thomas Cranmer who made sure that the break with Rome became clear by supporting the doctrine that the pope was the Antichrist: the seemingly holy figure who actually presided over a false church that led people to damnation. As he explained in 1549 to some "ignorant men of Devonshire and Cornwall" protesting thc church reforms, the "bishop of Rome's ordinances and laws" were wicked, ungodly, tyrannous inventions created "more than a thousand years after the faith of Christ was full, and perfect!"[11]

Cranmer's most important legacy for the church was the *Book of Common Prayer*. A guide for worship, the Prayer Book, as it came to be called, was designed to ensure that the church's thousands of clerics adhered to a uniform and officially sanctioned liturgy. Many of England's priests were neither committed Protestants nor highly educated. However, they could conform by following these printed prayers and the prescribed forms and order of worship. The Prayer Book became so important in creating English Protestantism that it quickly became a defining element of the Church of England. The two Edwardian parliamentary Acts of Uniformity relied on it. The first, in 1549, ordered all churches to use the *Book of Common Prayer* and required all subjects to attend its services. Those who missed too many services had to pay a fine. Cranmer then revised the *Book of Common Prayer* into a more overtly Reformed product that sanctioned only forms of worship that could be shown to have scriptural authority.

In 1552 the second Edwardian Act of Uniformity imposed this new version and threatened clergymen who refused to use it with punishment. In between, royal injunctions tried to smooth over any confusion by expressing a desire for religious unity and peace. People were admonished to not "'in any wise refuse or exclude' those who held different views from themselves 'from their companies, at any time when occasion shall be offered that they may come together charitably and Christianly.'"[12]

To give the Edwardian church a clearly Reformed theology, Cranmer then drew up forty-two articles of faith. Unfortunately, before they could be implemented and the Reformed character of the church confirmed without a doubt, poor Edward died of tuberculosis in July 1553. The rights of succession dictated that his older half sister Mary become queen. Daughter of Henry VIII's first wife, the Spanish princess Catherine of Aragon, Mary had remained a devout Catholic all her life. The Edwardian government, respecting her status, had not compelled her to conform. Terrified of the spiritual and political consequences of a return to Catholic rule, one of Edward's Protectors staged a coup in favor of a Protestant monarch: the sixteen-year-old Lady Jane Grey, Edward's nearest Protestant relative who was not a child of one of Henry VIII's wives. Lacking popular support, it failed. Backed by conservative elites, Mary was proclaimed queen a few days later.[13]

Queen Mary did not immediately restore the Roman Catholic Church. However, she made her intentions clear by rescinding her brother's Act of Uniformity, denying priests permission to marry, ordering a return to the liturgy of Henry VIII, and then marrying the Spanish prince Philip. Committed Protestants who could flee went into exile, finding shelter and inspiration in the Reformed territories of Switzerland and the Rhineland. The rest watched with dread as Mary's regime revived the old medieval statutes against heresy, including the 1401 statute permitting the burning of heretics, and proclaimed its determination to end the "errors and heresies which of late have risen, grown, and much increased within this realm." Calling "for order and conformity in religion" and commanding her subjects "to live in quiet and charity," Mary warned of the "great dangers" threatening "this realm through diversity of opinions in religion." In January 1555, her government repealed the Act of Supremacy and restored papal authority. In February, it began burning people for heresy. By November 1558, her government had executed about 280 Protestants, including Cranmer. It was an exceptionally ferocious campaign, accounting "for almost 10 per cent of the heresy executions in Latin Christendom between 1520 and 1565."[14]

Given time, the regime conceivably could have suppressed Protestantism. With brutal logic it targeted the most outspoken and committed Protestants, like Cranmer. As the geography of executions reveals, they were unevenly distributed across her realms, suggesting the limits of Protestant reform under Henry and Edward. The vast majority of Mary's victims lived in the south and east of England, especially London. These were not only the most economically developed parts of the country but also the areas with the closest ties to Protestant Europe. Her government found few, if any, individuals worth punishing in Wales or the north and west of England, and none in Ireland.[15]

Fortunately for the Protestant cause, Mary died suddenly on November 17, 1558. The national religion changed once again as her twenty-five-year-old half sister Elizabeth, daughter of Henry's first Protestant wife, Anne Boleyn, took the throne. However, Elizabeth and her advisors moved cautiously. Their instincts were more conservative than those of Edward's Protectors, and they feared a sudden return to the firmly Reformed policies of Edward's reign might provoke a revolt. The Catholic revival under Queen Mary had strengthened religious conservatives, and Catholics had already rebelled under Henry VIII (the 1536 Pilgrimage of Grace) and Edward VI (the 1549 Prayer Book rebellion). Only after several months of negotiation did Parliament pass a new Act of Supremacy in the spring of 1559. England's church was taken out of obedience to the pope for the last time. The subsequent Act of Uniformity established the contours of Protestant conformity for centuries to come.

The Elizabethan church began as a compromise, somewhere between the conservatism of the Henrician church and the Edwardian church's promise of Reformed Protestantism. Worship according to the *Book of Common Prayer* was restored, but the Elizabethan Prayer Book modified the 1552 Edwardian version to make it easier for religious conservatives to stay in the church. Several points of doctrine were deliberately rendered vague and practical concessions made, including the requirements that ministers wear the surplice (the priestly tunic that evoked their traditional sacramental role) and make the sign of the cross when baptizing a child. Another requirement that resembled Roman Catholic practice was having parishioners kneel when receiving communion. The doctrine of the church was not outlined until 1563, when the Protestant bishops and clergy meeting in Convocation drew up the Thirty-Nine Articles. Revised in 1571, the Thirty-Nine Articles became "the closest thing England ever had to a 'confession' or creedal document" like those of other Protestant churches. These too contained a degree of religious ambiguity that permitted Calvinist and non-Calvinist views to coexist within the same church.[16]

The compromises kept the door open for religious conservatives, but they affronted Reformed Protestants. The resulting controversy might not have mattered much if Elizabeth, like her siblings, had died quickly, or if she had been willing to endorse further reform. However, she not only lived an unusually long time but stubbornly resisted any changes to her religious settlement. Elizabeth's Protestantism was conservative, like her father's. She was not zealously anti-Catholic and allowed individuals with Roman Catholic ties and sympathies to exercise influence at her court. She did not care for clerical marriage. She liked a certain amount of ceremony, including candles, crosses, beautiful music, and the surplice—all legitimate according to her church settlement. She was not a fan of sermons, which Reformed Protestants considered to be the central and indispensable part of the church service. She thought ministers did enough when they simply read out from the *Book of Common Prayer*. She did not believe they all needed sufficient education to be able to preach on their own. Significantly, Elizabeth was a political conservative as well. She valued conformity as a demonstration of loyalty and obedience, qualities she and her leading advisors had already displayed. Although raised Protestant, Elizabeth had conformed to the Roman Catholic Church during Mary's reign. So had her leading minister, William Cecil, and her first archbishop of Canterbury, Matthew Parker. Conformity mattered more than one's personal religious predilections.[17]

Elizabeth's conservative religious and political attitudes are crucial because it was during her almost half century of rule that the bulk of England's population, and a small fraction of Ireland's, became Protestant. Her religious settlement had a lasting impact on English Protestant identity, not least by cultivating a deep attachment to the *Book of Common Prayer*. This was a religion of bishops and some ceremony, but it was also fairly easy to export overseas, with or without a minister. We have few records of actual religious practice on most of the early exploratory and colonial ventures, but we can assume it resembled that of Virginia in its first years. Robert Hunt was "an honest, religious, and courageous Divine" according to Captain John Smith, but he died within a year. The colonists stayed loyally conformist until "more Preachers came" by saying their "Prayers dailey, with an Homily on Sunday," likely read from the *Book of Common Prayer*. They lacked the sacraments that only a minister could perform and the elaborate material culture available in some parish churches. They did not lack religion.[18]

Conformity was a tricky basis for building a religion, however. Exactly what it meant and how it was performed could and did vary. The emphasis on legal forms and behaviors gave people some leeway to alter the character of the church by exploiting what Martin Luther identified as the "things indifferent" to religious worship. There were many areas where Scripture was unclear about how exactly to organize worship. Regarding these "things indifferent," or *adiaphora*, Luther believed that every country had the right to organize its church and enforce worship as it saw fit—so long as it did not alter the core matters that affected salvation. *Adiaphora* included superficial acts like kneeling for communion or wearing the surplice, which Luther and many conservative Protestant reformers favored because they felt that religious worship could and should reflect a country's social and political structure. Such gestures were important displays of political loyalty and obedience but had no significant religious consequences. English conservatives had been drawing on this theory since the 1530s to emphasize the Englishness of their church over its universality. The Church of England, they claimed, was not a Reformed Church like those on the Continent. Henrician churchmen praised their church as an "indifferent mean" between the two extremes of the "blind superstition" and "stiffness" of Roman Catholics and the "arrogant blindness" and "rashness and licentiousness" of Reformed Protestants. Henry VIII described it as sitting between those who were "too stiff" and those who were "too busy and curious."[19]

After 1660 it would become commonplace to affirm that the Anglican Church represented an ideal middle way, or *via media*, between the two extremes of Reformed Protestantism and Roman Catholicism. However, before then this ideal was just one of a variety of religious opinions within the Church of England. Less conservative churchmen emphasized the Bible, sermons, and the writings of Calvin. Nevertheless, they had to worship alongside the conservatives drawn to religious ritual. Elizabethan conformity thus comprised a spectrum of religious views that became more diverse over time, as some became partial conformists or even nonconformists to distance themselves from the aspects of religious worship they disagreed with without abandoning the church while others moved in the opposite direction and became what scholars now refer to as avant-garde conformists, who not only embraced strict conformity but infused *adiaphora* with more spiritual meaning than Luther had ever intended. In between was a fairly wide range of views and attitudes, all coexisting and sometimes struggling for supremacy in a system that gave each some leeway but denied all a final say over the fundamental character of the church beyond what had already been established in the Elizabethan church settlement.[20]

American historians are very familiar with puritans and their nonconformity, but are less clear about the avant-garde conformity they were reacting against. This trend emerged in the 1590s, after and largely in reaction against puritanism. It had strong links to Oxford University, the more religiously conservative of England's two universities. Here, where conformity had been strictly enforced since 1581, the conservative understanding of conformity gained philosophical heft in 1593 with the publication of Richard Hooker's *Of the Lawes of Ecclesiastical Politie*. This Oxford theologian argued, among other things, that the Church of England's peculiar mix of traditions, ceremonies, and practices was not, as puritans claimed, the result of an incomplete or imperfect reformation. On the contrary, it represented a distinctively English form of Protestantism that should be celebrated. Human reason, not Calvinist fundamentalism, should guide interpretations of God's law. Ceremonies and sacred music were not popish corruptions of the original truth but valuable "aids to devotion."[21]

Soon after Hooker's book was published, a theological dispute over the place of Calvinism within the church broke out at Cambridge University. Cambridge did not enforce conformity until 1616, giving it a puritan-friendly reputation that attracted students like John Cotton and John Winthrop who later became ministers and magistrates in New England. In 1595, William Whitaker, an "eminent Cambridge theologian and hard-line supralapsarian Calvinist" worried that the church was moving away from its Calvinist roots, responded to the dispute by drawing up nine points affirming the church's Calvinist theological core. If the archbishop of Canterbury, John Whitgift, would publicly confirm them, surely all controversy would be put to rest? Whitaker's points upheld several strict Calvinist propositions, including double predestination: namely, that God had predestined souls to be saved *and* damned. It was common doctrine in the church that some were predestined to be saved, but only the firmest of Calvinists insisted God had equally predestined others to damnation. Whitaker personally carried his propositions to Whitgift at his palace in Lambeth, where Whitgift shared them with a committee of theologians. They made some seemingly minor adjustments, and Whitaker carried these Lambeth Articles back to Cambridge. However, before he could do anything with them, he suddenly sickened and died. In the meantime, both Queen Elizabeth and her leading minister, William Cecil, expressed their opposition to Whitaker's propositions, especially double predestination. The Lambeth Articles never became official doctrine. They were not even published until 1651. A closer look at the alterations made by Whitgift's committee reveals something else: while not explicitly anti-Calvinist, they do, as one historian notes, transform "an unambiguously Calvinist proposition into one susceptible to a non-Calvinist reading." It seems Whitgift was attempting to create "a consensus document" that "could be embraced by all parties within the English mainstream." However, it failed because a number of influential figures—not least of all, the queen—felt it too was still too "harshly predestinarian."[22]

Nevertheless, what set avant-garde conformists apart was not so much their theology as their exalted view of *adiaphora*. They used set prayers, ceremonies, music, sacred architecture, interior design, ritual behaviors (like kneeling when receiving of communion and making the sign of the cross when baptizing), and traditional customs (like Sunday church ales and the churching of women) to give religion in their parish a distinctly different tone from what strict Calvinists like Whitaker demanded. An important early promoter of this trend was Lancelot Andrewes, the influential rector of a London parish. His career shows how the character of the Church of England could be altered from within, as he actively partook of two rather different visions of the church. Born under Queen Mary in 1555, Andrewes, like many early Elizabethan churchmen, began his career as an orthodox Calvinist. Then, in the mid-1590s, he began altering the liturgical practice in his church. For example, he moved the communion table back to the traditional position of the altar. Protestant Reformers had banished the altar, replacing it with a simple communion table that was explicitly given no special location or sacred status within the church building. It was just a table. Placing it where the altar had been threatened to bestow upon it some of the spiritual significance associated with Catholic altars. Andrewes also shifted his style of preaching and devotion, relying less on the Bible and more on *adiaphora*. His career flourished, and he rose to the position of bishop before his death in 1626. Thereafter, his legacy became an exemplar of the ambivalent possibilities of early seventeenth-century conformity. Calvinists admired his early work; anti-Calvinists his later sermons.[23]

A new regime offered a rare opportunity to make major changes to religious policy. Queen Elizabeth died on March 24, 1603, giving the many figures within the church who wanted further reform away from her compromise hope. The accession of the thirty-six-year-old King James VI Stewart of Scotland to the throne of England and Ireland as James I Stuart seemed auspicious. James was a devout Calvinist raised according to the strongly reformed Protestant priorities of the Church of Scotland. Not only was Protestantism now the dominant religion in two out of three kingdoms, instead of just one of two, but for the first time in English history the throne was occupied by a mature, experienced, and reliably Calvinist monarch. Even better, James had secured the Protestant succession by fathering two sons and a daughter. As he rode down from Scotland to take up the throne, opponents of avant-garde conformism organized a massive petition drive in favor of further religious reform. After allegedly acquiring one thousand signatures, this so-called millenary petition was presented to James, who agreed to host a public debate over religious policy the following winter.[24]

The debate at the royal palace of Hampton Court pitted four carefully chosen and not very radical puritans against four defenders of the existing episcopal order. Occasionally joining in on issues of doctrine and liturgical practice like the wearing of the surplice and making the sign of the cross at baptism, James ultimately concluded that there was no need for serious reform. He did assent to a few minor concessions, including a new translation of the Bible, the now classic King James Version. However, he came down firmly on the side of episcopacy, famously proclaiming, "No Bishop, No King." A few months later, he ordered the drafting of a new set of canons to govern the Church of England. These canons explicitly banned a wide range of activities and coping mechanisms that those who could not fully endorse conformity had developed during Elizabeth's reign. Ministers now not only had to swear to uphold all the canons of the Church of England, they also, in canon 36, had to swear that its government and ceremonies were scripturally sound. Those who did not would lose their post. Confronted with the demand to conform to the new canons, some three hundred ministers refused and lost their positions.[25]

Virginia was founded within the boundaries of this Jacobean conformity. The new rules discouraged puritans and encouraged avant-garde conformists to wiggle conformity ever further away from Calvinism. Even more influential in this process than Andrewes was Richard Neile (1562–1640). Unlike Andrewes, Neile had not begun his career as a Calvinist. He seems to have always loved ceremony and hated puritans. Wherever he was, he went out of his way to discourage sermons and insist that people kneel when receiving the sacraments. The son of a London tallow chandler, Neile had begun his career as household chaplain to William Cecil. He then served his son Robert Cecil in the same capacity. With their patronage, Neile embarked on a successful ecclesiastical career that included several bishoprics and culminated with his appointment as archbishop of York in 1632. The archbishopric of York contained the country's largest Catholic community. Neile strove to convert them, but his methods were not those of a Calvinist. Rather than deploy confrontational sermons, he preferred to appeal to Catholic sensibilities by beautifying local churches and encouraging the use of ceremonies. The powerful positions he held in the church and at court, first as clerk of the closet from 1603 to 1632 and then as member of the Privy Council from 1627, gave him significant patronage. He used it to support other men who also loved what puritans hated. Durham House, Neile's official residence in London while bishop of Durham between 1617 and 1628, became so infamous for its anti-Calvinism that the puritan-friendly Parliament of 1629 accused its residents of treason.[26]

Avant-garde conformists remained Protestants, but they sure looked popish to those who insisted that everything the church did had to be scripturally sound. Even more controversial and influential than Andrewes or Neile was William Laud. Like Andrewes, Laud, born in 1573 as the younger son of a wealthy clothier from Reading, had grown up in the Calvinist tradition of the Elizabethan church but turned against it in the 1590s when Calvinism seemed to become divisive, unpredictable, and disruptive. Laud valued the opposite qualities. After a long stint at Saint John's College, Oxford University, first as a student, then a fellow, he steadily rose through the ranks until he became archbishop of Canterbury in 1633. In between he resided at Durham House under Neile's patronage and served as bishop of London. Laud's influence over both the clergy and the policy of the church became so notorious that scholars often refer to the avant-garde conformity of the early Stuart era as Laudianism and its adherents as Laudians.[27]

Laudianism was not a theology so much as a holistic approach to religious life developed in explicit opposition to English puritanism. Laudians were social and religious conservatives who emphasized respect for the traditional hierarchies in church, state, and society. They zealously endorsed conformity and made a show of their complete submission to its demands. There was a strong communal dimension to their religiosity. Unlike supralapsarian Calvinists like Whitaker, Laudians refused to deny all hope of salvation to their neighbors. They also wanted to liberate the church from the power that the laity had acquired over it since the Reformation and recuperate some of its old institutional glory. Laudians favored royal and episcopal authority over just Scriptural authority. Indeed they developed a more exalted vision of bishops' role in the church than had been common under Elizabeth. Playing down the importance of preaching, they emphasized instead the power of set prayers. Some even argued that Jesus Christ was not the only divine figure to intercede in spiritual affairs. Saints, angels, and even certain priests had special powers to do so as well. They resented Calvinism because its emphasis on individual inspiration, spontaneous prayer, and charismatic preaching threatened to allow talented men of low social rank and questionable political views gain more power and influence than was their due.[28]

Calvinists frequently accused Laudians of being Arminians. Arminians followed the teaching of the Dutch Reformed theologian Arminius that humans may have some role in determining their own salvation. Arminius actually came out of the Calvinist tradition, but his position was often exaggerated into a crypto-Catholic belief in free will. Some Laudians were Arminians; others were not. Whether Laud was an Arminian is unclear. He kept his exact theological views ambiguous. Arminianism may well have appealed to him, but he and many other Laudians are better understood as anti-Calvinists. More than a specific theological point, it is their dislike of what they believed to be the unruly social and religious implications of anti-Calvinism that stands out.[29]

The consternation Laudians provoked in Calvinists is evident in a sermon by one of Laud's Oxford colleagues, Regius Professor of Divinity Robert Abbot. Perplexed, Abbott publicly berated Laud. "What art thou, ROMISH or ENGLISH? PAPIST or PROTESTANT?" Ventriloquizing the voice of Jesus Christ in heaven, Abbot wondered if Laud were a "Mungrel, or compound of both: A Protestant by Ordination, a Papist in point of Free Will, Inherent Righteousness, and the like. A Protestant in receiving the Sacrament, a Papist in the Doctrine of the Sacrament? What, do you think there are two Heavens? If there be," Abbot (as Jesus) concluded, "get you to the other, and place your selves there, for into this where I am ye shall not come."[30]

Laudians were Protestant, but is not hard to see why their critics believed they might be closet Roman Catholics. The phrase most closely associated with Laudians, "the beauty of holiness," aptly sums up their desire to restore splendor and majesty back to the church. Initially, they claimed they just wanted to improve the material fabric of the country's aging churches, which were, in fact, beginning to crumble after decades of Protestant neglect. However, Laudians went beyond just fixing up old buildings to introduce new elements like stained glass and remodeled church interiors. They enthusiastically deployed candles, exquisite music, and reveled in priestly costume like the surplice. They followed Andrewes in arranging communion tables like altars. Moving them back to the east end of chancels, they then enhanced their status by railing them off to separate them from the congregation, just as Catholics did with their altars. They also encouraged congregants to bow toward them as if they had altar-like spiritual power.[31]

Some of the suspiciously "popish" elements in Laudian reforms reflected their strategy for completing England's Reformation. They wanted to convert all the remaining Roman Catholic subjects of the English Crown while also preventing Protestants from backsliding. They felt their approach made it easier to bring Catholics into the church while satisfying the desires of Protestants who might otherwise be lured over to Catholic ceremonialism. In brief, Laudians targeted the conservative end of the spectrum of English Christianity. They did not think the differences between the Church of England and Roman Catholicism were as great as Calvinists insisted. Indeed, their respect for established authority and bishops was so strong that it extended to the church of Rome and the pope himself. Breaking with earlier orthodoxy, they stopped labeling the pope the Antichrist and calling the Roman Catholic Church a false church. Instead, some Laudians argued that Catholics erred in little more than their obedience to the *court* of Rome and the supremacy of the pope: the pope's claim to be supreme head of the church was misguided, but his role as bishop of Rome was legitimate. Some Laudians even looked favorably on that other ancient and episcopal Christian religion: Greek Orthodoxy. The ultimate results of their strategy were mixed. Some Catholics conformed to the Church of England. However, some Laudians converted to Catholicism.[32]

Under King James, Laudian influence extended to the top of England's government thanks in large part to Robert Cecil. Before his death in 1612, he actively shaped Jacobean religious policy through a number of his official roles, including serving as chancellor of Cambridge University and patron of Richard Neile. He had served Queen Elizabeth as an advisor alongside his father and continued to do so after his father's death in 1598. His key role in securing the Stuart succession prompted King James to make him his leading minister and even ennoble him as the Earl of Salisbury. Like his father, Robert Cecil privileged conformity over theological orthodoxy. However, his stance toward Roman Catholicism was more moderate, and several Catholic English aristocrats were close friends. At the same time, Cecil was not fiercely anti-Calvinist. Indeed, his parents had raised him so thoroughly immersed in Scripture that he occasionally lent a hand to Calvinist ministers who got in trouble with bishops. Nevertheless, his religious tastes were far from Calvinist. Pauline Croft has pointed out that bits of textual evidence indicate that his spirituality was "remarkably similar" to that found in Lancelot Andrewes's "preaching style and devotional fervour." More revealing of his inclinations is the private chapel he ordered built toward the end of his life at his estate of Hatfield House. It was, according to Croft, "expensively ablaze with colour, gold leafe, painting and stained glass." It underlined "the most notable feature of Cecil's mature religious outlook," namely, "its intimate connexion with his strong aesthetic interests," including religious art. King James would copy the aesthetics Cecil pioneered at Hatfield chapel when he had the chapel in his Scottish palace of Holyrood redecorated.[33]

In colonial America, evidence of Laudianism can be seen in the influence of people like the Ferrar brothers, who played an important role in early Virginia. Only William Ferrar actually went to the colony, where he—like so many others—soon died. However, his brothers Nicholas and John Ferrar were influential directors of the Virginia Company and remained involved with the colony for many years. Famous for their piety, the Ferrars did much to promote religion and piety in early Virginia. However, they also became notorious for their Laudian tastes. In the village of Little Gidding, they created a special religious retreat similar to the chapel at Hatfield House. A visiting Calvinist minister denounced it as "an Arminian nunnery." He was offended not only by its splendid decorations but also because of the prominent role the Ferrars's kinswomen had in its worship services. The Ferrars's version of conformity may not have been the same as that of other early Virginians. However, it had much in common with that of some of the most powerful people in England at the time Virginia was founded.[34]

*

Conformity was the essential building block of the Church of England. It was not a perfect tool for securing religious change. For three decades the English were buffeted back and forth between Roman Catholicism and Protestantism, producing a mixed bag of religious allegiances. Only during Queen Elizabeth's long reign did conformity successfully shepherd the great majority of English, and a few Irish, from Roman Catholicism to Protestantism. In the meantime, the repeated changes in official religion raised for some individuals more radical questions about the nature of national religion. Roger Williams, looking back from the 1640s, was amazed at "how easie it is to turne, and turne, and turn againe whole Nations from one Religion to another." After all, "within the compasse of one poore span of 12 yeares revolution, all England hath become from halfe Papist, halfe Protestant, to absolute Protestants; from absolute Protestants, to absolute Papists; from absolute Papists (changing as fashions) to absolute Protestants." If the national religion had changed before, could it not change again?[35]

Imposed from above by parliamentary laws and local magistrates, conformity emphasized external displays of devotion and loyalty but allowed room for internal differences of opinion. Since there was no Protestant inquisition to probe individuals' particular beliefs, those internal differences of opinion could and did persist for generations. So long as individuals fulfilled the external requirements established by law, they would not be punished for their beliefs. However, as the rise of the avant-garde conformists demonstrates, conformity was not immune to change even when the laws remained essentially the same. Some of the people who loudly proclaimed their loyalty to the official religion under King James were of a rather different breed than the men who had first created Elizabeth's church. Even as Virginians were being told to conform to the established church, these ostentatiously conforming individuals were subtly altering its shape and character from within. Those who experienced those changes as a violation of the church's ostensibly reformed Protestant character had increasing difficulty adhering to conformity. This dilemma was most acute for ministers, who were held to stricter standards and could lose their jobs for failing to uphold them, as several hundred discovered just three years before Jamestown was founded.

Conformity is an effective reminder of the degree to which political power shaped early modern English religion. It also points to the important jurisdictional, legal, and political limits on religious authority in the English world. Everywhere, at all levels, patronage was crucial to the success or failure of religious reforms. Laudians, who remained a minority within the church, derived their increasing power from Laud's successful use of patronage, but they never controlled the implementation of conformity everywhere. At the local level in various corners of the English world, patronage could also protect puritan sympathizers from the full demands of conformity. As Richard Neile's service in the archbishopric of York suggests, conformity could take on a different character in different jurisdictions within the English world depending on who had the power to interpret and enforce it. Understanding the interplay between who enforced conformity on who and how is essential for understanding colonial religious history, for each colony represented a new ecclesiastical as well as political jurisdiction. In Europe, the variety of jurisdictions allowed a range of religious differences to survive. In America, jurisdictional differences allowed pluralism to gain a foothold, even as the colonies officially conformed to England's church.

THREE

Jurisdiction: Ireland, Scotland, and the Limits of Authority

Protestant England's first encounter with America, a disastrous voyage to Newfoundland in 1536, offers a useful indication of the limits local authorities faced even within one of the most authoritarian of environments: a ship at sea. In this case, the ship had run out of food. In desperation, some of the crew turned to cannibalism. Although their captain warned them such behavior "offended the Almightie," and invoked "the Scriptures from first to last," the crew did not heed him. Fortunately, the "mercie of God" sent a French ship well stocked with food that "same night." The English seized it and sailed home, forgetting their mission. Their poor captain was not the only Protestant patriarch who failed to command his subordinates. While family patriarchs were responsible for the basic religious education and observance of the members of their households, even in arch-puritan New Haven colony Governor Theophilus Eaton could neither prevent his wife from becoming a Baptist nor stop her from abusing their servants, and John Davenport, the colony's fiercely puritan minister, could not prevent his young female servants from hosting drinking parties and having sex with young men in his own house. If even these local elites had trouble securing compliance with their demands, we should not wonder at the variety of ways official religion was defied and resisted across the English world.[1]

The texture of local religious life depended on a variety of factors, political, social, and economic. The church was, after all, a material institution as well as a spiritual entity. Its bishops were powerful, but they did not have a monopoly on wealth or power. Lay individuals exercised considerable influence through various forms of patronage, especially by controlling the advowson, or right to nominate the parish priest, and the impropriation, or the right to collect and dispense parish tithes. Ideally, these powers belonged to the church, but some laymen had acquired these rights even before the Reformation. Thereafter, especially where monasteries had played an important role in local religious life and impropriations often had been combined with the advowson, Protestant laymen inherited this significant influence over local religious life—as well as a chance to enrich themselves—along with the monastic property. They could select and protect ministers more sympathetic to their religious dispositions than those of their bishop. These possibilities extended to lecturers, ministers who supplemented the services of the parish priest by preaching public sermons outside the usual times of church, and the chaplains who worked for entities like the Virginia or East India Companies, the royal court, aristocratic households, or the army.[2]

In short, parish ministers were not the only source of local religious authority, nor were they immune from the politics of the day. The rector, or chief minister of each parish, was responsible for a parish's property as well as its spiritual life. On a number of issues, he had to work with the parish vestry, an elected committee of parishioners. Vestries could prove powerful allies in fulfilling his religious aspirations or could thwart them, especially if the minister was a curate fulfilling the obligations of a distant rector, as Robert Hunt did for Richard Hakluyt in Virginia. Curates could be effective leaders of their congregations, as Hunt evidently was, but they also could be poor men with little education who were easily dominated by their lay parishioners. This mix of lay and clerical influences helps explain the occasional gap between the religion officially prescribed and the religion effectively practiced on the ground.

Conformist religion was a matter of law, politics, and government as well as belief. From the monarch at the church's head down to commoners serving on the parish vestry, a "complex mosaic of jurisdictions" governed the religious life of the English world. England was a monarchy, but it was divided into so many different self-governing units that some scholars refer to it as a monarchical republic. Three hundred largely self-governing boroughs as well as a number of smaller exceptional jurisdictions, or liberties, from university corporations to aristocratic households, governed themselves without direct royal involvement. Although they depended on royal authority, their full compliance with the monarchical will was never guaranteed. Despite persistent demands for conformity, these jurisdictions could, in the words of one leading scholar, shelter "a diverse religious topography." The disjuncture between how religion was supposed to be and how it actually was on the ground is even more apparent when one takes in the rest of the English world, from jurisdictions as large as Ireland to those as small as the Channel Islands. The colonies were often explicitly modeled on the lordships and other territories scattered along the frontier of the English world. A survey of their post-Reformation religious history illuminates the religious diversity existing within conformity at the time the first permanent colonies were established.[3]

*

Ships of exploration were not typically incubators of religious pluralism. More often they were models of conformity and obedience. King Edward's chief explorer, Sebastian Cabot, saw these qualities as crucial to overseas exploration. A consummate conformist, he expected his sailors to follow his example. The son of John Cabot, Sebastian had previously lived as a Catholic in England and then Spain before returning to England and joining the Edwardian church. Around 1550, he drew up regulations that reveal what religious life aboard ship was supposed to be like. Every morning and evening, an officially approved prayer was to be read, along "with other common services appointed by the King's Majesty, and laws of this realm." Additionally, the Bible was "to be read devoutly and Christianly to God's honour." Ideally a minister would perform this religious service. However, if one was unavailable, a "merchant or some other person learned" could take over. Throughout the voyage there was to be no "blaspheming of God, or detestable swearing . . . nor communication of ribaldry, filthy tales, or ungodly talk" nor "brawling, fighting and oftentimes murder." Such behavior could lead "to the utter destruction of the parties, provoking God's most just wrath and sword vengeance."[4]

Nevertheless, the religious tumult of the later Tudor era meant that the voyages establishing England's first ties with sub-Saharan Africa, Russia, and America did not always live up to Cabot's ideal of conformity. Planned during King Edward's reign and largely led by Protestants, they were not launched until Queen Mary's reign. Sebastian Cabot had quickly conformed to the Roman Catholic Church, facilitating his appointment as head of the Muscovy Company, England's first major long-distance trading enterprise. Others, like the Protestant Thomas Wyndham, benefited from the initial tolerance of the Marian regime. In August 1553, shortly after Mary came to the throne, Wyndham led England's first expedition to the Guinea Coast of Africa. His ship had at least one Irish crewman who was likely a Catholic. That poor individual died of a fever along with Wyndham and many of the other sailors. Among the survivors was a young Martin Frobisher, who joined the second expedition to West Africa in 1554, while the Marian regime still upheld the standards of the Henrician church. Another ship sailing to Guinea in 1554 carried a "byble and service boke" (i.e., the *Book of Common Prayer*), but one of its shipboard merchants left money for the master and crewmen of his ship "to praye for me," suggesting a Roman Catholic belief in purgatory. A similar bequest to have "poore people" pray for him was made by a dying member of a 1558 expedition to Guinea. Traces of Catholic attitudes persisted on ships of exploration for several years after Elizabeth became queen. A sailor on a 1562 expedition to Guinea left money to the poor "to praye for my sowle." Nevertheless, Elizabethan shipmasters carried the *Book of Common Prayer* and sometimes more, like the man on a 1564 voyage owning a "paraphrase of the fowre Evangelistes" in addition to "one booke of service." Frobisher's expedition returned with gold, ivory, and "black slaves." The others hoped to acquire similar cargo. Here, as elsewhere, the quest for wealth did not create an exemption from the dynamics of early modern English religious life. It simply carried them overseas.[5]

The recently unearthed evidence of Roman Catholicism in early Jamestown should be understood within this context. If even within the small social scale of a ship a variety of religious opinions could exist, it should not be surprising to see them in colonial outposts as well. Archaeologists have found rosary beads and religious medallions of Catholic saints. Most striking is the find from the grave of Gabriel Archer, one of the first leaders of the colony. In 1609 he was buried in the chancel of Jamestown's first church near minister Hunt who had died several months earlier. On Archer's chest, someone had placed a silver reliquary containing a bone. Archer was a conformist, but he came from a Catholic family. There was no Catholic community in early Jamestown, but Catholicism was clearly present somehow.[6]

Along England's frontiers, such mixtures of Catholic elements in an officially Protestant outpost were especially common. The lordships that guarded those frontiers in Europe enjoyed a constitutional position similar to that of colonies. Like colonies, lordships derived their authority from the monarch, not Parliament. In the Middle Ages, lordships had helped monarchs expand their territory. A loyal lord could govern distant, even foreign lands, more effectively by adapting to local circumstances without having to force the people he governed to fully conform to the foreign law and customs of England. Colonial proprietors benefited from similar vice-regal powers. Also like the colonies, lordships varied in size, character, history, and location, factors that could produce rather different religious outcomes.

In 1497, English lordships stretched across a swath of territory reaching from modern France to Ireland. By 1607, some of that territory had been lost, but Scotland had been gained. On the easternmost frontier was Calais. An important port town and fortress bordering the northwest coast of France, Calais and its surrounding pale of towns had been English since they were conquered in 1346. In the 1520s, Calais's proximity to the Protestant-friendly towns of the Low Countries and northern France made it a hotbed of Protestant influence years before England's Reformation. In 1536, Calais lost its status as a lordship and was directly incorporated into both the Kingdom of England and its church. Religious conservatives worried it was a "nest of heretics," but not everyone in Calais supported the Protestant cause. Some clergymen, parts of the garrison, and even the governing lord deputy actively resisted reforms until Mary became queen. Thereafter, Protestant sympathies persisted among some of its elite until a sudden French attack captured the town in 1558.[7]

The loss of Calais is a useful reminder of the precarious nature of English expansion. Forcing overseas territory into an English mold did not guarantee it would stay that way, as the history of English Boulogne demonstrates. Captured from the French in 1544, Boulogne and the pale of territory surrounding it was immediately subjected to English laws—and the Henrician Reformation. The English destroyed monasteries and abbeys and confiscated their lands and redistributed them among English aristocrats. French people who wanted to remain in the territory had to swear an oath "to renounce the obedience of all other princes and potestates, and also the authority of the bishop of Rome." Some French nobles and townsmen showed an interest in the new religion. Most of the country people did not. In these and other ways, Tudor rule in Boulogne foreshadowed what would follow in Ireland and the colonies—until, in 1554, the French regained the territory.[8]

Only one small piece of France remained English long enough to exercise some influence on American colonization. The French-speaking Channel Islands were the sole piece of England's ancient Norman inheritance that had not been subsequently lost to France. Nominally, the bishop of Winchester presided over them, but he was too far away to have much influence. More important were the islands' long-standing connections to Normandy, which drew them into the orbit of French Protestants. Following Huguenot practice, in 1576 the Channel Islanders organized their church on presbyterian lines. England's monarchs largely accepted the situation, along with the islands' other distinctive liberties and privileges, well into the seventeenth century. After a long struggle, an "attenuated" conformity to the Church of England was achieved on the island of Jersey in 1620, but Guernsey successfully resisted a similar fate. This small exception to episcopal rule offered a compelling alternative for England's more radical Protestants.[9]

More important for understanding colonial developments was the lord bishopric of Durham. Sitting on the ancient frontier with Scotland, it was one of three counties palatine created along the embattled borderlands facing the Welsh and Scots. Durham's distinct constitutional status, whereby lord bishops ruled with vice-regal powers in both the secular and ecclesiastical spheres, provided the model for a number of early colonial charters—most famously that of Maryland. The lord bishops sat in the House of Lords, but their county did not get representation in the House of Commons until the 1670s. For much of the period from 1530 to 1559, the lord bishop was Cuthbert Tunstall. Neither he nor Durham's other Tudor era lord bishops were particularly enthusiastic about the Reformation. After all, they had much more to lose. Tunstall used Durham's political liberties to blunt religious reform in a career that saw him presiding over trials of both Protestants and Catholics, depending on what the official religion of the monarchy was. A humanist in the mold of Erasmus and Sir Thomas More, he believed persuasion, not coercion, produced the best Christians, and generally favored mercy when confronted by religious dissent. His exercise of tolerance was not politically insignificant. It proved a key factor in allowing Roman Catholicism to survive the Reformation in the north of England. The people of Durham joined two major revolts against the Reformation: the 1536 Pilgrimage of Grace and the 1569 Northern Rising.[10]

Northern England's other two lordships, Lancashire and Cheshire, had lost most of their distinctive powers by the sixteenth century. However, they too produced conservative Reformations. Lancashire became the home of Protestant England's largest Catholic community. Cheshire's Catholic community was smaller, but there was a steady influence as it sat between Lancashire and the pilgrimage site of Holywell in Wales, making it one of the major axes of post-Reformation British Catholicism. Few militant Protestants appeared in either of these territories, although in the 1650s Lancashire became the home of Quakerism.

The Gaelic societies of Wales and the Isle of Man, furthest removed from the radical Protestant influences emanating out of the Low Countries, likewise followed a conservative path, adopting conformity with little fuss in a gradual process of religious change that left few Catholics or puritans in its wake. Wales, a rural region with a largely Gaelic-speaking population, had been broken up into small lordships and a principality. It did not become a unified territory until it was formally annexed to England between 1536 and 1543. Most Welsh elites supported and benefited from the change and, since the Tudors had a Welsh ancestor, they could imagine it as the fulfillment of a national destiny rather than their colonization by their larger, more powerful neighbor. Poverty and cultural differences slowed the religious change to Protestantism. The church was in poor condition, Welsh-language bards and peasants resisted sudden change, and there were few Protestant materials available in the Welsh language. The *Book of Common Prayer* was not translated into Welsh until 1567, the Bible in 1588. Nevertheless, those same factors ensured that Wales's Reformation was ultimately successful, albeit conservative. Poor, lacking direct contact with Roman Catholic Europe, and heavily dependent on England's economy, Wales had few means to resist. Indeed, the small bits of Catholicism that survived confirmed Wales's reliance on England. Welsh Catholic communities lay not deep in the mountainous interior but along the English border, around Holywell in the north and near Hereford's English Catholic community in the south.[11]

A similar mix of geographic and economic factors produced similar results on the Isle of Man. A thoroughly Celtic society, the Isle of Man had an ancient tradition of political independence. Its Reformation had to be imported from elsewhere in the British Isles along with its Protestant churchmen. Nevertheless, the Manx also had few resources to resist. Spared the attention of both convinced puritans and committed Catholics, this overlooked corner of the English world became thoroughly, but conservatively, conformist.[12]

Ireland, on the other hand, was big and wealthy enough to remain Roman Catholic despite the Reformation. In 1607, Protestants were a distinct minority, most of them recent immigrants from Britain, generally known as the New English to distinguish them from the Old English descendants of the Anglo-Normans conquerors and subsequent immigrants. The church of the pope had been a traditional source of Old English authority in Ireland since the conquest, and they largely remained Roman Catholic. So did Ireland's Gaelic majority, the Old Irish. By the time the Reformation began, Gaelic resistance had effectively confined the power of the Old English to the eastern and southern fringes of Ireland: the capital of Dublin, its surrounding pale of English settlement, and port towns like

Wexford, Cork, and Galway. The papacy, by contrast, oversaw the church across the whole island and had proven itself adept at mediating the demands of Gaels and English. The Irish had few reasons to complain about papal influence. With no real indigenous desire for religious change, Roman Catholicism was in a stronger position in Ireland than elsewhere. Crucially, Old English elites were willing to use their wealth and their mercantile connections to France and Iberia to keep the "Old Religion" alive well after the Tudor lord deputy convinced the Irish Parliament to pass an Act of Supremacy in 1536. Some Irish elites profited from the seizure of monastic estates that followed, but that did not imply a sudden embrace of Protestantism. The act did not impose Protestant doctrine or even make significant changes to church liturgy. Instead, it kept the current bishops in place. Only a few priests were compelled to swear the new oath of supremacy. Roman Catholicism was able to survive virtually unchallenged for decades within this technically antipapal church.[13]

Queen Mary's reign cut off the first efforts at Protestant religious reform and gave the Irish enduring hope that Catholicism could be restored again, even years after the return to a Protestant monarchy under Elizabeth. In July 1565, for example, Catholics in Kildare celebrated the (false) news that there had been an "alteration of religion in England." In the meantime, in 1560 Elizabeth's Irish Parliament had passed a second Act of Supremacy and an Act of Uniformity. Church attendance was compulsory, and all officeholders had to take the oath of supremacy. A further act in 1567 established the church's Twelve Articles of Faith. They were both simpler and more clearly Calvinist than England's Thirty-Nine Articles. As Ireland's church took on a more firmly Reformed character than England's, the bulk of its population remained Catholic. By the end of Elizabeth's reign, the country was effectively divided into three ecclesiastical zones. In the most Catholic and Gaelic regions, like Ulster, religious reform could not be enforced at all. In other regions, where the Act of Supremacy was enforced but not the Act of Uniformity, Catholic practice more or less continued under a light Protestant oversight. The third, most Protestant, zone was largely confined to the pale and other areas of New English strength like parts of Munster. Here, authority and demographics made it possible to fully enforce Protestant conformity. Yet even there, few native Irish converted. Prominent among the few who did was the Ussher family in Dublin, including the outstanding Irish Protestant churchman James Ussher, who benefited from the founding of Ireland's first university, Trinity College, Dublin, in 1591. Before then, and even for years afterward, the Church of Ireland relied heavily on English and

Welsh clerics for its preaching clergy. Its Reformed character attracted men with puritan sensibilities who were also driven by a strong sense of mission to overthrow popery and idolatry. While their anti-Catholicism appealed to the thousands of New English immigrants who began to fill the church's pews in the 1580s and 1590s, it only alienated the native Irish further from the church.[14]

Significantly, Ireland had become a church before it became a kingdom with the 1542 Crown of Ireland Act, suggesting something of the unnatural fit between the two institutions and the island they were supposed to govern. Ireland's Reformation began late and was blunted by its entanglement with Tudor political and legal reforms that sought to bring Ireland firmly under royal authority by replacing Irish norms with English customs. Anglo-Irish and Gaelic aristocrats resisted these changes in a long series of intermittent revolts large and small running from 1534 to 1608. These revolts helped stall the religious Reformation, but their repeated failures steadily opened up Irish lands to colonization. The Catholic Queen Mary actually pioneered the policy of seizing the lands of rebels and turning them over to English planters, but under Elizabeth these colonial plantations become synonymous with Protestantism. Beginning with small claims on the border of the Pale, New English colonists went on to claim extensive tracts of land in Munster in the 1580s. After 1609, with Ulster's traditional aristocracy having been destroyed after over a decade of fighting, this province was opened up to an even more thorough colonization. By the early 1620s, approximately twelve thousand Scots and English immigrants lived in Ulster. Planners hoped Ulster would soon become the most loyally "British" and Protestant part of Ireland. Altogether, this history reinforced the distinctly colonial character of the Church of Ireland. It was the church of the New English, not the Irish.[15]

Occasionally, Ireland's lord deputies considered tolerating Roman Catholicism, the religion of the bulk of the population they were trying to govern. Charles Blount, Baron Mountjoy, proposed such a plan in 1602. At the height the Nine Years' War (1593–1603), with English victory still uncertain, Mountjoy argued that the Irish were not yet civilized enough to become proper Protestants. Even if they were, the government did not have the means to instruct them in the faith. While hoping that "this ignorant and wilful people may be brought to the true knowledge of God's holy Word for the salvation of their souls," Mountjoy proposed a "toleration of religion" that would last "for a time not definite" as a "matter warrantable by religion and in policy of absolute necessity." Inspired by the recent Edict of Nantes ending the French Wars of Religion, he said it could be geographically restricted, applying everywhere "except in some principal towns and precincts after the manner of some French edicts." Then, especially in the towns "where the people is capable thereof," he suggested that "some good preachers, specially of that sort which are vehement and zealous persuaders and not scholastical" be recruited to convert the Irish, albeit only through the persuasive power of the Word not the coercive power of the state. In the end, Mountjoy managed to crush the rebellion without these concessions. His proposal for a religious peace was forgotten.[16]

Before the English managed to defeat the Earl of Tyrone and Ulster's other Irish rebels, the province had been the place where Protestant influence was weakest and Catholic Gaelic power strongest. The MacDonnell clan's influence was so powerful that it reached across the Irish Sea to the Highlands and Western Isles of Scotland inhabited by the Scottish MacDonalds and revived Roman Catholicism in that remote corner of Scotland with the help of Gaelic-speaking missionaries. By 1609, Ulster's most prominent Irish Catholic leader was Randal MacDonnell, the Earl of Tyrone's Catholic relative by marriage. He had earned the favor of King James by remaining loyal to the monarchy. James made him Earl of Antrim. Antrim helped preserve a Catholic presence in Ulster, but did not let religion get in the way of profit. He was happy to take advantage of the influx of Protestant colonists to develop his lands.[17]

By the 1620s, Ireland reflected the growing religious complexity of the English world. First of all, some of the Scots and English colonists were actually Catholic. Then, just as Antrim relied on British Protestant tenants, many Protestant landlords could not resist using native Irish Catholics as a cheap source of ready labor. In Ulster, many Old Irish hung on as tenants of Protestant landlords. This religious diversity affected the Church of Ireland, which became divided among a similar mix of religious opinions as Britain's churches. Many of the largely English and Welsh clergy were plain Calvinists, but not all. In Limerick, a distinctly nonpuritan English visitor of 1620 admired how, "by the provydence of the Bishop," the cathedral had been "beautifyed within, and as gloriously served with singing and organs." Ireland's Scots were split into two camps, reflecting the basic divide in Scottish Protestantism. Graduates of Aberdeen University tended to favor episcopal standards of religious conformity. Those of Glasgow University generally favored presbyterianism. Some of these Scots gathered with those of the New English who shared their hostility to bishops and worshipped as dissenters outside of the established church.[18]

This unsettled religious mix entered the colonies at an early date. Since the colonization of Ulster coincided with the colonization of America, there were already in 1607 schemes to weaken Ireland's Catholic community by shipping troublemakers overseas. One suggestion was to send about eight thousand Irish "swordmen Called kerne" to colonize Virginia in the expectation that time would "Eate them out or amend them." Later, when some Irishmen protested the expansion of the English plantation in Wexford, they were condemned to be transported to Virginia, to "terrifie others of the same unquiet spirit." Local magistrates recommended that any other resisters should also be sent "thither after their Countrymen." A suggestion from 1623 proposed to solve the challenge of Ireland's rapidly growing population of poor people by forcing some to work on public works while shipping others to "Virginia or some other of the newly discovered lands in the west." While it is unclear how many Irish were actually sent to Virginia, a ship full of servants, "many of them being Irish," was stranded near Plymouth colony in 1627. They spent the winter and spring in Plymouth before sailing on to Virginia. Plymouth's governor said nothing about their religion—and if they had revealed themselves to be Roman Catholics, he certainly would have noticed—but he felt there were "many untoward people amongst them; though there were also some that carried themselves very orderly all the time they stayed." More Irish Catholics went to work in the new Caribbean colonies, where they became a crucial source of labor.[19]

The Munster plantation, by contrast, suggests how a joint sphere of militant Protestant enterprise could link England, Ireland, and colonial America. Munster attracted a number of Englishmen with ties to the emerging colonies, including members of the Winthrop and Gookin families. Sir Vincent Gookin, one of the wealthiest New English colonists in Munster, was notoriously outspoken in his anti-Catholic and anti-Irish views. His brother Daniel began trading cattle to Virginia in 1620. Buying a plantation at Newport News, he successfully defended it from attack during the Powhatan War, then continued to ship cattle and servants to Virginia. Other Irish traders followed his example. Most were fellow Protestants, but the occasional merchant who was Catholic, or at least had Catholic connections, attempted to profit off of Virginia's booming tobacco trade. In 1624, for example, Samuel Tuchin was banished by the Virginians after it was discovered that he had refused to take the oath of allegiance in Ireland. Worse, he had connections to the Spanish that made the Virginians fear "that he should become a Pylott to a fforeen Enymie."[20]

Like Ireland, Scotland's initial link to America was punishment. In 1618, King James's Star Chamber court suggested that if the notorious Scottish borderers—people who had profited from cross-border raid during the centuries when England had a different monarch—refused to keep the peace, they could be sent "into Virginia or to sum remote parts, to serve in the wearris or in collonies." The Scottish Privy Council rejected this suggestion, but the idea of sending obstreperous Scots to America persisted. In 1619 the archbishop of Saint Andrews threatened ministers who opposed the controversial Articles of Perth with banishment to America. While the proposal fell through, the incident suggests how ferocious the religious divisions within Scotland's church had become.[21]

The archbishop of Saint Andrews was the traditional head of Scotland's church, representing its episcopal continuity with the era before the Reformation. The Scottish Reformation had been hard on bishops, depriving them of most of their special authority, but by 1619, they were making a comeback, especially in the more religiously conservative north and east of Scotland. Scotland's Reformation had been much more radical than that of England, especially in the Lowlands of the south and west, the part of Scotland closest to Ireland and the source of the majority of Scottish immigrants to Ulster. The men the archbishop threatened to deport were defending the Church of Scotland as it had been before James became king of England and Ireland. The archbishop was enforcing the new church order. Within two decades, the conflict between these two positions would have major consequences for early American religion.[22]

Where England's Reformation had been largely directed by the monarchy, Scotland's monarchy had played almost no role in changing the country's religion. Instead, the Scottish Reformation involved a series of civil wars, dynastic coups, and foreign interventions. It began while King James's mother, Mary, Queen of Scots, was living in France as the young bride to the French dauphin. Her mother, the French noblewoman Mary of Guise, governed Scotland. In the spring of 1560, a number of Scottish lords who had converted to Protestantism overthrew Mary of Guise's government with the help of English allies, undoing Catholic Scotland's ancient anti-English alliance with France. These so-called lords of the congregation then had Scotland's Parliament declare the country to be officially Protestant. In the meantime, Mary, Queen of Scots' French husband died, and she returned home in the summer of 1561. Still devotedly Roman Catholic, she had to promise not to change the official religion without consulting Parliament first. To secure the succession, she married an English aristocrat and gave birth to James in June 1566. Unfortunately, James's father soon became estranged from Mary. He died suddenly, a few months later, when the Edinburgh house he was lodging in suddenly blew up one night. Suspicions pointed to close associates of Mary, fueling a revolt that in 1567 forced her to resign in favor of her infant son. A year later, she fled for help to England. Instead of helping, Queen Elizabeth placed her under house arrest for the next eighteen years, then had her executed for treason. In the meantime, Protestant Protectors governed Scotland on behalf of the young James Stewart while George Buchanan, one of Scotland's leading ministers, gave him a strictly Calvinist, and not very affectionate, upbringing.

During the generation it took for James to reach adulthood, a remarkably thorough Reformation sank its roots into Scotland, even in the remote Highlands and Isles of the West. It enjoyed the active support of many local elites, most Scottish aristocrats (who were more powerful than their English counterparts), and Scotland's Parliament (which was less powerful than its English counterpart). Replacing the Roman Catholic system of bishops and monasteries with a system of councils run by ministers—each theoretically equal to the other—the Church of Scotland was organized by and large along Presbyterian lines. Councils met in an ascending hierarchy from local presbyteries to regional synods that culminated in the General Assembly of the national church—a far more powerful force than the Church of England's Convocation. The General Assembly was even more powerful than the Scottish Parliament. Bishops did not completely disappear, but they were largely indistinguishable from other ministers. Church councils took over most of their usual administrative functions.

As in England, all Scottish subjects were automatically members of this established church or Kirk, as it was commonly known. Unlike in England or Ireland, the Scots were subjected to a clearly Calvinist doctrine and ethos. Individuals' behavior was closely monitored by so-called Kirk sessions, a parish level committee composed of the parish minister and a dozen or so lay elders who enforced moral discipline. Church buildings had neither altars nor images. Ministers wore no priestly garments like the surplice. Sermons and Bible reading formed the basis of worship services. Traditional holidays were abolished: Scotland had no official Christmas from 1560 until 1958. Only in seventeenth-century New England and the Cromwellian 1650s would the English attain anything like this level of Calvinist purity. Still, religious change was almost never as swift or thorough as many reformers desired. Only after 1572 did church members have to give a confession of faith. Only in 1581 did the General Assembly adopt what in later years would be known as the Negative Confession: a National Covenant denouncing Catholic beliefs and practices, pledging loyalty to the Reformation, and virtually abolishing bishops. The pace of change varied from parish to parish. However, as one historian points out, this gradualism may "unintentionally have aided the eventual success of the reformers" in various ways, not least by forestalling opposition.[23]

By the 1580s, Scotland's Kirk had become one of the most purely reformed in Europe, with notoriously strict standards of worship and discipline. Roman Catholicism barely survived, being almost completely wiped out not by the English strategy of penal laws but through mockery and scorn. Denying Catholics a chance at martyrdom and glory, Scottish reformers also prevented them from developing an effective resistance. Scottish Catholicism survived, but only in isolated pockets, mostly a few powerful aristocrats in the conservative northeast and a few urban elites. Most everywhere else the Kirk ruled over a firmly Protestant population. Only its comparative neglect of the Highlands and Isles allowed the MacDonalds, the region's traditionally dominant clan, to return to the Catholic fold with the help of Irish missionaries around 1590. However the MacDonalds' rivals, the upstart Campbells of Argyle, responded by becoming Calvinist champions. They then benefited from King James's program of "civilizing" the Highlands and Isles, which basically involved reducing the power of the MacDonalds.[24]

Scotland's Kirk was strong, but it unfortunately had little room for royal authority. King James had endorsed the Negative Confession, while still an immature boy, but once he attained his majority in 1584, he began to make his independence felt. His experience of governing Scotland and its church would have important consequences for his government of England, Ireland, and their churches. For James, governing was a survivalist art. With his father murdered shortly after he was born and then his mother exiled and, in 1587, executed, James had a rough and lonely childhood. He grew up as a hapless political prize being fought over by powerful factions of aristocrats. To survive, he developed a distinctive political style of balancing those political factions off against each other. Instead of becoming fully dependent on one or the other, he engaged with all of them, playing them off against each other until he had carved out an irreplaceable role for himself as the true center of power. That was no mean feat in a country where the monarchy had been the weak tool of aristocrats for generations.[25]

James's strategy of balancing factions extended to the Kirk. As the one institution that reached into all corners of his country, the Kirk was a politically as well as religiously vital institution. As his famous pronouncement of "No Bishop, No King" demonstrates, James clearly came to see bishops as essential representatives of his royal authority by the time he became king of England. Indeed, as soon as he came of age in 1584, he worked with aristocrats who disliked Presbyterianism to get Parliament to pass a set of acts affirming royal authority over the church by, among other things, restoring royally appointed bishops to the Kirk. Their powers and authority were limited, but nonetheless important figures within the Kirk opposed bishops as unnecessary if not downright anti-Christian, and denounced these so-called Black Acts. A long series of disputes over royal church policy followed, during which James's strategy of balance led him to occasionally abandon the episcopal cause. For example, in 1590 he and his council joined the General Assembly in affirming the Negative Confession. According to one historian, he wanted "neither overmighty bishops nor overmighty ministers" but "pliable men who relied upon him for their status" and whom "he could depend upon to carry out his government." He resented subjects telling him how to govern his church and kingdom, regardless of their religious views. Still, Presbyterians were the first to get in trouble. A number of them advocated a thorough separation of the spheres of church and state to protect the Kirk from royal interference. They also urged the king to eradicate Catholicism and abolish episcopacy. For their pains, they lost their positions, were arrested, or even exiled. The important church reformer and educator Andrew Melville, for example, died alone in exile in France after standing up to James in the name of Presbyterianism. By the time James became king of England in 1603, he had secured his authority over the Kirk as much as the monarchy.[26]

James was an unusual monarch in a number of ways. For one, he was willing to publish his ideas. His *True Law of Free Monarchies* was a firm defense of the absolute authority he claimed (but did not always in fact possess). It also had an important religious inspiration. Both radical Presbyterians and Roman Catholics, especially Jesuits, had developed theories justifying resistance to monarchs who obstructed their version of a pure church. James's defense of his royal prerogatives was partly a response to this dual threat. In his personal experience, however, Catholics had proven more loyal and less dangerous than militant Presbyterians. His preference for personal loyalty and obedience over religious orthodoxy allowed him to cooperate with Catholic lords in the Highlands in the name of preserving the peace of his kingdom. Although he was a Calvinist, he was not going to force his subjects to convert. This favor toward Catholic aristocrats extended to his court, where several educated Catholics served as royal advisors. Around 1601, some of them persuaded his

Lutheran wife, Anne of Denmark, to convert. When she informed James of her conversion, he characteristically respected her choice but insisted she prevent it from becoming a political issue. She did. Keeping her religion private, she continued to attend church services but did not receive communion. Disloyal Catholics, on the other hand, suffered his wrath as much as disloyal Protestants. The fate of the Jesuit John Ogilvie, the one Scottish Catholic martyr of James's reign, is revealing. A Protestant who had converted while studying in Germany, Ogilvie returned to Britain in 1615. After some personal contact with James, he went to Glasgow where he was caught proselytizing. In court, Ogilvie denied James's authority over the church. The harsh sentence meted out to him is believed to reflect James's sense of personal betrayal. Usually, Jesuit missionaries were simply exiled. Only witches, who rejected not only his authority but also the authority of God, felt James's unremitting ire. Witchcraft became a capital crime in England after he became its king.[27]

After becoming king of England, James rarely returned to Scotland. Instead, he came to rely increasing on bishops to represent his interests in the Kirk. Since their authority depended on him, it seemed unlikely that they would challenge his influence in church affairs the way presbyterians did. When several Scottish ministers spoke out against having bishops in the Kirk in 1606, James banished them. Soon afterward, he began bringing the liturgy of the Scottish church closer to that of the Church of England, which he regarded as a more obedient and reliable church and a better model for his hoped-for reunion of Christendom. Those efforts culminated with the Five Articles of Perth, which had several provisions many Scots found obnoxious, including the requirement for communicants to receive the sacred host while kneeling instead of sitting, as presbyterians preferred. The articles also permitted the celebration of major festivals like Christmas and Easter. Passed by the General Assembly of the church at the king's urging in 1618, they were ratified by the Scottish Parliament in 1621. Thereafter, neither James nor his successor Charles permitted the General Assembly to meet again until 1638. For twenty years, Scots were left to stew or resist these reforms as best they could without any institutional recourse.[28]

*

Religion in the early modern English world was inevitably a political as well as spiritual phenomenon, involving institutions, economic resources, and power. As such, it cannot be separated from these other struggles, which varied according to the different jurisdictions within which they played out: kingdoms, lordships, cities, and towns. Once permanent colonies emerged after 1607, the colonies joined this dynamic as a new set of jurisdictions within this complex "monarchical republic." The variety of those jurisdictions, their relative independence from each other, and their very different histories, cultures, and conditions, undercut the demands for religious unity emanating from the center. The religious pluralism of the English world owed a good deal to these constitutional units with their separate prerogatives, executives, courts, assemblies, and laws.

In both theory and practice, elements of this governmental diversity affected colonial America from the beginning. Colonial laws insisted on religious unity, but conformity could look rather different in the different corners of the English world. The challenge of religious unity became all the greater after 1603. Not only was the Church of Scotland added to the mix, but King James I brought a very different attitude to the problem of religious diversity from that of the English Tudors. The harsh lessons of his Scottish experience had taught this firm Calvinist the benefits of a certain degree of tolerance, as long as it was linked to political loyalty. Those who were not loyal could suffer exile and banishment, and it was under James that schemes to ship obstreperous Irish and Scots to America were first proposed.

James was not an advocate of pluralism as such, but he did recognize that religious diversity offered opportunities for him to exercise his absolutist inclinations. It gave him a choice of religious and political factions to draw on for support without compelling him to rely exclusively on any one of them. Here, the failure of Tudor England to fully achieve conformity within England—or, alternatively speaking, the ability of both Roman Catholicism and dissident Protestantism to survive the Elizabethan regime's efforts to suppress them—proved another crucial factor in the emergence of pluralism in colonial America. English Calvinists could not question James's religious orthodoxy, but they were flummoxed by his reluctance to suppress religious difference. James would not only reject what by the end of Queen Elizabeth's days had become an extremely harsh system of religious repression; he would actively encourage a variety of religious opinions to flourish within the churches of Britain and Ireland. His strategy of balance required a diversity of opinions, religious and political, and it was under his much looser umbrella of conformity that some of that variety was able to find its way into the colonies virtually from the beginning.

FOUR

Dissent: English Papists, Puritans, and Others

If the dramatic religious changes under the Tudors had taught their subjects one thing, it was that, since the official religion had changed more than once, it could change again. Some radical Protestants, like Roger Williams, eventually concluded that "whole Nations are no Churches under the Gospel." God was not going to redeem "unto Himselfe any Nation or people as he did this people of Israel." Accordingly, by the end of Elizabeth's reign, a growing number of individuals were beginning to separate their religion from that of the state. In Williams's case the relentless quest for religious truth took him from being a member of the Church of England to a puritan dissident, to a Separatist who broke with the church, then a Baptist, until ultimately, as one biographer describes it, he came "to believe that all churches invariably contained an unacceptable mixture of God's true saints and unregenerate men and women." Leaving Rhode Island's "Baptist congregation a mere four months" after he had helped found it in 1638, he "prayed only with his wife for the remainder of his life." Along the way, he became an outspoken advocate for religious tolerance and liberty.[1]

Roger Williams's spiritual journey is especially important because it led to the creation of the colony of Rhode Island, but he was just one of thousands of people threading in and out of the Church of England by the early seventeenth century. The pressure to conform posed a persistent challenge to those who tried to maintain their individual spiritual purity, for it could never be a purely religious decision. The very use of terms like nonconformity, dissent, and recusant indicates just how the religious life of the English world was defined by membership in the established church. The ability of thousands of individuals to slip back and forth between nonconformity and occasional conformity posed a continual challenge to "the Reformation by arguing about what conformity signified." By conforming just enough to avoid what could sometimes be very severe penalties, Protestant and Roman Catholic dissenters could enjoy the benefits of conformity, which included attending university and holding public office. John Calvin, complaining about Huguenots who attended Roman Catholic services, had labeled such individuals Nicodemites, after the biblical story of Nicodemus who, fearing to be seen with Jesus during the day, visited him by night. In England, conservative conformists worried about puritans, while their militant colleagues worried about "church papists," a papal fifth column sitting in their churches protected by the thin veneer of conformity. They wanted proof of thorough, internal, conversions before they would accept those individuals as Protestants. In one extreme case, militant Protestant magistrates forced a group of imprisoned Catholics in York to listen to sermons for an entire year (1599–1600). The Catholics responded by blocking their ears and using other petty tactics to prevent the Protestant message from entering their bodies and spoiling their souls. Although reduced to a minority by the 1570s, their continued existence provoked a running debate about religious pluralism long before it manifested on America's shores.[2]

Puritans also became the subject of talk about religious pluralism in Elizabethan England—something they vehemently opposed. This group of would-be Reformed Protestants had expected to build on the momentum for reform from Edward VI's days. Frustrated by Elizabeth's refusal to modify her church settlement, they struggled to reform the church from within while resisting full conforming to its misguided demands. By the 1580s, some broke off to prioritize their personal spiritual state over that of their country. Rejecting conformity completely, they formed new religious groups. Separatists sought to develop a pure Reformed Church order out of voluntary, or "gathered," congregations of godly individuals. Baptists challenged the traditional church hierarchy even further by rejecting the common sacrament of infant baptism. Only knowing adults could become proper Christians. Others dabbled in various forms of mysticism. All of these dissenters from conformity, Catholic and Protestant alike, insisted they were politically loyal. However, their defiance of the monarchy's religion exposed them to charges of treason.

Few of these religious dissidents viewed America as a refuge. Instead, their involvement in colonization demonstrates, once again, how colonization was an extension overseas of the religious dynamics of the English world, not an escape from them. Inevitably, some of those who traveled to the early colonies under the guise of conformity harbored sympathies for one or more of these divergences from the official religion, but there was no clear or consistent relationship between religious dissent and colonization. Some did seek opportunity in colonization, especially a small circle of Roman Catholics who continued to engage and invest in colonial enterprises long after their country officially turned Protestant, but colonization was a way to carve out space within the English world, not escape from it. Most preferred to stay home. Nevertheless, a shifting mix of factors allowed (or compelled) Roman Catholics, puritans, and Separatists each to take a stab at setting up an American colony at some point before Elizabeth died. None of them succeeded, but as the complex dynamic of religion, politics, and colonization continued under her successors, some of their fellows would find a place in the colonial religious landscape, albeit not officially recognized.

*

Elizabeth's religious settlement may have satisfied most of her subjects, but it alienated a significant minority of individuals at both ends of the Christian spectrum. To begin with, twenty-seven of the church's twenty-eight bishops and about three hundred of its roughly two thousand clergymen chose to lose their positions rather than conform to the Protestant church. They were quietly pensioned off in the hopes that Roman Catholicism would die out along with them—many of them were old. Without priests to perform the Mass and other religious services, Roman Catholics could not sustain their religion. The strategy might have worked if some key individuals had not determined to preserve the faith of their ancestors.

Resistance to Protestant conformity took two forms. The first was open rebellion. In 1569, the northern counties, where Roman Catholicism remained strongest, rose up in the Northern Rebellion, the last Roman Catholic rebellion against the Tudor Reformation. The revolt was sparked by several conservative northern noblemen who, outraged at being marginalized at court, retreated home and denounced the "new found religion and heresy." A massive uprising ensued. Rebels publicly celebrated Catholic Mass in Durham cathedral and spoke out in favor of Mary, Queen of Scots' claim to England's throne. Currently under house arrest in England, the Roman Catholic Mary, the granddaughter of Henry VIII's sister, had the most legitimate of all claims to replace the unmarried and childless Elizabeth. The papacy then aggravated Protestant concerns about Catholic loyalty by endorsing the rebellion. Its 1570 bull, *Regnans in excelsis*, excommunicated Elizabeth, labeled her a heretic who provided a "refuge" for heretics while supporting "the persecution of the faithful," declared her "deprived of her pretended title" to her throne, and formally absolved her Roman Catholic subjects of their obedience to her. Those who insisted on obeying her laws and swearing the oath of supremacy were excommunicated. The pope was too late to save the rebellion, which Elizabeth's forces already had brutally suppressed, hanging hundreds of rebels in their villages. Nevertheless, some Catholics continued to scheme in hopes of reclaiming the throne by replacing Elizabeth with Mary, Queen of Scots. There was the 1571 Ridolfi Plot, the 1584 Throckmorton Plot, and then the 1586 Babington Plot, after which Mary was executed for her alleged involvement in the conspiracy. Her loss put a damper on the conspiracies, but Catholics did not give up hopes that the throne could be theirs again.[3]

In the long term, the more effective resistance came from a group of younger priests inspired by the Counter-Reformation teachings that had spread during Mary's reign. A number of them chose to go into exile rather than conform to Elizabeth's church. Most important was William Allen. Scion of a family of Lancashire gentry, Allen had held a position at Oxford. Returning home for a brief visit in 1563, he discovered to his horror that conformity was taking hold among his former neighbors. Determined to prevent England from falling completely into the abyss of apostasy, in 1568 Allen established the English College at the new University of Douai in the Spanish Netherlands to train English Catholic priests. In 1571 its graduates began infiltrating back into England. Additional seminaries were then established in Valladolid, Seville, and Rome. These seminaries and the expatriate community they sustained kept England's small Catholic community alive until the French Revolution. At the time Virginia was established there were about eight hundred seminary priests working in England. While they could not prevent the drastic decline of the English Catholic community, they did keep it alive. In 1607, roughly forty thousand of England's approximately 4 million people, or about 1 percent of the population, were Roman Catholic.[4]

Seminary priests were essential to the survival of English Catholicism, but, as in Ireland, their efforts would have meant little without the support of elite families. Catholic gentry and peers of the realm used their mix of court connections, personal wealth, and local patronage to defy the laws on conformity, protect their poorer coreligionists, and covertly support the priests, giving them shelter and a place to worship in their homes and other secret locations. English Catholics clustered around the elites willing to dedicate their honor and fortunes to preserving the faith. They could be found in small numbers almost everywhere in the countryside, but only in a few corners of Lancashire were they anything approaching a local majority. London was their focal point. There they could take advantage of the liberties enjoyed by the embassies of Catholic France, Spain, and Venice to openly attend religious services in their foreign chapels, sustain a national network, and influence government policy through personal connections and private negotiations.

Despite their small numbers, Roman Catholics had a wide range of experiences and attitudes regarding the relationship between their religious and political loyalties. Few fit into a simple image pitting Catholics against Protestants. Some Catholics had never been Protestant. Others converted after being raised as conformists. Most vacillated somewhere in between conformity and resistance. The most noticeable part of the Catholic community was the recusants. Technically a recusant was anyone who failed to attend church, but since Catholics were the original targets of the law—and the vast majority of early offenders—recusancy quickly became synonymous with English Catholicism. Some Catholics boldly made little effort to hide their recusancy, but most tried for years to avoid prosecution by meeting the minimum requirements of conformity. Some occasionally attended church. Others designated one member of the family (usually the husband/father) to attend while the rest stayed home. During church services, individuals could adopt a variety of tactics to avoid spiritual contamination. In the early years of Elizabeth's reign, one man sat "so far that, he neither heareth nor can hear" the sermon; another walked "up and down in time of divine service in a place so far off that he cannot hear"; another "read so loud upon his Latin popish primer . . . that he troubleth both the minister and people."[5]

Stances toward conformity varied over time partly because Catholics were increasingly subject to an expanding series of penal laws designed to pressure them to conform. First, a 1571 act made it high treason to import papal bulls like the one excommunicating Elizabeth. In 1577, at a point when Protestant concerns about the Spanish threat were reaching a peak, the seminary priest Cuthbert Mayne became this law's first victim. While priests like Mayne trained in the Spanish Netherlands, Spanish armies were fighting to suppress the Dutch Protestant revolt. Would not English Protestants be Spain's next victim? Subsequent legislation targeted seminary priests with a declaration that anyone who left the country without permission for longer than six months—say, for an extended course of study at a seminary—could have his lands seized by the government.[6]

To the shock of many Protestants, the political prospects of English Catholics changed dramatically shortly after Cuthbert Mayne's death. Between 1578 and 1581, the aging Queen Elizabeth entered into negotiations to marry Francis, Duke of Anjou, the Roman Catholic youngest son of France's King Henry II. This so-called Anjou Match promised to restore English Catholic influence at court and even, one anticipated, "freedom for their faith." Catholics had been requesting toleration since 1563, hoping for an arrangement like that of the Holy Roman Empire, with a few Catholic churches existing in specific places in exchange for a financial subsidy to the monarchy. Hoping to take advantage of the Anjou Match, the Jesuit order launched a mission to supplement the work of the seminary priests. In 1580, Edmund Campion and Robert Parsons arrived in England. The Jesuits wanted to stop Catholics from practicing occasional conformity and instead create a distinct, visible, English Catholic community to whom a formal grant of toleration could be made. By blurring the confessional divide, occasional conformity allowed the English government to think there was no Roman Catholic community in the country. Campion and Parsons claimed it went against Catholics' religious duty and insisted Catholics make a complete break with the established church. Firmly proclaiming their political loyalty, the missionaries insisted they were not encouraging political disobedience. They simply wanted to make plain the reality of England's religious pluralism. As Parsons argued, England actually had "fower known religions": "the Catholickes, the Protestants, the Puritanes, and the howsholders of Love" (a small, new mystical sect). Catholics were "the first, the auncientest, the more in number, and the most beneficial to al the rest." They were also generous. Rather than simply ask for toleration just for themselves, they aspired to "equall tolleration with other religions disalowed by the state."[7]

Protestants responded with a stepped up anti-Catholic campaign. They urged Elizabeth to clamp down on English Catholics at home and support the Dutch Protestant rebels across the North Sea. In 1581, Parliament passed a new penal law in response to the Jesuit mission. The Act to Retain the Queen's Majesty's Subjects in their True Obedience made it treason to convert anyone to Catholicism or "withdraw" them "from their natural loyalty to her Majesty to obey the usurped authority of Rome." It also raised the fine for failing to attend church services to the enormous sum of twenty pounds after just one month of proven recusancy. Edmund

Campion was captured shortly afterward and executed for violating this law. While Campion became the most famous of Elizabethan Catholic martyrs, Parsons escaped to Italy, where, after Cardinal Allen died in 1594, he took over as head of England's expatriate Catholic community.[8]

Against this increasingly tense background, several English Catholics entered into negotiations with Humphrey Gilbert to create a Catholic enclave in what is now Rhode Island. Several of them had earlier requested permission to colonize Antrim in Ulster, where the established Protestant church was weak, and lacking England's increasingly harsh penal laws. The petition had been rejected, but mostly because they had wanted the Crown to help fund their plantation. The American colony they would fund themselves. Two gentleman within the group, Sir Thomas Gerard from Lancashire and Sir George Peckham from Buckinghamshire, were so important to Gilbert's enterprise that he made them the executors of his will. He trusted these Catholics to run his colony until his children came of age. Joining these men was an important figure at Elizabeth's court, the enigmatic John Dee. The so-called Arch-Conjuror of England, Dee was a noted scholar, healer, and astronomer whose respect at court derived from his deep knowledge of the occult arts. He advised Elizabeth on a variety of issues from health complaints to espionage. Dee's nebulous religious loyalties were emblematic of the age. During Queen Mary's reign, he had been suspected of heresy for casting Elizabeth's horoscope. For two and a half decades after Elizabeth became queen he conformed, but in 1585 he reconciled with the Catholic Church.[9]

These men's relationship to conformity may have been ambivalent, but their enthusiasm for colonization was genuine. Peckham wrote an account of Gilbert's voyage that made the most thorough case for English colonization yet published. Dee purchased the rights to seven islands and over eight million acres, and Sir Humphrey Gilbert granted the Catholics the power to execute "all lawes Ecclesiasticall temporall politique marshall and Civill" in the colony they planned to create on Narragansett Bay. Although they left no public record of their motives, they doubtless harbored a desire to escape ecclesiastical scrutiny while patriotically profiting off of colonial expansion—apparently with the connivance of Elizabeth's government. Elizabeth's privy councilor, Sir Francis Walsingham, a man deeply involved in the world of espionage and intrigue, had approved their petition to establish a colony for recusants after they agreed that they would not use it as a way to leave English territory for "any other foren Christian realm." Although there is no evidence of an explicit grant of toleration, the Spanish ambassador believed they had gained permission "to live in those parts with freedom of conscience." Certainly, with a location some 1,500 miles away from Gilbert's base on Newfoundland, this "Dee River" colony could have allowed Catholics to live free of harassment even if no formal religious toleration was proclaimed. Alas, the plans came to nothing. Gilbert died on the return journey, and then in 1584 Peckham was imprisoned for his connection to the Throckmorton Plot.[10]

Gilbert's cooperation with English Catholics is an important reminder of the murky religious origins of the British Empire. Indeed, the very idea that the empire should be called "British" rather than English has a Catholic taint. John Dee coined the term while advising Queen Elizabeth on foreign policy in 1577. He joined the voices urging Queen Elizabeth to support colonial ventures by suggesting England had an ancient right to America thanks to the long ago conquests of King Arthur. Harkening back to this period was a wise bit of antipopish nationalism that nevertheless cleverly avoided anti-Catholicism. It found favor with the militant Protestant faction at court led by Robert Dudley, Earl of Leicester, since the main point of Dee's argument was not to justify the colonization of America but to prompt Elizabeth to intervene in other territories once allegedly owned by King Arthur, namely, the Low Countries. In 1585, just as Dee returned to the Catholic fold, Leicester finally convinced Elizabeth to join the Dutch war against Spain.[11]

Another link between John Dee and American colonization adds to this picture of a religiously mixed culture of early Elizabethan colonization. Sir Humphrey Gilbert's younger brother Adrian wanted to discover the Northwest Passage. Dee consulted the spirits on his behalf to determine the voyage's chances of success, explaining, in March 1583, that Adrian would "cary the name of Jesus among the Infidells to the great glory of god, and the recovery of those miserable people from the mowth of hell into Jesus." One spirit suggested that Dee spoke "prop[h]esy." However, by July the matter had become muddled. Asked again about Adrian's "intended voyage," the spirit replied, "He is not in the true faith." When Dee asked the spirit why a few months earlier it had suggested that Adrian "should be the setter forth of God, his faith and religion among the infidels," the spirit could only reply "That is a mystery." Adrian never made the voyage.[12]

In the end, the English Catholics' failure to establish a colony in America pleased William Allen. Since 1582 he had been complaining about those who wanted "to send the poore Catholikes whom they have ruined at home, to *Terra Florida*, there to exercise their religion and to have freedom of conscience." Allen believed it was a trick, "a strange coozenage [i.e., deceit] and craft, to be rid of the poore gentlemen under pretence of their preferment." Allen suggested the puritans should be sent to America instead. After all, "most men of the realme wish rather the puritans" to be gone than Catholics. Puritans had a "humor that our commonwealth had more need to be purged of."[13]

Puritans did not agree with William Allen on much, but they did agree that it was better to stay in England than go to the colonies. Like Allen's mission to save English Catholicism, puritanism had begun as a reaction against Elizabethan conformity. Disappointed by the compromises with religious conservativism, some ministers refused to wear the surplice. They claimed the "rags of Antichrist" tainted the wearer and confused the congregation by suggesting it was the minister's sacramental functions as a priest, not his sermons, prayers, and preaching, that led to salvation. They also took a selective approach to the 1559 Prayer Book, rejecting the points they felt had no clear scriptural sanction. Until 1566 their nonconformity was not an issue. Then, Queen Elizabeth insisted all ministers fully conform to her church settlement. Matters came to a head on March 26 when Edmund Grindal, the bishop of London, was forced to summon 140 of the ministers of his diocese to his palace. Grindal had been a Marian exile. He sympathized with those who refused to wear the surplice. Unfortunately, his position as bishop meant that, when push came to shove, he had to obey the queen. With Matthew Parker, the archbishop of Canterbury, standing at his side, Grindal explained to the assembled men that they must sign an agreement saying they would wear the surplice or lose their positions. Thirty-seven refused. Despite protests from their congregations, they were dismissed. Nonconformity was now the official stance of a sizeable minority of England's trained ministers. The puritan movement had begun.[14]

These nonconformists did not reject the established church. They simply hoped to complete its reformation by abolishing the ungodly elements the Elizabethan settlement had preserved. Unable to preach from their pulpits, some of the deprived ministers began holding semiprivate religious services for their former parishioners. They gathered in and around London in private houses and warehouses and on ships. A few took the more dramatic step of forming a congregation of their own, appointing their own ministers and worshipping without regard to parish boundaries. In June 1567, close to a hundred people were arrested during a clandestine religious service at Plumbers' Hall. This step toward separation from the established church was not intended to make a complete break with it. Rather, the idea was to model how the church could operate along reformed lines, like the churches of Scotland and Switzerland. The essence of being puritan was to struggle for reform *within* the church, not to separate from it. Only when such reform seemed impossible would some puritans take the drastic step of separation.[15]

Frustrated by their failure to alter the terms of conformity, in the 1570s puritans conspired to alter the church's ecclesiology. In 1570, the Cambridge University professor Thomas Cartwright made the case for reforming the Church of England along presbyterian lines in a series of lectures. Presbyterian churches varied in specifics, but in general they built up from the congregation rather than down from bishops. At the bottom was the consistory (in Scotland, a session), which managed each congregation. Several consistories grouped together formed a classis (in Scotland, a presbytery). Several classes together formed a synod, the ultimate authority within a presbyterian church. Laymen, usually church elders, played a more active role in church governance, as each of these assemblies was made up of delegates of ministers and laymen from the lower level of organization. Surely a presbyterian church controlled by the ministers and laity would serve the cause of Reformed religion better than an episcopal church subservient to the monarchy? Presbyterian churches took hold easily in republican societies like Switzerland and the Dutch Republic, and in Scotland, where reformers did not have to contend with a strong monarch. Exactly how it would work when confronted with a determined monarch like Elizabeth was unclear. England's "classis movement" was vague on the role of royal authority within the church as well as the relationship between its synod and Parliament, although Cartwright argued that a presbyterian system was not only scripturally sound but also most appropriate for England, whose mixed and balanced political constitution, with its monarch, House of Lords, and House of Commons, functioned very much like the series of councils in a presbyterian church. Others disagreed and deemed his lectures seditious. The university's statutes were changed so that he could be dismissed. While Cartwright went into hiding to avoid prosecution, in 1572 sympathizers of the classis movement published *An Admonition to Parliament* advocating presbyterianism. The subsequent "Admonition" controversy saw the pamphlet denounced as a seditious libel. Its authors were imprisoned, and the authorities began going after the classis movement more broadly.[16]

While the classis movement struggled, puritans seeking a less confrontational approach to reform worked on improving the quality of preaching in the church. In a system of so-called prophesyings, ministers from neighboring parishes would gather before a knowledgeable audience of other ministers and laity to discuss doctrine and practice giving sermons. However, Elizabeth had not authorized the gatherings. They too seemed to threaten her control of the church and in 1576, only months after poor Edmund Grindal had become her new archbishop of Canterbury, she ordered him to suppress the prophesyings. This time, Grindal refused. Instead, he reminded her "that you are a mortal creature" and "He which dwelleth in heaven is mightier." For this act of disobedience, Elizabeth confined Grindal to house arrest for the rest of his life. Many of his responsibilities were turned over to a committee headed by John Aylmer, bishop of London. Aylmer, an ambitious conformist, lacked Grindal's sympathy for puritans. He happily enforced Elizabeth's command that "no manner of public and divine service" or "other rites or ceremonies, be in any sort used in the Church but directly according to the orders established by our laws." When Grindal died in 1583, puritanism was on the defensive.[17]

Domestically and internationally, the scene suddenly improved for puritans and their sympathizers in 1585, when Elizabeth finally heeded their calls to help the Dutch and declare war against Spain. The ensuing Anglo-Spanish war, lasting until 1604, unleashed a wave of anti-Catholic sentiment that confronted England's Catholics with an increasingly brutal penal regime. A 1585 "Act against Jesuits, Seminary Priests and such other like Disobedient Persons" condemned them as political agents who strove "to stir up and move sedition, rebellion and open hostility within her Highness' realms and dominions." Ordered to leave the country in forty days, the priests and those who sheltered them were threatened with punishment for treason if they refused to leave or returned after they left. Between 1586 and 1603, 123 of the 146 Catholics executed by the Elizabethan regime were indicted under this statute. Most were priests, but some were laypeople. An additional penal law passed in 1593 sought to prevent "popish" plotting by requiring all recusants over the age of sixteen to live in their family home and forbidding them to travel more than five miles without official permission. Catholics suffered under heavy fines, which now became both a new source of revenue for the state as well as an effective way to bog down Catholics in legal affairs to protect their property. Other recusants were sent to prison, where many suffered or even died in the unhealthy conditions. Under this repression, Catholic efforts to set up an American colony vanished.[18]

The new archbishop of Canterbury, John Whitgift, supported the repression of Roman Catholicism as part of his broader campaign to enforce conformity, which targeted puritans as well. Catholics complained it was religious persecution. Defenders of the regime, like Secretary of State William Cecil, denied that it was about religion. The campaign against Catholics was purely political. Magistrates were simply enforcing public religious unity, a political virtue essential to security. A "state co[u]ld never be in safety where there was tolleration of two religions," he later wrote, "For there is no enmytie so greate as that for religion, and they that differ in the service of God can never agree in the service of theire Contrie."[19]

The Jesuit Parsons actually agreed with Cecil on this point. Despite his earlier pleas for toleration, there was, he wrote, "no one thing to be so dangerous, dishonourable, or more offensive to Almighty God in the World, than that any Prince should permit the Ark of Israel and Dagon, God and the Devil, to stand and be honoured together, within his Realm, or Country." Parsons made this statement in 1588, when the mighty Spanish Armada gave him hope that England could be returned to the Catholic camp. His plan to re-Catholicize the country had a place for tolerance—but only as a temporary means to facilitate the restoration of Roman Catholicism. Taking inspiration from the successful re-Catholicization of the Spanish Netherlands, Parsons advised England's Catholic conquerors "not to press any Man's Conscience at the beginning for matters of Religion, for some few Years." There should be a "certain Connivence or Toleration of Magistrates" but "only for a certain time" and "limited, and with particular Conditions," namely, "that no meetings, assemblies, preaching or perverting of others be used." This was not a "Liberty of Religion to live how a Man will." That, Parsons felt, should not "be permitted to any Person in any Christian Commonwealth." Instead, his tolerance would allow those "quiet and modest People" who "have never heard perhaps the grounds of Catholick Religion" to "use the freedom of their Consciences, to ask, learn and to be instructed for the space prescribed, without danger of the Law or of any inquiry to be made upon them to inform themselves of the truth." Parson did not want to coerce individual's consciences, but, like the Christian humanists Erasmus and Sir Thomas More, he felt that, ultimately, in the case of "wilful Apostates, or malicious Persecutors, or obstinate Perverters of others," force could compel the recalcitrant. As God "hath had a sweet hand to cherish the well-affected," Parsons concluded, "so hath he a strong arm to bind the Boysterous, Stubborn, and Rebellious." Once Catholics had the upper hand again the tolerance would end.[20]

In the favorable atmosphere of the war against the Spanish Catholic Empire, puritans finally embraced colonization as part of the broader struggle against the Antichrist. The Roanoke colony may have been their first endeavor. It had been launched on the eve of the war, in an atmosphere of strong anti-Catholic sentiment. Although little is known of the colony's religious history, the connections of several colonists within London suggest that at least some of them were puritans or puritan sympathizers. Puritans certainly would have been happy with the way Ralph Lane, Roanoke's first commander, understood the colony's importance as part of the global struggle for "the Churche of Chryste thoroughe Chrystendom" against "Spayne (beynge ye swoorde of yt Antychryste of Rome and hys secte)."[21]

Puritan Hispanophobia was now patriotic. Puritan attacks on bishops were not. In 1588–89, the surviving classis movement could not resist publishing a savagely funny satire of episcopacy. Calling bishops "petty popes and petty antichrists" who "usurp the authority of pastors," these so-called Martin Marprelate tracts got the movement in deep trouble with Archbishop Whitgift. An investigation led to another campaign to enforce conformity that eventually suppressed the classis movement. Whitgift failed to find the author of the Martin Marprelate tracts, who remains anonymous to this day, but Cartwright was imprisoned for several years along with a few other ministers. Powerful and wealthy patrons prevented their conviction, but others were not so lucky. John Penry, a Welsh puritan associated with the secret press that had published the tracts, was hung for sedition in 1593. He had criticized the government in print for not doing more to evangelize Wales and leaving it in "spiritual misery . . . for want of the preaching of the Gospel."[22]

Suppressed in England and Wales, presbyterianism survived on the margins of the English world. Channel Islanders offered Thomas Cartwright, "the true progenitor of English presbyterianism," a welcome refuge for a couple of years in the mid-1590s. There he had a chance to practice running a genuinely presbyterian church. Later, at the Merchant Adventurers' church in Antwerp, Cartwright also had the support of reform-minded individuals to organize a congregation along presbyterian lines. In Amsterdam, the new English church was managed in a similar fashion, while the Church of Ireland welcomed puritans willing to work with sympathetic bishops. For the next several decades, these jurisdictions, safely removed from the authority of England's Parliament, kept presbyterian dreams alive.[23]

Within England, however, authorities in church and state undermined puritan ministers and strengthened episcopacy. Laws steadily reduced the arenas in which puritan ministers had been able to acquire special charismatic authority—by performing exorcisms and combatting witchcraft, for example. Ministers who once gained fame by using the classic puritan techniques of fasting and prayer to liberate individuals possessed by Satan could now be convicted of fraud. This antipuritan trend culminated in 1604 with the passage of canon 72 of the church forbidding ministers from performing exorcisms without a license from their bishop. King James, who famously believed in witches, had opposed the wish of some conservative clergymen for an outright ban on exorcisms. Keeping them under the control of bishops was enough.[24]

During these years of repression, puritan energies turned away from church reform and toward the cultivation of personal spiritual purity. Lay religion gained in importance as individuals sought to distinguish themselves from their ungodly fellow parishioners by developing an alternate religious life within and around their parish churches. Adopting ostentatiously pious behavior, they admonished their neighbors to live a more godly life, formed groups for private worship, and traveled to parishes where a minister they considered godly was preaching. This custom of sermon "gadding" also made clear which ministers were deemed to be ungodly. Puritan clergymen, meanwhile, developed nuanced ways to conform just enough to hold their positions. This process of "modified subscription" to the church's articles worked better at some times and places than others. A lucky few found sympathetic ecclesiastical niches within the church, where parishes vestries, patrons of parishes, chaplaincies, lectureships, and so forth, provided shelter, support, and employment without the pressure to fully conform.[25]

Some individuals went further and turned to alternative forms of Protestantism. From the earliest days of the Reformation, there had been those who emphasized that the conscience would voluntarily comply only with true religion. To knowingly conform to false religion was cowardly, misleading, dishonest, and spiritually dangerous. People who conformed merely because the law compelled them to could not be trusted. In the 1580s and 1590s, these attitudes carried the nonconformity of some into outright separation from England's church.[26]

Radical religious developments in the Low Countries were a major source of influence. Dutch Anabaptists rejected the whole system of established churches, including specially trained priests and ministers, and put ultimate religious authority in Scripture alone. Their distinguishing practice derived from their conclusion that there was no scriptural basis for infant baptism. Only a fully consenting and properly converted adult could be baptized (hence "Ana-baptism" meaning baptized again after the traditional infant baptism). Although virtually no English people became Baptists before the seventeenth century, some Dutch Anabaptists lived in England. Elizabeth's regime executed several of them. It also executed a few Englishmen who held Anti-Trinitarian views (whether Arian or Socinian is unclear) that possibly derived from their Dutch connections. Other, more mystically inclined individuals in East Anglia picked up on the esoteric theology of the German-Dutch mystic Hendrik Niclaes. Inspired by visions to develop a distinct path to salvation, Niclaes did not require his followers, called the Family of Love, to create a separate church. Instead, they could comfortably conform to parish religion while practicing their true faith in private. Only a few people became full-fledged Familists, but their ideas, like those of Anabaptists and Anti-Trinitarians, hung around the radical edge of puritanism.[27]

The influence of this growing range of beliefs and attitudes gradually undermined any puritan consensus over what a properly Reformed Church should be like. Most significant was the rise of Separatism. Opponents, in an effort to discredit them as mere sectarians, labeled them Brownists or Barrowists, after their early leaders Robert Browne and Henry Barrow. Particularly strong in the puritan hotbeds of East Anglia and London, Separatists believed the government's failure to fully reform the Church of England was a sign of its woeful corruption. It would be impossible to find salvation within it. To establish a pure church that could offer salvation, it was necessary to break with parish worship and create a separate, alternative church. Between the early 1580s and 1620, they worked out their new church system with much soul searching and strife, based on an individual "gathered" congregation, a voluntary association of people who recognized the saintly qualities in each other. Unlike geographically based parish congregations, membership was not automatic. Instead, it depended on two basic requirements: a disavowal of all Christian fellowship with the national church and a refusal to accept anyone as a minister who did not first deny the legitimacy of their ordination within the Church of England.[28]

Separatists were Calvinists and so not liable to be burned as heretics like Anti-Trinitarians. However, they were schismatics: people who believed much the same thing as the established church but refused to join in communion with it. Accordingly, they could be considered traitors and hung. Fear of this ultimate punishment led some, including Robert Browne, to recant upon being arrested and condemned for sedition. Others, like the important preacher Henry Ainsworth, sought safety in exile. In the 1590s, Ainsworth briefly conformed upon being caught, then fled to Ireland, where a hostile critic claimed the bishops permitted "papists, puritans, Brownists, atheists . . . to preach, to reason, to prate, to gather conventicles." Apprehended again, Ainsworth again briefly conformed before moving to Holland, where Separatists had been finding refuge since the 1580s. Amsterdam in the 1590s became the seat of a Separatist congregation that would exercise an outsize influence on puritans in England and the Americas.[29]

Repression drove other Separatists to consider an American colony—but only because they had no other choice. Parliament's 1593 "Act for Retaining the Queen's Subjects in their due Obedience" targeted both Separatists and Catholics by commanding that all adults who refused to attend church or who attended separate religious meetings ("conventicles") be imprisoned for sedition until they agreed to conform. Two Separatist leaders, Henry Barrow and John Greenwood, were executed under its provisions. Dozens of their followers languished in prison. Trapped alongside Roman Catholics in unhealthy conditions, some began to die. Given three months to conform or face a choice between exile and execution, some of them agreed to set up a colony in the mouth of the Saint Lawrence River on behalf of some merchants. The Magdalen Islands were prime walrus-hunting grounds with easy access to the rich fishing on the Grand Banks off Newfoundland. A colony there could give the English a head start on the fishing season. In 1597, the Separatists sent out their minister, his brother, and two others to set up a base. The rest would join them later. The result was a case study in why colonization was no easy solution for dissenters. The Separatists quarreled constantly, about the godliness of the minister's recent marriage, among other issues. Then, one of their two ships wrecked off the Newfoundland coast. When they finally found a suitable harbor in the Magdalen Islands, a group of French and Basque fishermen allied with the local Micmacs to drive them off. A plan to return was discouraged by the Privy Council, who feared provoking a war with France.[30]

All the attempts to establish a colony during the Anglo-Spanish War failed. Roanoke, weakened by poor relations with its indigenous neighbors and cut off from England by the assault of the Spanish Armada, vanished after 1588. In 1602 Bartholomew Gosnold led the final colonial expedition of the Elizabethan era. At what is now Buzzards Bay, Massachusetts, he established a trading post. However, it only lasted a few weeks. His men, fearing they would not have enough food to last through the winter, fled home.[31]

Circumstances changed significantly after James became king. In 1604 he made peace with Spain and released English Catholics from the oppression of the Elizabethan regime. Encouraged, some once again looked for profit in American colonization. In the spring of 1605, the mix of religious interests evident in Sir Humphrey Gilbert's venture was revived in George Weymouth's voyage to New England (then known as North Virginia). Weymouth's father, patriarch of a Protestant Devonshire shipping family, had invested in Gilbert's enterprise. Sir Thomas Arundell, another important investor in Weymouth's voyage, had connections with the Peckhams who had worked with Gilbert. Arundell was a zealous enough Catholic to have been imprisoned for his beliefs under Queen Elizabeth, yet also enough of a patriot to support the resistance to the Spanish Armada. After 1588 he avoided trouble in England by serving the Holy Roman emperor against the Ottomans for a number of years. Back in England by the fall of 1604, he recognized that the ending of both the Nine Years War in Ireland and the Anglo-Spanish War left a number of English and Irish Catholic soldiers at loose ends. Perhaps they could be used for colonization? Weymouth, who had sailed in search of the Northwest Passage for the East India Company in 1602, seemed to be thinking along similar lines. In 1604 he had presented King James with a manuscript treatise that used his skills in math and navigation to demonstrate the techniques successful colonizers would need, from shipbuilding to gunnery and fortification.[32]

Around the same time as Arundell was planning his expedition, probably between November 1604 and March 1605, Tristram Winslade, a Catholic from Cornwall who had fought in Spanish service, devised an elaborate plan for a colony to employ discharged British and Irish Catholic soldiers. We no longer have the plan, but we know about it because he submitted it for approval to the Jesuit Robert Parsons, who wrote up his comments in March 1605—just as Weymouth's expedition began its voyage to America. Parsons's reaction indicates why Catholics did not automatically see America as a place of refuge. Parsons liked Winslade's "intention," especially the conversion of North America's "barbarous people to Christianitie," but he saw "many great difficultyes, which seeme to me scarsly to be superable." He believed the king and his Privy Council "will never allowe" the "transferring English Catholiques to the Northern Partes of America." It would strike them as "not onely dishonorable . . . but dangerous." The dishonor lay in forcing "so many of thire naturall subjectes to flie and abondon thire owne countrey" because they suffered "persecutione." The danger lay in the chance that the government could deny Catholics leave to sell their property and bring their families to America with them. Without government support, Catholic colonists would face "many and great difficulties or rather impossibilities." Consequently, he doubted "that the better and richer sort, in respecte of theire wealth and commodities at home and of the love of the countrey and feare of the state," would want to go. The "poore sort without the riche will be of smal importance." Winslade's plan to get financial backing from the Holy Roman emperor Rudolf II, his younger brother the Archduke Albert (currently ruling the Spanish Netherlands along with his wife, an infanta of the king of Spain), and some Italian princes, seemed equally implausible. Worse, it would taint English Catholics by association with foreign princes. That could make them the laughingstock of "the Heretickes" who would joke about the "evacuatione of Papistes," as they had during Humphrey Gilbert's enterprise. Since then, the idea of a colonial refuge had become "most odious to the Catholick partie." Or so Parsons claimed. He personally feared that if English Catholics moved to America, it "may be very prejudiciall to the increase of Catholicke religione in England." By "decreasinge the number of Catholickes" and rendering those who remained behind "more contemptible to thire adversaryes," the English Catholic community would become poor and weak. Who would take care of the priests? Catholics needed to stay home.[33]

Parsons's comments may well have discouraged Arundell's plans to set up a colony. He had sent two servants with Weymouth, both of them Catholic. One, James Rosier, was a Cambridge graduate and recent Catholic convert. Rosier wrote the public account of the voyage, describing how the expedition explored what is now Maine and set up two crosses before returning home. It was a boosterish account praising his backers and the region's potential for colonization. Touched by the cooperative attitude of the Indigenous people he met, Rosier added his "prayers to God for the conversion of so ingenious and well disposed people." However, while Rosier was in America, Arundell changed his mind. King James made him Baron Arundell of Wardour (where the family had a castle) in May and gave him command of a regiment of English Catholics in Spanish service in the Low Countries. Arundell took up the post in September. Rosier had to seek alternate employment. Eventually he made his way to Rome and joined the Jesuit order. Planning to become a missionary to England, Rosier apparently never mentioned his participation in Weymouth's exhibition to Parsons. Sadly, he died in Italy in 1609 on his way back home.[34]

Nevertheless, other Roman Catholics continued to show an interest in colonization. In 1606, Sir John Zouche led a group of investors, including London fishmongers, who wanted to get involved in a colonial project. They contacted Sir Ralph Bingley, a well-connected veteran of the Nine Years War currently commanding the royal guardship on Ireland's southern coast. Details are scarce. The plan seems to have been to recruit Irish Catholics for Virginia. A ship was outfitted and sent to Ireland, but Bingley never made it to America. He seems to have gotten caught up in piracy against the Spanish instead, then turned to colonizing Ulster in lieu of America.[35]

*

Although the Tudor dynasty failed to establish a permanent American colony, its legacy for early American religion was nonetheless essential. It was under the Tudors that the religious diversity that later filtered over to the colonies first developed. This religious diversity also pushed the English to debate and contemplate religious pluralism and toleration. Few saw any good in either. Toleration was repeatedly rejected as an official policy both at home and in the colonies. Even among the dissenters, broader toleration was only endorsed, as in the case of the Jesuit Robert Parsons, when it seemed a useful tool to secure religious privileges for one's own faith. Nevertheless, by 1607 pluralism had become very much of a reality in the English world—and it was increasing. It was impossible to shield the American colonies from the many individuals whose commitment to religious conformity, or even Protestantism, was less than complete. The colonies did not offer an escape or alternative to English repression. Rather, they represented just one of a number of possible outlets, among them Ireland and the Low Countries, for exile and refuge, resistance and intrigue.

Given the complexity of Elizabethan religious politics, it should not come as a great surprise that individuals holding various religious views became involved in colonial projects. The mix of Catholic and Protestant interest in America indicates that the efforts of religious minorities to set up an overseas colony did not begin as a desperate response to religious repression but rather depended on official support. After all, colonies needed royal approval to succeed as a legitimate enterprise. Catholics got a green light to colonize within Humphrey Gilbert's patent. Separatists were encouraged to set up a colony off the Canadian coast. Nevertheless, America was no one's first choice to live. Religious dissidents wanted to stay home. If they had to leave, they preferred not to go far away. Separatists went to Holland while Catholics went to the Spanish Low Countries.

Those who showed the most enthusiasm for colonization were the merchants, soldiers, and others in need of new sources of wealth and glory. They had little interest in creating a religious refuge. Still, as the Virginia Company assembled its first expedition to America, the different religious interests kept their eyes open for opportunities.

PART 2

Jacobean Balance, ca. 1607–1625

FIVE

Balance: Virginia, Bermuda, Newfoundland, ca. 1607–1618

Anglo-American religious life began as an embattled middle. Virginia's first minister was praised as "a man not any waie to be touched with the rebellious humors of a popish spirit, nor blemished with the least suspition of a factius scismatick." Bermuda's first colonists pledged "to continue in that faith into the which we were baptized in the Church of England, and to stand in defence of the same against all Atheists, Papists, Anabaptists, Brownists, and all other Heretiques and Sectaries whatsoever, dissenting from the said Word and Faith." These statements echoed the religious policies of King James, who emphasized political loyalty and mistrusted religious extremes. Nevertheless, religious pluralism first trickled into the colonies under the cover of such solidly conformist statements. With conformity increasingly defined by what it was not rather than what it was, religious polemicists of various stripes recognized that the way to win was to successfully claim the middle ground. As the competing factions within the Jacobean Church of England adopted this strategy to their own ends, the shifting boundaries between the extremes opened up space for a variety of religious attitudes. Calvinists used it to support puritans; conservatives to support Catholic recusants. Beneath the profusion of moderate rhetoric, the church was deeply, and increasingly, divided. The reasonable middle varied significantly depending on who drew the lines and where.[1]

King James was an important influence on early American religion, not least because he presided over an enlarged and expanding English world. For the first time in history, the entire British archipelago from the Shetlands to the Channel Islands together with Ireland was united under one ruler. The religious possibilities and challenges he confronted were greater than those of the Tudors. He governed three kingdoms, each "somewhat diverslie affected in Religion," as Sir John Harington, courtier, author, inventor of the flush toilet, and godson of Queen Elizabeth, recognized. The English were "for the greater parte, according to the now established forme, being Protestant." The Scots, "enclyned to a purer manner of doctrine, which they take from the reformed Churches beyond the seas," were "in England blamed as Puritans." Meanwhile, "Ireland, and much of Wales, either for lack of instruction, or perhaps by so much instruction, is in manner altogether Catholique." Clearly, it would take much "wysdome, learning, and temper . . . to frame three so diverse enclyned nations to one due uniformity." Harington was writing in 1602 to persuade "all trew Englishmen that feare God and honor the Queene," be they "Protestantes, or Puritans, or Papists," to support James's right to the throne. In an ostentatious show of impartiality, Harington drew on authors from each of these religious camps to incline "all our myndes to a due obedience, and a moderat temper" toward James, who was "like to have no occasion to be partiall of any syde or to uphold any faction." He urged all Englishmen to "quietly and peaceblie" accept James as king and "beseech" him "as a true father to sett a peace between his children, if it be possible; that they may not one devoure and spoil another as they now doe, but at least in civill carriage agree orderlye." However, his pleas had their own partisan purpose. Harington was a religious conservative who opposed clerical marriage, was amenable to church papists, and sympathized with recusants. His plea for moderation aimed to block puritans' campaign for further church reform.[2]

Harington was not alone in hoping that James's accession to the throne would resolve the religious strife in England and Ireland. His policies seemed promising. After decades of war and confessional strife, James favored peace over war and moderation over radicalism. Domestically and internationally he assumed a religiously irenic stance.[3] Alas, far from resolving the religious problems of his kingdoms, James ended up exacerbating them. His Scottish-bred habit of balancing out religious and political factions rather than wholeheartedly identifying with any one of them tended to multiply rather than reduce the contests for influence. As it became clear that he privileged personal loyalty above any specific religious position, those seeking his favor learned to insist on their loyalty and claim their position as the reliable middle between competing—and disloyal—extremes. Unfortunately, the middle and the extremes were never identified. However, they clearly shifted over the course of James's reign in a gradual turn against Calvinism. Thus, while we can say that

English America's first churches were conformist, that does not mean they were all exactly the same.

*

Insisting in his opening speech to Parliament that he was "loath to be thought a Persecutor," James set a noticeably different tone for England's religious politics. He acknowledged that only "one *Religion*, and that which is by myself professed," was both "the true Religion" and "publicly allowed, and by the Law maintained." Nevertheless, he recognized that "lurking within the bowels of this nation" there was "another sort of Religion," which he described as "the falsely called Catholics, but truly Papists." Catholic derived from the Greek word for universal. Insisting that the Protestant church was the truly universal one, James deliberately labeled Roman Catholics "papists" to suggest that by following the pope they were not part of the truly universal religion. As for "the *Puritans*" or "*Novelists*," James called them a "private sect." Labeling them a "*Sect* rather than a Religion" emphasized that they "do not so far differ from us in points of Religion, as in their confused form of policy and parity." Puritans were "ever discontented with the present Government, and impatient to suffer any superiority," be it a bishop or a king. For James, that made "their sect insufferable in any well-governed Commonwealth." On the other hand, Roman Catholics' capacity for political loyalty made James willing to "put a difference betwixt mine own private profession of my salvation, and my politick Government of the Realm for the weal and quietness thereof." Assuaging the antipopish fears of Parliamentarians, he affirmed that he shared their faith and constancy in "Gods Truth." His attachment to the established religion was especially secure because he "found it agreeable to all reason, and to the rule of my conscience." At the same time, James's respect for reason and conscience also led him to reject the idea of "inthralling of my Subjects in matters of conscience" by strictly enforcing conformity. That would be subjecting them to "persecution" in the name of a foolishly "Precisian" (a word usually associated negatively with puritans) policy of coercing "all my Subjects to my private opinions."[4]

James's speech reveals both his capacity for tolerance and his priority to balance, rather than eradicate, religious differences. It also shows James to be more concerned with the political implications of religious difference than theological orthodoxy. James was theologically Calvinist but politically antipuritan. Rather than make England's church more reliably Calvinist, as puritans wanted, James preferred to allow a range of religious views and attitudes to proliferate within it. He may not have fully agreed with the anti-Calvinist views of some "avant-garde" conformists, but he did appreciate their outspoken devotion to his church. Puritans—like Scottish presbyterians—annoyed James by questioning and resisting his authority in church matters. Their hope of transforming the church into an institution more compatible with the international Reformed Protestant churches was not as soothing as conformists' professions of loyalty. Some conformists insinuated that puritans could be no more trusted than Scottish presbyterians and deliberately positioned themselves against them. Puritans criticized bishops. Avant-garde conformists praised them. When puritans questioned royal policy, they professed unquestioning obedience to it. Where puritan sermons threatened to sow consternation and instability, they stuck doggedly to the Book of Common of Prayer, diminished the importance of sermons, and enhanced the role of ceremony in their church services.[5]

The question of how James would cope with England's religious diversity had been an urgent political issue in the years preceding his succession. Elizabeth's refusal to countenance any public discussion of the succession exacerbated these tensions by giving the impression that her court was losing touch with the needs of the country. In the anxious and dangerous political struggles of the final years of Elizabeth's reign, the upper echelons of English politicians congregated loosely into two factions. On one side were William Cecil and his son Robert. Originally members of the gentry, they recently had been ennobled for their decades of loyal service to the queen. The Cecils' long hold on power restricted the possibilities for patronage and glory to a small group of their court friends and favorites. They generally accepted her long-standing policy of resisting change, defending conformity, and suppressing Catholics and puritans.[6]

Those frustrated and vexed by the Cecils' influence rallied around one of the wealthiest and most powerful noblemen in the country: the young Robert Devereux, Earl of Essex. A member of the old aristocracy and a war hero who had fought in France and the Low Countries as well as serving on several naval expeditions against the Spanish, Essex looked down on upstarts like the Cecils. He moved in similar circles to the Elizabethan colonizers Ralegh and Gilbert but at a far more exalted level. Essex represented a number of things: the landed aristocracy versus the new service aristocracy; the active warrior against the paper-pushing bureaucrat; the young versus the old. He was also a strong supporter of James's candidacy who adopted a more open approach to religious matters than the Cecils and their insistent conformism. While keeping his true opinions to himself, he cultivated a degree of religious ambiguity that enabled him to gain the reputation as a protector of *both* puritan ministers *and* Catholic priests. This approach kept Essex's political options open and attracted the support of disparate groups who could see in him someone able to promote their agenda: either a workable coexistence (the Catholic hope) or cultural dominance (the puritan hope). His influence in national politics reached a pinnacle in 1599 when he was made lord deputy of Ireland and put in command of a huge expedition of sixteen thousand men to decisively defeat the Irish rebels. Alas, he failed and was cast out of court. In a desperate effort to regain influence, he led a revolt in the streets of London against the Cecil faction in 1601. It sputtered. Essex was captured and executed as a traitor. For the next several years, his supporters lived under a cloud of suspicion.[7]

Given his reputation for tolerance, Essex was a prime target for those who opposed religious pluralism. The Jesuit Robert Parsons suggested he lacked principles as well as true religion. In a 1595 pamphlet purporting to convey a conversation that took place in Amsterdam among "Gentlemen of divers nations, qualities and affections, as wel in religion as otherwise," he mocked Essex's ecumenism. The text also cast doubt on James's candidacy for the Crown in favor of other, Catholic, candidates. Essex's ability to maintain friendship with "both sorts & factions, both of Catholicks and Puritanes, as they terme them," threatened conformists as well. After his downfall, one of Essex's old friends, Francis Bacon, publicly lambasted him to save his skin. He criticized Essex's religious policy as a transparently disingenuous design to gain the support of the masses, "turning his outside to the one, and his inside to the other." Essex was a hypocrite. His policy was "profane." He made puritans happy "by professing zeale, and frequenting sermons, and making much of Preachers." However, at the same time he was "secretly under hand giving assurances" to his Roman Catholic followers "that (if hee might prevaile in his desired greatnesse) hee would bring in a toleration of the Catholike religion."[8]

The man serving as archbishop of Canterbury when Virginia was first colonized was even more violently hostile to religious diversity. Richard Bancroft was born in Lancashire but made his career in London. Rising to become bishop of London in 1597, he worked as assistant for the aging Archbishop Whitgift before replacing him upon his death in 1604. Between then and his own death in 1610, Bancroft made opposition to Protestant nonconformity a priority. Since the 1580s he had been portraying the Church of England as caught between the hostile extremes of puritans and papists, lamenting the many "false prophets" who "now remaine amongst us: Arrians, Donatists, Papists, Libertines, Anabaptists, the Familie of Love, and sundrie other (I knowe not of what opinion)." Preaching against schism he insisted that religious diversity undermined piety. The "many sectaries and schismatikes" caused some Protestants to "revolt daily to Papistrie," while others "are become meerly Atheists, and the best do stand in som sort at a gaze." Five years later Bancroft published a compilation of "dangerous positions and proceedings" held by Scots and English clergymen who wanted to make the established church presbyterian "under pretence of Reformation." Bancroft's main foe was "our pretended reformers, the Consistorian Puritanes" of the classis movement. Nevertheless, they were just one of the "two sortes of men that especially disturbe the Church of England." The other was the "Seminary Priests and Jesuites." Both offended Bancroft's sense of religious order. Puritans were "lewd and obstinate." Roman Catholic priests perpetrated "divelish and traiterous practices." Nonconformity or even partial conformity was disobedience to royal authority. Bancroft posed the issue this starkly to increase the church's authority, wealth, and influence at a time when they seemed threatened from all sides. However, his mix of anti-Catholicism and antipuritanism also encouraged the growing shift within the church away from its Calvinist roots.[9]

King James's appointment of Bancroft had reinforced the royal antipuritan turn taken after the Hampton Court conference in the winter of 1604. The church's new set of canons targeted puritans in various ways. James's insistence that ministers conform to them forced about three hundred ministers to lose their positions. However, in a classic tactic of the Jacobean balance, after this initial campaign, subscription to the canons was not strenuously enforced. James allowed puritans to still serve as ministers. However, they lived under the constant threat of being confronted with the demand to fully conform. If they became troublesome or seemed disloyal, they could be confronted with the demand to conform or resign.[10]

Some puritans attempted to exploit James's priorities for the greater good of their cause. In 1605, the moderate puritan minister Andrew Willet attempted to persuade James to moderate his religious policies by stressing puritans' capacity for loyalty and drawing an important distinction between toleration and connivance to argue in favor of the latter (for Protestant nonconformists) and against the former (for Catholics). A prolific author most famous for his massive compilation of Protestant controversies with Roman Catholicism, *Synopsis Papismi*, Willet praised

James for "professing to love and honour the grave men and preachers of either opinions," especially "all faithfull, sound, and sober preachers of the truth," which could include puritans. He also commended the king for "rooting out all idolatrie and superstition, and rejecting all confused motions of a Babylonicall Toleration" of Roman Catholics, maintaining "justice and righteousness against the adversaries of truth in the land." Willet then turned to the peers of the realm overseeing James's campaign for conformity (Lord Mountjoy, the Earl of Devonshire, and Robert Cecil), and pled for "tolerance and forbearance towards friends and brethren" (i.e., puritans) in a policy of "brotherly connivance." Years later, his son Thomas would take the more radical path of joining the Separatist community in Holland before moving to the Plymouth colony and eventually becoming the first mayor of New York City.[11]

Unfortunately for Willet, James's antipuritanism was stronger than his anti-Catholicism. English Catholics, aware of James's tolerance of Catholics in Scotland, believed their position could improve under his rule. Even before he became their king, they drew up petitions asking him for a formal grant of toleration. Rumors circulated that "the recusant Catholics . . . may perhaps be . . . freed from persecution for their religious acts in private." James's leading Scottish advisor, Edmund Bruce, Lord Kinloss, offered no promise of formal toleration, but he told the Venetian ambassador that English Catholics would "neither be hunted nor persecuted" if they "remain quiet and decently hidden." And, in fact, James did tone down the ferocious anti-Catholicism of the Elizabethan regime. He spoke favorably of the pope (who had not excommunicated him), remitted the recusant fines scheduled to be imposed for the next year, and negotiated an end to England's war against Spain. He then ordered that his Catholic mother be reburied in Westminster Cathedral. His declaration "that she suffered for no other cause than for her religion" seemed to endorse the Catholic perspective on their relationship to the English state. However, and once again in the classic form of the Jacobean balance, James's benevolence toward Catholics had limits. He refused Spanish demands that he grant Catholics a formal toleration, and, after the peace was concluded, he ordered all Jesuits and seminary priests to leave England. In November 1604, he reimposed the penal fines. Catholics, like puritans, were to remain dependent on his favor.[12]

In the meantime, their improving circumstances encouraged some English Catholics to get interested in colonization again. Former friends of Essex helped. James sympathized with the Essex faction and was gradually rehabilitating them, but in the meantime colonial projects offered them a way to demonstrate their patriotism while hopefully turning a profit. For American history, the most notable of these figures was Sir Ferdinando Gorges who played a leading role in the early colonization of New England, first as a member of the Plymouth Company and then of the Council for New England. More representative of Essex's religious ambiguity was his good friend Henry Wriothesley, the third Earl of Southampton. A member of a leading Catholic dynasty, Henry had been raised a conforming Protestant by William Cecil. His father had died when he was young after a stint in prison for recusancy wrecked his health. This connection to Robert Cecil later saved the young third Earl of Southampton's life. Southampton had served with Essex in Ireland, forging a close friendship that led him to join Essex's revolt. On trial for his life, Cecil pleaded his case effectively enough to earn him life in prison rather than execution. In 1603, James pardoned Southampton, freed him, and restored him to his honors. Southampton then became involved in several colonial schemes, including the Virginia Company, the East India Company, and the Somers Isles Company in charge of Bermuda.[13]

In the spring of 1605, Southampton collaborated with his Catholic brother-in-law, Sir Thomas Arundell, to support George Weymouth's voyage. Had a major political crisis not suddenly intervened that fall, Southampton may well have become a conduit for further Catholic colonial projects. The Gunpowder Plot struck just a few months after Weymouth's return. In November 1605, a group of disgruntled English Catholics attempted to blow up King James, his eldest son, Prince Henry Frederick, his leading ministers, and the members of Parliament at the inauguration of Parliament. Mere hours before the session opened, investigators discovered Guy Fawkes sitting in the basement of the building where Parliament was to meet, surrounded by kegs of powder with matches in his pockets and spurs on his boots. Fawkes was not born Catholic, but he was from Yorkshire, one of the northern counties with many Catholics. After his widowed mother married into a recusant family, he had converted to Catholicism as a young man, then gone to serve in the Spanish army in the Netherlands. He was exactly the sort of person Tristram Winslade and Arundell wanted to recruit for their American colony. Instead, Arundell was one of the figures Fawkes implicated in a confession obtained under torture. The full details and ambitions of the plot were lost when the rest of the plotters were killed a few days later during a failed attempt to start an uprising in the Midlands. They seem to have feared that James's tolerance would weaken the English Catholic community. They hoped a rebellion would provoke a galvanizing conflict with the Protestant state.

Resentment at having a Scottish monarch also played a role, as well as a desperate plan to kidnap James's nine-year-old daughter, Elizabeth, convert her, and marry her to a Catholic monarch.[14]

Unsurprisingly, this astonishingly ruthless plot provoked a fierce anti-Catholic reaction. In later years the event would be turned into a national and imperial holiday with November 5 commemorated with bonfires, fireworks, and sermons celebrating God's providence in saving both King James and Protestant England. James would be remembered as a Protestant hero. However, in the immediate wake of the Gunpowder Plot, he actually disappointed militant Protestant expectations by refusing to turn the incident into a national campaign against Catholicism or even to label all Catholics an intrinsic threat. Instead, he did no more than propose a new loyalty oath designed to address what he considered the real problem: Catholic loyalty to the foreign power of the pope. The oath required his subjects to renounce the pope's power to excommunicate rulers and absolve their subjects of their obedience, as the 1570 bull *Regnans in excelsis* had done. Depriving monarchs of their right to rule was a "damnable doctrine" that was "impious and heretical." They then had to swear that the pope could in no way absolve them of the oath, regardless of any papal "pardons and dispensations to the contrary." Passed by Parliament in 1606, the oath would be written into the new colonial charters, beginning with Virginia.[15]

The Virginia Company received its first charter in this atmosphere of anxious anti-Catholicism and disappointed puritans. Its 1606 charter recalled the 1593 penal law against Jesuit missionaries and Separatists by forbidding colonists from withdrawing colonists "from their due allegiance" to the Crown. In its 1609 charter, King James reiterated that he was "loath, that any person should be permitted to pass, that we suspected to effect the superstitions of the church of Rome" and commanded everyone who entered the colony to take the oath of supremacy as well as the oath of allegiance. Those who could not swear the oaths would have to leave. That same year, a pamphlet encouraged investors in the Virginia Company not to allow "Papists, professed or Recusant," or anyone "seasoned with the least taint of that leaven, to be setled in our plantation, nor in any part of that countrie." If any be found in the colonies, they should "weede him out, and shippe him home for England, for they will ever bee plotting and conspiring, to roote you out if they can." Do not believe them, it went on, "howsoever they sweare, flatter, and equivocate."[16]

Similar anti-Catholic rules and attitudes permeated the other early Jacobean colonies, from the Newfoundland Company (1610) to the failed

Sagadahoc colony in Maine (1607–8), which, as with the previous efforts to establish an outpost in "Northern Virginia," was done in by harsh weather and scant supplies. Known as "Popham's Colony," it was notable for the prominent role several members of the Popham family took in funding and running it. Sir John Popham, the lord chief justice, and his son Francis, a member of Parliament, supported it from England. Sir John's nephew George Popham was the colony's governor. The Gunpowder Plot had directly threatened the Pophams, like a number of those involved in the Virginia and New England Companies. As members of Parliament or royal officials, they would have been present when Parliament blew up. For them, the oaths of supremacy and allegiance were instrumental to their safety and religious liberty. Many of their Protestant colonists agreed. As Virginia's governor and council explained to the Privy Council in 1629, the "freedome of our Religion" meant that "noe papists have beene suffered to settle their aboad amongst us."[17]

Roman Catholics were not the only individuals suspected of disloyalty. Puritans and Separatists were liable to similar charges. James tolerated a diversity of opinions within the church (what historians of toleration call horizontal or ecclesiastical tolerance and contemporaries termed *concordia*). He was less willing to tolerate those who stood outside of his church (what historians of toleration call vertical or civil tolerance and contemporaries termed *tolerantia*). From them he expected demonstrations of political loyalty. Compliant Catholics benefited from a reduction in recusancy fines; outspoken ones were harassed with the penal laws. Similar standards applied to puritans: those able to work with the church suffered little more than occasional admonishments for their nonconformity. More outspoken puritans, together with Separatists who refused to recognize the legitimacy of the national church, were driven into exile. Most of the Separatists who eventually wound up in the Plymouth colony, for example, derived from a group that formed in Lincolnshire in 1607 but had to flee to Amsterdam for safety in 1608. There they joined with the London Separatists who had opted for exile after the failure of the Magdalen Islands colony in 1597.

By driving Protestant dissent out of the country, King James inadvertently allowed England's Protestant fringe to evolve beyond his control. In Holland a growing mix of radicals lived alongside English presbyterians who kept alive the aspirations of the classis movement. In the relative freedom of the Dutch metropolis, Separatists entered a turbulent but creative phase that laid much of the groundwork for Congregationalism, the religion that twenty years later would dominate New England. In the meantime, the Amsterdam congregation splintered. Some, including most of the future Plymouth colonists, left Amsterdam to form Separatist congregations elsewhere, like Leiden. Others, like John Smyth, stayed in Amsterdam and, influenced by Dutch Anabaptism, became Baptists. A few went off in more idiosyncratic directions.[18]

Among the Amsterdam dissenters was Henry Jacob, an important figure in the development of Congregationalism. The son of a Kentish yeoman, Jacob had studied for the ministry at Oxford, spent time in London as a lecturer and, possibly, served as a chaplain for the Merchant Adventurers. In the 1590s he began carving out a middle ground between Separatism and conformity, entering into theological disputes with the Separatist Robert Johnson, on the one hand, and the bishop of Winchester, on the other. In 1603 he played a leading role in organizing the millenary petition. Disappointed by James's response, Jacobs began arguing that parishes should be given more autonomy from episcopal oversight to pursue reform on their own. When that failed, he petitioned James for tolerance in 1609. Pointing to James's lenient "proceediges towards some of a Romish and disaffected spirit," Jacob believed the king had demonstrated "that it shalbe lawful for each loyall and religious subject without prejudice to his life or libertie" to supplicate him for religious boons. Denying he had "the least spark of disloyaltie to your Persone and Crowne," and acknowledging James as "the Lords Lieutenant," Jacob requested "toleration and libertie to enjoy and observe the ordinances of Christ Jesus in the administration of his Churches." He wanted to be protected from "the Prelates, our professed adversaries, and their officers" through "an entier exemption" from their "jurisdiction." Nevertheless, he would "live under the command of your subordinate civill Magistrates." To bolster his case, Jacob claimed "that the church-government solicited by us, is more compatible with your Imperiall scepter and more advantageable thereto, then that of the said Prelates," never mind Roman Catholics. James did not grant his request. By 1610, Jacob was living in the Netherlands, associating with William Ames, John Robinson, and other progenitors of Congregationalism.[19]

It was not long before the ideas about church ecclesiology and theology developing in Holland began filtering back into England. First came the Baptists. With Thomas Helwys as their minister, they established England's first Baptist congregation in London in 1612. In 1616, Henry Jacob returned to establish an early version of a Congregational church. Ignoring parish bounds, it was composed of individuals who voluntarily joined together through a solemn covenant in a church fellowship—not unlike a Separatist church. However, Jacobs's church was expressly not Separatist. He claimed there were still enough godly people scattered about the Church of England to justify a tenuous communion with it. Jacobs allowed his church members to worship and take communion in certain, specific parish churches, primarily that of the noted puritan minister Henry Roborough. Nonetheless, his church treaded dangerously close to Separatism. Many puritans viewed it with more criticism than admiration.[20]

Back in Amsterdam, the Separatist congregation continued to divide, with repercussions soon felt in Virginia. Having determined that ultimate religious authority lay in the congregation, not a bishop nor a presbyterian council of ministers, the congregation's two Separatist ministers, Henry Ainsworth and Francis Johnson, fell out over the question of who had ultimate authority within the congregation: the bulk of its members or the minister and elders? Johnson supported the authority of the minister and elders. Ainsworth's group supported the lay majority. Ainsworth's group gained control of the building where they met, forcing Johnson and his followers to look for a new home. In 1613 they crossed the border to Emden. Several years later they went to Virginia.[21]

Virginia had not begun as a puritan-friendly colony, as the praise of its first minister for not being "blemished with the least suspition of a factius scismatick" suggests. However, Hunt soon died, and some his successors proved more amenable to puritan ideals. As early as 1609, there was an "unhappy dissension" over the preaching of the colony's second minister. Complaining that he was "as they say, somewhat of a Puritan," the "most part" of the colonists "refused to go to his services and hear his sermons." However, "by the other part he was supported and favored." Virginia's third minister, and the first minister at Henrico, was Alexander Whitaker, son of William Whitaker, the Cambridge University professor who had composed the Lambeth Articles in 1595. Alexander is mostly famous as the man who baptized Pocahontas. However, his experience in Virginia suggests that the colony had more puritan potential than is usually recognized. His father had been intimately familiar with the classis movement: in 1589, while he was out of town, it had held a national synod in his lodgings. As a student, Alexander had studied alongside future Massachusetts luminaries like John Cotton and John Winthrop. No doubt hoping to attract some of his former colleagues to join him in Virginia, in 1614 Alexander wrote an open letter wondering aloud why "so few of our English ministers that were so hot against the surplis [surplice] and subscription [to the Jacobean canons of the church] come hither where neither is spoken of."[22]

Ministers could shape the religious climate in early Virginia toward their own ideal—but few of them survived to leave a lasting impression. The colony's notorious mortality posed a serious challenge to institutional continuity, as did the often temporary status of their tenure. Ministers either died or returned to England after their time of service ended. Hunt had died within a year. Alexander Whitaker died crossing a river in 1617. His younger brother Jabez, also a minister of puritan inclinations and a desire to convert Native Americans, followed him to Virginia, but died soon after arriving. It is difficult to pin down early Virginia's religious climate, but it clearly contained the full range of opinions available within Jacobean conformity.[23]

Whitaker's case suggests how a distant colony, like other peripheral regions of the English world such as Ireland and the Channel Islands, could preserve the Calvinist heart of the Church of England even as authorities in England turned against it. Much hinged on the predilections of local elites and key individuals within the companies governing the colonies. A 1609 sermon preached before the Virginia Company in London suggests how some of its members grappled with the range of religious views within and without the established church. "Popery was a mint of treason," the preacher insisted, pointing to the Gunpowder Plot and blaming the Jesuits as particularly dangerous. However, he saw problems on the Protestant side of the fence as well. The "Brownists and Barrowists" were the real "peace-breakers of the Church," but "our mother the Church" was also plagued by the "calamity" of "divers opinions striving in her wombe," much as Esau and Jacob did within Rebecca. The preacher was less hostile to nonconformists than Archbishop Bancroft. He called them "neerer friends to our Church (men for their diligence and other good partes worthy of much prayse)." However, he belittled the scruples that prevented them from fully conforming. They were "so impatient at the ceremonies of our Church, that they be scarce willing (in obscuring of them) to ioine with us." Urging puritans to "maintaine the unity of the spirit, and in the band of peace," he challenged them to "not be so conceited of" their "holinesse, as to distate all mens company" and the religious unity of the church. It was "a sinne indeed to halt betweene two opinions, to have a knee for God, and a knee for Baal."[24]

The church in early Newfoundland likewise sat between threatening extremes. More famous for fish than religion, Newfoundland began to be colonized by the English in 1610. Sources are few, but the writings of Robert Hayman offer a rare window on its likely official character. In 1617, Hayman served as governor of an outpost on the northern edge of the Avalon Peninsula. He then returned regularly before going to Guiana, where he died. While in Newfoundland, he wrote a book of epigrams. Lovingly dedicated to King Charles I, it contained attacks on puritanism as well as Catholicism. Hayman characterized "Puritaines" as "blind-hearted, Proud, Vaine-glorious, Deepe Hipocrites, Hatefull and Envious, Malicious, in a fell high excesse, and full of all Uncharitablenesse." On the other hand, he also dismissed "Poperies chiefest absurdities." One epigram complained, "Our common Whores turne Roman Catholicks, By that meanes they get Pardons for tricks."[25]

Another source suggesting the character of early Newfoundland's conformity comes from Sir William Vaughan, a Welsh landowner who tried but failed to establish a colony there between 1616 and 1619. He later published several books defending the established church and attacking its critics, going out of his way, like Hayman, to disparage Catholics and puritans. Vaughan and Hayman's views likely affected their choice of ministers for Newfoundland. Although we know little about them, Hayman spoke well of one, suggesting a shared conservative approach to conformity. Another is known to have deliberately positioned himself between puritans and Catholics at a later date. Newfoundland, in brief, seems to have begun as a rather conservative bastion of conformism.[26]

Bermuda, however, was even more puritan friendly than Virginia, notwithstanding the stolidly conformist name of its main port and capital: Saint George's. The uninhabited island was discovered by accident in 1609 when a Virginia-bound ship wrecked on one of its reefs. The survivors eventually made it to Virginia, but one, Sir George Somers, an original patentee of the Virginia Company and a privateer who had been knighted for his service against Spain, later returned to Bermuda, where he died. In his honor, the Virginia Company subsequently referred to Bermuda as the Somers (or Sommer) Isles. In 1612 they sent out a group of people to colonize them. In 1615, a separate Somers Isles Company took over control. By 1625 the colony had about eight hundred inhabitants.[27]

Membership in the Somers Isles Company overlapped with that of the Virginia Company, but had a noticeably more puritanical slant. Like other colonial charters, its patent said little about religion because the assumption was that the established church would prevail. All inhabitants had to swear the oaths "of supremacy and allegiance." The company's governor and assistants, who supervised the colony from their headquarters in

London, appointed its ministers and other officers. Colonists were supposed to "live together in the feare and true worship of Almighty God, christian peace and civill quietnes each with other." As in Virginia, "no person addicted to the Superstition of the Church of Rome" was to "bee at any tyme permitted to pass unto the said Islandes." The importance the Virginia Company attached to religion is evident in its commission to Bermuda's first governor, Richard Moore. Insisting that "Religious Government" was the best way to "bynd men to pforme there duties," it ordered Moore to ensure "that prayers be saide euery morninge ane eueninge . . . to preserue peace and Concord amongst yourselves." The company also provided him with "diuers good books . . . to be imployed for the said service."[28]

The puritan twist that could be given to these run-of-the-mill endorsements of official conformity became evident the day after Moore and his fifty colonists arrived on Bermuda. Together with their minister, George Keith (a Scot), they celebrated the Sabbath, which they "dedicated to God in the best manner we could." They then subscribed to a pledge of religious unity, promising to defend the Church of England "against all Atheists, Papists, Anabaptists, Brownists, and all other Heretiques and Sectaries whatsoever," who dissented from its "Word and Faith." However, this apparently enthusiastic endorsement of conformity affirmed several puritan priorities, such as the strict observance of the Sabbath and forbearing from swearing, stealing, or quarreling. Affirming the colonists' loyalty to King James, it closed with an oath to defend their commonwealth and "the Gospell wee professe."[29]

Bermuda's early religious history shows how, at the local level, the Jacobean church could be bent toward puritan ends given the right combination of patrons and minister. In such a geographically and demographically small environment, a single minister could exercise a great deal of influence over the tenor of local religious life. Bermuda was divided into "tribes" that functioned like parishes. Each ran its own church through a council of local overseers working with the minister, but rarely in the early years was there more than one minister in the whole colony. George Keith, Bermuda's first minister was "no Minister" and "a poor Scholar" in the opinion of its second minister, the puritan Lewis Hughes. Hughes, on the other hand, had once called all bishops antichrists and in 1602 lost his position as rector of a London parish for performing an exorcism. He arrived in Bermuda in 1614 and stayed until 1623. Keith left in 1617. The third and fourth ministers both died shortly after arriving in the colony. Hughes thus exercised the most influence over the first decade of the island's religious life. He dismissed the ceremonies of the church and its *Book of Common Prayer*, used a liturgy that resembled that of Geneva more than contemporary England, and emphasized preaching and catechizing. Hughes later fondly remembered how, during a famine not long after he arrived, he took heart from colonists' "forwardnesse to heare Gods word," as he preached, weak from hunger, from a "lowe rocke, on the side of an hill" while they sat "in rowes upon the ground." To reinforce Bermuda's puritan potential, he encouraged the immigration of those that "have grace to serve God," were willing to work and "endure hardness," and would "bring Bibles, and other good bookes" for "the comfort of their soules." He discouraged "Idle persons" and "such as are profaners of the Sabboth, and come to the service of God but when they list." Daniel Tucker, governor from 1616 to 1619, was not a puritan. However, he tolerated Hughes's machinations for the sake of preserving the civil peace—and out of a desire to have some ministerial services in the absence of any other options. Still, he wished Hughes would use the *Book of Common Prayer*.[30]

In the meantime, Catholics' interest in colonization revived as their position within Jacobean England became increasingly stable. Surprisingly, King James's loyalty oath was key to this process. Of course, it posed a moral dilemma for Catholics, as it required the swearer to acknowledge limits on the pope's authority that the pope himself did not accept. Some took it; many others resisted. In practice, however, James deployed it strategically. Rather than enforce it systematically, James preferred to keep it on the books as a way to demand Catholic loyalty when necessary. Indeed, it was not enforced in earnest until a French Catholic murdered the French king, Henry IV, in 1610, provoking James's long-standing fear of being killed by a religious fanatic. In the meantime, Catholics struggled to find a way to swear loyalty without denying the legitimate authority of the pope. An extended series of complex negotiations between the Jacobean regime and English Catholics never entirely resolved the dilemma. However, they gave Catholics a new degree of political legitimacy, for they provided a forum for developing a new relationship with the state. In short, where the Elizabethan regime had oppressed Catholics with an expanding array of penal laws, James kept Catholics within the political nation—albeit at the margins. He never granted them a formal toleration, although he was willing to contemplate it for diplomatic reasons. Nevertheless, they benefited from a "limited degree of tolerance" in other ways. For example, once the furor over the Gunpowder Plot died down, James favored a more lenient enforcement of the penal laws. Then, in

1611, the cash-strapped king created the expensive honor of baronet as a way to both create an honor above that of knighthood and raise money. A number of English Catholics purchased the honor.[31]

In this comparatively tolerant atmosphere, Catholics drew up a new plan for colonization. In June 1609, "three Hundred Catholic Housholds" from England sought to obtain a license from the king "at theyre owne cost & Charges, to depart this Land to inhabit Virginia to hold such part as shalbe allotted to them." They expressed themselves willing to accept "such Conditions as his Maiestye with the Advice of his Counsell shall sett downe, so that they be not against theyre Consciences." The Spanish ambassador reported that they were also "negotiating with the Baron of Arundell" to have him join them "with 500 Englishmen, and with as many Irishmen to settle in Virginia, to fortify themselves there, and to take the necessary supplies, so as to put it in the best state of defence." Arundell wanted a separate "patent by this king, and" financial support. The "patent, they dare not give it to him," the ambassador claimed. As for money, "they have none." The plan sputtered.[32]

In the meantime, English Catholics turned on each other in a fight to see who would be in charge of the community. On one side were the Jesuits and other religious orders. They treated England as if it were a mission territory like India or America, ignoring parish and episcopal boundaries and authorities. On the other side were the secular clergy who wanted to recreate something like the parish system of old. These seminary priests crafted an image of themselves as loyal Englishmen by portraying the Jesuits as international conspirators. Their self-conscious posture of loyalty mirrored a similar split among James's Protestant subjects: Catholics and Protestants affirmed their loyalty to James by disparaging the reliability of their coreligionists. James encouraged these divisions. They kept the different religious factions weak and divided and increased the importance of his royal authority as a mediator between them. These divisions within and between England's Christians within and without its church would have tremendous ramifications for colonial American religion.[33]

*

In Scotland, the Jacobean balance had succeeded in both strengthening royal authority and restoring peace to a violent country. Elsewhere, however, it had a polarizing effect. James's English subjects, Protestant and Catholic, were divided when he first took the throne and became more so over the course of his reign. James refused to condone the sort of persecution that the Elizabethan regime had unleashed on Catholic and Protestant dissenters, but he also avoided officially tolerating them. Instead, he preferred to indulge a range of religious views within and without the church, so long as they professed their loyalty to him. Rather than fully endorse the reformist platform of the puritans and their sympathizers, he preferred to keep the scope of the established church broad, initially by favoring antipuritans like Richard Bancroft. However, he did not want to be beholden to antipuritans like Bancroft anymore than he did to puritans. Upon Bancroft's death in 1610, he appointed George Abbot, a stern Calvinist and steadfast anti-Catholic, as archbishop of Canterbury. James's strategy of balance allowed both groups to persist within the church, but it also encouraged them to fight for his favor and prove their loyalty.

In this atmosphere of royal semi-tolerance, the Jacobean balance, English Christianity planted its first roots in America. Conformity was the official norm, but it took on different connotations from place to place as influential individuals pushed local religious life in different directions. The small scale of colonial life generally gave a few key individuals tremendous influence over colonial religious life. In Newfoundland, it was religious conservatives. In Bermuda, it was puritans. In Virginia, it was a constantly shifting mix. None of these conditions was permanent. Regular changes among the local elite in church and government due to death or transfer out of the colony kept the door open to new influences from within the broad cope of Jacobean conformity. Through this dynamic the religious variety of Jacobean England began to work its way into the colonies under the cover of conformity. When religious politics became increasingly polarized across Europe after the outbreak of the Thirty Years War in 1618, even the extremes of the Jacobean religious world—Catholics and Separatists—would be able to gain footholds in America by playing along with the Jacobean balance, insisting on their loyalty and playing down their differences from the official religion. In this way colonial religious pluralism emerged even as the toleration of religious difference remained anathema.

SIX

Polarization: Plymouth, Avalon, Nova Scotia, New England, 1618–1625

In the early 1620s, concerns rippled across the English world that it was becoming too tolerant. Captain John Bargrave, a man deeply involved with the Virginia Company, complained that the person currently in charge of its colonial policy, Sir Edwin Sandys, wanted "to give leave to the Brownistes and Separatists" to settle in the colony and "erect a free state in Virginia." Sandys was promising that "they shall have no Govermt putt upon them but by their owne consents." If the Separatists had their way, "their doctrine clayminge a libertie to disagreeing" with monarchical government would turn Virginia into a republic on the model of Geneva. Around the same time, England's ambassador to Istanbul, Sir Thomas Roe, who had once commanded an expedition to Guiana, was fighting against "diverse rumors and reports lately spread abroad, to the dishounor of his Matie and scandall of the Church of England," that King James "had granted a tolleration of Popish Religion and liberty of conscience in England, and had suppressed all lecturers and lectures." In England, the outspoken parliamentary leader John Pym warned that if King James showed his Roman Catholic subjects any favor, "they would expect toleration. After 'toleration they will look for equality, after equality for superiority, and after superiority they will seek the subversion of that religion which is contrary to theirs.'"[1]

The Jacobean balance was getting off kilter. The primary culprit for this state of affairs was King James's efforts to marry off his children. Royal marital politics do not figure much in early American histories, but in this case they inadvertently opened the door to pluralism in the colonies. Prince Henry Frederick, a committed Protestant for whom puritans had high hopes, had died suddenly of a fever in 1612. Before dying, he had approved his sister Elizabeth's marriage to the firmly Calvinist Elector of the Palatinate, Frederick V, which took place in early 1613. King James then decided to balance out the religious polarization of Europe by finding a Spanish Catholic wife for his son and heir, Prince Charles. Negotiations over this so-called Spanish Match dragged on from 1614 to 1623. To appease the Spanish, James treated his Catholic subjects with calculated tolerance. He even entertained the possibility of a formal toleration. Was he abandoning the Protestant cause? When the Parliament of 1614 objected to his plans, James dissolved it after only eight weeks. For the next seven years, he governed without it. Meanwhile, western Europe began its spiral into the Thirty Years War. Rather than join the Protestant cause—headed by his son-in-law Frederick V—James hoped the Spanish Match could help him broker a peace. Irish and English Catholics hoped that a Catholic queen could bring "a relief of their grievances so long suffered for their religion." However, when his need for money became desperate, James had to summon Parliament again. After several years of agitation, it managed to compel James to abandon the match and then declare war against Spain. Shortly thereafter, in March 1625, he died.[2]

The controversy over tolerance sparked by the Spanish Match took place at a time when travelers, including several directly connected to the Virginia Company, were beginning to inform the English public about the religious pluralism practiced in the rich and powerful empires of the Ottomans and Mughals. Clearly, it was an effective strategy for building the largest and wealthiest empires in the world. The English rejected this model of empire building, but pluralism nevertheless crept into their colonies. Four factors proved decisive in this process. First of all, Ireland was increasingly drawn into colonial projects. Second, the Spanish drove the English and Irish out of Guiana, forcing them to turn their energies to the Caribbean and North America, where they gained a permanent foothold. Third, Virginia loosened up its land policies, allowing colonists to set themselves up at a significant distance from the direct supervision of Jamestown and its church. The policy deliberately encouraged nonconformists and Separatists to move to America, including the small but stubborn knot of Leiden Separatists whose ship accidently carried them to New England instead. Finally, in the course of the Spanish Match negotiations, George Calvert developed a close relationship with King James that led him to grant Calvert a colonial charter. Calvert was a conforming Protestant at the time, but from a Roman Catholic family. Before moving overseas he would return to their faith. Consequently, by the time Prince Charles succeeded his father as king, the religious extremes of early modern England—Protestant Separatists and Roman Catholics—had gained access to American colonies without any formal recognition or toleration.

*

For a time in the 1610s, puritans had had reason to hope that the church could turn back in their direction. In his first several years in office, the Calvinist Archbishop of Canterbury George Abbot reversed the anti-Calvinist ambitions of his predecessor Bancroft and instead encouraged Calvinist preachers. Abbot believed the really important struggle was the one against Catholics and their religion, not the disputes between Protestants. Strict conformity was far less of a priority for him than Bancroft. Abbot gladly tolerated mild acts of nonconformity as long as they did not lead to overt heresy or open disloyalty to the church. That he did not tolerate. Indeed, in 1612 Abbot approved the last burnings of Protestant heretics in England: two Arians. Separatists and anti-episcopal puritans like William Ames also suffered. Ames was denied a position in the church and went into exile in the Netherlands, where he developed ideas about congregational church government that later influenced New England's puritans. On the other hand, puritans willing to work within the church did well. Unfortunately, as Abbot began to disagree openly with James over policy questions, especially the Spanish Match, he steadily lost power and influence. James's royal favor shifted to the antipuritans within and without the church, a pattern continued by his son Charles. By the time Abbot died in 1633, he had become little more than an impotent relic.[3]

James's drift away from the Calvinism represented by Abbot is evident in his response to the 1618–19 Synod of Dort, a major international event that established Calvinism as the orthodoxy of the Dutch and other Reformed Churches. The Dutch Republic had been plagued by a running dispute between Calvinists and Arminians over the theological question of the role of human agency in receiving God's Grace for salvation. Hardline Calvinists said everything depended entirely on God's preordained will. Arminians argued there was some space for human agency. The dispute culminated in the Calvinist faction staging a political coup and calling for a national synod to be held in the city of Dort. Since similar questions were troubling Reformed Churches across Europe, the synod became an international assembly. King James sent several delegates but refused to explicitly endorse the synod's affirmation of strict predestinarian Calvinism. He did not create new canons or otherwise clarify the doctrine of the Church of England beyond what already had been done at the beginning of his reign. James always insisted that all good Protestants agreed on the fundamentals. However, he preferred not to specify exactly what they were. This ambiguity gave him an important degree of wiggle room, enabling him to support anti-Calvinists like William Laud as well as Calvinists like Abbot. To adopt the findings of Dort would remove this politically valuable room for maneuver and strengthen the Calvinists who were currently annoying him by their refusal to either fully conform or support the Spanish Match.

Instead, James published the *Book of Sports*. This controversial text struck a deliberate blow against puritan efforts to enforce a strict observance of the Sabbath by publicly authorizing physical recreation after divine services on Sundays. There was no national sabbatarian policy, but in Lancashire, the county with the most Catholics, puritans had effectively enforced sabbatarian policies and banned traditional Sunday sports. James only found out about this local initiative when he happened to pass through the county. He ostensibly published the *Book of Sports* to defend the established religion against the calumniations of the "two sorts of people, wherewith that countrey is much infected (Wee meane Papists and Puritanes)." His son Charles reissued the declaration after he became king.[4]

This increasingly anti-Calvinist atmosphere prompted puritans and Separatists to look afresh at America. Virginia was struggling to survive. Until 1617, it had proven a better consumer of English lives than a producer of valuable products. Hundreds of people had moved to the colony, but its population remained stuck at about four hundred. Desperate to attract more inhabitants, in 1618 the Virginia Company implemented a new land policy. Colonists would be allowed to set up plantations away from Jamestown—and the immediate supervision of its church. The Virginia Company did not make a formal grant of toleration, but it was clearly not going to ask many questions about immigrants' religious views. The policy worked. By 1624, some four thousand people had arrived, including several hundred puritans and Separatists, several of whom became respected colonists, even burgesses in the assembly. They tended to settle across the James River and downstream from Jamestown, where the counties of Isle of Wight, Nansemond, and Upper Norfolk became known for puritan sympathies. Their impact on the religious character of the colony was limited because colonists kept dying. The first Separatist move to Virginia in 1618, for example, ended in disaster. Francis Johnson, the congregation's minister, died before the ship sailed. His successor, Francis Blackwell, died during the long voyage to Virginia. The unhealthy, overcrowded

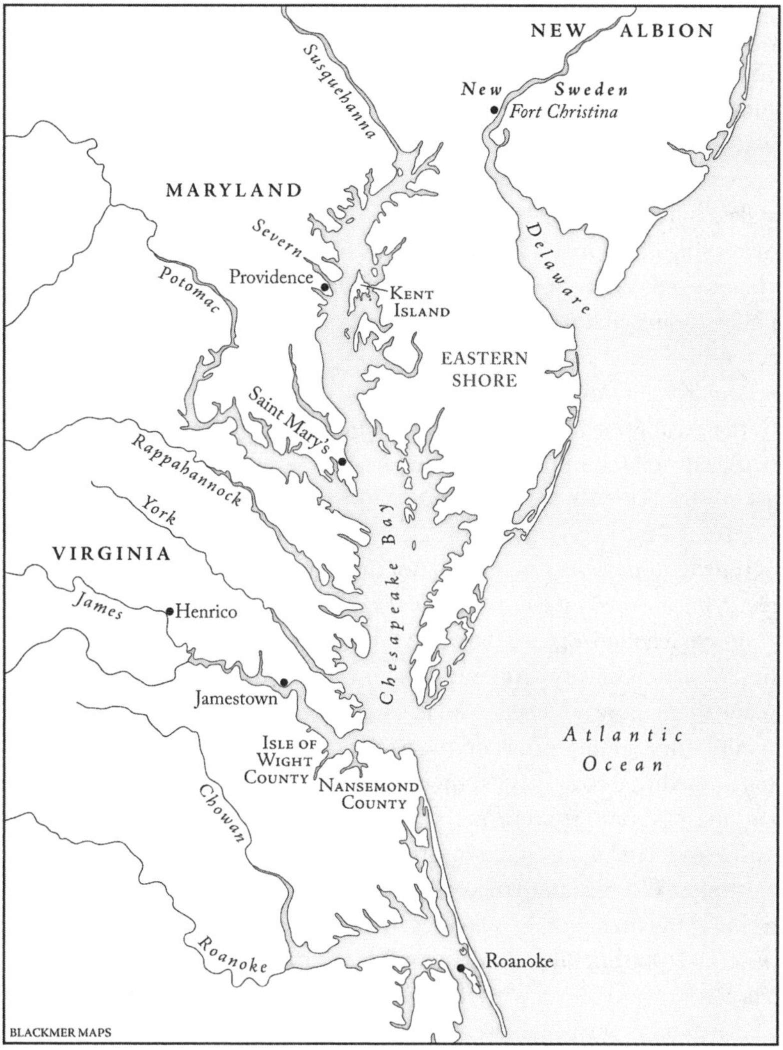

FIGURE 5. English Chesapeake before 1660

conditions also killed most of the 180 other passengers. Only a handful of these Separatists managed to set foot in Virginia. Henry Jacob, the pioneer of Congregationalism, decided to go to Virginia in 1622. It's not clear if he ever made it, but by the spring of 1624 he too was dead.[5]

Nevertheless, Virginia's religious climate was noticeably altered by the newfound tolerance. It was not a formal policy of toleration but simply a relaxation of the enforcement of conformity that allowed a wide range of

Protestants to carve out a home, thousands of miles away from any episcopal oversight. With only one or two ministers working in the colony at any given time, there were few resources to strictly enforce conformity beyond Jamestown anyway. However, this was more than simply a pragmatic policy designed to populate the colony. It drew some inspiration from hopes to reunite Christendom under one church again. King James had staked his ecclesiastical and international policy on this dream, while the increasing familiarity with the religious diversity of the Muslim world also encouraged some of the company's directors to reconsider tolerance as a policy for expansion. For example, the same year the Virginia Company received its first charter, Richard Knolles, a headmaster of a grammar school in Kent, published his translation of *Six Bookes of a Commonweale* by the great French legal theorist Jean Bodin. Bodin attributed the power of the Ottoman Empire to its willingness to "permitteth every man to live according to his conscience" and openly tolerate "foure divers religions, viz. That of the Jewes, that of the Christians, that of the Grecians, and that of the Mahometanes." Bodin did not think toleration per se was a positive good, but he recognized its political value.[6]

English colonizers, on the other hand, saw little to admire in this Muslim toleration of very different religions. Instead, their encounter with it made them more attached to an interconfessional tolerance within Christianity. For example, after serving as the chaplain on George Weymouth's 1602 expedition to seek a northwest passage, John Cartwright visited the Ottoman Empire. He returned hoping that the current war between the Turks and Persians would allow the "divers parts of Christendome to refresh themselves, and to increase their" strength so that they could unite against "the Great Turke." Likewise, the first chaplain the Levant Company sent to Aleppo openly looked forward to the time when God "will cast out" the "Turks" and "restore" Syria "to the true owners, the Christians." True, the Ottomans permitted men "of all Countries, of all Religions" to trade in Aleppo, but they were still "usurpers." Even more negative was the assessment of the gentleman traveler Henry Blount. He claimed the Ottomans actually wanted "to extinguish Christianitie" through toleration. Christians were tolerated, but also singled out for extra taxation and military service as Janissaries. Rendered "poore, wretched, taxed, disgraced, deprived of their children and subject to the intolerance of every Raskall," many eventually converted to Islam to be liberated from those burdens.[7]

Sir Edwin Sandys contributed to this discussion in 1605 with his *Relation of the State of Religion.* The son of a bishop and a client of the Cecils, Sandys was a convinced conformist who is believed to have converted his distant relative Henry Wriothesley, Earl of Southampton, from Catholicism. However, during extensive travels through Catholic and Protestant western Europe in the 1590s, he had developed a cosmopolitan approach to Christian religious differences. His book was a travel narrative that professed a deep desire for religious unity but argued it was practically impossible. Catholics and Protestants would not be reconciled anytime soon. However, in the meantime, Christian Europeans should exercise mutual tolerance. He took this attitude to Parliament, where he became an influential figure in the 1610s. It also informed his approach to colonial policy. An entrepreneur with substantial investments in the Virginia, Bermuda, and East India Companies, he took the lead in promoting Virginia's tolerant new land laws after he was elected an "assistant," that is, director, of the Virginia Company in 1616.[8]

Sir Edwin Sandys never visited Virginia, but his younger brother George Sandys did in 1621. Also a member of the Virginia Company council in London, George accompanied their kinsman, Governor Sir Francis Wyatt, to Virginia, where he served on the governor's council until 1625. George had developed his own views in favor of pan-Christian solidarity during earlier travels in the Mediterranean. He found that, although the Ottomans granted Christians "unreproved exercise of their religion," they also forced them to live in a country "defiled" with the "superstitions" of their Turkish rulers. In Virginia, George's ideal of Christian unity took on a lethal aspect when he led the first counterattack against the 1622 Powhatan uprising.[9]

The Sandys brothers' willingness to tolerate puritans and their sympathizers on the colonial frontier was opposed by some investors in the Virginia Company, like Captain John Bargrave. Bargrave's brother Thomas had replaced Alexander Whitaker as minister of Henrico (but died in 1621). Another brother, Isaac, was chaplain to Prince Charles. Bargrave, a former soldier with some university education and important contacts on both sides of the Atlantic, preferred an antipuritan colonial policy. Worried that Sandys's policy would encourage Virginia to become religiously radical and independent, he drew up a "Forme of Polisie to Plante and Governe Many Families in Virginea, Soe as It Shall Naturally Depend one the Soveraignteye of England." With conformity the key to loyalty, there was to be no tolerance for religious dissent. Bargrave insisted that the "true word and service of God . . . accordeing to the doctrine, rightes, religion, and eclesiasticall forme of governement now professed and established in England" be practiced "not onely within everie the sayde severall collonies, but alsoe as much as they may amongst the savage people."

Ideally, Virginians should take the oath of supremacy "once everie yeare at the least." With Separatists and Roman Catholics in mind, Bargrave claimed that those who "shall refuse to be governed by our eclesiasticall government established," or "whoe shall professe any doctrine contrarie to oures," or "shall attempt to withdrawe any of our people . . . from the same government" would be considered "as a resister of our soveraigne power." Offenders would be imprisoned "untill hee shall throughly reforme himselfe." Those who refused to reform and conform would "be banished Virginea and sent to England" for punishment.[10]

The lack of consensus on Virginia's religious future was just one of the Virginia Company's many troubles in these years. Factional infighting was rife. Then the devastating Powhatan War, provoked by the rapid expansion driven by Sandys's new land policy, drove the company into bankruptcy. With the company's competency now called into question, King James dissolved it in 1624. After much controversy, Virginia became a royal colony. The colony's religious policy became less indulgent of nonconformity and more attuned to royal tastes in conformity.

Bermuda, in the meantime, became even more puritan friendly. Nathaniel Butler, governor from 1619 to 1622, was very sympathetic to the ambitions of the puritan minister Hughes. He even translated the French presbyterian liturgy used on the Channel Islands to give Hughes a claim for legitimacy within the Jacobean church. Butler also supported Hughes's efforts to enforce godly social values. When one poor soul drank himself to death, Butler treated it as a suicide. Ordering his former drinking companions to bury the man "in the high way, with a stake driven through him," he also forced each of them to wear "a paper on his backe with this superscription, *These are the Companions of him, which killed himselfe with drinking*." Two of the men were then whipped, while the third, a soldier, was forced to "ride the Cannon" as it was "shot off full charged, which did shake him terribly." Obviously, not all Bermudans had puritan inclinations, but subsequent ministers and magistrates managed to sustain this largely puritan regime into the 1650s.[11]

The effective cooperation between governor Butler and minister Hughes shows how elites could set the terms for local religious life, but they ultimately were limited by their subordination to the Somers Isles Company back in London. While its original leadership had supported Hughes's efforts, that changed when a turnover in leadership replaced his puritan allies with antipuritans like Nicholas Ferrar. Their antipathy to Hughes derived from accusations by former governor Tucker and others that, among other offenses, Hughes's sermons tended to "speake against the Church of England, to raile upon Bishops, and to say that the Booke of Common Praier is but an olde Wifes tale." Hughes responded by first suggesting the colonies were too far away to engage in the religious disputes roiling England: "it were too much peevishnesse for me, to meddle with the Bishops there, where they could not meddle with me." He then claimed that he actually had been preaching against "the Romish Lord bishops" who "are the greatest supplanters of Christian Religion and shedders of Christian blood." The "Bishops of the Church of England, as it now stands," on the other hand, were people he honored "for the good that I have and dayly doe receave out of their godly and learned Works." Neither lying nor telling the complete truth, Hughes was doing what many other nonconformist ministers facing similar accusations did to maintain their jobs. In this case, the tactic failed. The directors punished Hughes by refusing to pay his back salary. Hughes appealed to the Privy Council, but never did get it.[12]

In the meantime, militant Protestants believed English America could become a bastion of anti-Spanish Protestantism. Thomas Scott, an outspoken puritan opponent of the Spanish Match, gave it that role in his influential anti-Spanish polemic of 1620, *Vox populi, or News from Spayne*. Adopting the voice of the Spanish ambassador to England from 1613 to 1622, the aristocrat and soldier Diego Sarmiento de Acuña (made Count Gondomar in 1617), the text claimed that once the English "begin to inhabit" America "and to fortifie themselves," they "may in tyme there perhaps raise an other England to withstand our new Spaine in America, as this old England opposeth our present State." Gondomar claimed England's profitable trade with the Ottoman and Mughal empires actually benefited Spain by bringing corrupting luxuries into England and killing many of its seamen through disease and hardship. In America, on the other hand, the English could trade "for commodities without wast of their treasure, & often returne gould for knives, glasses, or the like trifles, and that without such losse of their Mariners as in other places." Virginia and Bermuda "could help" the English by serving as "draines to unloade their populous State, which else would overflow its own bancks by continuace of peace, and turne head upon itself or make a body fit for any rebellion." To undermine these colonies, Gondomar strove to persuade "most of the Recusants who were sharers" in colonial ventures to withdraw their investments and "discourage the work" of colonization. *Vox populi* concluded with a call for "the publike purse" to build up the English presence in America.[13]

This heroic puritan vision of America soon had to compete with other endeavors. First came the Scots, who Captain John Mason, governor of Newfoundland, encouraged to invest in his colony.[14] In 1622, they received their own colony when Sir William Alexander, a loyally conformist poet and courtier, obtain a charter for Nova Scotia. Hiring a ship in London, he sent it to recruit colonists in the west of Scotland. Unfortunately for Nova Scotia, the ship never arrived at its destination. Stopping at Saint John's, Newfoundland, it dropped off the colonists then headed back to London for supplies. By the time a relief ship arrived in 1623, most of the colonists had hired themselves out to the fishing fleets, while the "Minister and Smith (both for Spirituall and Temporall respects the two most necessary members)" had died. Some of the remaining colonists joined the relief ship, which then explored the Nova Scotia coast. However, it returned without setting up an outpost. The Scots did, however, gather enough information for Alexander to have a map made and printed in his 1624 promotional tract, *An encouragement to colonies*.[15]

Sir William Alexander faced several challenges in developing a Scottish colony. Scotland's mercantile community was oriented to the North and Baltic Seas, not the Atlantic. Scotland had a surplus population, but Nova Scotia was not its most convenient outlet. Potential Scottish colonists had opportunities closer at hand to either fight as mercenaries in the Thirty Years War or join the plantation of Ulster. Alexander turned to King James for help. He responded with a fund-raising scheme he had already used to effect in England: the purchase of baronetcies. Drawing up a new charter for Nova Scotia in 1624, James offered baronetcies to any Scot who would plant a certain number of colonists there, or pay Alexander to do so. The first (and one of the few) to take up the offer was Sir Robert Gordon, a courtier who enjoyed the favor of both King James and Charles. This well-educated younger son of the Earl of Sutherland had grown up in the north of Scotland. Although a loyal conformist to Scotland's church, his religious commitments were somewhat suspect, as his mother was the daughter of the Earl of Huntly, one of the great northern Scottish lords who remained Roman Catholic after the Reformation. Gordon, like Alexander, remained loyal to the Jacobean Kirk even as it became less presbyterian and more episcopal. Only when push came to shove in the revolutionary 1640s did he accept the Presbyterians. His nephew, the Earl of Sutherland, became a Covenanter leader.[16]

Sir Robert Gordon proposed to set up a colony on Cape Breton Island. He named it New Galloway, after the region in the southwest of Scotland where he had recently acquired a lordship. Desiring the "blessing of God" on the colony, Gordon emphasized that colonists would have to swear the oath of allegiance and "conforme themselves in Religion" according to the Church of Scotland. He also wanted them to adopt a "reformation of life, and manners" and promised to have "the transgressours, and contemners of the same bee severelie punished." Gordon expected the colony's ministers to "bee the factours of Christ for the gaine of Soules: and to propagate his Trueth: and enlighten those that are captivate in Ethnicke darkness." Offering them free passage to New Galloway, he would further encourage "true religion" by not charging them for freighting their wives, children, or household goods. Even better, he would pay their salaries for the first three years. By then the colony should be big enough to create parishes able to support them. Within New Galloway, ministers would be treated with "such reverence, and respect . . . as appertaineth unto their place and calling." Alas, New Galloway, like Nova Scotia, fizzled.[17]

New England, meanwhile, showed little hint of its puritan future. Had Sir Ferdinando Gorges had his way, it likely would have remained within the Church of England. Ferdinando had been a friend of the Earl of Essex since they met while fighting against the Spanish in Holland and France. After Gorges was wounded in battle, Essex had knighted him. He then recommended Gorges to command the fort guarding Plymouth harbor, a position that kept Gorges comfortable for the rest of his career. Partially implicated in Essex's revolt, Gorges was imprisoned for a time but, thanks to the patronage of Robert Cecil, Gorges was soon restored to his command at Plymouth. Then, like several other former members of the Essex faction, he turned his energies toward colonization. In 1606 Gorges helped secure the charter for the Plymouth Company to colonize what was still known as North Virginia (it was not called New England until 1614). After the initial efforts, including the Popham colony, failed, Gorges helped revamp the Plymouth Company into the Council for New England in 1620, becoming one of its leading members. It's charter, like all colonial charters, enjoined conformity by giving the council or its deputies the power to "administer oaths of allegiance and supremacy to all who shall go to New-England" or otherwise be "employed for their honest and faithful discharge of service."[18]

The Council for New England had the backing of important courtly interests, none of them known for their love of puritans. Those interests are evident in the land grants to such important figures as the Duke of Buckingham, the Duke of Lennox, the Earl of Arundel, the lord bishop of Lincoln, and George Calvert. Although they did little to develop the region, their backing encouraged Gorges to spend much of the 1620s trying and failing to turn New England into a profitable—and conformist—

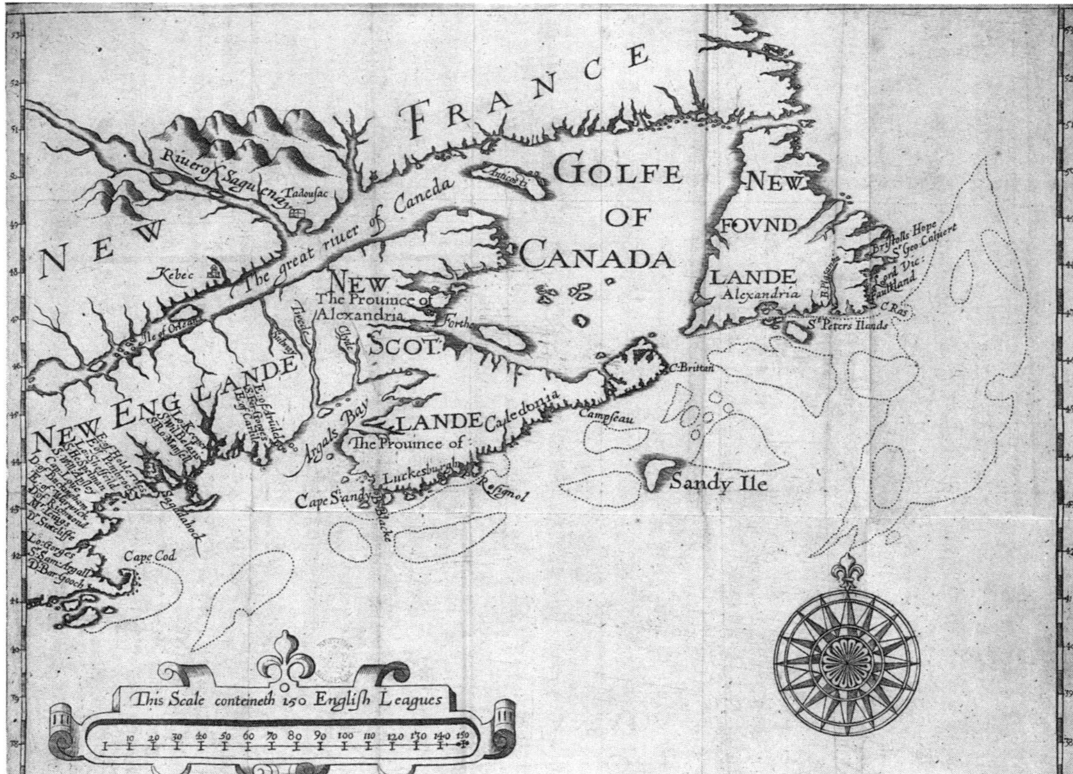

FIGURE 6. Map of New Scotland, © The British Library Board, from Sir William Alexander, *An encouragement to colonies* (London, 1624), shelfmark C.21.b.36

colony. In the end, he established little more than a few scattered outposts along the coast between Cape Ann and the Penobscot River. Operating in what later became New Hampshire and Maine, they busied themselves with a modest trade in fish, fur, and lumber. Attempts to found similar outposts further south did not last long. Thomas Weston took a group of men to Wessagusset in 1622, but abandoned it after a hungry winter. The Dorchester Company, based out of the puritan city of Dorchester, set up a somewhat more successful fishing colony at Cape Ann in 1623, but it too folded in 1626. "Mount Wollaston," named after its leader Captain Richard Wollaston, was established in 1624, but also failed. Weston, Wollaston, and others moved down to Virginia, leaving behind only a few of the servants they had hired.[19]

Gorges's most significant contribution to colonizing New England came in 1623, when he sent his son Robert Gorges to serve as governor general of all of New England. It was the most ambitious, largest, and best supplied expedition yet sent to the region. It included women, children, several mechanics, two clergymen, and six gentlemen. They set up camp in the recently abandoned post of Wessagusset while Robert Gorges traveled up and down the coast to make his authority known. One of the chaplains, William Morrell, dreamed of becoming the head of New England's church. Yet, once again, a hard winter brought disaster. When spring came, Robert Gorges retreated to England. Morrell followed him a year later. Only a handful of the colonists stayed on, contributing a slight nonpuritan leaven to the future colony of Massachusetts Bay. One, Samuel Maverick, eventually became one of its most outspoken critics. Another, Gorges's second chaplain William Blaxton, greeted the puritans with sympathy when they landed at Boston. However, he judged the creation of a Congregationalist church a step too far and in 1635 moved south to Rhode Island.[20]

Had Gorges been more successful, New England could have remained within the Church of England. Gorges's legacy was strongest in northern New England, where he and Captain John Mason began a colony in 1622. Christopher Levett, a merchant from York, wrote a pamphlet to promote it. Dedicated to the Duke of Buckingham and the rest of the Council for New England, Levett's pamphlet said almost nothing about religion. However, it clearly assumed the region's religious future was conformist. He made a reference to "Christmas" and urged bishops and aristocrats to donate money for the colony. To populate it, he proposed recruiting poor men from parishes around England—not godly upstanding puritans.[21]

David Thomson, a Scott and protégé of Gorges and Mason, planted the first outpost in what later became New Hampshire. In 1625, he wrote to the Earl of Arundel with a plan to unite New England's scattered fishing outposts into fewer, larger settlements under a strong governor. Thomson said little about religion, but his conformist expectations are implied in his annoyance with the "Brownists" of New Plymouth, who caused "infinit greevances amongst us," governed as they were by "a rude ignorant mechanicke" who could not provide justice. Thomson suggested they be allowed "to continue where they are, for as they desyre the Societie of none but such as are of their owne profession, soe I am sure non regardes them or their fellowship." This toleration was not to be a model for the region, however. Thomson wanted the conformist Mason to serve as the region's governor. However, instead of uniting New England, in 1629 Mason and Gorges decided to divide its northern half in two. Gorges took Maine; Mason, New Hampshire. Both colonies officially conformed, but their colonists increasingly harbored puritan sentiments.[22]

As Thomson's comments suggest, New Plymouth had not been part of the Council for New England's plan. Nor had the Separatists originally intended to go there. They were supposed to be in Virginia. In 1617, disenchanted with life in the tolerant Dutch Republic and worried about the renewal of war with Spain, the Leiden congregation contemplated moving to America. After some earnest fasting and prayer, they decided to go to Virginia rather than Guiana. In the negotiations for a colonial patent that followed, they somewhat deceptively presented themselves as puritans, not Separatists. Emphasizing how close their ideas were to other Reformed Churches, they even endorsed the Church of England's confession of faith (although that was no more than a simple recognition of a shared Calvinism). The Privy Council was skeptical, but before it could challenge the Leideners' petition, Sir Edwin Sandys and the Virginia Company arranged for Secretary of State Sir Robert Naunton to take it directly to the king. Naunton was a staunch Protestant known for his support of an anti-Catholic and anti-Spanish foreign policy. He was also a distant cousin of the most influential man at court: James's favorite, George Villiers, the Duke of Buckingham. Naunton portrayed the Leiden congregation as nonconformists, not Separatists. They merely sought the chance to live in America with some liberty of conscience for their qualms about full conformity. James did not object to the idea, but, after conferring with Archbishop Abbott and the bishop of London, he seems to have agreed to simply not interfere with the emigration rather than formally endorse it. Plymouth colonists would later claim that he had explicitly granted them "liberty of conscience," but there is no record of it.[23]

Chance, through a series of accidents and misrepresentations, sent the Leiden Separatists to New England instead of Virginia. First, with their patent delayed by political infighting among the Virginia Company, the Leideners contemplated moving to the Dutch colony of New Netherland. When the leader of a group of London "adventurers" arrived in Leiden with a patent for land on the northernmost boundary of Virginia, in today's New Jersey, and a promise of financial backing, the congregation hesitated. It decided to send out a small group first. The rest, including their minister, would follow later. As is well known, the ship carrying these "Pilgrims" missed its target and landed instead on Cape Cod in the fall of 1620.[24]

Before landing, the colonists gathered on the *Mayflower* drew up a "Combination for Foundation of Government." This "Mayflower Compact" proclaimed the colonists to be "loyall subjects" of King James who had come to the "Northerne parts of Virginia" for the "glorie of God, and advancement of ye Christian faith, and honour of our king and countrie." The compact was a "covenant" for "a civill body politick" but said nothing about religion or swearing the oath of supremacy. Plymouth's government only required its inhabitants to swear an oath of loyalty. As with previous attempts at colonizing New England, the first winter was brutal. Half of the roughly one hundred colonists died. However, the survivors hung on with help from their Wampanoag neighbors, reinforcements arrived, and the colony survived. Rather than move south into Virginia's jurisdiction, they applied for a patent from the Council for New England for the territory they were already on. The patent gave them the right of self-government but said nothing about setting up an independent church.[25]

Years later, Sir Ferdinando Gorges would recall that the Plymouth colonists had desired "liberty of conscience" when they asked him for help in getting the patent. Like Sandys in Virginia, Gorges was desperate for colonists and agreed. Later, on the recommendation of the Earl of Warwick, he would also approve the Massachusetts Bay patent for those "disaffected to Episcopall Governement." However, Gorges insisted that he had not intended New England to become "a receptacle for the divers sorts of Sects and Schismes which contemn'd the Ecclesiastical Government" of England. That had happened "very much contrary to his expectations." When a royal order came "that none should be suffered to passe into New-England, but those that should take the Oaths of Supremacy and Allegiance," Gorges supported it.[26]

It seemed unlikely that the Separatists would be able to create their own church in America. Their colony was small (about 180 people in the early 1620s) and religiously mixed. Separatists predominated, especially at the upper levels, but some of the colonists were puritans. The rest, mostly servants, were run-of-the-mill conformists. In his later years, William Bradford, who served as Plymouth's governor and principal leader from 1621 until his death in 1657, remembered how these conformists tried to maintain the customs of the established church. They appear in an anecdote about his proud refusal to tolerate them. This incident "of mirth" took place in 1621 on "the day called Christmas Day." As a good Reformed Protestant, Bradford abhorred the holiday. Rather than acknowledge it, he called everyone "out to work as was used." Some newly arrived servants "excused themselves and said it went against their consciences to work on that day." Bradford replied, "that if they made it matter of conscience, he would spare them till they were better informed," and left to work the fields. Returning at noon, he "found them in the street at play, openly; some pitching the bar, and some at stool-ball and such like sports." It was all perfectly legitimate behavior according to King James's *Book of Sports*. However, Bradford "took away their implements and told them that was against his conscience, that they should play and others work." He told them that if "they made the keeping of it [Christmas] matter of devotion, let them keep their houses, but there should be no gaming or reveling in the streets." And so Christmas was banned in New Plymouth. Bradford noted with satisfaction that since then, "nothing hath been attempted that way, at least openly." Once again, local elites on the margins of the English world were effectively supporting an alternative to the established religion. Without their minister, they met together on Sundays to pray and listen to the lay preaching of the talented William Brewster. However, John Robinson, their minister, was needed to have a fully operational church complete with sacraments.[27]

Reports of Plymouth's rejection of the established religion soon made it back to London, troubling the Adventurers who had financed their voyage. The Adventurers were puritans, not Separatists, and determined to prevent a Separatist church from taking root in America. They decided not to send over the rest of the Leiden congregation, and especially not Robinson. However, rather than completely deprive the colonists of religious services, they sent over John Lyford, a puritan minister who had served previously in Ulster. He arrived in 1624, along with a new group of colonists. At first, he got along well with the Plymouth colonists. Lyford made a confession of faith and joined Brewster in preaching. However, when it came time to be ordained as minister, Lyford refused to renounce the Church of England as a false church or denounce his calling as a minster of that church as unlawful: the two fundamental demands of the Separatists. They then refused to accept him as their minister. Lyford responded by privately setting up an alternative congregation and administering the sacraments, especially baptism: vital as the colonists were starting to produce children. Lyford also wrote back to England, attacking Plymouth's church system and urging the Adventurers not to send over the rest of the Leiden congregation. When the Separatists discovered what he was up to, they banished him and his chief ally, another puritan. Other Lyford sympathizers then left voluntarily.[28]

In the meantime, New Plymouth's comrades in Leiden were troubled by the royalization of Virginia. They worried that the king's "full resolution is, to the end that there may be one uniform course of government, in, and through all his whole monarchy." Surely, to make Virginia "immediately depend on himself" rather than "any company or corporation," was but the first step toward imposing on the colonies "the same civil and ecclesiastical government that is in England." They asked their fellows in Plymouth if they "feared the danger of being suppressed." They doubted whether it was a good idea "for our pastor and church to come to you." Some did; many others did not. They were getting old, and some were dying. In the spring of 1626, word arrived in the colony that Robinson and Robert Cushman, the Separatists' mediator with the London Adventurers, had died. It seemed the congregation might never be restored.[29]

Certainly many hoped that the bishops would take over America, but if King James had a plan to vigorously impose the Church of England on the colonies, his penchant for favoring loyalty over orthodoxy undermined it. While Plymouth struggled to protect itself from puritans, James was inadvertently opening up the colonies to Roman Catholic influence by granting a colony to his loyal, conformist, secretary of state Sir George Calvert. Calvert had been born into a Catholic family in Yorkshire, but chose religious conformity when he was young. Conformity allowed him to attend Oxford and embark on a successful political career. Beginning as a secretary to the Privy Council, he rose to become secretary of state alongside Sir Robert Naunton. However, where Naunton, like many in Parliament, firmly opposed the Spanish Match, Calvert not only supported it but also took the lead in advocating improved relations with both Spain and English Catholics. For James, Calvert's Catholic associations actually enhanced his appeal and usefulness, and, in 1623, when Calvert was at the height of his influence, he granted him the patent for Avalon. The year 1623 was a good one for Calvert. It seemed like the Spanish Match would finally succeed. More importantly, he enjoyed the favor of the all-powerful royal favorite, the Duke of Buckingham, another supporter of the match. Calvert later acknowledged Buckingham's help in obtaining the Avalon patent.[30]

Avalon gave Calvert the chance to finally run his own colony. Like many colonial entrepreneurs, he had already been actively investing in other colonial projects, including the Virginia Company, the East India Company, and, since 1621, Newfoundland fishing operations. The Avalon charter was more generous than other recent grants in Newfoundland. It gave Calvert rights to the entire Avalon Peninsula and a virtual monopoly on all English activity in the region, including its valuable fisheries. The powers he received resembled those Sir Humphrey Gilbert had had, including the power to establish and patronize all churches within his colony, with the caveat that "no interpretation" of this grant could be made "whereby Gods holy & true Christian religion, or the allegiance due to us, our heires & successors may in any thing suffer any prejudice or diminution." Avalon began promisingly. Calvert sent over two small groups of colonists who built a sturdy manor house at Ferryland and began fishing. When they requested a "godly minister," Calvert sent over a Church of England minister, who served for a year then returned. Few people stayed in Ferryland for long. It was, as one man later put it, the "coldest harbor in the land."[31]

Avalon conformed, but its charter was, as one historian points out, "curiously vague on the matter of religion." Unlike the Newfoundland Company's charter of 1610, it did "not require . . . that all going to the island take the oath of supremacy." Calvert said nothing about his initial religious hopes for the colony, but the colony's name offers a hint. Avalon was a patriotic name, but it was not particularly Protestant. Like John Dee's "British" empire, it was a nationalist evocation of early Christian England. An account from 1670 explained that it was a deliberate reference to "Avalon in Somersetshire where Christianity was first received in England." This associated it with the legends of King Arthur, a mythology with well-known Catholic resonances. In the late Middle Ages, the monks at Glastonbury had deliberately encouraged the Arthurian myth to bolster the fame of their abbey, making it a thriving center for Catholic pilgrimage and devotion. Even after the dissolution of the monasteries under Henry VIII, an air of nostalgia hung about the place. It has been argued that the name indicates Calvert's desire to pull English Protestants, especially antipuritan conservatives attached to ceremony and ritual, back to Roman Catholicism. However, neither Calvert nor any of his partners ever described Avalon, or the colony of Maryland for that matter, as a haven for Catholics or a factory for converting Protestants. Instead, they portrayed both as mission stations, opportunities to convert America's native peoples while extending the reach of English Christianity overseas. Avalon is perhaps best glossed as a patriotic desire for Christian expansion: it would be to America as Glastonbury was to England. Still, its Roman Catholic resonances cannot be overlooked.[32]

Regardless of what Calvert originally intended, everything changed just a few months after he launched the colony. The Spanish Match suddenly collapsed, and his political fortunes took a disastrous turn for the worse. In a crazily naive gesture mixing romance and frustration with the interminable negotiations, Prince Charles and the Duke of Buckingham had made a secret visit to the Spanish court to try and woo the Spanish infanta directly. While a few Spanish theologians favored the marriage, seeing it as a way to eventually "convert heretics," including Prince Charles, and prevent the "perversion" of England's Catholics, most of the court was shocked by this breach of protocol. They never let the Englishmen come close to meeting the infanta, and Charles returned home empty-handed. To his surprise, he discovered that his romantic failure abroad was a political success at home. Enormous crowds celebrated his safe return and the end of the Spanish Match in almost equal measure. Charles and Buckingham then joined Parliament in opposing the Spanish Match and pushing for a declaration of war against Spain. James finally obliged in March 1624.[33]

Calvert, so intimately associated with the Spanish Match policy, lost all political credibility. He fell into a personal crisis and, sometime in October or November 1624, returned to the ancient faith of his family. A few months later, he informed James of his change of religion. James did not retract the Avalon grant. Instead, he allowed him to resign his post as secretary of state with honor and, in recognition of Calvert's years of loyal service, allowed him to retain a seat on the Privy Council. He even ennobled him with the grant of the Irish title of Baron Baltimore. As an open Catholic at the Jacobean court, Calvert might still have had an important career. Roman Catholic issues remained central to royal policy. Indeed, James was now negotiating for a French Catholic princess to marry Charles. Unfortunately, James died in March 1625, and King Charles, currently posing as a Protestant hero in the war against Spain, insisted that all his privy councilors take the antipapal oath of allegiance. Calvert refused, resigned, and moved to Ireland with his family. Charles respected Calvert as a loyal servant of his father and, bearing him no personal animosity, did not revoke his colonial charter either. Now Avalon was English America's first Catholic-owned colony.[34]

*

The uncertainty over Avalon's religious purpose reflects the atmosphere of puritan anxiety and Catholic hope into which it was launched. Between 1618 and 1625, colonization took place against a backdrop of political and religious polarization across Europe. Within England, the clash turned primarily on the question of relations with Spain and England's Catholics. King James's peace policy led many Protestants to fear (and Catholics to hope) that a formal toleration of Catholics was possible. Those hopes and fears ended dramatically with the failure of the Spanish Match and the declaration of war against Spain in 1624. America now had the chance to prove itself as the militantly Protestant bastion puritans hoped it would be. However, in the meantime it also had surreptitiously acquired a Catholic-owned colony.

Notwithstanding, or perhaps because of, the polarization at home, tolerance of some sort was becoming a factor in colonial policy. The Sandys brothers had used their influence in the Virginia Company and colony to tolerate nonconformists and even Separatists, hoping it would help populate the colony. Protestants could enjoy a newfound unity in the non-Christian Powhatan country. Hundreds of Separatists, including the famous "Pilgrims" from Leiden, took advantage of this opportunity to move to America. Catholics entered America through royal patronage. Sir George Calvert's close ties to King James had secured him the colonial patent, which King Charles confirmed even though he knew Calvert had become a Roman Catholic. No formal grant of toleration was made in either case, but some were clearly seeing it as a viable strategy for colonial expansion. Colonial promoters were aware of the accounts about the Islamic world, where religious pluralism was an effective tool of empire. Although they rejected an Ottoman-style toleration of different religions, some of the English were clearly willing to overlook certain differences among their fellow Christians in the name of a greater cause.

Formal toleration was thus on the table in the first decade of permanent English colonization. Although officially rejected, pluralism was beginning to take root in a rather sneaky fashion. The Plymouth colony's arrival in New England was a surprise, and not necessarily one bound to succeed. The Separatists had to fight against other colonists and the Adventurers who financed them to control the colony's religious life. Thanks to a mix of luck and their predominance among the local elite, they were winning. Still, Plymouth colony seemed more an unwelcome exception to the rule of conformity than the beginning of a trend. On Bermuda, a similar blend of luck and preponderance among the local elite gave the colony a strongly puritan character despite resistance on both sides of the Atlantic. Puritanism was by no means destined to triumph in America, however. Other contenders remained active. Loyal Scots were trying to plant the official version of the Church of Scotland in Nova Scotia. In religiously conservative Newfoundland, the Avalon colony offered a possible base for Catholic colonization. This mix of possibilities was the unexpected fruit of the vagaries of royal favor and local elite ambitions. Over the following decade, those factors would undermine colonial religious unity even further.

PART 3

Caroline Transformation, 1625–1638

SEVEN

Favorites: Saint Christopher, Barbados, Maryland, 1624–1632

We associate the trope of the errand into the wilderness with puritan New England, but in the fall of 1629, the minister of the Caribbean colony of Saint Christopher preached a sermon that placed it firmly within a conformist framework. Rather than use the trope to sanction religious refuge, he made it a lesson in obedience to absolute power, divine and royal. Standing in London before a group of colonists about to accompany him back to the Caribbean, John Featley, the minister, compared them to Joshua, who had been commissioned by the "Divine Authority" of God to give the "promised Land of Canaan to the Israelites." They were leaving their "Native Soile, that we may possesse the Land of the Hittites and Amorites, the Habitations of Salvage-Heathens, whose understandings were never yet illuminated with the knowledge of their Maker," he proclaimed. Featley reminded them that God's "Authority will not bee questioned, therefore his will must be obeyed." Of course, "this Command is loving too, and out of that affection which hee had both to the People and to Joshua." Absolute, omniscient, and omnipresent, God had accompanied and protected Joshua and the Israelites on their "Voyage." Likewise God would accompany and protect them to "secure our happinesse," Featley assured the colonists, but only if they avoided "disobedience." Obedience would not only give them God's protection "in forraigne-parts" but also "enrich us with Prosperity."[1]

Featley's sermon is permeated with Laudian religious priorities, suggesting that conservative conformity could travel overseas as well as puritanism. Between 1624 and 1630, England's colonization of the Americas took place against a backdrop of wars against Spain (1624–30) and France (1627–29) abroad and the rise of the anti-Calvinism at home. Hispanophobes believed this was their chance to undermine the Spanish Empire in America. They drew up ambitious plans, including one to coordinate colonial efforts by founding a West India Company and another to forge an anti-Spanish alliance with the indigenous peoples of Chile that would also lead to their conversion with the help of a Calvinist catechism. These ambitious plans fell through, but the English did manage to expand their American claims in the Caribbean and Canada. On Saint Christopher and Barbados, the first permanent Caribbean colonies took root, while Nova Scotia was revived and French Canada conquered. For a moment it seemed like the British would win North America for the Protestant cause. However, it was not entirely clear what sort of Protestantism would triumph.[2]

In the end, the wars did not go well, the colonies struggled, and England's religious and political divisions worsened, raising the concerns about obedience that Featley preached about. Some blamed the military failures of the war on King Charles's reliance on incompetent and corrupt royal favorites, especially the all-powerful Duke of Buckingham. No colonial charter, religious reform, or major political initiative could get far without his support. Indeed, in these years King Charles seems to have switched from issuing colonial charters to companies to only issuing them to aristocrats who enjoyed Buckingham's favor. The charters farmed out the supervision of colonial religious life to a series of royal favorites whose relationship to conformity varied. Most extreme was the case of the Roman Catholic George Calvert. Protected by Charles's favor, Calvert turned Avalon into an American outlet for his religion, then, several years later, obtained a permanent North American home for the English Catholic community with the grant of Maryland. It was just one of several examples of how the royal penchant for rewarding political loyalty could poke holes in colonial religious uniformity.

*

Under King Charles, the decades-long antagonism between "Puritans" and "Arminians" tilted decisively against the puritans. William Laud, a protégé of the Duke of Buckingham's, rose to a position of prominence in royal councils. Laud's rise began rather late in his life. After decades at Oxford, his acquisition of the modest bishopric of Saint David's, Wales, in 1621 allowed him to finally enter court politics. With Buckingham's help, Laud rapidly rose to be dean of the Chapel Royal and, in 1628, bishop of London. Along the way, Laud developed a close connection with

King Charles that ensured he would succeed George Abbot once the archbishop of Canterbury died in 1633. Sensing the change in the wind, those eager to demonstrate their loyalty in hopes of royal favor adopted the Laudian style of piety.[3]

Puritans meanwhile became increasingly frustrated and furious at their exclusion from power and influence. They accused Laudians of promoting popery. While Laudians were Protestants, not crypto-Catholics, puritans had reason to fear that England was going soft on Catholicism. King Charles had begun his reign as a Protestant anti-Spanish hero, but that had quickly changed several months later when he followed through on his obligation to marry the French princess Henrietta Maria, the youngest sister of King Louis XIII and a devout Catholic. The marriage treaty guaranteed her an officially tolerated Roman Catholic chapel. She used that privilege to transform her household into the center of the first openly tolerated Catholic community in the British Isles and Ireland. Her circle became a steady source of French and Catholic influence on Charles's government, which was all the more effective once Charles fell deeply in love with her. Charles's Catholic subjects saw their situation improve as he suspended recusancy laws in England and Ireland and even contemplated a formal toleration. Of course, what was good for Roman Catholics was not so good for Reformed Protestants, whether in England, Ireland, or France. As King Louis XIII waged a war against Huguenots to reduce the autonomy they had enjoyed since the Edict of Nantes, some began to think an American colony might be a better place to sustain the militant Protestant cause.[4]

The Duke of Buckingham's influence over colonial policy derived from his tremendous influence over the young, inexperienced, politically naive, and spiritually devout King Charles. Only twenty-five when he became king, Charles was short of stature, insecure in personality, and lacking in the political savvy and subtlety of his father. Where James had managed for years to balance out the competing religious, political, and diplomatic tensions of three very different kingdoms, Charles preferred to stick to his principles, intimate friends, and loyal servants. Nevertheless, by 1625 both James and Charles had come to the conclusion that "puritans" posed a threat to royal authority. Puritan militancy provided a convenient explanation for Parliament's stubborn resistance to the royal will. Buckingham encouraged this reading of current politics, as did William Laud. While puritans grumbled about bishops and royal interference in the church, Laud ostentatiously asserted his loyalty and submission to both. In a characteristically pretentious restatement of James's pronouncement,

"No Bishop, no King," Laud argued that those who "would overthrow *sedes ecclesiae*, the seats of ecclesiastical government, will not spare, if ever they get power, to have a pluck at the throne of David."[5]

Laud was a reformer who dreamed of restoring the church to its ancient power and glory. He claimed his reforms complimented the king's political ambition to impose "order," obedience, and uniformity on his subjects. Speaking the language of tradition that was so dear to Charles, Laud insisted he simply wanted to restore decency and order to worship. However, his efforts to enhance episcopal authority and reclaim the church lands, revenues, and autonomy that had been lost in the course of the Reformation involved a sustained set of political, economic, and religious changes that, in the words of a recent biographer, amounted to a "revolutionary programme" with a "radical vision of the nature and significance of the institutional church and of its role in society." Had Laud succeeded, he would have undone many "of the effects of the Reformation, and would have transformed the social and political balance of the country as a whole." By the 1630s, Laudian reforms were spreading to the Church of Ireland as well.[6]

Laudian religion favored aesthetic beauty, ceremony, wealth, traditional hierarchies, and social order—none of them in much evidence in the raw American colonies. Nevertheless, one can find evidence of Laudian sensibilities. The best example comes from the island colony of Saint Christopher (often abbreviated to Saint Kitts), England's first permanent Caribbean outpost. Begun in the last year of King James's reign, Saint Christopher pioneered the colonization of the Leeward Islands as well as the development of plantation slavery. The colony's founder, Captain Thomas Warner, had been one of the Guiana colonists who had survived by trading tobacco with the Dutch until the group's leaders began to die off. Then, when "all authoritie" was "dissolved," as Captain John Smith later described the situation, this lack "of government did more wrong their proceedings, than all other crosses whatsoever." Warner and a couple of companions returned to England "to be free from the disorders that did grow in the Amazons for want of Government amongst their Countrey-men, and to be quiet amongst themselves." This enthusiasm for order and authority suggests the conservative nature of Warner's religion as well as his politics.[7]

Captain John Smith knew Warner's story because Saint Christopher's origins were closely linked to Virginia. From the time the first expedition to Virginia had stopped at Nevis for refreshment, the Leeward Islands were a regular resting point on the voyage to the Chesapeake. In 1607, the English had found the islands "unhabited" apart from the "Indians" whose "treacherie" they feared. When Warner arrived on a Virginia-bound ship with fifteen men in 1623, he found a few Frenchmen had preceded them. After an initial scare that the French would "set the Indians upon us," the English managed to become "friends" with both groups. Dividing the island into French and English zones, the Europeans planted tobacco and traded with passing ships for supplies. After a few more Englishmen arrived in 1624, Warner returned to England to secure a royal patent for the colony (granted on August 30, 1625, as the island was "inhabited by a Savage people, and not in the possession or government of any Christian Prince or State"). Appointed governor, Warner returned in 1626 with one hundred colonists and John Featley, the island's first minister. When, in 1627, Lord Carlisle received a patent for the Caribbee Islands that included Saint Christopher, Warner continued as governor under Carlisle's auspices. Maurice Thompson, a former Virginia colonist turned merchant entrepreneur, then sent over some sixty enslaved Africans, "the first recorded English slaving voyage ever made to an English settlement." Surviving a devastating hurricane and near starvation, the colonists divided the island with the French by formal treaty (the English got the middle, the French the two ends) and then fought a war against the island's Caribs that "forced" them "out of the Ile" by 1628. With ever more colonists and supplies arriving, Saint Christopher became a highly profitable tobacco colony. Thomas Warner governed until his death in 1649.[8]

Judging by the evidence we have on Warner and Featley, the church on Saint Christopher was loyally conformist and conservative. Institutionally, it was thin on the ground. The first church building was only erected in 1640. The island was not formally divided into parishes until 1655. As late as 1676, there were only two church buildings. However, as in other early colonial settings, what mattered more than institutional infrastructure were the attitudes and actions of local elites. Warner, a Suffolk landowner's son who, before going to Guiana, had served as captain of King James's bodyguard and lieutenant of the Tower of London, had an authoritarian streak. In 1630 he had a man whipped for four days and then sent back to England in chains "for speaking against Bishop Abbott." We know nothing else about the incident, but we do know that John Featley's uncle, Daniel Featley, was a chaplain to Archbishop Abbott. Daniel was also a press censor, or licenser, controlling what could be published in England. A Calvinist conformist, Daniel was also noted for his learning and skill as a polemical foe of Catholics, Arminians, Separatists, and Baptists. Sympathetic to some aspects of puritanism, he encouraged the publication of certain puritan works, especially anti-Catholic ones. However, he rejected their nonconformity and censored it in print.[9]

On Saint Christopher, Daniel's nephew John set the tone for the island's official religious life during an extended stay from 1626 to 1635 followed by a short return in 1643–45. Judging by his published sermons, John Featley's sympathies were Laudian and antipuritan, possibly acquired during his student days at Oxford. Our first glimpse of his views comes from the sermon he published in 1629 while visiting London with his "very dear friend" Warner. Preached on the eve of their return to Saint Christopher, this "briefe, yet orthodoxall" sermon was dedicated to Lord Carlisle, proprietor of the Caribbees. Preaching on Joshua 1:9, "the Lord they God is with thee withersoever thou goest," Featley pointed out that Joshua had been commissioned by the "Divine Authority" of God to colonize Israel. Of course, God's "Authority will not bee questioned, therefore his will must be obeyed." Echoing God's encouragement to Joshua, he told the colonists who were about to go to the Caribbean "not to be afraid, neither bee dismaid." Obeying God's will, their exemplary obedience would "teach the Salvages what we obey," while their "Precepts" would show "whome we obey." The "Sinceritie" of the colonists' religion would persuade "those ignorant Infidels observing our religious Conversation" to "joyne with us in a happy Resolution." Featley included an antipuritan rebuke to "the forwardnesse of our Times." Archly alluding to Parliament's refusal to cooperate with the king, he complained that some, "not knowing the burden of Authority, thinke themselves happy to weare the favour of a Title," yet remained "ignorant in the dutie attending it."[10]

Further evidence of what Featley likely preached during his nine years on Saint Christopher comes from 1635. He had returned to England to act as curate for his aging uncle. With Laud as archbishop, Daniel's continued opposition to Arminianism was getting him in trouble. Perhaps to compensate, John Featley gave a sermon exuberantly praising Laudian values. *Obedience and Submission* urged people to submit themselves "to every Ordinance of Man for the Lord's sake," including the royal "prerogative of Supremacy, and the loyalty of the Subject." They should also submit to the church, which was "subordinate to sacred Majestie." Praising the benevolent rule of bishops, Featley contrasted them to puritans "beyond the Seas" who disregarded the social order and traditional hierarchies. Whether as a "schismaticall Sectarie," a "self-conceited railer," "grave-bearded Brownists," a bunch of "down-look't Separatists," or "disorderly Anabaptists," they listened to "Apron preachers" and "illiterate, pettish Baulers" who were "the Authors of distraction, not order; and the ringleaders to mutinie and rebellion, not the composers of differences." They were living testimony to the ways the "deceiving Serpent" was whispering "into the Laity a contempt of the Clergie" and encouraging England's "rude vulgar" to "sit in judgement upon their Pastours." While "forward censures hurrie them into errours," a "feare of conformity" inspired them to "quit our countrey to flie into their Canaan" of New England. These "spirits of contradiction," who disdained "the confines of our flourishing kingdomes," seemed "begotten for rebellion." Featley wished to "be no more troubled with their schismaticall censures, and clamourous disturbances." He wanted to live in a world where everyone performed their duties "in obedience and submission to the powers below, for the sake of him who sitteth above." He assured his listeners that by freeing their lives "from distraction here," they would find "our deaths shall open to us the gate of eternity."[11]

Obedience and Submission bears likely hallmarks of Featley's colonial experience. His attacks on nonconformists suggest he had gotten to know some of them all too well: "Did ye but heare them in their Conventicles in those Countries where they have gained their freedome, you would wonder that men should be sold to such folly," he confided. They spoke "undigested crudities" most "gravely" and would "father their contradictions upon the blessed Spirit." In fact, Saint Christopher had a significant puritan tinge. In addition to the puritan slave-trader Maurice Thompson, the noted navigator Captain Charles Saltonstall spent a year growing tobacco on the island in 1627. This cousin of the Saltonstalls who later colonized Massachusetts would later serve the Parliamentary cause in the civil war. Then there was William Collins, a young preacher "full of zeal" who, according to John Winthrop, converted "divers" of the colonists to the evangelical cause in the early 1630s. When Warner "persecuted" Collins and his converts, they took their tobacco and families up to New England, then "dispersed themselves here and there, and some returned to Ireland." To Winthrop's disgust, Collins became a supporter of Anne Hutchinson and married her daughter. Winthrop had just seen her banished from Massachusetts for her radical unorthodoxy.[12]

Although on a much smaller scale, the cooperation between Warner and Featley—the secular and religious authorities—mirrored that between Charles and Laud, who Featley praised for having "corrected the furie of" the puritans' "disorder." Some historians have suggested that King Charles shaped church policy more than Laud, arguing that we should term the religious style of his reign "Carolinism" instead of Laudianism. However, others have shown that Charles's role was generally secondary to Laud's. Moreover, especially when it came to the American colonies, he was inconsistent, as we can see with his grant of Maryland to the Roman Catholic George Calvert.[13]

Charles tended to favor political loyalty over religious conformity. Between 1626 and 1628, this instinct led him to divide up much of what became English America among a number of Scottish and English aristocrats. Like his father, Charles had financial difficulties, and American lands offered a convenient and cheap way to reward loyal service. In 1626, Sir Robert Gordon, who earlier had received a patent for New Galloway, acquired another patent to colonize the "Insula Caroli," an island somewhere off the coast of Brazil. He never colonized the island, fitting out a privateer instead, but a more influential Scot, Charles's secretary of state, James Hay, Earl of Carlisle, received the Caribee patent in 1627. Carlisle, an investor in the plantation of Ireland and a former director of the Virginia Company, took an active interest in his colony, which included Barbados and the Leewards. By contrast, the lord chamberlain, William Herbert, Earl of Pembroke, and his brother, Philip Herbert, Earl of Montgomery, did little with their grant of Trinidad, Tobago, Barbados (for a time), and the island of Fonseca, a "mythical island" believed to lie near Central America. The English attorney general Sir Robert Heath, meanwhile, was granted Carolana, which included both the future Carolinas and the Bahamas. The Duke of Buckingham received the coveted territory of Guiana.[14]

Each of these patents came with the vice-regal powers of the bishop of Durham, just like Calvert's Avalon charter. Charles was effectively delegating control over most of colonial America's church to a series of proprietors whose stances on conformity varied significantly. The Earls of Pembroke and Montgomery were puritan sympathizers. Pembroke, one of the most influential peers at court, was a leader of the Protestant cause in Parliament until his death in 1630. Montgomery shared his brother's support for godly Protestantism, anti-Spanish causes, and hostility to Laudianism, but was more interested in hunting than politics. He did little to develop the grant, but when he sold it in 1638, he sold it to another great aristocratic champion of the puritan cause, Robert Rich, the Earl of Warwick. Gordon, Heath, Carlisle, Buckingham, and Calvert, by contrast, had much less sympathy for puritans.[15]

For puritans, getting involved in colonial projects in these years let them demonstrate patriotism, fight the Catholic enemy, turn a profit, and hide out far from the prying eyes of Laudian conformists. With the help of a cadre of aristocratic puritan courtiers, puritans began investing in, and promoting, additional colonies. The Viscount Saye and Sele and Lord

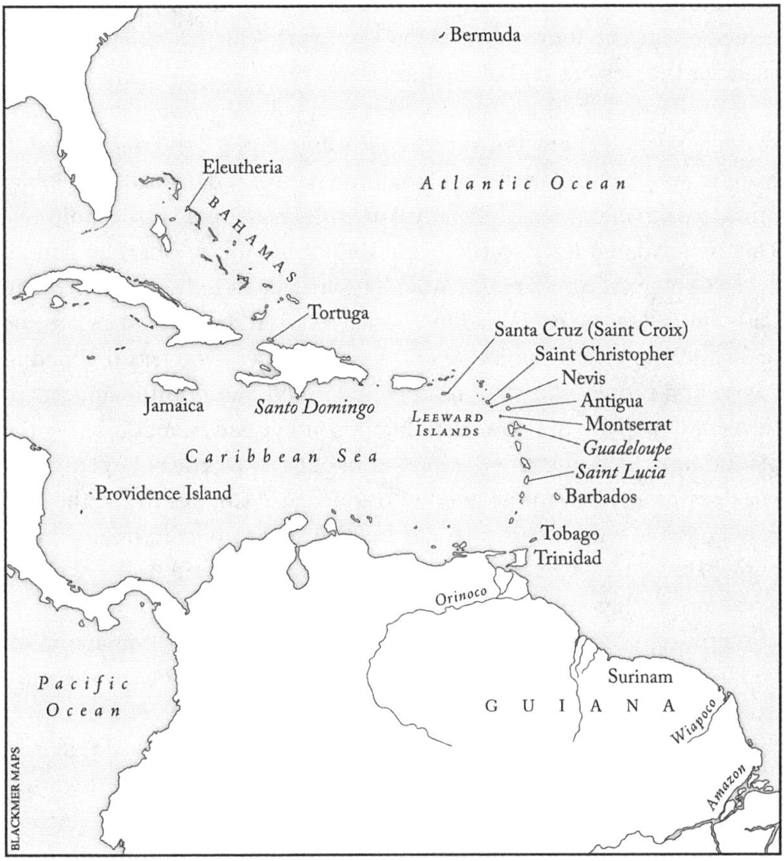

FIGURE 7. English Caribbean ca. 1590–1660

Brooke invested in New Hampshire and created the Saybrook Company, which played a role in the early colonization of Connecticut. Most important was Robert Rich, the Earl of Warwick. He had been advocating aggressive action against the Spanish colonies since 1614, when he became a founding member of the Somers Isles, or Bermuda, Company. Now he enthusiastically backed the creation of the English West India Company and, in various other capacities, assisted other puritan colonies. He had supported the Plymouth colony's effort to gain a patent. His continuing support, combined with the colony's poverty and obscurity, helped it to survive. It largely flew under the radar of the king and his favorites. In 1628 Warwick was instrumental in securing the Massachusetts Bay Company patent, a more powerful colony that neither Charles nor Laud could ignore. John Winthrop later acknowledged Warwick had "incouraged our proceedings, & offered his helpe to further us in it." In 1629, Warwick also helped create the Providence Island Company, which colonized a small island at the western end of the Caribbean.[16]

Had Warwick had his way, the English colonies would have had a strongly puritan character. Yet Charles's apparently deliberate decision to move away from chartering colonial companies and instead tie colonial privileges directly to individual royal patronage checked those ambitions. This policy dated back to the beginning of his reign, when he had allowed George Calvert to retain Avalon. Charles knew Calvert was a Roman Catholic, but, as he explained in a 1628 letter to Ireland's lord deputy, he had confirmed the colonial patent because he was "no less inclined to favour and protect the plantations of our good and faithful subjects in those remote parts of the world" than his father had been. Claiming the plantations "tend much to the honour of our Crown, the enlargement of our dominions, and to the good of our people," Charles urged the lord deputy to allow Baltimore to travel freely from any port in Ireland bearing whatever he wished to support his colony. He said nothing about Baltimore's religion.[17]

Baltimore did not immediately transform Avalon into a Roman Catholic refuge. After he converted, he instead duly appointed a second minister, Erasmus Stourton, who attended the colonists at Ferryland over the course of 1626. Stourton was probably something of an anti-Calvinist religious conservative, judging by the praise he received from the conservative conformist Robert Hayman. He seems to have had a connection to the Duke of Buckingham. Stourton, like the duke, was originally from Leicestershire and would later benefit from his family's patronage.[18]

Baltimore never formally tolerated Roman Catholicism in Avalon, but he clearly thought the colony could offer opportunities for English and Irish Catholics. In the summer of 1627, he moved to the colony along with him most of his family, a couple dozen Catholic colonists, and two seminary priests. Returning to England with one of the priests, Baltimore went back to Avalon in 1628. This time he brought about forty Catholic colonists and another seminary priest. Among the colonists was his Irish son-in-law Sir Robert Talbot. Scion of an Old English family from county Kildare that had lost land to New English planters, Talbot may have represented the sort of person Calvert was hoping to attract to Avalon: disgruntled and dispossessed Old English gentry. Calvert may even have had the support of the current lord deputy, Viscount Falkland, to recruit them. The king certainly encouraged Falkland to help Baltimore. Many of the new colonists may have been recruited from Irish Catholic neighbors of Baltimore's estates in Wexford.[19]

British and Irish Catholics certainly saw Avalon as both a missionary opportunity and a safe haven, as some English Catholic correspondence with the Congregatio de Propaganda Fide demonstrates. The Congregatio was founded in Rome in 1622 to support Catholics living in non-Catholic countries. In 1626, the English friar Simon Stock, a Discalced Carmelite, had complained that "the heretical Englishmen have established in North America" a town "called Plimouth" that "was built upon hills like those of Rome and a fort." It threatened to "corrupt" the "pagans" of the region "by their heresy." To prevent that, Stock expressed his willingness to go to New England if the Congregatio would support him. However, he did not want to abandon the "many converts" he had made in England. The following year, Stock's missionary interest turned to Avalon. The Catholic priest who had accompanied Calvert reported that the Indians "are all poor" and the Europeans "have become as savage as the bears of the country, and that men of 70 years have never been baptized." In 1630, papal agents reported that Catholics "gladly went along" with "Protestants" to Avalon "to avoid the persecution which was just commencing" in England.[20]

Without a doubt, the wars against Spain and France between 1625 and 1630 exacerbated anti-Catholicism in England. In Ireland, however, Catholics benefited from a semiofficial royal toleration. Defying standard anti-Catholic logic, King Charles did not repress his Irish Catholic subjects during these wars against Catholic powers. Instead, he inaugurated an era of comparative tolerance to keep the Irish at peace—and to get some of their money. England's Parliament was refusing to give him enough money to fight the wars, so Charles decided to negotiate a deal with the Irish Parliament, where Catholics retained an important presence. They even enjoyed a slight majority in its House of Lords. In return for a pledge of loyalty and regular subsidies he offered them relief from various aspects of the penal laws. The negotiations over these so-called Graces lasted from 1625 to 1634, during which time the king suspended the enforcement of anti-Catholic legislation in Ireland.

Given the disruptive and dangerous role that Ireland had played during Elizabeth's war against Spain, Charles's approach to Ireland was not unreasonable. It kept Irish Catholics loyal and discouraged foreign interference. However, it alarmed many of his Protestant subjects. John Winthrop—the future governor of Massachusetts—had been planning to join his relatives in Munster, but abandoned the idea upon hearing about the Graces. Only then did he start looking to New England. The Church of Ireland, meanwhile, vociferously objected that any relief from the penal laws amounted to an unacceptable toleration of Roman Catholicism. The archbishops and bishops enumerated its terrible effects in a 1626 petition. First of all, merely negotiating with the Catholics threatened "to set religion to sale" along with "the soules of the people, whom Christ hath redeemed with his most precious blood." Tolerating Catholics would be a "grievous sinne," because Roman Catholic "faith and Doctrine" was "erroneous and Hereticall" and their church "Apostaticall." Worse, it would make the Church of Ireland "accessarie, not onely to their Superstitions, Idolatries, Heresies, and in a word, abominations of Poperie, but also" as a consequence, "to the Perdition of the seduced people" who would perish in a false religion.[21]

However, the wars against the Spanish and French were going horribly wrong. Charles was desperate. Parliament had demanded the Anglo-Spanish War in hopes it would save the Protestant cause in Europe. It did not. Much of the blame fell on the Duke of Buckingham, who Charles had put in charge of the war effort. Buckingham, lacking both military competence and the political trust of Parliament, accomplished little. His most notable expedition against the Spanish was a failed attempt to capture Cadiz in 1625. Thereafter, the English watched helplessly as Spanish forces conquered Protestant provinces across the Holy Roman Empire. King Charles's sister Elizabeth and her husband the Calvinist Elector of the Palatinate had to flee for safety.

To the frustration of the losing war against Spain was added the frustration of the losing war against France. This second conflict was the awkward fallout of Charles's marriage to Henrietta Maria. The marriage alliance with France failed to bring French into the war against Spain. Instead, King Louis used English ships to capture the Huguenot stronghold on the Île de Ré. When Louis then laid siege to the crucial Huguenot port city of La Rochelle, Buckingham joined the outraged Parliament to demand a war against France to protect their Protestant cousins. Alas, Buckingham's campaigns against the French proved even more disastrous than his efforts against Spain. Despite several costly expeditions, the English utterly failed to either recapture the Île de Ré or relieve La Rochelle.[22]

Buckingham's military failures combined with Charles's domestic policies to inspire a murderous anger among their opponents. First, a London crowd beat to death one of Buckingham's friends and confidants, John Lambe. Allegedly, Lambe exercised a pernicious influence over the duke and the king: in addition to favoring the Spanish, he was rumored to practice black magic, engage in homosexual sex, and molest children. Then, just as the Duke of Buckingham was about to embark on a new expedition to relieve La Rochelle, a former army officer assassinated him. Partly disgruntled at the failure of the previous campaign, the assassin was mostly inspired by the hostile propaganda of his puritan critics. Two months later, this last bastion of Protestant France fell to the armies of Louis XIII.[23]

The murders of Lambe and Buckingham demonstrated the extent of anti-Catholic nationalists' alienation from Charles's court and their willingness and ability to mobilize popular politics to put pressure on the king. That frustration also found an outlet in overseas colonization, although here too, the war presented a series of setbacks. Spanish, Portuguese, and Native American forces destroyed the budding colonies of Saint Christopher, Nevis, and Guiana and stymied efforts to colonize Trinidad, Tobago, and Tortuga. Nevertheless, Sir Thomas Warner managed to revive Saint Christopher while other veterans of Guiana helped colonize Barbados. In 1627, the merchant who led the initial expedition to Barbados used his connections to encourage several native Guianese to accompany him to the then uninhabited island. He promised to "bring up their children to Christianities" and develop "a constant trade betweene" Barbados and Guiana. Instead, the Barbadians enslaved these poor individuals, who eventually merged into the island's expanding population of enslaved Africans and Native Americans.[24]

Politically, Barbados got off to a tumultuous start. For several years, contesting claims to the island pitted factions of colonists against each other. Religiously, however, Barbados began on a solidly conformist foundation. A minister was on the island within the first year. Once his authority as proprietor was confirmed, the Earl of Carlisle seems to have left the island's religious government up to local authorities, who around 1630 began laying out parishes. By 1645 the island had reached its full modern complement of eleven parishes. Most of them were staffed most of the time. Compact, wealthy, and populous, Barbados would be better supplied with clergymen than any other colony outside of Massachusetts.[25]

Barbados and Saint Christopher were the principal colonies established during these turbulent years, but there were a number of other attempts and plans. Notable was the first Huguenot scheme to settle within the English colonies. Sir Robert Heath encouraged Huguenot refugees from La Rochelle to establish a colony in Carolana. He had not yet managed to occupy the territory and hoped that their misfortune could prove his good luck. Accordingly, Antoine de Ridouet the Baron de Sancé, his aide, Monsieur de Belavene, and Hugh L'Amy, drew up a plan for a Huguenot refuge. Like Heath, they were former clients of Buckingham. Their colony, located on the northern frontier of Spanish Florida, would be a militantly Protestant and fundamentally anti-Catholic stronghold. It had no room for toleration. Only committed Protestants would be allowed in. Ideally, most would be Huguenots or Reformed Protestants from the Dutch Republic. People would have to bring a certificate from their pastor proving that they were Protestants in good standing. Huguenots who could not have their certificates confirmed by the Huguenot pastor in London would be sent back to France. Once in America, the colonists would have to lay their hands "upon the Bible thereby to acknowledge themselves to be true Protestants & faithfull to their commanders & planters and true to their king and cuntrie." The Huguenots sent out a ship to get the colony going, but it wrecked on the Carolina coast. A lack of funds prevented them from sending another. King Charles was no more eager or able than Heath to sink money into an uncertain colonial project. Anglo-America's first Huguenot colony faded into oblivion.[26]

On the brighter side, the war against France revived the flagging enterprise of Nova Scotia. It even (briefly) made Canada British. In 1627 Sir William Alexander organized another expedition of three ships to Nova Scotia led by his son, also Sir William Alexander. Technical difficulties prevented them from leaving until 1628, at which point Alexander's small fleet joined up with three privateers sponsored by an English company with French connections. Gervase Kirke, a London merchant who had settled in Dieppe, France, led the company with the help of his three sons by a Huguenot wife: David, Lewis, and Thomas. Each son commanded one of the privateers. David, the eldest, was in overall command. Together they captured Tadoussac, the French fur trading post at the mouth of the Saint Lawrence River and defeated a French fleet sent to supply Quebec. The Kirkes then returned to England for more supplies while Alexander's colonists spent the winter in Saint John's, Newfoundland.[27]

Over the winter of 1628–29, Alexander, his fellow Scottish investors, the Kirkes, and other English merchants formed a company to conquer Quebec and plant colonists in Nova Scotia. David Kirke led the expedition against Quebec, which was captured in August 1629. He sent the French colonists and their priests back to France and made Canada a British Protestant colony. Meanwhile, Sir William Alexander the Younger went to Cape Breton Island with a group of Scottish and English colonists, including a minister, apparently a Scot who conformed to the Church of England. Depositing sixty colonists and the minister on Cape Breton under the command of Sir James Stewart, Lord Ochiltree, Alexander sailed on to occupy the abandoned French post at Port Royal. He spent the next year there engaging in the fur trade. About half the Nova Scotia colonists died over the harsh winter, but a second party arrived in the summer of 1630. A third arrived in 1631 with cattle.[28]

On Cape Breton, Lord Ochiltree worked energetically to entrench his colony. The official atmosphere among his mix of English and Scots colonists likely favored puritan sensibilities. Ochiltree's family had long been supporters of the militant Protestant cause in Scotland. One ancestor was father-in-law to John Knox. Other relatives were active in the Ulster plantation. However, those credentials were not radical enough for all of the colonists. To the surprise of everyone, and the disgust of the colony's minister, eight households revealed themselves to be "Brownists." Shortly after coming ashore, they broke off to live apart from the rest of the colonists. In the disapproving words of the minister, "they will admit none to their society without publick confession, they allow no pastorall function." However, they did not leave their neighbors in peace. The minister complained that they were "great Seduceers." Evidently they tried to make converts. The minister must have debated with them, for he got to know their views, which he characterized as, "censorious above measure, holding all papists damned, raylors against superiours, refractory to powers especially to Bishops, and the Setled State of Englands church." The minister hoped the "good Lord" would "deliver all plantations from such people, and root them out, or convert them where they live." Instead, a few weeks later, a French expedition captured the colony. Ochiltree, shipped back to Europe with his colonists, including the Separatists, remained undeterred. By April 1631 he had secured his freedom and become a baronet of Nova Scotia. He was making plans to recolonize the area in conjunction with other Nova Scotia baronets when he falsely accused another Scottish lord of treason. For the next twenty years, he sat in prison. The Scottish Cape Breton colony was forgotten.[29]

Port Royal, however, survived and showed promise of becoming the seed of a Scottish American empire. Nova Scotia's resurgence revived hopes of using America to solve Scottish social problems. At some point in 1629, Sir William Alexander entered negotiations "with some of the heads of the Chief Clannes of the Highlands . . . for transporting themselves and thar followers, to settle themselves into New Scotland." In October, King Charles informed the Scottish Privy Council that he did "very much approve of that course for advancing the said plantatione, and for deburdening that our kingdome of that race of people which in former times hade bred soe many troubles ther." Since it would be for "the publick good and quiet thereof," he urged the council to arrange for a "voluntarie contributione" to support it.[30]

Nova Scotia benefited from the strong support of King Charles. In April 1629, he granted Sir William Alexander land at Largs, on the Firth of Clyde outside of Glasgow, to build a port for trade with his American colonies in Nova Scotia and "Canada." To reinforce this royal patronage, Charles then raised Sir William to the peerage as Viscount Stirling and Lord Alexander of Tullibody in 1630. Alas, while Largs would become a popular seaside resort in the nineteenth century, it was not a good location for a transatlantic port. The scheme to make it the hub of a Scottish colonial empire came to nothing.[31]

In the end, diplomatic pressures combined with King Charles's need for money undid both Nova Scotia and British Canada. The war with France had ended in March 1629 with the Treaty of Susa. Quebec, captured in April, was to be returned, although the Kirkes managed to forestall the turnover until 1632. The French also insisted that Nova Scotia be relinquished. King Charles held out on Sir William Alexander's behalf until July 1631. He then suddenly changed his mind when the French promised to pay the remaining half of his wife's dowry. The Treaty of Saint-Germain-en-Laye, signed in 1632, handed over both Quebec and Nova Scotia to the French. Most of the Scottish colonists left Nova Scotia, but a couple stayed on. One was a woman whose two sons converted to Catholicism, married French women, and sired a large Acadian dynasty.[32]

To compensate for their lost colonies, King Charles gave David Kirke a knighthood in 1633 and raised Alexander to Earl of Stirling and Viscount of Canada; then, in 1635, Stirling secured a grant from the Council of New England for what is now eastern Maine and Long Island. Preoccupied with the increasingly difficult task of managing Scottish affairs for his royal master, Stirling took no active role in colonizing those lands. However, New England puritans had to negotiate with his representatives to settle within the limits of the Stirling patent on Long Island, the eastern half of which later became part of Connecticut.[33]

Meanwhile, in Avalon the influx of Catholics provoked a crisis that almost cost Baltimore his colony. The controversy began in Baltimore's manor house at Ferryland, the only built space big enough to host religious services. In England, where households had become the fundamental religious unit for prohibited Catholic worship, priests like Richard Broughton had turned this necessity into a positive virtue. In a clandestinely published collection of prayers, Broughton insisted that Roman Catholics "can not goe to the Church" when "misbelievers" and "the wicked occupy the place." Instead, they "must flee from that place, because it is prophaned by them." Segregation was a sacred duty. "Let not the godly pray neither at home with an heritike, for *what society is there betwene light & darknesse?* (Corinthians 6)." Instead, Catholics should "assemble together" either at a private home or other secret meeting place. If that was impossible, the worship of "true believers" could be reduced to the individual level: "let every one by themselves, singe, reade, pray." But it was better to gather together in small groups, "for *where there be two or three gathered together in my name, there am I in the middle of them.* (Matthew 16)." As historian Lisa McClain describes it, Catholic priests proposed three different ways Catholics could keep themselves spiritually separate in a world dominated by heretics. They could either create "a physical separation, with each side occupying a different space," a "ritual separation, with each side performing different gestures or speaking different words in either a shared or separate space," or, as a last resort, make their faith purely "imaginative, occurring in the minds of believers either in a shared or separate space." The exclusion was as important as the inclusion. The ultimate effect was "to buttress Catholic identity, build a community of believers (however small), provide opportunities for meaningful worship, and strengthen individual faith."[34]

Baltimore did not have the luxury of turning his manor house into an exclusively Catholic place of worship. His Protestant colonists were already using it for Protestant worship. Instead, he attempted a sort of domestic *Simultaneum*. Like in the Holy Roman Empire, where some churches were split into Catholic and Protestant sections, Calvert divided his manor house into two sacred precincts. Erasmus Stourton led Protestant services in one wing while Baltimore and his fellow Catholics were "at masse" in the other. Or, as Catholic sources described it, "under one roof Mass was celebrated in one part of the house, while the heretics held their services in another part." It was the first experiment in religious coexistence in the English overseas world. It was not a success. Stourton resented seeing the two Catholic priests performing "the ceremonies of the church of Rome in as ample maner as tis used in Spayne." Worse, "the childe of one William Poole a protestant was baptized according to the orders and customes of the church of Rome" against "the will of the sayd

Poole." Baltimore had allegedly insisted on the baptism and served as "a witness" to it. The outraged Stourton, threatening to submit a complaint to the Privy Council, sailed back to England in the fall of 1628.[35]

Publicly supporting Roman Catholic worship could have been grounds for voiding Baltimore's charter. Stourton's chances of getting a favorable hearing from the Privy Council seemed very good. He evidently had some sort of link to the all-powerful Duke of Buckingham, for soon after his return he was appointed chaplain to Buckingham's less distinguished younger brother, Christopher Villiers. Worse, Calvert's friendship with Buckingham had evaporated after the collapse of the Spanish Match. There is every reason to think that Buckingham, under fire for his failures as a military leader and his support of Laudianism, would have seized on the Ferryland scandal to bolster his sagging reputation as a Protestant hero. Alas for Stourton, Buckingham was assassinated six weeks before he made it back.[36]

Buckingham's misfortune was Baltimore's luck. Stourton's complaint went nowhere because Calvert's relationship with the king remained strong. Indeed, in the wake of Buckingham's murder the poor king seems to have remembered Calvert with extra fondness. In a 1629 letter exchange, a nostalgic Charles called Baltimore a person of "qualitie" who was especially dear to him because he had "beene so neare a servant to our late deare father of blessd memorie." Calvert also benefited from other close connections at court. Less than two weeks earlier, Charles had added Thomas Wentworth to the Privy Council, shortly after having raised him to the peerage. Wentworth, a fellow Yorkshireman and old friend of Calvert's, was rapidly rising to the position of Charles's new chief minister. Shortly after Baltimore thanked Charles for protecting him "against calumny and malice which hath already sought to make me seem foul in your Majesty's eyes," he also thanked Wentworth.[37]

It was these court connections more than anything else that gave English Catholics a permanent foothold in America, but not in Avalon. Between the disruption of trade caused by the war with France and Newfoundland's harsh climate, Baltimore lost hope for his colony. Charles tried to discourage Calvert from wasting his fortune and energy on further colonial efforts, but Baltimore was determined to try again. In 1629 he sailed south to the Chesapeake to seek a new site for a colony. Returning to England in 1630, he pressed his case with the sympathetic king. After several years of negotiations, the charter for Maryland was confirmed in June 1632. Since George Calvert had died five weeks earlier, his son and heir, Cecil Calvert, received it. The second Baron Baltimore was only twenty-seven years old, but, if anything, even more committed to Catholicism. He had converted to Catholicism a year before his father, while on a trip to Rome. He was also married to Anne, the Roman Catholic daughter of Thomas Arundell, first Baron of Wardour: the Catholic soldier who tried to establish an American colony at the beginning of King James's reign, before being implicated in the Gunpowder Plot.[38]

Maryland was no more intended to be a Catholic colony than Avalon. Like Avalon, it was granted as a personal favor to George Calvert, "in whose Fidelity, Prudence, Justice, and provident Circumspection of Mind," King Charles claimed to "repose the greatest Confidence." Historians have treated Maryland's charter, with the bishop of Durham's civil and ecclesiastical powers, as distinctive, but it only seems so in retrospect. Maryland survived whereas the other early Stuart proprietary colonies with the same powers did not. Those powers included "the Patronages, and Advowsons of all" the colony's churches, "together with License and Faculty of erecting and founding Churches, Chapels, and Place of Worship." However, unlike other charters that often left conformity to the Church of England implicit, Maryland's charter contained an explicit command that its churches "be dedicated and consecrated to the Ecclesiastical Laws of our Kingdom of England." On the other hand, apart from insisting that the province and its inhabitants be "of our Allegiance," and that "no interpretation . . . be made, whereby God's holy and true Christian Religion, or the Allegiance due to Us, our Heirs and Successors, may in any wise suffer by Change, Prejudice, or diminution," the charter did not include the typical clauses explicitly excluding Roman Catholics. Officers and immigrants were not explicitly required to swear the oaths of loyalty and supremacy.[39]

Once again, our best clue for the colony's religious vision comes from its name. A manuscript from 1670 claims it was the king's idea. Lord Baltimore thought to name it "Crescentia or the Land of Crescence," but left the space blank on the charter. When Charles asked him what name he would like, Baltimore loyally replied he wanted it to be "something in Honor of his Maties name but the he was deprived of that happinesse there being already a Province in those parts called Carolana." King Charles then suggested "a name in Honor of the Queen . . . Mariana." Baltimore protested that Mariana was the name of a Jesuit (Juan de Mariana) "that wrote against monarchy." The king then proposed the name of "Terra Maria in English Maryland." It was, in historian Antoinette Sutto's apt phrase, "a name both loyal and royal." It was also an obvious reference to the Virgin Mary. Indeed, early Maryland's history would be distinguished by its elite's propensity for both royalist loyalism and Roman Catholicism.[40]

*

The creation of Maryland was not the beginning of something new so much as the culmination of a Caroline pattern of colonization that depended heavily on royal favor and aristocratic patronage. Associated with royal favorites, especially the Duke of Buckingham, it reached its peak during the years of war against Spain and France. These years proved pivotal for several reasons. They forced English enterprise to move away from South America and into the Caribbean, where it gained permanent footholds on the islands of Saint Christopher and Barbados. Here, Laudianism found its first American home. More immediately relevant to the future United States, the war against France persuaded Lord Baltimore to abandon his Avalon colony and move the seed of Anglo-American Catholicism to the Chesapeake. Meanwhile, Charles's fiscal, military, and diplomatic weakness led him to trade away Canada and Nova Scotia, rendering North America a field of Anglo-French competition for the next century and a half.

Puritans benefited from the same aristocratic pattern, as the influence of the Earl of Warwick indicates. More important, though, was the pattern of colonization often described as a religious refuge that derived from their increasingly oppositional relationship to the Stuart regime. That relationship reached a crisis point during the unsuccessful wars against Spain and France. Charles had never been fond of puritans. The killing of his beloved Duke of Buckingham made him downright hostile to them. He blamed them for the assassination and for Parliament's resistance to his policies, foreign and domestic. Convinced that neither Parliament nor puritans could be relied on for help, Charles tried to force his subjects to contribute money to support his troops without parliamentary authorization. In 1628, Parliament protested, presenting the king with a "Petition of Right" that denounced his maneuvers as unconstitutional. Charles signed it, ostensibly believing the petition only affirmed existing constitutional rights. He received five subsidies from Parliament in return. However, Parliament's next session in the winter of 1629 ended less happily. Parliament complained about the introduction of "popery or Arminianism" into the Church of England and refused to grant more money until Charles put an end to "innovation of religion." Charles dissolved it and refused to call another Parliament until 1640. The stage was set for his so-called Personal Rule—and the great puritan migration to New England.[41]

EIGHT

Puritans: New England, Providence Island, the Leewards, 1629–1638

Looking back from the 1690s, Cotton Mather, colonial America's most famous puritan minister, had no doubt as to why his grandfathers—puritan ministers John Cotton and Richard Mather—together with several "Thousands of Good men" (aka other puritans), had suffered "much Poverty and Misery, with daily fears of Massacre from Indian Salvages, in a bleak Region, a Thousand Leagues from ones own Country." They "judged" those sufferings, "not so sad and so hard, as that of being in the Griping Talons of Archbishop Laud." With their "Persecutions," William Laud and his fellow "Ceremony-Mongers" had driven those seeking "the Liberties of the Gospel" into the "American Wilderness, now known by the Name of NEW-ENGLAND." Such "ceremony-mongers," insisted Mather, "ever were, and ever will be Enemies to all the true Interests of the Nation."[1]

The great puritan migration to New England began after King Charles disbanded Parliament in March 1629. Complaining that the House of Commons had been expanding "their privileges" against his rightful powers, he blamed "some turbulent and ill-affected spirits" for intimidating "the sincerer and better part of the House" into what he clearly saw as an illegitimate way of proceeding. Affirming that he would always "maintain the true religion and doctrine established in the Church of England, without admitting or conniving at any backsliding either to popery or Schism," Charles urged his subjects not to "abuse" their "ancient and just rights and liberties" by turning them "into licentiousness" or "a lawless liberty" against "lawful and necessary authority." However, puritans had good reason to think they were losing those liberties. Just two months earlier, King Charles had given the Laudian cause decisive public support by forbidding any preaching about predestination. Ostensibly, the decree was designed to suppress religious polemics on both sides of the Arminian debate. However, few bishops enforced it in a balanced matter, especially not Laud, then bishop of London. He claimed to be enforcing it evenhandedly, but on closer inspection, it is clear he used the decree to intimidate Calvinists and to favor Anti-Calvinists. Thousands of otherwise upstanding subjects—not at all the typical sort of colonist—began looking for shelter overseas.[2]

Between 1629 and 1640 some fifteen thousand puritans, or members of puritan households, migrated to New England. It is difficult to think of a more dramatic statement of dissent from royal policies. This was no ordinary migration in search of opportunity. It started at a very specific moment, then suddenly ended when circumstances changed in England. The move was so closely connected to English politics that about three thousand of its participants returned to England after the migration stopped. Some went for prosaic reasons. Others joined the revolution that brought down England's monarchy and its church.[3] England's present, not America's future, was their primary concern. The descendants of those who stayed in America, like Cotton Mather, would remember the migration as a flight from persecution. However, to judge by its contemporary effect, it might be better to think of the puritan colonies in the 1630s as the advanced beachheads of the English revolution of the 1640s.

The puritan colonies permanently altered the religious makeup of the emerging empire by creating a series of puritan-dominated jurisdictions. New Englanders understood the power their colonies gave them to set up ecclesiastical bulwarks of resistance. Instead of forcing people to swear the oath of supremacy, they preferred to ensure their attachment to their specific jurisdiction and its religious arrangements. New England's oaths professed loyalty to "this present plantation," "this jurisdiction," "the Colonie," "this people," or "this government," phrases emphasizing local specifics over a generic conformity. Puritan New England quickly developed a new church order, Congregationalism, which spread from Massachusetts to Plymouth, Connecticut, Bermuda, New Hampshire, Providence Island, and eventually England. It was a new model for a righteous church order, neither episcopal nor presbyterian.[4]

*

Puritans' interest in colonization corresponded closely to their loss of influence within England. The 1630s was a time of peace—and no sitting Parliament. Scholars have suggested King Charles was crafting a proto-absolutist "Personal Rule" that allowed him and Laud to shut down the institutional loopholes through which puritans had preserved their cause and their clergy, like the feoffees of impropriations. Formed in 1625 by John Davenport and a group of puritans in London, the feoffees bought up impropriations, advowsons, and landed property, then used the legal powers and privileges they thus acquired to protect, patronize, and support nonconformist ministers, curates, and lecturers across England and Wales. Laud recognized them as a threat to his control over the church, and the feoffees were shut down at his urging in 1633. By then, many of its members had become involved in puritan colonial companies, like Massachusetts Bay and Providence Island. Such colonies became part of a broader transatlantic effort to shelter puritans, especially their ministers, from the full force of Laudian conformity.[5]

In the right circumstances, puritans could dominate colonial church life virtually unchallenged. They gained power through various means, from aristocratic patronage within England to local political struggles in the colonies. In New England, their hegemony began with the Dorchester Company's fishing outpost on Cape Ann, where John Lyford and his puritan allies found refuge when they were exiled from Plymouth. One of Lyford's allies, Roger Conant, was the brother of a puritan minister in England and friend of the moderate puritan John White, a leading investor in the Dorchester Company. When the company folded in 1626 and shipped its servants home, White encouraged Conant to stay on while he and some other investors in the company worked to acquire a new patent for what they called the New England Company, a collaborative effort with a group of London merchants and East Anglian gentlemen. Lyford took some of his followers south to Virginia, but Conant stayed on and explored the Cape Ann peninsula, discovering the excellent harbor of Naumkeag that became the New England Company's first American outpost. To reflect the company's religious ambitions, Naumkeag was renamed Salem in 1628. Salem was where God had "his tabernacle, and his dwelling place in Zion" (Psalm 76:2).[6]

Plymouth's Separatists, meanwhile, continued to suppress manifestations of conformity to the Church of England across the region. On May Day 1627, the group of Englishmen who stayed behind at Mount Wollaston after Captain Wollaston had left for Virginia set up a May pole (a traditional custom detested by puritans), renamed their outpost "Ma-re Mount" (or, as the puritans claimed, Merrymount), and celebrated with drinking and dancing. Leading the celebrations was Thomas Morton, a proudly antipuritan poet, lawyer, and writer. He had joined the captain's former servants and become the outpost's leader. He evidently delighted in annoying the Plymouth colonists, gleefully offending their religious sensibilities and developing better relations with the nearby Massachusett nation that led Mount Wollaston's fur trade to surpass that of Plymouth. Provoked, Plymouth sent its military commander, Miles Standish, with some militiamen to arrest Morton in 1628. The Separatists then deported Morton to England for trading in arms and ammunition and "living without all fear of God or common honesty." Morton replied that the "cruel Schismaticks" were deliberately driving out their religious and economic competitors. He returned to New England the following year, but was banished again along with other colonists who insisted on using the *Book of Common Prayer*.[7]

Shortly after Morton's first deportation, the New England Company's first governor, John Endecott, visited Mount Wollaston. Renaming it Mount Dagon, after the temple of the Philistines destroyed by Samson (Judges 16:23–31), he hewed down the Maypole and rebuked the remaining colonists "for their profaneness and admonished them to look there should be better walking." To the delight of Plymouth's Separatists, religious conformity was now suppressed in southern New England. They called Endecott a "worthy gentleman," "a second Burrow" (referencing the executed Separatist leader Henry Barrow), and "a friend to us all."[8]

Having cleared out the conformists, Salem's puritans and Plymouth's Separatists entered a dialogue over the spring and summer of 1629 that led to the creation of New England Congregationalism. There are surprisingly few details about exactly how it happened. It seems to have begun when Plymouth sent Samuel Fuller, the colony's doctor and a church deacon, to Salem, which was coping with an outbreak of disease. In May 1629, Endecott thanked William Bradford for sending Fuller, commenting that "God's people are all marked by one and the same mark, and sealed by one and the same seal." Endecott added that Fuller had "satisfied" him "touching your judgments, of the outward forms of God's worship" and was convinced that what Fuller told him was "no other than is warranted by the evidence of truth, and the same which I have professed and maintained, ever since the Lord in mercy revealed himself unto me." With these words, Salem started down the road to Congregationalism.[9]

Back in England, the Massachusetts Bay Company replaced the New England Company. Its first governor, the wealthy puritan merchant Matthew Cradock, stayed in England and made Endecott his deputy. Of course, the company's charter, like all colonial charters, required the "governor and his Deputy, or any assistants to administer the oathes of supremacy and allegeance to al persons that goe thither," but the colonists could enforce these rules as they saw fit. In April 1929, the first group of Massachusetts Bay Company colonists embarked along with three nonconformist ministers. They affirmed their religious intentions in a letter to Cradock and his council, proclaiming the propagation of the Gospel was "above all" their "ayme in setlling this plantaccion," and expressing their confidence that their carefully selected, godly ministers would preserve them "in the knowledge of God." Hopefully, "in Gods appointed tyme," their American neighbors would then "bee reduced to the obedyence of the gosple of Christ." Despite their "good hope" of "love and unanimus agreemt" among their ministers, however, they worried that religious disagreements could undermine the "peace and unitie" of the colony. If "some busie psons (led more by their will then any good warrant out of Gods word)" were to "take opportunitie of moving needless questions to stirr up strife . . . and bring men to declare some different jugmt (most commonly in things indifferent) from wch small beginning great mishcheifs have followed," they urged the company's council to "suppress them." They most likely feared conformity might intrude into their puritan enterprise.[10]

Before the colonists left, an old presbyterian had advised them to settle on a church system. They did not. Had they done so, Massachusetts Bay might have gone in a presbyterian direction. Instead, they landed in July, open to suggestions, and found that the people of Salem had already made the decision on the colony's church order. Endecott and the Salemites had rejected the use of the *Book of Common Prayer* and were modeling their church along the congregational lines of Plymouth. Rejecting the parish system of the established church, which automatically made everyone within the parish a church member, Salem's church was now a gathered congregation. "Visible saints" who could convince their fellows that they were among the elect predestined by God to be saved (or very likely to be so) could become church members. Others still had to attend the town's church, but they could not receive its sacraments or have a say in how it was run.[11]

Congregationalists' enemies described their churches as "Independent" because they rejected higher ecclesiastical authorities like synods or bishops. The Congregational system placed supreme ecclesiastical authority within each locally gathered church. Consequently, the members of each congregation had a tremendous amount of authority over local religious life. Self-governing, they selected their own ministers and disciplined their own members through a system that mixed lay and clerical authority. Church elders (or "presbyters") were divided into "teaching" elders (i.e., the minsters, ideally two per congregation, a pastor and a teacher—an expensive and ultimately unsustainable ideal) and "ruling" (or lay) elders. A separate group of deacons oversaw the business of the congregation and its meetinghouse. Congregationalists rejected the idea of "church" buildings with special spiritual qualities: that was deemed superstitiously popish. Since each congregation was equal to every other congregation, decisions involving more than one congregation had to be reached through agreement in religious fellowship, for no single entity had the authority to command the congregations. Lesser matters could vary from congregation to congregation, but there was a broad affinity on more important issues, creating a fellowship similar to a church establishment, albeit one very different from England's established church.[12]

The Salemites quickly persuaded the newcomers to accept their new church order, which was important because the three ministers that accompanied them allowed it to become fully operational. The newcomers still had to prove their spiritual worth first before they could become fellow church members of Salem's congregation. At a special meeting, Salem accepted the two ministers the Massachusetts Bay Company had assigned to it. The third minister went to the new outpost at Charlestown, whose church was not yet Congregational. Among the new colonists were about thirty-five of the Leiden Separatists, who finally rejoined their companions. Ralph Smith, one of the new immigrants, became Plymouth's first minister. In August, with Plymouth's governor William Bradford and members of the Plymouth church present, Salem's church selected ruling elders and deacons and offered the hand of fellowship to Plymouth's church. Salem and Plymouth now shared essentially the same Congregational church system. Thereafter, as Plymouth quickly became the poor cousin of its larger, thriving neighbor, its ministry would depend on the help of migrants to Massachusetts.[13]

Back in England, John Winthrop, unaware of the creation of Massachusetts's Congregational church, was preparing to emigrate. He drew up a list of justifications for "the Intended Plantation" that gave it a bold but ecclesiastically vague religious purpose. It would be "a service to the Church of great consequence to carry the Gospell into those p[ar]ts. Of the world, to help on the cominge in of fulnesse of the Gentiles and to rayse a Bulworke against the kingdome of Antichrist, w[hi]ch. the Jesuites labour to rear up in those parts." He then led the next group of colonists, who arrived in a large fleet in the spring of 1630 along with some more members of the Leiden congregation. To their surprise, the only person Salem's church accepted as a fellow member was a man from Henry Jacob's London church. The rest had to join Salem's covenant first. Two colonists protested against this obvious break with the established church. They were sent back to England. Winthrop and the rest took the covenant. Then Charlestown also adopted the Congregational church order, helped along by several Plymouth colonists and a mortal outbreak of disease that gave the decision divine urgency. Hopefully having a pure church would "pacify the Lord's wrath."[14]

Massachusetts quickly doubled down on its new church establishment. It restricted the political franchise to church members and prohibited any alternative form of worship within its borders. In the spring of 1631, one of the first acts of the colony's newly elected General Court (its colonial assembly) ordered that "noe man shalbe admitted to the freedome of this body pollitícke, but such as are members of some of the churches within the lymitts of the same." In March 1635 a law required everyone to attend "church meeteings upon the Lords day" or face a fine. The colonies' governors had to pledge their "best endeavor to draw on the natives of this country, called New England, to the knowledge of the true God, and to conserve the planters & others coming hether, in the same knowledge & feare of God." One did not have to be a Congregationalist to live in Massachusetts Bay, but one could not otherwise gain access to church sacraments, the vote, or political office. The "residents" who did not hold the franchise had to swear a separate oath of loyalty from the "freemen" who did.[15]

While New England worked out the kinks in its church system and developed a strict sense of acceptable theological orthodoxy, Congregationalism spread around the English Atlantic. In Rotterdam, Hugh Peter helped to establish a Congregational church before joining the stream of people moving to Massachusetts. Other English churches in Holland nourished similar tendencies. The exact mix of influences, ideas, and theology at work remains a topic of some debate, but clearly the interplay between puritans and Separatists on both sides of the Atlantic was important. As with Henry Jacob's London congregation, the main difference between Congregationalists and Separatists remained the refusal to completely disavow the Church of England and episcopal ordinations. Congregationalists professed to maintain communion with portions of the Church of England, even though they had an increasingly difficult time in specifying exactly which parts. Equally significantly, they rejected presbyterianism, which remained popular among many puritans. This developing split within English puritanism would ultimately destroy puritans' ability to reform the Church of England and break up what once had been a fairly unified movement into irreconcilable fragments.[16]

Congregationalism flourished in New England because its demographic and constitutional situation was unique. Unlike most colonies, it attracted educated families with property and children. Its unusually dense concentration of puritan laymen and ministers meant that the exclusive character of its Congregational church was not particularly problematic: most of the original colonists could become church members with comparative ease. More importantly, the colonists had full control over their government because, at Cradock's suggestion, a large number of the company's founding members had moved to Massachusetts Bay along with the Winthrop fleet and taken their charter with them. Thereafter, the company's General Court was not based in London, as was usual with other colonies; it was in the colony. This decision put the colony's government and church out of easy reach of royal authority and allowed the colonists to act quickly and decisively and without contradiction from company directors back in England, unlike Bermuda or Virginia. Once he was elected governor of Massachusetts, for example, John Winthrop could rule without worrying what a governing board based in London might think.[17]

Massachusetts's unusual qualities made it a beacon for Protestant dissidents around the English world. In Ireland, Englishmen and Scots who resented having bishops and did not want to conform to Laudian norms formed conventicles in Ulster and Dublin. John Winthrop Jr. attended some of them while a student at Trinity University. In 1635, he persuaded a group of Irish Scots to move to New England. A tremendous storm at sea prevented them from making it to America. They interpreted it as a providential sign to stay in Europe. Other Irish Protestants did successfully emigrate. In March 1631, after having traded to Virginia for a decade, Daniel Gookin, petitioned the king for a patent to colonize the mysterious island of Saint Brandon. "English Travellers Merchants and other gent expert in maritane affaires and discoveries" believed it lay three hundred leagues southwest of the westernmost Irish islands. Claiming a colony there would not only help enrich his monarch's kingdom, but would also be for "the glorie of God for the propagating of Christian Religion in places where for the most savage and heathen people did live and inhabit," Gookin asked for, and received, the same "preheminences and Immunities" as Sir William Alexander had received for his Nova Scotia colony "to discover and plant the same Island." Alas, no such island was found before Gookin died in 1633. He bequeathed his Virginia lands to his sons, one of whom, his namesake, later became an important figure in Massachusetts.[18]

Massachusetts was a special case, representing just one end of the spectrum of "Puritanism." It was not long before some began to dissent from the Massachusetts church, although not from its principle of church establishment. Minister Thomas Hooker thought it was too restrictive in its requirements for church membership. In 1636 he led about a hundred other puritans overland to the Connecticut River Valley, where they established the towns of Windsor, Hartford, and Wethersfield, where church membership was less demanding. Two years later they united to form (without a royal charter or authorization) the new colony of Connecticut in the name of "the Allmighty God" and "the wise disposition of his divyne prvidence." To "mayntayne the peace and union" among them they announced their decision to have "an orderly and decent Government established according to God . . . to maytayne and prsearve the liberty and purity of the gospell of our Lord Jesus wch we now prfesse, as also the disciplyne of the Churches, wch according to the truth of the said gospell is now practised amongst us." In 1637 a new group of emigrants from England including John Davenport decided that Massachusetts's church membership requirements were actually too lax. They moved on, likewise without a royal patent, to establish a "civill Governmt according to God" and gather a church in what became the colony of New Haven, where church membership was more restrictive than in Massachusetts. Guided by the prayers and advice of their minister, John Davenport, they determined to set up a government according to "Scripture," and followed Massachusetts in restricting the franchise and the right to hold office to members of the colony's church. Both colonies retained fellowship with the Massachusetts churches, but their separate jurisdictions allowed their differences to coexist within a broad Congregational system.[19]

Meanwhile, Lord Saye and Sele and Lord Brook, proprietors of the Saybrook colony situated between Connecticut and New Haven, objected to both Massachusetts's high standards for church membership and its decision to limit political power to church members. As historian Karen Kupperman has explained, they felt it placed "the decision-making power of the congregation above that of the state" and "overturned the basis of good order and true liberty." These aristocrats were willing to grant the church and its clergy a great deal of autonomy, but they insisted on holding the church in a politically subordinate role to the laity as a whole, not just its godly church members. That was how the church on Providence Island was organized. It also figured in Saye and Sele and Brook's pro-

FIGURE 8. New England ca. 1650

posals for church reform in England. In Massachusetts, minister John Cotton responded that if the rights of freemen "be committed to men not according to their godliness, which maketh them fit for church fellowship, but according to their wealth," the traditional basis of English political rights, it risked putting control of the church in the hands of "worldly men." If "worldly men" then became a majority, "as soon they might do, they would as readily set over us magistrates like themselves, such as might hate us." Wealthy, ungodly magistrates could "turn the edge of all authority and laws against the church and the members thereof, the maintenance of whose peace is the chief end which God aimed at in the institution of magistracy."[20]

New Englanders were clearly posing a direct challenge to the church of Laud and their king. To avoid drawing too much attention to Massachusetts, Governor Winthrop did what he could to keep radicalism in check. Criminals crossing the Atlantic to flee punishment were sent back to England. When Roger Williams questioned the king's right to grant American lands to his colonists by saying only Native Americans could sell those rights, he was banished. A bigger scandal came in 1634. John Endecott, at a muster of Salem's militia company, lost patience with the idolatrous cross of Saint George that decorated the commonly used English flag. Cutting it out with his sword, he then trampled it on the ground. Some colonists were shocked at this defacement of their national symbol. Others agreed that Endecott had struck a righteous blow against idolatry. Winthrop worked out a compromise whereby the king's arms (a different flag) flew over the colony's fort on Castle Island while the militia bands received new sets of colors—without the offending cross. In the meantime, the colony built up its defenses—evidently preparing to defend itself from intervention from England as much as from invasion by foreign enemies.[21]

Despite Winthrop's efforts, it was clear that his colony was deviating from conformity. In his 1631 guide to erecting colonies, Captain John Smith expressed optimism about New England's religious future. It seemed likely to "grow a good addition to the Church of England." The colonists had "Preachers erected among themselves, and Gods true Religion (they say) taught amongst them, the Sabbath day observed, the common Prayer (as I understand) and Sermons performed, and diligent catechizing, with strict and carefull exercise." Nevertheless, Smith, who had dedicated his book to the archbishops of Canterbury and York and proudly noted how "Ecclesiastical government in Virginia" drew its "authority" from the archbishop of Canterbury, was concerned. It was "not well understood" by which authority the New Englanders "have sought for the government and tranquility of the Church." His "suspicions of factions in Religion" led to a lecture on the importance of religious unity. Drawing on his experience with the Ottoman Empire, Captain Smith emphasized that the "greatnesse of the Turks Empire" owed much to the fact that "Turkes are generally of one religion." Christians, on the other hand, are "in so many divisions and opinions, that they are among themselves worse enemies than the Turkes." Echoing the view of a number of other writers on this issue, Smith claimed that it was the divisions among Christians that allowed the Ottomans to expand at Europe's expense. New Englanders should "beware faction in that nature" and maintain "an orderly authority" under "the prime authority of the Church of England." After all, they could not "have any certaine releefe, nor long subsist without more supplies from England." It would be "lamentable in a . . .

Common-wealth . . . such as yours," he warned, to bring in "hypocrisie and corruption." Corrupt laws would undermine their colony. Making their conformity clear "would clearly take away all those idle and malicious rumours."[22]

By 1632, reports were reaching England that Massachusetts refused to use the liturgy of the Prayer Book, refused to accept all English Christians as members of their church, and openly endorsed Calvinist theology. In response to this news, a Commission for Regulating Plantations was established in 1633. Headed by William Laud, now the archbishop of Canterbury, it included Archbishop of York Richard Neile and other members of the Privy Council. In February 1634, the commission began policing emigration to New England. Complaining that "divers persons" known "to be ill affected, and discontented, aswell with the Civill as Ecclesiastical Government" were moving there "whereby such confusion and disorder is alreadie growne there, especially in poynt of Religion," it worried that they would lead to "the ruine of the said Plantation" and "the Scandall both of the Church and State here." It then ordered a fleet of ships sitting in the Thames ready to depart for New England, as well as two more ships in Ipswich, to halt until their masters could "enter into severall Bonds" to observe and enforce several articles. These included the severe punishment of anyone who "shall blaspheme or prophane the holly name of God," a promise that shipboard religious services be conducted according to the *Book of Common Prayer*, "and that they cause all persons aboard their said Shippes to be present at the same," and that only those who could prove they had taken "both the oaths of Allegiance and Supremacie" be allowed on their ships. Only then were they permitted to depart. In December the commission ordered all port officials to ensure that immigrants, especially those heading to New England, display letters from their parish certifying that they had taken the oath of allegiance and supremacy from their minister, who also had to certify that they were members of the church in good standing. These measures did not prevent puritans from making their way to New England, but they did cause some to take more roundabout routes.[23]

England's ruling elites understood New England posed a political as well as religious challenge. During a visit to Oxford University in August 1636, King Charles and Laud watched an antipuritan play whose main conclusion was that puritans should take their disorderly passions and go live in the "suburbs" or "new-England." A satirical ballad circulating in taverns urged those of "ye Purfidian sect / I meane ye counterfeit Elect" to "goe to New-England / To build new Babell strong & sure / now called a Church unspotted, pure." In 1638, Laud complained to Thomas Wentworth about the "universal running to New England, and god knows whither," sighing, "this it is, when men think nothing is their advantage, but to run from government."[24]

When Laud got a chance to punish a New Englander, he seized it. In 1635, Edward Winslow, one of the leading colonists of New Plymouth, returned to England to take care of important business for the colony. On behalf of the Council for New England, Sir Ferdinando Gorges used a complaint from Thomas Morton about the irregularities of religious life in the colonies to have Winslow brought before the Commission for Plantations. Laud grilled him about Plymouth's church matters and other reported anomalies, like civil marriage (a Dutch but not an English custom) and allowing church elders who were not ordained ministers to preach. Winslow was then imprisoned for several months at Laud's urging.[25]

If Massachusetts's enemies had had their way, the colony and its church system would have been suppressed. The same year that Laud prosecuted Winslow, the Privy Council issued a writ of *quo warranto* requiring the Massachusetts Bay Company to submit its charter for review and possible revocation. Sir Ferdinando Gorges had encouraged a group of the colony's critics to petition the Privy Council against the patent. If Massachusetts lost its royal privilege to govern itself, it would fall under the less sympathetic authority of Gorges's Council for New England. In May 1637, the Privy Council decided the *quo warranto* case against the Massachusetts Bay Company and its officers. They had to surrender its charter. However, since the charter was in New England, Sir Ferdinando Gorges had to go seize it. He ordered a large ship built to carry him and a number of supporters to Boston. Alas, it was so poorly constructed that it broke apart on launching. Gorges lacked the money to build a new one. Rumors circulated that Laud planned to send over a bishop with a military escort to impose conformity, but neither Laud nor the king could afford such an expedition. Nevertheless, Laud did successfully propose that overseas territories be placed under the oversight of the diocese of London and that a board of royal administrators, consisting of both of England's archbishops and nine privy councilors, be established to govern the colonies.[26]

Fortune had spared Massachusetts and its new church order for the moment, but Charles and Laud were beginning to build an imperial apparatus that could finally bring some order to the religious arrangements of the English overseas world. Laud first worked to gain control over the English churches in Holland then turned his attention to Bermuda. In

1633, Bermuda's governor, Captain Roger Wood, had tried to persuade a nonconformist minister to emigrate to the colony by claiming Bermuda's isolation meant ministers "may use thier discretion in god ordinances, for wee are growin soe poore that no Byshops will looke after us." Unlike New England, which was attracting so many wealthy men "that when they have well settled themselves they must be brought under the Archbishop of Canterburie and have a suffragan sent to reduce them into the fould of their old shepheards," Wood claimed that "noe great prelate will leave his Pontificall pallace to take his journey to live upon a barren rock" like Bermuda. However, when he remarked that the "king will not be quit of his subjects wheresoever they live under his lawes and obedience," Governor Wood spoke more truly than he realized. In 1637, Laud ordered Bermuda to fully conform. The *Book of Common Prayer* was to be used in all of its churches; ministers were to make the sign of the cross during baptism; parishioners were to receive the sacrament of communion in "the reverent posture of kneeling." In 1638, the Privy Council complained to the Bermuda Company that ministers "who are unconformable to the discipline and Ceremonyes of the Church here, have and doe frequently transport themselves unto the Sommer Islands and other his Majesties plantations abroad, where they take libertye to nourish and preserve theire factious and Schismaticall humors to the seducing and abuse of" the king's subjects "and the hindrance of that good conformitye and unitye in the Church" the king desired "throughout his Dominions." It ordered the company to only allow clergymen approved by the archbishop and the bishop of London to serve in the colony. Those already in Bermuda "without such approbation" were "to be remanded back hither." Two years later, Laud reiterated the demand after being informed "that a great part of" the Somers Isles Company, "the Governor and Council, and others in special, are non-conformists."[27]

Laud's informants were not wrong. Nonconformity had become the status quo on Bermuda with the encouragement of many of its directors, including the Earl of Warwick. A series of (mostly) nonconformist ministers had given the colony's church a distinctly Calvinist and non-Laudian flavor. Two of the longest serving ministers were Scots. Patrick Copland served for twenty-one years, George Stirk for fifteen. In conjunction with English nonconformists like Lewis Hughes, they created a church that did not use the *Book of Common Prayer* or the ceremonial gestures that offended puritans, such as making the sign of the cross while baptizing a child and kneeling to receive communion. Bermuda did not adopt Congregational standards of membership, but, being in regular contact with

Massachusetts, it was aware of its Congregational church order. Some Bermudans began contemplating a move in that direction, but for the time being the colony's dependence on its governing board in London limited their room for maneuver.[28]

Many of the puritan sympathizers involved with the Somers Isles Company, including prominent puritans like the Earl of Warwick and John Pym, were also members of the Providence Island Company, whose general court also remained in London. This bold endeavor took over a small island off the coast of Honduras in 1629. Originally, the plan was to populate the colony with the same sorts of people as were migrating to New England. Unfortunately, most godly emigrants preferred the comparative safety of Massachusetts to the fiercely contested Caribbean. Many of the colonists who did finally go to Providence Island were not puritans. Even those who were did not agree on church matters. Hope Sherrard, the colony's longest serving minister, had several confrontations with the governors over the godly standards he wanted in the church. Finally, in 1638, Sherrard set up a gathered congregation. He then persuaded the newly arrived minister, Nicholas Leverton, to abandon the *Book of Common Prayer* and join him. Conformist colonists were left without any church services. Outraged, they staged a political coup and deported both ministers, sending them home with complaints about their nonconformity. The sympathetic company directors sent Leverton back, but in the meantime the island had fallen to the Spanish: a reminder of the contingent nature of all the colonies' existence.[29]

The English footholds in the Leewards fared better than Providence Island. In the 1630s the English expanded from their base in Saint Christopher to claim nearby Nevis and Antigua. They also set up a small outpost on Santa Cruz (Saint Croix). Little is known about the religious life on these islands, but a few scraps of information allow us to make a rough sketch. Nevis evidently leaned toward Reformed Protestant sensibilities. From an early date, it contained a number of Scots who, while they conformed to the English church, seem to have encouraged a puritan-friendly environment. When the puritans on Saint Christopher were persecuted in the 1640s, Nevis was one of the places they fled to. In the 1650s, a Cromwellian official judged its governor, Luke Stokes, to be a "most sober, godley and discrete person."[30]

Around 1631, men from Nevis colonized Tortuga, a small island off the coast of Santo Domingo. They placed themselves under the protection of the Providence Island Company, which referred to it as Association Island. Importing the economic habits of the Leewards, they grew tobacco with enslaved labor. Virtually nothing else is known about the colony, never mind its religious life. Nevertheless, the associations with Nevis and the Providence Island Company suggest it likely had a puritan tinge. In any case, it did not last long. A mutiny by enslaved people disrupted the colony; then, in 1635 a Spanish attack drove off the English. Thereafter, Tortuga became notorious as a haven for pirates. Elsewhere in the Caribbean, Spanish and Indigenous resistance limited English expansion. In 1640–41 the Kalinago drove English colonists from the islands of Saint Lucia, Trinidad, and Marie-Galante and almost recaptured Antigua.[31]

Antigua struggled to survive but also may have leaned in a puritan direction. It attracted one of John Winthrop's puritan sons, Samuel Winthrop, who became a prominent planter. In the 1650s, its governor, Colonel Christopher Kaynell, petitioned the Cromwellian government for help in "peopling" the island. In particular, he requested "men and women servants . . . out of England, Scotland and Ireland" to defend it from the "Indians" and "the Spaniards." Cromwell's government agreed "that all convenient encouragement be given . . . to any of the Protestant Religion of what nation soever, that either are at present Inhabitants upon the said Island of Antigua or shall . . . desire to come and live under the English Government in the said Island."[32]

Puritans thus had a strong presence in the Caribbean, but it was constantly contested from without and within. Laudianism retained its hold on Saint Christopher and was gaining ground in Virginia. Around 1629, the Ferrar brothers, whose domestic piety was labeled "Arminian" by a critical puritan, began working with the new royal governor, Sir John Harvey, to move the colony's religion in their direction. One of the brothers, William Ferrar, even went to Virginia to help see the reforms through. Harvey is remembered for presiding over Virginia's economic recovery and expansion after years of devastating war and other disasters, but he also strove to strengthen the institution of the church. His official instructions ordered him to provide every congregation with a minister and ensure each minister had a parsonage to live in and a glebe to support him. To clear and enclose the glebe lands, every one of the "Parishoners for three years" was to be ordered to "give some daies labours, of themselves and theire servants." Admonished to "Suffer noe Innovation in matters of Religion," Harvey was ordered to "be carefull to appoynt sufficient and conformable Ministers, to each Congregation that may Catechise and instruct them, in the grounds and principles of Religion."[33]

Harvey also worked to bring Virginia's church in line with Laudian standards of conformity. Even before he went to the colony, Harvey called for "six grave and conformable ministers" to instruct colonists "in matters of their salvacon, and to yield due obedience to his Matie and his government." Once he and William Ferrar arrived, Harvey had the Virginia General Assembly pass a series of acts reinforcing this Laudian turn. First, in 1630, the assembly passed an act of uniformity for its clergy: "all ministers residing and beeing, or who hereafter shall reside and bee within this colony, shall conforme themselves in all thinges according to the cannons of the church of England." Anyone who "shall refuse for to conforme himselfe" would, after due notice, be censured. Two years later, another act extended this demand for conformity to all colonists, ordering "a uniformitie throughout this colony both in substance and circumstance to the cannons and constitution of the church of England as neere as may bee." Every colonists was to "yeald readie obedience unto them uppon penaltie of the paynes and forfeitures in that case appoynted." Further acts regulated ministerial salaries and ordered churches to be built and repaired. In 1632 the churchwardens of each parish were commanded to enforce attendance and combat vice. Religious holidays like Easter were to be respected (something puritans preferred not to do). Clerical authority was bolstered by protecting ministers from being criticized in any way "whereby the minds of his parishoners may be alienated from him and his mynistrie prove less effectuall." The penalty for such criticism was "payne of severe censure of the governor and councell." Meanwhile, ministers were enjoined to catechize the colonists according to the tenets "sett forth in the booke of common prayer." Finally, in the "remoate places" of large parishes, ministers were to appoint a deacon to read from the *Book of Common Prayer*. No puritan-style preaching would be permitted.[34]

Unfortunately, the absence of other records makes it impossible to determine how deeply these demands penetrated into the countryside. The better-documented southeastern portions of Virginia certainly managed to maintain their puritan ways into the 1640s. Virginia continued to attract puritans. John Lyford, the puritan minister expelled from Plymouth colony, served there until his death in 1629. In 1635 another puritan minister, John Haydon, offered, "voluntarily to leave this kingdom and go to Virginia" if he was released from jail. He had gotten in trouble with the Court of High Commission for continuing to preach "since his degradation" and otherwise flaunting the authority of the court.[35]

Finally, evidence from Newfoundland suggests its religious life was also being molded along Laudian lines. After Baltimore left Avalon, Sir David Kirke, former conqueror of Canada, moved into his manor house in Ferryland and, from 1638 to 1652, presided over a colony on the southern part of the Avalon Peninsula. Since no minister seems to have been stationed in Newfoundland in these years, Kirke likely supervised religious services with readings from the *Book of Common Prayer*. A few scraps of evidence suggest that he was more than amenable to Laudianism. In 1639, he wrote to Laud. Boasting about "our strict observance and use of the rites and service of the Church of England," he also joked that only Jesuits and Protestant Schismatics found the weather intolerable. Recently, an intriguing piece of archaeological evidence in the form of a gilded baroque cross has been found at Ferryland. Archaeologists interpret it as a Laudian rather than a Catholic symbol likely buried in 1652, when Kirke had to surrender his colony to a Cromwellian fleet.[36]

*

Looking back from the 1640s, Governor Bradford of Plymouth colony was impressed by what New England had accomplished. From "small beginnings greater things have been produced." By actively suppressing attempts to maintain religious conformity within or near their jurisdictions, he and other Reformed Protestants had secured their dominance over New England. Their allies also exercised local hegemony in the Caribbean, in colonies from Bermuda to Providence Island. Bradford gave the credit to God, who made New England like a "small candle" that could then "light a thousand." The "light here kindled hath shone . . . in some sort to our whole nation," he beamed. In other words, the Congregational church order was spreading around the English Atlantic. For Bradford, New England in the 1640s was not a refuge. It was a religious model for the English world.[37]

Before 1638, however, puritan New England's triumph was far from certain. One could not escape the clutches of William Laud simply by moving overseas. New Englanders were free from Laud's interference only for the moment. Laud and his allies had plans to bring them back into the conformity. Indeed Laud was the first archbishop of Canterbury to actively try and impose religious uniformity across the English world, and not without a number of local successes. Bermuda and New England were coming under the sort of pressure that was forcing the English churches in Holland to conform. Laud had a vision, royal support, and the will to implement what he believed to be the proper religious order for the English world. Laudianism was a centralizing force, but it also had local supporters in colonies from the Leeward Islands to Newfoundland

and was gaining ground in Virginia. Had Laud had his way, the religious and political history of the British Empire would have been very different. Unfortunately for Laud, he had to contend not only with puritans and other sectaries, but with King Charles as well. While puritans fled his attempts to impose his ideal of conformity, the king continued to allow loyal Catholics into the colonies.

NINE

Catholics: Montserrat, New Albion, Maryland, 1632–1638

Thanks to the great puritan migration, almost 60 percent of the English in America lived on the North American mainland in 1640. Of the roughly fifty-one thousand people from the British Isles and Ireland who lived in the Americas, about twenty thousand of them lived in closely built towns scattered along the coast from Maine to New Haven. Virginia's population, at roughly eight thousand, was just less than half that of New England, even though it was the oldest in English America. Maryland, by contrast, was small and compact. Almost all its roughly six hundred colonists lived within a short range of the capital of Saint Mary's, only about three times the more or less two hundred people living along Newfoundland's Avalon Peninsula. The remaining approximately 40 percent of colonists lived in the Caribbean: about ten thousand on Barbados, another ten thousand or so in the Leewards and other small islands, and about two thousand on Bermuda. Folded into this mix was a minority of English and Irish Catholics, who included several hundred of the Marylanders, and, at most, a couple of thousand of the Caribbean colonists.[1]

Most of this demographic strength had been accumulated over the previous decade, during the Personal Rule of Charles I. The logic behind the Personal Rule involved financial, political, and religious motives. Parliament, mistrusting royal policies at home as well as abroad, had refused to grant Charles the funds he demanded to fight his war. It also objected to his religious, political, and financial ambitions. Unable to manage Parliament, Charles dismissed it and relied on a mix of trusted advisors—mostly conservative aristocrats and obsequious churchmen like Laud. For puritans, this style of governing was an outrageous affront to their political and religious liberties. For Roman Catholics, however, the Personal Rule offered unprecedented access to royal favor and colonies, as the Calvert family and others discovered. In Ireland, moreover, Catholics continued to benefit from Charles's willingness to consider toleration in exchange for loyalty and financial support. These favorable conditions encouraged more Irish Catholics to look for opportunities overseas. Altogether, these factors led to the creation of a permanent English and Irish Catholic presence in the colonies, especially Maryland and the Leeward Islands. The majority of these colonial Catholics were Irish servants who provided labor for the Caribbean plantations. On Montserrat they formed the majority of the population. Nevertheless, in a colonial world that still professed conformity, no formal grant of toleration was ever made. Instead, everything depended on political connections at court and local enforcement (or lack thereof) in the colonies.[2]

Historians looking at Virginia, the one and only royal colony, or listening to the fears of New England's puritans, who were openly defying royal government in church and state, might think that the era of the Personal Rule was a time of centralization, that the court was attempting to take direct control of the colonies and royalize them. However, a broader perspective suggests Charles had no such plans. To assume direct control over the colonies would be expensive, to say the least. Instead, the king preferred to govern the colonies as he did Britain and Ireland, by delegating authority to individuals he trusted. Proprietary colonies like Lord Carlisle's Caribbee Islands or Lord Baltimore's Maryland reflected this priority. Virginia was an awkward exception; New England, a defiant anomaly. The king's willingness to delegate authority to trusted individuals explains why his regime favored a number of Roman Catholic colonial ventures in the 1630s. Catholics were trustworthy. They were also ambitious for the sorts of political and economic opportunities that were denied them at home. Although most of their colonial endeavors did not bear fruit, closer attention to them illuminates the unusual religious politics of this decade of colonial history. The Personal Rule was more a time of individual privileges than royalization or centralization. Under the shelter of individual proprietors, loyal Catholics gained a foothold in English America.

*

While John Winthrop was moving to America, an Old Irish soldier, aristocrat, and convert to Protestantism was drawing up his own plans for a colony. Sir Pierce Crosby was unusual in a number of ways. Very few

Old Irish were Protestant. Even then, they tended to be consigned to the margins of British society. However, Crosby had good family connections at court that helped him to pass for Old English. Rendered thus socially acceptable, he had been able to marry a wealthy Old English widow and to secure the patronage of the Duke of Buckingham, who allowed Crosby to raise a regiment for service in the war against France. Crosby's regiment was unusual by British standards as it was composed of Irishmen—not all of them Protestant. Moreover, it fought well. During the otherwise disastrous 1627 English expedition against the Île de Rhé, Crosby's troops ably protected the hasty retreat of their English comrades, salvaging some dignity out of an otherwise humiliating defeat. Upon returning home, Crosby's regiment was stationed in Ireland.[3]

The approaching peace threatened to disband Crosby's beloved regiment. More than just an act of patriotism, raising a regiment was an investment that could pay handsomely. Regimental commanders controlled the distribution of the funds that paid their soldiers. They also enjoyed the patronage of appointing the officers needed to staff the regiment. Military commissions were economic opportunities that were not easily acquired or relinquished. In 1630, in a bid to preserve his regiment, Crosby submitted a proposal offering to colonize "a rich and fruitful part of America, not inhabited by any Christians." Like all other colonial proposals, Crosby insisted his colony would support "the propagation of religion" as well as "the inlarging of his Maties dominions and increase of trade." Asking for the same "liberties and privileges as have been formerly granted to others in like cases" as well as "a good proportion of land," Crosby then revealed the unusual part of his proposal: his colonists would be his regiment. It is a terse, soldierly petition, concluding with the brief note that it "is to be observed that the main part of the officers and many of the souldiers are protestants." The rest, of course, were Catholics. Nevertheless, the Scottish courtier-poet Sir William Alexander was willing to let them settle in Nova Scotia and made Crosby a Nova Scotian baronet. What would American history have been like if an Irish military colony had been founded in Nova Scotia at the same time as puritans were fleeing to Massachusetts? Fortunately for America's puritans, King Charles aborted this ecumenical experiment when he returned Nova Scotia to France in 1631. Crosby then tried to place his Irish troops in the service of the Swedish king Gustavus Adolphus, but that militantly Protestant monarch refused to hire Catholic soldiers, so Crosby again looked to America. In 1632 he petitioned for a West Indies colony. King Charles granted his request, but by then Crosby had turned to a new line of work: recruiting

Irish troops for French service. Instead of moving to America, he became increasingly involved with Irish politics. When Ireland's Catholics rose in revolt in 1641, he joined them, and, shortly before his death in 1646, converted to Catholicism.[4]

Sir Pierce Crosby and his Irish regiment never made it to America, but the very fact that they received royal permission to set up a colony there says volumes about the peculiar religious and political atmosphere of the Personal Rule. It highlights not only what was possible—Irishmen, including Catholic soldiers, colonizing America on their own terms—but also what, in the eyes of puritans, was going wrong. Within Ireland, the drawn-out negotiations over "the Graces" chafed Protestants. Forced to refrain from using the law to suppress Roman Catholic worship, they had to practice an unaccustomed tolerance. The man in charge of restraining Ireland's Protestants, Lord Deputy Henry Cary, Viscount Falkland, was a loyal servant of the king. Previously known for promoting the plantation of Ireland and persecuting Irish Catholic priests (and not only because his wife, to his chagrin, had recently converted to Catholicism), Falkland complained in 1628 that the "universal toleration of religion" implied by this religious détente was "dangerous, and ought to be interrupted." He advised a more selective approach, to "banish some Papists and regulate others so that the loyal Papists may have full liberty, yet with absolute security and safety to the State."[5]

Cary was knowingly appealing to Charles's priorities. Other Irish Protestants were less circumspect. In 1633, Sir Vincent Gookin, one of the wealthiest men in Munster and a relative of the Gookin colonists in Virginia, circulated a memorandum to the lord deputy arguing that Catholics were only demanding liberty of conscience and a greater role in government so that they could "get good laws repealed," namely, the laws upholding Protestant supremacy. Mistrusting everything about his Catholic neighbors, Sir Vincent believed that "were it not for the sword of justice by which we are governed we had better lived in the Indies than here for safety." Sir Vincent's naked display of contempt for his neighbors caused a scandal that forced him to flee to England for safety, where he died several years later.[6]

Irish Protestant fears about Irish Catholics' growing confidence were not unfounded. Thanks to the Graces, Ireland's Catholic Church was having a heyday. Freed from persecution, the Catholic hierarchy was returning to places that had not seen Catholic bishops since the 1580s. Increasing numbers of priests, many of them members of one of the religious orders (especially Franciscans, Jesuits, and Cistercians) circulated through the country. Inspired by the reformed Catholicism of the Council of Trent, these continentally educated men led a religious revival that attached Irish Catholics to Counter-Reformation Catholicism. For the first time in the country's history, the ancient sense of ethnic and political differences that had divided Gaels, English, and Scots began to fade in the face of a common religious experience. As Sir Vincent Gookin expressed it, the Old English "hate and scorn the name, but will be Irish, and never so much as at this time."[7]

Ireland's Catholic revival varied by province and even by town. As ever, local religious life depended a great deal on elites. Ulster had few Irish Catholic landlords. With its Catholic population too poor and scattered to support a steady supply of priests, they relied on itinerants willing and able to work for meager reward and uncertain protection from the Protestant authorities. Where the influx of Protestants was heaviest, like eastern Ulster, it was virtually impossible to maintain any sort of Catholic presence. However, in the west, where Connacht's population remained overwhelmingly Catholic and Gaelic, Catholicism was remarkably visible. The situation in Munster was more mixed, as English Protestants regained the predominance they had lost during the Nine Years War. Still, even in Dublin a Jesuit church and school could operate in a back lane, as the future puritan revolutionary Sir William Brereton noticed in the 1630s. Traveling down to Wexford, Brereton watched Catholic women walk through the town on a court day, each with "a crucifix, tied in a black necklace, hanging betwixt their breasts." He was astonished that Wexford's Catholics "are not ashamed of their religion, nor desire to conceal themselves." On Sunday, he watched the town's mayor and sheriff walk the Protestant judges to the town's church. They then "left them there, and went to mass, which is here tolerated, and publicly resorted unto in two or three houses in this town." Wexford had "many papists" but "very few Protestants, as appeared by that slender congregation at church where the judges were."[8]

Alas, the negotiations over "the Graces" came to a disappointing climax for Irish Catholics. In 1634, the new lord deputy, Sir Thomas Wentworth, agreed to grant all but two of the Graces. Unfortunately, those two were the crucial ones. Worse, Wentworth refused to guarantee the land rights of Catholic owners in Connacht. Irish Catholics had more reason to feel betrayed than they realized: Wentworth was not only secretly planning a Protestant plantation in Connacht, but also hoping to get the Catholics to conform to the Protestant church. Like Laud, he believed the Laudian style of piety was likely to draw them in, and so he encouraged its adoption within the Church of Ireland.[9]

Notwithstanding the disappointing conclusion to the Graces, conditions remained comparatively benign for Irish Catholics, encouraging some to become increasingly involved in colonial projects. A few had been involved with Guiana. Now, with the help of Anthony Hilton, an enterprising merchant from the religiously conservative bishopric of Durham, they began to get involved in the Caribbean. Hilton had visited Saint Christopher while en route to trade for tobacco in Virginia. Stopping off in Ireland on his way back, he persuaded some Irish merchants that the Caribbean would be "a better place then Virginia" for growing "tobaccoes." They then supplied him "with men & all things necessary" to begin a plantation on Saint Christopher. When the Kalinago destroyed the plantation, Hilton got additional backing from English merchants and a commission from the Earl of Carlisle to colonize a new island in 1628. Rejecting Antigua and Montserrat, he chose Nevis. The following year a Spanish expedition destroyed the plantation: his Irish servants ran over to the Spanish, crying "out 'Liberty, joyfull Liberty.'" However, the Spanish failed to permanently drive out the Irish and English. Survivors from the Guiana colony rejuvenated the plantations on Nevis and Saint Christopher with the help of Irish and English merchants. Ever after, Ireland would remain an important source of trade and labor for the Leewards, sustaining an Irish community that was both Protestant and Catholic.[10]

In the early 1630s, Irish Catholics from Saint Christopher also colonized Montserrat. Soon they made up the majority of the island's free, European population—and would continue to do so into the eighteenth century. Montserrat, like the other Leeward Islands, officially conformed to the Church of England, but their demographic preponderance gave Irish Catholics a certain influence. It helped that they tended to be governed by Protestants who came from the same parts of Ireland as they did. Montserrat's first governor was the New English Protestant Captain Anthony Briskett. In 1636, Briskett reported that he was "erecting a Church of Stone and Brick, for the glory of God, and your Majesties honor." However, it was years before a Protestant minister arrived. When Briskett died in 1649, his brother-in-law Colonel Robert (Roger) Osborne, also an Irish New English Protestant, succeeded him. Osborne had a brother serving as a minister in Cornwall, but that did not stop him from treating the Catholic majority with a certain indulgence. Montserrat's religious life resembled that of Ireland's, where religious conformity was the law but

Catholics sustained their faith with the help of sporadic, clandestine visits from traveling missionaries who knew "they would not permit a priest on that Island." One Irish Jesuit arrived in 1650, disguised as a merchant. Claiming to be collecting wood in a forest, he held services and secretly bestowed the sacraments for a few weeks. Others followed. If they kept a discreet profile, they seem to have been left alone. Protestants gossiped, but by remaining in the private realm, Catholicism managed to survive into the nineteenth century without any formal toleration.[11]

Some Irish Catholics, perturbed by the limits imposed on them by the Protestant English world, began taking their entrepreneurial ambitions to other countries. A few took the bold step of negotiating with Spain for a colony in the Guiana region. Between 1630 and 1632, "Gaspar Chillan" (probably Jaspar Sheehan) argued such a colony could prevent Guiana from being overrun by the Dutch and "other nations" to "the great damage" of "the Holy Catholic faith." Sheehan would send over a group of Irish, "all Catholics," to drive out the Protestants in the name of the Spanish king. Then they would remain to protect Guiana from further incursions. His prospective colonists included five Irish survivors of the Guiana colony established by Sir Thomas Roe. They had learned the Indigenous language and customs and could ensure a profitable trade. Unfortunately, Ireland's peculiar situation meant it could not be a purely Irish colony. They would need some English or Dutch experts with special knowledge of navigation, war, and construction. Sheehan promised that only a handful of such experts would be allowed in but, as a vassal of the king of England, he would have to also get permission from King Charles to ensure no one else interfered with the colony. He tried to sweeten the deal by promising the Spanish it would cost them nothing. His brother would secure financing from Ireland. The plan intrigued Spanish authorities, including King Philip IV. However, his Council of State opined that there were too many "inconveniences" involved. Sheehan was an English subject. English Catholics and "heretics" would likely "mix" with the Irish and possibly betray the colony to the king of England. The proposal was rejected. In another case from 1635, a report reached the English government that William Gayner, "a Romish Catholique," was working "with others of that religion . . . to raise unto themselves a plantation" in Guiana under Dutch protection that would be "exempte from ye English government." Pointing out that it would infringe on the English claims to the area, the government ordered Gayner to desist. Apparently he did.[12]

Clearly, Ireland had the potential to become an active participant in American colonization. Some of King Charles's subjects thought that it could provide a useful check on a budding empire full of puritans. In 1632, Lord Deputy Wentworth granted a colonial charter to Sir Edmund Plowden. This English Catholic landowner and lawyer proclaimed that his mission was to "conquer on Indians, and convert Pagans, and civilize them, and bring them to the obedience of our Soveraign." Sir Thomas Wentworth's grant used a rare invocation of the Kingdom of Ireland's royal powers to expressly declare that Plowden's colony existed "without appeale or subiection to the Governour or Company of Virginia." Wentworth seems to have thought it could pioneer a way for Ireland to help King Charles govern his kingdoms without relying on England's Parliament. An Irish-centered colony could help build up Ireland's economy and provide an outlet for ambitious Old English loyalists. New Albion had tremendous potential, as it laid claim to the entire mid-Atlantic region of North America between the Hudson and the Delaware River Valleys. As with Avalon, Plowden never claimed it to be a Catholic colony, but its name patriotically recalled Britain's ancient Catholic past. Plowden's religious affinity is further apparent in some of the other names he chose for his colony. For example, he proposed renaming the island of Manhattan "Syon," after the wealthy and famous Bridgettine abbey that had existed just west of London before the Reformation.[13]

Nevertheless, it was unusual for the Kingdom of Ireland to grant a colonial charter, especially to an English Catholic who had no particular connections to the place. Plowden evidently chose this path because he lacked George Calvert's exalted connections at court. Instead, Plowden's connections led him to Wentworth. The most likely link was Toby Matthew, who was serving a brief stint as Wentworth's secretary at the time Plowden received the New Albion patent. Son of an archbishop of York and a noted Catholic convert, Matthew was a friend of George Calvert's from their days at Oxford. Within the English Catholic community, a further bond united the Calverts, Plowdens, and Matthew: all favored the Jesuit mission to England over that of the archpriest. After converting in 1607 while traveling in Italy, Toby Matthew had become a priest, writer, and translator of Catholic devotional works. While his refusal to take the oath of supremacy kept him in exile for much of his life, his Catholic connections occasionally made him useful to the Crown. He worked with Calvert on the Spanish Match negotiations. King James knighted him for those services in 1623. That honor enabled Matthew to stay in England until 1641, when hostile Protestants forced him to seek safety in exile again. In the meantime, Matthew appointed Plowden's father, a lawyer, one of the executors to his will. He named Sir Edmund as a substitute executor.

Plowden could have made his colonial dreams known to Matthew, who then raised the possibility with Wentworth.[14]

Like Avalon and Maryland, New Albion was more a dynastic enterprise than a religious refuge. Plowden reveled in the palatine rights that came with his colonial charter and proudly clung to the title "Earl of Albion" until his death. He apparently had been made an Irish earl as well. Clearly, he aspired to transform his family from wealthy but beleaguered (because of their religion) gentry into people who could almost look a peer of the realm in the eye. A 1648 pamphlet promoting his colony says nothing about his Roman Catholicism, nor does it make any special appeal to Roman Catholics, but it does talk a good deal about his "ancient family" whose distinguished ancestry stretched back twelve hundred years to "the Saxons in England." It also goes on at length about the special role of earls and counts palatine in English history, boasting that, unlike the Lord Baltimore, Plowden had "a special creation of an Earle Palatine." He used his privilege to bestow numbingly dull royalist titles on his family: the "Baron of Mount Royall," the "Baron of Roymont," the "Baronesse of Princeport." He also boldly renamed Long Island "Plowden Island." The pamphlet praised Plowden as a man "in whom Pietie, Religion, Honor, Justice, Learning, Valor, Judgement, Temperance, and Policie shines." It suggested that with his palatine powers he would create courts that were "fit to compose differences, reconcile debates, to unite hearts, to settle the factious and seditious in any other English colonies or Countries."[15]

Alas for Plowden, an unusual combination of difficulties at home and in America undercut his beloved colony from the beginning. Unlike Calvert or Matthew, Plowden had been a recusant his whole life. Consequently, he lacked their education, opportunities, and connections. Securing a charter through the Crown of Ireland was an intriguing use of that country's sovereign powers, but it came with distinct limitations. New Albion's legal foundation was dubious. Plowden could not recruit colonists in England. Then family troubles and political opposition, especially from members of the government connected to the Virginia Company, delayed his departure by almost a decade. When he and a party of relatives and indentured servants finally arrived on the Delaware River in 1641, they found the Swedes had gotten there first. When Plowden's small company attempted to build a fort, agents of New Sweden arrested them. Eventually, the Swedish governor let Plowden move to Virginia, where he waited in vain for reinforcements until 1648. With none forthcoming, he returned to England to make one last attempt. His hopes were gutted when, soon after his return, the king was executed, the monarchy abolished, and Ireland invaded and conquered. For the next century and a half, New Albion's fragile claim to American territory lingered, but Plowden's descendants entered American history as inhabitants of other people's colonies, not his own.[16]

New Albion's failure is a useful reminder that flexibility on religious and even political matters was no guarantee of colonial success. Plowden's promotional pamphlet from 1641 gave no indication of New Albion's Catholic links. It simply mentioned that, "my Lord of Baltamore will be glad of Sir Edmunds Plantation and assistance against any enemy or bad neighbour." Readers might infer that a shared Catholicism could be a source of solidarity, but when Plowden got in trouble he sought refuge in Virginia and befriended the group of Protestant Virginia colonists, led by William Claiborne, who opposed Baltimore's claim to Maryland. Plowden was politically adaptable. Notwithstanding his love of his palatine powers, in 1648 the revolutionary atmosphere of England prompted him to endorse religious tolerance and guarantee that a "Parliament or Grand Assembly" would make the colony's laws. Since the colonists could not follow the current religious example of England, where religion was "yet unsettled," he proposed that New Albion's "Parliament" would pass an act "to settle and establish all the Fundamentals necessary to salvation, as the three Creeds, the Ten Commandements, Preaching on the Lords day, and great days, and Catechising in the afternoon, the Sacrament of the Altar and Baptisme." Once basic Christian beliefs and practice were legislated, there would be "no persecution to any dissenting." Instead, dissenters would be allowed to have "free Chapels." The religious establishment would not rely on coercion, but instead use "argument or perswasion . . . acted in mildenesse, love and charity, and gentle language, not to disturb the peace or quiet of the inhabitants." As long as they obeyed "the Civill Magistrate," Christian dissenters could live in peace. Only "seditious" people who would "bitterly rail and condemn others" would be prosecuted. Plowden did, like any good Catholic, worry that the "severall Translations of Bibles" could be "expounded to each mans fancy" and thereby breed "new Sects." That sort of religious pluralism was not welcome.[17]

It was an extraordinary offer of religious tolerance. Yet no one took it up. Instead, Maryland remained English North America's only Catholic-owned colony. Neither Baltimore nor King Charles ever described Maryland as a Catholic colony or refuge, however. Charles insisted he had made the grant for pragmatic reasons: "there being land enough for the entertainment of many thousands, and the work more easily overcome by multitudes of hands and assistance." In reality, the Calverts benefited because they were well connected and demonstrably loyal. Cecil Calvert had been named in honor of his father's patron, Robert Cecil, the councilor to both Queen Elizabeth and King James. As long as Charles was alive, Cecil benefited greatly from royal privilege. Charles was aware that he had created a special jurisdiction in Maryland—one of several he had granted to his friends and allies. In 1638 he ordered his Privy Council to draft a new charter for the Virginia Company that would explicitly protect the rights and privileges of the neighboring "Province of Carolana" and "Province of Maryland." Charles made it clear he wanted to prevent "any future question or preiudice to" those colonies' proprietors and to preserve and confirm "theire said severall Interests and Jurisdictions and other rights."[18]

It was Virginia Protestants who insisted that Maryland was a Catholic colony—and should therefore be abolished, as it claimed territory they believed was theirs. The Virginians argued that letting Catholics immigrate to Maryland would end hopes of ever getting them to conform. Worse, the immigrants would subvert England's penal laws by taking their wealth out of England and over to Maryland. Finally, Maryland's Catholics could pose a security threat. If they declared independence and turned their province over to the Spanish, Maryland could become a base for conquering New England and Virginia. Lord Baltimore responded that America was too poor, the distances too large, and English Catholics far too outnumbered by Protestants for any of this to be possible, never mind logically desirable. After all, if English Catholics had religious liberty under the English Crown, why would they turn to a foreign prince? They needed the Crown's protection from foreigners—and hostile Englishmen. The Privy Council agreed and dismissed the Virginians' objections. Once again, the Calverts benefited from royal support.[19]

The need to defend against the legal and political threats to Maryland's charter prevented Cecil Calvert from following his father's example as an active colonial leader. Staying in England to defend his proprietorial rights, he sent out his younger brother Leonard Calvert, also a Catholic, to serve as governor in his stead. Leonard had some colonial experience, having lived in Avalon in 1628–29, and proved a capable governor. Baltimore also had another reason to stay behind: to shore up his position within England's divided Catholic community. The Archpriest, or Appellant, Controversy had recently flared up, pitting the seminary priests against the missionary orders like the Jesuits. In 1624, during the marriage and alliance negotiations with France, the pope had appointed a Catholic bishop (or "archpriest") at the urging of King Louis XIII. The archpriest's efforts to assert control over not just all of England's Catholic priests, including Jesuits and other religious orders, but also personal aspects of lay Catholic life like marriage and the probate of wills caused a scandal among Protestants as well as Catholics. Headed by George Calvert, many English Catholics came down on the side of the Jesuits and other missionaries. They were more willing to accommodate themselves to the constraints of Protestant England—especially on the question of the loyalty oath—than the seminary priests supporting the archpriest. These regular priests were also more deferential to the Catholic gentry. Flustered by this resistance, the archpriest fled into exile in France in 1631, but tensions persisted.[20]

For Maryland, Baltimore's experience of the Archpriest Controversy had two important consequences. First, he determined to rely on the Jesuits to supply it with priests. Second, he crafted a special loyalty oath for Maryland. The oath modified the official oath by pledging loyalty without rejecting the pope's power to depose monarchs. Some (but not all) Catholics would be able to swear it. Those who did would be able to slip across the sea to Maryland without having to swear the oath of supremacy.

The first band of Maryland colonists was religiously mixed, but not equally so. The elite was predominantly Catholic. Several were rather wealthy. Most were younger sons of gentry families, like Leonard Calvert, who had few opportunities in England. The Protestants were mostly their servants. To facilitate coexistence between the colony's Catholics and Protestants, Baltimore favored a policy that downplayed religious difference and controversy. The requirement to support the Church of England was never repudiated. Roman Catholicism was never formally tolerated. Instead, Baltimore preferred to avoid ostentatious endorsements of Catholicism. Already before his colonists left for America, he gave the Catholics instructions on how to behave, ordering them to restrain themselves, to "be very carefull to preserve unity and peace amongst all the passengers" on the voyage and "suffer no scandall nor offence to be given any of the Protestants, whereby any just complaint may heereafter be made, by them, in Virginea or in England." Catholics had "to be silent upon all occasions of discourse concerning matters of Religion" and treat Protestants with "as much mildness and favor as Justice will permit." As for their religion, it was to be practiced "as privately as may be."[21]

Nevertheless, some of the Catholic colonists favored a more explicitly Catholic vision of Maryland, as a manuscript account of the first voyage to the colony reveals. Written by Andrew White, one of Maryland's first Jesuit missionaries, it was very conscious of English Protestant

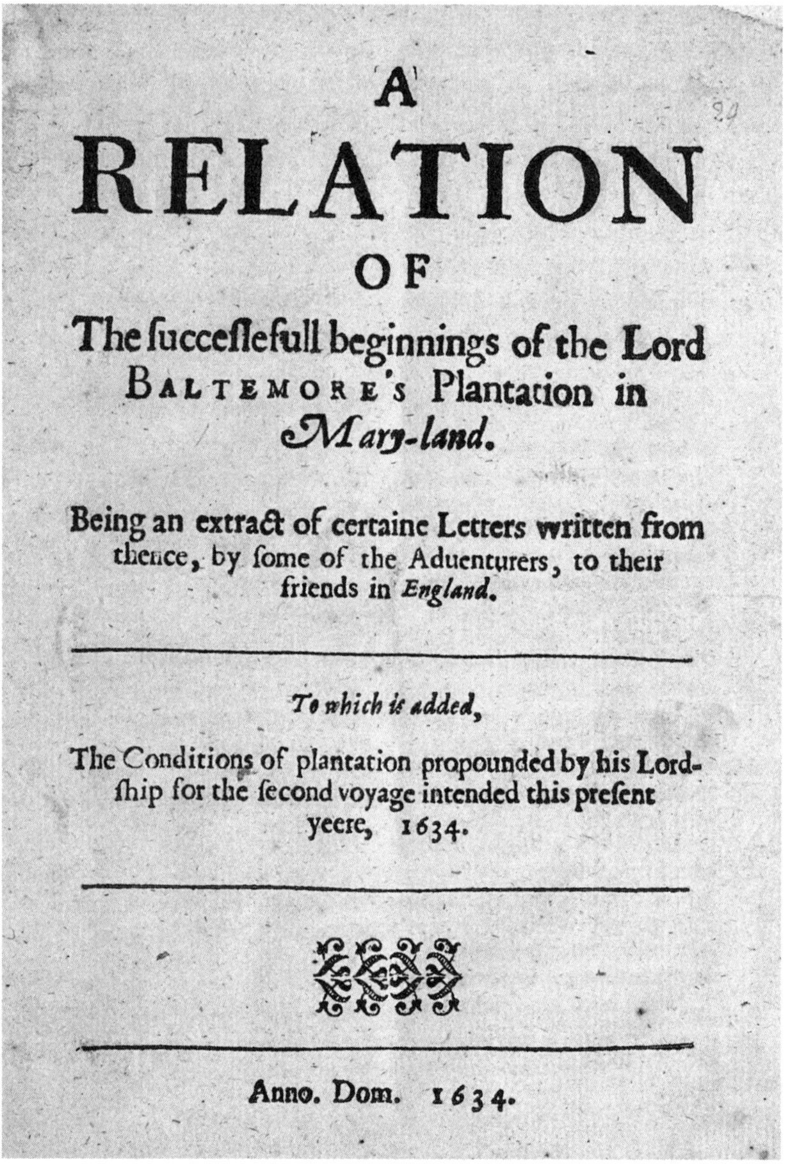

A
RELATION
OF
The ſucceſſefull beginnings of the Lord BALTEMORE'S Plantation in *Mary-land.*

Being an extract of certaine Letters written from thence, by ſome of the Aduenturers, to their friends in *England.*

To which is added,

The Conditions of plantation propounded by his Lordſhip for the ſecond voyage intended this preſent yeere, 1634.

Anno. Dom. 1634.

FIGURE 9. Andrew White, *A Relation of the successfull beginnings of the Lord Baltemore's Plantation in Mary-land* (London, 1634), courtesy of the John Carter Brown Library

hostility to the colony. Their departure was actually delayed by rumors that not everyone had taken the oath. Even the sailors tried to stall, saying "that they expected a messenger from London with letters" to prevent the Catholics from emigrating. Fortunately, White reports, "God interrupted their wicked designs, for the same night a favorable, but strong wind" sent them out to sea. They were then tested by a series of storms at sea, prompting White to place "the principal parts of the ship under the protection of God, the most holy Mother, St. Ignatius, and all the other guardian angels of Maryland." He was pleased by the strong spiritual response of the storm-tossed "catholics," which included prayers and "vows in honor of the most blessed virgin Mother, and her immaculate conception, of St. Ignatius, the patron of Maryland, St. Michael, and all the tutelary angels of the place." At one point, White, fearing "the loss of the ship and of my life . . . declared to the divine Christ, the most blessed Virgin, St. Ignatius, and the angels of Maryland, the purpose of this voyage, to honor the blood of the Redeemer in the salvation of barbarians, and to erect to the same Saviour a kingdom." However, it was only after he promised "that I would consecrate another gift to the immaculate Virgin Mother, and many similar things," that the storm abated. The rest of the voyage was smooth and safe.[22]

Maryland's religious purpose was clear to all, as the mixed reception the Jesuits encountered upon arriving in America suggests. The Leeward Islands were remarkably friendly. They spent a day on Montserrat, which they found "inhabited by Irishmen who have been expelled by the English of Virginia, on account of their profession of the catholic faith." This story was likely a garbled account of the Irish leaving Saint Christopher, but perhaps some Irish who had been to Virginia were also there. The Marylanders then spent ten days on Saint Christopher after being "invited to do so in a friendly way by the English Governor [Captain Thomas Warner] and two catholic captains." They also met the "Governor of the French colony, in the same island," who treated Andrew White "with the most especial kindness."[23]

One of the Catholic captains on Saint Christopher was probably Sir Henry Colt, a Catholic gentleman who had previously fought in Spanish service. Colt had sailed to Saint Christopher with a well-supplied ship in the spring of 1631. To help instruct his son, who was to follow him, Colt wrote an account of his journey that liberally mixes the practical with the pious, offering a rare glimpse of the mentality of a lay English Catholic colonizer. He carefully described the preparations for the voyage, including the "ordringe of our ship towards ye service of God from whose divine power & providence, we must expect all our secruitye & happinesse in this voyage." Colt's decidedly nonpuritan religious inclinations are evident in his response to a "work of God" that struck his ship after it docked in Saint Christopher. A number of his sailors were working in the rigging when a bolt of lightning hit the main mast, killing several of them instantly. Rather than read this as a message of God's providence, Colt submitted himself to God's will: "what is strange or new to this great God above to whose will & power we must obey & submit ourselves, & not pry or search to neer into ye secrets of his decrees & ordinances, for who is he yt cann finde them out?" Colt's piety is evident throughout the account, from his criticism of Barbadians' drinking habits to his regular thanks and prayers to God. His Catholicism is most explicit when discussing international affairs. Where puritans hated Spain and supported the Dutch Revolt, Colt admired the Spanish and mistrusted the Dutch. After almost being attacked by a Spanish ship, Colt mused that if the king of Spain would only demonstrate "his goodnessse towards us," he would "allwayes be readye to pray to ye Almighty god, for ye long prosperitye & happinesse of his Catholic maiestye." After all, "we" were also "Catholicks." The Protestant Dutch, on the other hand, annoyed him with their "blinde zeale & vayne superstition, doubtlesse moor then ever was commanded or observed by ye Jewes." This anti-Semitic jab reflects Colt's contempt for Dutch capitalism, which he portrayed as "a religion" that "was never read nor heard of amongst Christians untell this present time." Nevertheless, he professed a willingness to tolerate them, to "leave them to ther opinion, bycause I know itt nott." This attitude no doubt helped him fit in to the officially Protestant climate of Saint Christopher.[24]

When the migrating Marylanders left the Caribbean for the Chesapeake, they encountered much hostility in Virginia. The found the inhabitants were "under arms" in response to a rumor that "six ships were approaching, which would reduce all things under the power of the Spanish." Fortunately, the Marylanders found that letters "which we brought from the King and the Chancellor of the Exchequer to the Governor" offered sufficient protection. Once again, royal patronage protected Cecil Calvert's enterprise. Governor Harvey helped the Marylanders with supplies because, as the Jesuit noted, Harvey wanted to retain King Charles's favor. He also "hoped" that "by this kindness to us," he would be able "to recover the more easily from the royal treasury a great amount of money due to him."[25]

With Harvey's help, the Marylanders arrived safely in the territory that would become their colony in February 1634. Leonard Calvert chose a high spot on the Potomac River just across from northern Virginia as the site for the colony's capital. Its name, Saint Mary's, had conformist as well as Catholic connotations. The colonists went on to fill Maryland's landscape with other such saints' names (Saint Gregory, Saint Michael, Saint Clement, Saint Catherine, Saint Cecilia). Then, on "the day of the annunciation of the Holy Virgin Mary, on the 25th of March, in the year 1634," Andrew White performed "for the first time, the sacrifice of the mass: in this region of the world it had never been celebrated before." After the mass, they took "up on our shoulders the great cross which we had hewn from a tree, and going in procession to the place that had been designated," Leonard Calvert, together with the "commissioners, and other catholics" (but not the Protestant colonists) participated in a "ceremony." They "erected" the cross "as a trophy to Christ the Saviour, while the litany of the holy cross was chaunted humbly on our bended knees, with great emotion of soul." Soon thereafter, the Jesuits established relations with their indigenous neighbors and began their mission to convert them to Catholicism.[26]

A long historical tradition dating back to the era of the American Revolution traces the beginnings of American religious freedom to Maryland. The distinction between the Catholic religion of some colonists and their priests and the official Protestant religion of the English world looks, in hindsight, like the first effective separation between public and private worship. It was an awkward and improvised arrangement. Maryland's rulers exercised their obligations toward the Church of England largely in the negative. While no official action was ever taken against Protestantism, little was done to encourage it either. George Calvert had supported a Protestant ministry in Avalon, but his son did not in Maryland. Nor did he build churches. While the Jesuits took care of the Catholics, Protestant religious practice was largely left to the discretion of private individuals. Since they were generally poor servants, they made do with readings from the *Book of Common Prayer* and other texts. Occasionally, a minister visited them from Virginia.

Lord Baltimore did make at least a superficial effort to fulfill his religious duties as colonial proprietor. At his urging, the colony's assembly set land aside for the church and agreed, in its first comprehensive set of laws (the Ordinance of 1639), that the church should enjoy its traditional liberties. However, the assembly never specified exactly which church it had in mind or what those liberties were. The hint that this support for "the church" could apply to the Roman Catholic Church has been a matter of inference and dispute ever since. The assembly also affirmed that all

Christian colonists enjoyed English liberties without the discriminatory sanctions that existed in England. In other words, the penal laws levied against Catholics did not apply in Maryland.[27]

Few colonists embraced Lord Baltimore's vision of religious coexistence. In practice, Maryland's tolerance amounted to the socially and politically dominant Catholics restraining themselves in the face of the false religion of their inferiors. It did not always work. In the cramped quarters of the colony, some Catholics could not help but provoke confrontations with their Protestant neighbors. When religious conflicts erupted, Baltimore's government sided with the Protestants. No Protestants were convicted for upsetting Catholics. Several Catholics were punished for provoking Protestants. The first recorded instance involved William Lewis, overseer of a Jesuit-owned plantation. In 1638, his Protestant servants drew up a petition to the governor of Virginia, complaining that Lewis would not let them have any Protestant books in the house they shared with him. One can understand why. When they had good Protestant literature—like a book of sermons by the Elizabethan puritan Henry Smith—they read from it very loudly in Lewis's presence. Nettled, Lewis told them their "Ministers are the Ministers of the divell." For his pains, he was convicted for disturbing the peace. The servants were permitted to continue reading aloud from their Protestant books. In a second incident from 1642, a Catholic was convicted for taking Protestant books out of the colony's chapel then locking the door so that Protestants could not use it for their religious services. In both cases these devout Catholics were following the dictates of Catholic priests urging them to preserve their sacred spaces from contamination by heretics. Lord Baltimore's agents forced them to forgo this clerical imperative.[28]

Lord Baltimore did not interfere with the Jesuits' evangelical agenda, however. Although the Jesuits came to America to convert Native Americans, their mission soon included their Protestant neighbors as well. Indeed, English Protestants were their first converts. With both groups, Jesuits focused on vulnerable, poor, and sick individuals. In 1638, for example, after noting their inability to make any headway with their Indigenous neighbors, the Jesuits reported how in "the interim," they were "more earnestly intent on the English, and since there are protestants as well as catholics in the colony, we have labored with both, and God has blessed our labors." They claimed to have converted "almost all" of "the protestants who came from England this year . . . besides many others." Those other converts included "four servants" from Virginia "that we bought for necessary use," and two "of five workmen whom we hired for a month." One of those workmen had "not long after, departed this life, being well prepared by the sacraments for dying." One Jesuit confounded the zealous opposition of a Protestant colonist and managed to convert another who was "zealous in the religion of the protestants" while curing him from a snakebite. In 1639, twelve "heretics" gave up their "former errors" and "returned to favor with God and the church." More conversions followed. The Jesuits also worked to preserve Maryland's Catholic community, to the point of redeeming "two catholics who had sold themselves into servitude in Virginia." To all appearances, Maryland was a net gain for English Catholics: there were no reports of Catholics apostatizing. Still, it was a rather small increase. By 1640 Maryland's few hundred inhabitants barely amounted to twice the size of the Plymouth colony.[29]

In the meantime, anti-Catholicism did not abate among Maryland's neighbors. Governor Harvey's aide to the first colonists had contributed to a developing political crisis that weakened his government. His irascible efforts to subject Virginians to royal policy had already alienated most of the colony's political elite. Harvey's willingness to help Maryland's Catholics only discredited him further. Some colonists said "they would rather knock their cattle on the head before they would sell them to Maryland." In 1635, his councilors arrested him and sent him back to England for trial. Among their accusations was that Harvey was "a favourer of the Popish religion." Another claimed that Harvey "said it was lawful and meritorious to kill a heretic King." After Harvey denied "that he countenances the [Popish] religion in Maryland, and that there is public mass there," King Charles dismissed the charges and sent him back. Only in 1639—when Charles was distracted by bigger problems closer to home—were Harvey's enemies able to persuade the Privy Council to replace him with Sir Francis Wyatt.[30]

*

Under the protection of the Personal Rule, Roman Catholics gained a permanent foothold in the Americas. Unlike the puritan migration to New England, Catholic colonization was not a large, coordinated movement. Instead, Catholics entered the colonies with a mix of motives. To thrive, they depended on individuals with good political contacts, as Maryland demonstrated. Lacking that as well as luck, New Albion failed. Colonial America's Catholic population was not united. English Catholics were a minority, and often wealthier than their Irish compatriots, who made up the bulk of colonial Catholics. Uncounted hundreds of Irish Catholics, mostly young men, worked as servants in the Caribbean. On most islands they were a beleaguered minority, but on Montserrat they were the majority. While the expansion of Catholicism in the colonies was haphazard and disjointed, it nevertheless represented an important exception to the official rule of religious conformity. It was also a crucial step in the direction of colonial religious pluralism.

Pluralism was spreading without any official plan or formal grant of toleration. New Albion never got off the ground, even after advocating toleration in the 1640s. Montserrat resembled one of the places in Ireland where the established Protestant church was just a thin layer wrapped around a thick Roman Catholic core. Maryland officially upheld the authority of the Church of England but in reality did nothing to sustain it. Its much-vaunted tolerance rested on the lack of enforcement of penal laws supporting the church—not unlike in Ireland during the period of negotiations over "the Graces." As in Ireland, by not enforcing conformity, Maryland allowed Roman Catholic life to flourish. Moreover, English Jesuit missionaries were not only able keep the colonial Catholic community strong but also increase it by converting Protestants and Native Americans. Virginia, meanwhile, was divided between official Laudian imperatives and those who resented them, a situation aggravated by the arrival of the Marylanders.

For the moment, this emerging pluralism was still papered over by the official fiction of a shared conformity. On the ground that was clearly not the case. Maryland and New England were moving in very different directions, for example. It would not take much to send these colonies spinning off on completely separate religious trajectories. All that was needed was a breakdown in the political and religious authority at the center of the English world. That is exactly what began to happen in the spring of 1638.

PART 4

Civil Wars, 1638–1649

TEN

Fragmentation: Rhode Island, Madras, Trinidad, 1638–1643

If King Charles's emerging empire had a puritan problem, New England had a Rhode Island problem. In 1642, the governor of Massachusetts complained to the governor of Plymouth that Rhode Islanders were not only politically "divided from us, but in very deed they rend themselves from all the true churches of Christ and, many of them, from all the powers of magistracy." Worse, Rhode Islanders were infiltrating Massachusetts to make "public defiance against magistracy, ministry, churches and church covenants, etc., as antichristian." They sowed "the seeds of Familism and Anabaptistry, to the infection of some and danger of others." Massachusetts rejected the idea of "any league or confederacy at all" with Rhode Island.[1]

The existence of Rhode Island was just one small symptom of the religious and political fragmentation that broke out once the veneer of religious unity collapsed in the 1640s. King Charles and Archbishop Laud had spent the 1630s trying to bring the three kingdoms and their dependent territories into an ideal of religious unity and political obedience..They imagined it as a system of order, submission, and conformity. As long as the Personal Rule lasted, they could delude themselves into thinking they might succeed. Unfortunately for them, their real success was in antagonizing tens of thousands of people in Scotland, Ireland, and England. Starting in 1638, each rose up in turn to reject the Personal Rule, albeit for different reasons.[2]

As the three kingdoms fell into confusion, Charles's government lost contact with the overseas colonies, leaving them to work out their futures on their own. This breakdown of authority at the center is a crucial moment in early American religious history, for it allowed colonial American religion to evolve and consolidate without interference from England. Few colonists took advantage of this opportunity to pursue the cause of religious liberty. Instead, from New England to the Caribbean, most chose to consolidate and shore up their religious establishments. Pluralism was not their goal. Even Rhode Island was guided by a special Protestant vision. The problem was their religious establishments were not the same. In the end, the colonists proved no better than Charles and Laud at creating religious unity at anything above the provincial level. As England fell into civil war, the colonial religious order broke up into discrete, mutually antagonistic, units.

*

The fragmentation in the colonies began in New England, where the consolidation of Congregationalism produced a growing radical fringe as ever more puritans fell outside the pale of its orthodoxy. The most dramatic part of this process was the so-called Antinomian controversy of 1636–38, which drove a number of leading colonists out of Massachusetts, including the wealthy Anne Hutchinson and the minister John Wheelwright. Wheelwright and his followers found refuge in New Hampshire; Hutchinson and hers, in Rhode Island. Freshly established as a refuge from New as well as Old England by a hodgepodge of individuals who could not conform to the religious establishment of any of the other New England colonies, Rhode Island, like Connecticut and New Haven, had no royal charter. Unlike those colonies, it had no formal church establishment either. Instead, it sheltered a variety of Protestant misfits, beginning with Roger Williams. Williams had arrived in Massachusetts as part of the great puritan migration but was disappointed to find that the churches of neither Boston nor Plymouth had separated themselves sufficiently from the corruptions of the Church of England. For a time he served as an assistant to Salem's minister and enjoyed significant support in the community. However, his vehement insistence on a range of radical positions, including that Salem's church should fully separate itself from communion with the Church of England as well as denying that magistrates had the right to enforce religious conformity, got him banished. Rather than go back to England, Williams fled to Narragansett Bay in the winter of 1636. He then forged a friendship with the Narragansett nation, who sold the land on which the colony of Rhode Island was erected.[3]

Additional refugees from Massachusetts's religious order joined Williams until, by 1640, Rhode Island's several hundred inhabitants represented a remarkable swath of the range of religious views coming out of England's puritan underground. Most important were the Baptists. Having established their first congregation in London in 1611, Baptists set up several congregations in the English countryside in the 1620s, then moved out to the colonies in the 1630s. With the help of Roger Williams, they established their first American congregation at Providence, Rhode Island, in 1639. For a few months, Roger Williams was a Baptist. Then he decided that all churches in this fallen age were too flawed and imperfect to merit his membership. He became one of a growing number of English Protestant Seekers, most of them people with some ties to the puritan community, whose radical views could no longer fit into any existing church order. For example, Edward Wightman had spent time in puritan circles before being burned for heresy for not only denying the Trinity but also claiming to be a prophet with access to divine inspiration. Others also claimed special inspiration, proclaimed mystical truths, or asserted that they could attain perfect holiness here on earth. In England, frustrated puritan ministers had begun denouncing some of the more heterodox individuals to the Laudian authorities. Massachusetts expelled them.[4]

The colony of Rhode Island and Providence Plantations attracted Protestant religious dissidents of all stripes because it had neither an official church nor a strong government. It did not begin with a proclamation of religious liberty for the colony as a whole. Instead, its religious policy emerged in successive spurts from its four major towns, each with its own distinct religious texture. Providence, where Roger Williams lived, was first. In August 1637 Williams joined the other inhabitants, many of them Baptists, in signing an affirmation (they rejected oaths) to form a town government that would have power "only in civil things," publicly rejecting the ecclesiastical jurisdiction of the state. Anne Hutchinson took her supporters to Portsmouth, which in 1641 affirmed "Libertie of Conscience in point of Doctrine." When the merchant and aspiring authoritarian William Coddington, a man of Baptist views who wanted to rule "according to the lawes of God," fell out with the Hutchinsonians, he moved south with some followers to found Newport. In 1641, Newport's court ordered "that none bee accounted a delinquent for Doctrine: Provided, it bee not directly repugnant to ye Government or Lawes established." Meanwhile, the mystical spiritualist Samuel Gorton quietly surrounded himself with a small but dedicated group of idiosyncratic followers in Shawomet.[5]

Not until 1647 was this variety of local religious arrangements united under a common civil law code. Structured by biblical, not common law, categories, Rhode Island's law code was a clear statement of Protestant priorities. There was no formal provision made for a church. Instead, there was radical religious liberty: "all men may walk as their consciences perswade them, every one in the name of his God." Furthermore, so as not to impinge on "different consciences," individuals were permitted to make "a solemn profession or testimony" instead of the "taking of an oath."[6]

Massachusetts's other neighbors also offered refuge to puritans disappointed with its religious establishment. Some, especially those of presbyterian inclinations, went to the Dutch colony of New Netherland. Connected to the greatest mercantile power of the day, this small but dynamic colony attracted some English radicals as well, including Anne Hutchinson who moved there from the comparative backwater of Rhode Island. New Netherland was a firmly Reformed Protestant colony but, as everywhere else in the Dutch world, it did not compel its inhabitants to conform to its official church, offering them a liberty of conscience instead. Unlike Rhode Island, the Dutch did not permit worship outside of the Dutch Reformed Church, but in practice the Dutch exercised only sporadic oversight over religious life in the English towns that sprouted along its eastern border. The several different towns each had their own locally dominant religious culture. In some, Baptists and other radicals worshipped quietly in their homes. Elsewhere, presbyterians joined the official Dutch Reformed Church establishment.[7]

Northern New England offered other alternatives. New Hampshire, like Rhode Island, was comprised of four separate towns. It also lacked a strong central government able to impose a uniform religious order. Although it did not endorse religious liberty, each town was able to go its own way. Dover and Portsmouth (or Strawberry Bank) were not particularly puritan. Begun in the 1620s as fishing and lumbering outposts, they were populated mostly by servants who favored conformity. In 1640, Portsmouth even hired a conformist minister and gave him a parish glebe. Little other information is available about these towns' religious life. They likely read from the *Book of Common Prayer* and other acceptably conformist texts. By contrast, New Hampshire's other two towns were offshoots of the puritan migration to Massachusetts Bay. Hampton was established in 1636 with the help of the puritan minister Stephen Bachiler. It would have fit in well with Massachusetts. In fact, it served as Massachusetts's base of influence in New Hampshire. John Wheelwright and his followers established Exeter in 1638 after they were exiled from Massachusetts. They did not oppose the Congregational church, only certain aspects of the way Massachusetts implemented it.[8]

In Maine, Governor Thomas Gorges watched the developments in Massachusetts with a sympathetic but skeptical eye. He was a man of puritan sympathies, but saw "noe ground" for "the church covenant" practiced in Massachusetts and "could not tolerate it." In 1640, when John Wheelwright contemplated a move to Maine with thirty families of followers, Gorges explained that in his colony, "for the civill we steared as neere as we could to the course of Ingland. For the ecclesiastical we forced noe man to the common prayer booke or to the ceremonies of the Church of Ingland but allowed the Liberties of Conscience in this particular, for they are not used in this province as yet." In other words, Maine was and was not conformist. Sympathizing with, but not embracing, the New England Way, it practiced a horizontal, ecclesiastical tolerance among English Protestants that avoided a formal break with the Church of England.[9]

New Hampshire and Maine, like Massachusetts, had patents from the New England Company. As long as the Personal Rule lasted, these little alternative jurisdictions to Massachusetts Congregationalism were protected by their connection to England. As long as England was able to uphold the patents that legitimated the colonial governments, this delicate balance could be preserved. If England were not actively in the picture, the equation changed radically. That is exactly what happened in 1638, when the Scots rejected King Charles's efforts to reform their church.

Charles believed he was building on his father's efforts to reinforce episcopal authority in Scotland. Unfortunately, James's policies already had created a dissident movement within Scottish presbyterian opinion that had much in common with England's puritan movement. In the 1620s, as ministers who refused to conform to the Articles of Perth began losing their positions, some embarked on careers as itinerants. Conventicles of worshippers gathered to avoid churches that used what was widely regarded as an "English" liturgy. In small groups, they met in homes or barns. In larger groups, they gathered outdoors in fields and valleys, sometimes coming together for so-called Holy Fairs: large, semiannual communion festivals that attracting hundreds of people from miles around. These extraordinary experiences provided a welcome communal dimension to an otherwise individualistic Calvinism and facilitated many a Calvinist conversion experience. They also strengthened opposition to the Stuart church reforms in Scotland and Ireland. Beginning in Galloway in the 1590s, they spread to Ulster in the 1620s. In 1634, the minister Samuel Rutherford, a future leader of the revolutionary Presbyterian cause, elicited from the dying nobleman John Gordon—son of the proprietor of the New Galloway colony—the admission that he believed the ceremonies introduced by kings James and Charles were "plain Popery," "Idolatrous and Antichristian, and come from Hell." Only those "who are nick named Puritans," Gordon confessed, gave "comfort to my soul."[10]

King Charles's reforms of the Scottish church culminated in 1637 with an effort to impose a new *Book of Common Prayer*. Although a committee of Scottish bishops had approved it, its similarities to that of England led most Scots to reject it. Even the Scottish Privy Council sympathized with the opposition. Churchmen who tried to introduce the new Prayer Book faced boisterous protests. The most important of these Prayer Book riots took place in the new cathedral church of Edinburgh, where opposition to the Prayer Book combined with opposition to the bishops. The riots not only prevented the new Prayer Book from being used; they sparked a resistance movement. Over the winter and spring of 1638, much of the population pledged itself to a national covenant in defense of their church and country from "popish" innovations. Proclaiming that they "abhor and detest all contrary religion and doctrine, but chiefly all kind of papistry," these Covenanters pledged to "root out of their Empire all heretics and enemies to the true worship of God." Their goal was to "recover the purity and liberty of the Gospel as it was established and professed before the aforesaid novations." The Scottish National Covenant did not explicitly reject episcopacy, but when the church's General Assembly met in November 1638, it complained of "the many and great innovations and corruptions lately by the Prelats and their adherents intruded into the doctrine, worship, and discipline of this Church." Rejecting the king's order to disband, the assembly abolished episcopacy. To restore the "great puritie" that previously "to our unspeakable comfort" had been "established amongst us," it declared the Church of Scotland to be a Presbyterian church.[11]

Charles's plans to bring Massachusetts back in line were forgotten as the king lost control of Scotland. He devoted all his efforts to regaining control of his northern kingdom. It was the beginning of a conflict that would take up all his energies over the next decade—and eventually, his life and that of Laud. The conflict, variously known as the Wars of the Three Kingdoms, or the British Civil Wars, saved the New England puritan experiment.

To regain control of Scotland, Charles planned an elaborate three-pronged invasion for the spring of 1639. This first of two so-called Bishops' Wars was an embarrassing failure. The naval expedition was unable to land; the Irish army failed to invade; the English army was full of unwilling conscripts and poorly equipped militiamen who tended to sympathize with the Scottish cause; Scottish royalist forces were too weak to rise up and help. Although the Covenanters' army was smaller, it was strengthened with veterans of the Thirty Years War. It also had strong morale and a clear sense of purpose. In June, Charles was persuaded to stop at the border and negotiate the Pacification of Berwick.[12]

During this truce, a member of England's leading Catholic family, Thomas Howard, Earl of Arundel, became proprietor of a new colony in Madagascar. Arundel's life had a number of parallels and connections to that of the Calverts. Like George Calvert, Arundel came from a Catholic family but had conformed to the Church of England. He also had a longstanding interest in colonization, having invested in Newfoundland, supported Ralegh's 1617 voyage to Guiana, advocated a new Guiana Company in 1618, and served on the Council for New England. Like Calvert, he also had actively promoted the "Spanish Match" and lost favor at court when it collapsed. Again like Calvert, Arundel returned to royal favor after Buckingham's murder. Unlike Calvert, Arundel never recanted his religious conformity. Nevertheless, he was surrounded by Catholic connections, including his wife, Aletheia, their sons, and almost all of his extended relatives, including Cecil Calvert's wife, Anne. These Catholic associations strengthened Arundel's position at court, for Aletheia became close to King James's Catholic wife, Anne, and then part of Henrietta Maria's inner circle, which, from 1636 to 1639, included an agent from the pope: the Scottish Catholic George Con. Arundel did not fully approve of the way Henrietta Maria's circle tried to convert various courtiers, but that did not stop persistent suspicions that he was a crypto-Catholic. He had reached the peak of his political influence in the spring of 1639 when he was made commander of the English army mustered to fight against the Scots. His command was controversial for allowing over fifty Catholic officers to serve in the army with priests secretly administering to them. To make it easier for them to serve, he even devised a special oath of allegiance for the army. Like Cecil Calvert's loyalty oath for Maryland, Arundel's oath dropped all references to papal supremacy. It also implicitly condemned Calvinist resistance theory. When the two leading puritan peers serving in the army, Lord Brooke and Lord Saye and Sele, refused to take it they were imprisoned.[13]

Arundel's failure to defeat the Covenanters likely revived his interest in colonization. He announced his plans to become a colonizer in the first week of September 1639. King Charles, regretting "the loss of the Earl Marshal's services" but approving "his generous intentions," granted him the rights to Madagascar and "the other islands not inhabited" in the region, including Saint Helena. Arundel was not the first English person whose claim to Madagascar Charles had supported. In 1635 he had given a trading license to Sir William Courteen, who had overseen the initial colonization of Barbados, allowing him to build a base on Madagascar. In reality, Courteen wanted to break into the East India Company's trading monopoly. The ships his company sent out went for trade and never colonized Madagascar. In vain, the East India Company had protested against both Courteen's and Arundel's threat to their monopoly.[14]

Arundel's attention had probably been drawn to Madagascar through his close connections to the royal family as well as his Catholic court connections. He had learned from "all that have been there of the riches and plenty of those places," and wanted to seize Madagascar for England before some other nation claimed it. His informants were likely courtiers as well as merchants, for in 1636–37 there had been a proposal to send King Charles's nephew Prince Rupert, son of Frederick V, the Calvinist Elector of the Palatinate, and Charles's sister Elizabeth, to colonize Madagascar. Arundel was close to Rupert and his brother Louis, who he had brought to England after Hapsburg armies conquered the Palatinate. Arundel's wife and George Con then tried to persuade Prince Rupert to convert to Catholicism, claiming it would help persuade the Holy Roman emperor to restore the Palatinate to his family. All that came of these discussions was a 1638 poem by the playwright William Davenant. "Madagascar" imagined Rupert conquering the island and receiving the submission of its Indigenous inhabitants, a "long-lost, scatter'd-parcell of mankind," and people of other faiths, including "He that from cursed Mahomet derives his sinfull blood" and (in a not so subtle dig at the Scots) even "the mighty Presbiter." It was an absolutist vision of a pluralist colony, one that likely appealed to Davenant's friends Henry Jermyn and Endymion Porter, to whom he had dedicated the poem. Like Arundel, they were conformist courtiers closely tied to Catholic interests. Jermyn was intimate enough with Queen Henrietta Maria to generate gossip about their relationship. Porter had lived in Spain and was a promoter of various get rich schemes and projects, including the colonization of Madagascar. His wife, Olive, was one of the first women at court converted by Father Con and part of Aletheia Arundel's campaign to convert people at court.[15]

Initially, Arundel's Madagascar plan seemed promising. He had the express support of the king, who not only gave him leave to go, but, as Arundel announced, was sending "one of his best shipps" to assist "mee." Arundel commissioned a glorious portrait from Anthony van Dyck of himself and Aletheia presiding over a globe with Madagascar positioned in

FIGURE 10. *The Madagascar Portrait of Thomas Howard and his wife Aletheia Talbot*, by Anthony van Dyck (1599–1641), His Grace the Duke of Norfolk, Arundel Castle/Bridgeman Images

clear sight. His announcement said almost nothing about the colony's religious life, beyond the standard claim it would propagate the "Christian Religion." Instead, he emphasized that "I am resolved to goe me selfe in person," driven by "powerful inducements of honor and profitt both to my Countrey and perticuler." Ships were provisioned and men were recruited, but the colony was never launched. The aging Arundel became mired in the growing political crisis at home and died a few years later after escorting Henrietta Maria's mother to safety in the Spanish Netherlands.[16]

England's slide into civil war put an end to Arundel's family's involvement in colonization. This included his son's plan to colonize Carolana. In 1638–40, Henry Frederick Howard, Lord Maltravers, had been busy laying the groundwork for a colony, appointing a governor and securing the support of Virginia and the king. Like his father, Maltravers had a strong interest in colonial projects. He had supported the idea of the English West India Company, joined the Council for New England, and even acquired rights to land there. Like his father, Maltravers conformed but labored under suspicions of recusancy. Sir Robert Heath likely knew that. When he renewed his patent for Carolana in April 1632, Heath annulled all previous grants in favor of the new one to Lord Maltravers. Until then, he had continued to work with Huguenots and Samuel Vassall, a wealthy puritan merchant of French ancestry. Vassall had sent two expeditions to Carolana. The first had explored the area. The second, in 1633, carried forty colonists, but never made it to Carolana. Vassall's appointed governor, fearing he could not adequately supply the colony, turned back upon reaching Virginia. Those earlier efforts help explain why Maltravers's patent excluded "Straungers," that is, Huguenots, and nonconformists, insisting that only those who "submit and conforme themselves to the discipline of the Church of England" would be admitted to Carolana. In the end, Maltravers opted to fight for the king instead. Losing control of his estates, he died in 1652.[17]

Arundel and Maltravers represented the last gasp of the Caroline age of favorites under whose guise the Calverts had created Maryland. It was not the end of England's reliance on Roman Catholics in the colonies, however. In India, the East India Company was beginning to develop Madras, its first proper colony in Asia. Having purchased a spit of coastland from a local lord in 1639, the company built a trading outpost and then Fort Saint George, which would serve as their headquarters in India for the next century. Until their first permanent chaplain arrived in 1647, Madras's handful of English factors and soldiers read from the *Book of Common Prayer* in a room above their warehouse. Meanwhile, a few thousand Indians, many of them from a community of Portuguese mixed with Indians about three miles to the south called Saint-Thomé, settled in an adjacent town. Allegedly the last resting place of Saint Thomas, Saint-Thomé had been occupied by the Portuguese since 1523. Many of its inhabitants were Roman Catholics, and the company employed them as laborers, soldiers, weavers, and merchants. To make them feel at home, Madras's English governor persuaded a French Capuchin passing through in 1642 to stay to serve them. French Capuchins would preside over Madras's flourishing Indo-Portuguese Catholic community for decades to come. In 1660 its roughly three thousand people greatly outnumbered the small English community of about eighty merchants and soldiers. Despite occasional complaints that the priests visited sick "Christians belonging to our congregation" and "like the Devil, endeavour to . . . seduce them if they can to their idolatrous custom of setting the Images of Saints before them, that they may pray to them," and otherwise pushed religious boundaries, the English tolerated them and the Catholic community—so vital to Madras's economy and defense—well into the eighteenth century.[18]

Back home in Britain, however, anti-Catholicism had become a politically explosive issue. The first Bishops' War had taught King Charles that he could neither win nor pay for a war against Scotland without Parliament's help. Summoning it in the spring of 1640, he was grievously disappointed that it refused to grant him any funds for the Scottish war unless he first addressed its many complaints. Those complaints included the accusation that the Personal Rule was part of a Roman Catholic conspiracy threatening England, and denunciations of "the great encouragement to them of the popish religion by a universal suspension of all laws that are against them" and their admission "to public places of trust and power." The MP John Pym argued that Laudianism, or the "divers innovations in religion amongst ourselves," was surely part of a plan to return England to Roman Catholicism. Puritans were not the problem but simply "godly men who truly profess the Protestant religion, as though men could be too religious." Pym then criticized the royal institutions that operated outside of parliamentary jurisdiction: the High Commission for ecclesiastical affairs, which punished nonconformist ministers, and the Star Chamber, the highest executive court in the country, which tried cases, including those involving religious dissidents, quickly and without a jury.[19]

Perturbed, Charles dismissed this "Short Parliament" after a few weeks. Turning to Sir Thomas Wentworth, whom he now raised to the status of Earl of Strafford, he again tried to wage war without parliamentary support. The second Bishops' War was an even worse disaster than the first. Now the Scots invaded England and captured the northern counties of Northumberland and Durham. Defeated, Charles negotiated another, less favorable, truce in October. The Treaty of Ripon allowed the Scottish army to occupy the north of England until a final peace was negotiated while Charles paid the costs of their occupation. In need of money, he summoned Parliament again. Taking their seats in November, its members first revived the Short Parliament's demands then attacked the men they blamed for the hated royal policies, beginning with Wentworth. Accusing Wentworth of "a great and dangerous treason" that ostensibly would have involved, among other things, using Irish troops to crush the king's critics in England, Pym led the prosecution for his impeachment, claiming that if his "treason had taken effect our souls had been enthralled to the spiritual tyranny of Satan, our consciences to the ecclesiastical tyranny of the Pope, our lives, our persons and estates, to the civil tyranny of an arbitrary, unlimited, confused government."[20]

To Charles's grief, this Parliament turned out to be the "Long Parliament." It would continue to sit, on and off and in different guises, for the next twenty years, becoming more radically antimonarchical with each passing year. In December, Londoners presented Parliament with the so-called Root and Branch Petition calling for the abolition of the current government of the church by "archbishops and lord bishops, deans and archdeacons." Allegedly signed by fifteen thousand people, it objected to a long list of royal policies, reiterated the claim that the Personal Rule had punished good puritans and favored Catholics, and insisted that Laudian religious policies had led to the "discouragement and destruction of all good subjects," many of whom "have departed the kingdom to Holland and other parts" while "the Romish party" harbored hopes that "their superstitious religion will ere long be fully planted in this kingdom again." A week later, the aged Archbishop Laud was arrested, impeached, and imprisoned in the Tower of London. Then Parliament abolished the courts of Star Chamber and High Commission.[21]

A constitutional revolution was on hand. The hapless King Charles saw little choice but to cooperate. His low point came in May 1641, when he felt compelled to give permission for Wentworth's execution by attainder. He immediately regretted the decision. Still, there was some hope for peace. In August 1641 the Treaty of London was signed. Scottish troops marched home. The Bishops' Wars were over.

However, the Scots had been radicalized. They formally abolished episcopacy and made the Church of Scotland Presbyterian. Again, King Charles consented under duress. Covenanter leaders hoped that the other two kingdoms would adopt a similar ecclesiastical system, believing that only by having a common Presbyterian Church in all of the three kingdoms would true Christian salvation be promoted—and Scotland's church be finally preserved from meddling. The Scots also wanted a stronger federal union between the kingdoms. Demanding more of a say in foreign affairs and trade, they also insisted on more autonomy in their domestic affairs. Charles resisted these demands, but the Covenanters did not abandon them.[22]

Meanwhile, a group of ministers tried to encourage reconciliation by redirecting Britain's energy toward American colonization. William Castell, a puritan minister from Northamptonshire, petitioned Parliament (but not the king) to join with Scotland in a vigorous program of colonizing and missionary work. He had endorsements from seventy English and six Scottish ministers, including the leading theologian Alexander Henderson. The petition attacked Spain's much-vaunted missionary accomplishments as done "very corruptly," and "accompanied with many idle, absurd, idolatrous Inventions of their owne," but also criticized the British for being "exceeding remisse in performing this so religious, so great, so necessary a worke." Ultimately, the petition was less a comprehensive plan for evangelization than a call to protect and support the existing colonies by creating a powerful new colony "South of Virginia." It would provide a home for the "multitude of people" currently burdening England and Scotland. It would surely succeed, because the colonists would go "in Gods cause, for the promoting of the Gospel, and inlarging of his Church."[23]

In the event, Castell's vision of a puritan Carolana was quickly forgotten in the wake of another major crisis. In October, Catholic Ireland suddenly erupted in revolt. Irish elites' experience of the Personal Rule under Lord Deputy Wentworth (1633–39) had been unpleasant. Wentworth's close ties to the king and Laud had given him tremendous power to suppress any dissent or resistance. After the negotiations over the Graces ended, he had used that power to actively promote colonization schemes and to renew pressure on the Irish to conform to the established church. Protestants were still a tiny minority. Where the population of England and Wales was about 5 million, Scotland about 1 million, Ireland had roughly 1.5 million people, but only about one hundred thousand were Protestant, mostly living in Ulster (roughly eighty thousand) and Munster (about twenty thousand). This minority's vastly disproportionate access to land ownership rankled the overwhelmingly Catholic majority. When Wentworth left to assist his king during the Bishops' Wars, he left behind a population that was antagonized from all directions. The Old English and Old Irish Catholics resented his land and religious policies; English and Scottish Protestants resented his Laudian reforms.[24]

Angry Irish Catholic elites had provided evidence against Wentworth during his impeachment trial. However, while delivering their testimony in London, they realized England's Parliament posed an even bigger threat. Not only was it intensely anti-Catholic: it was assaulting the very monarchical institutions that were their greatest shelter. Returning to Ireland, a small group of Irish Catholics took inspiration from the Scots' success in using armed resistance to bring the king to the negotiating table and launched their own uprising in October 1641. It was supposed to be a limited strike to draw attention to their grievances. It turned out to be a horrible miscalculation. Beginning in Ulster, the revolt's leaders quickly lost control as Irish Catholics across the kingdom randomly attacked their Protestant neighbors. Irish Catholic resentment of English, Scots, and foreign Protestant domination combined with a desire to protect the religious gains that had been made since the 1620s to produce a dreadful civil war.

Land may have been the original inspiration for revolt, but it could not be separated from religious issues. Catholic clergymen, claiming their church was in danger, blessed the uprising as a struggle for the religious liberty of the Roman Catholic Church. Within a few months, the rebels had killed as many as five thousand Protestants. Many others were despoiled and driven from their homes in the middle of winter. Rebel priests encouraged captive Protestants to convert. Some did. Many others chose to suffer for their faith. Meanwhile, British Protestant fears and anger about Catholic treachery were stoked by accounts that drastically exaggerated the number of Protestants killed. It was commonly claimed that 150,000 Protestants fell victim in the initial uprising: that was fifty thousand more than Ireland's entire Protestant population. Depicting the uprising as a purely religious war, Protestant accounts claimed the Catholics intended to massacre all the Protestants in Ireland. A flood of hostile propaganda created shock and outrage as it spread throughout all three kingdoms and overseas. Protestant attitudes toward Irish Catholics were embittered for years to come.[25]

The Irish rebels gained control of much of the countryside, but crucially failed to capture Dublin. Making Kilkenny their capital, they established a confederacy to govern the territories they controlled. Irish Protestants, meanwhile, driven by a sense of aggrieved victimhood, joined the royal army to counterattack in the spring of 1642. It was not long before they had killed about as many Catholics as the Catholics had killed Protestants. Scotland also sent a small army to protect its countrymen in Ulster. It took advantage of the breakdown of royal authority to formally establish the Presbyterian Church in Ulster. For the first time, there was an official Protestant alternative to the Church of Ireland. Everyone on all sides professed their loyalty to King Charles, but no one really trusted him. Indeed, only a handful of Irish Protestants, led by James Butler, Duke of Ormond, were truly sympathetic to Charles's cause. However, neither the Irish Confederacy, nor the royalists, nor the Scots, nor, later, the English Parliamentarians had enough power to subdue the rest and pacify the country. Unable to decisively resolve the expanding conflict, they spent the next ten years fighting a bloody, grueling war.[26]

In the Caribbean, the Irish rebellion evidently inspired a wave of repression against Irish Catholics. To escape it, the Irish Barbadian planter Richard Hackett led several hundred of his countrymen from Barbados and Saint Christopher to Spanish Santo Domingo in 1642. There they established a small settlement on the under-populated north shore and petitioned for Spanish protection. Hackett explained that the Irish had suffered under "the heaviest of yokes" imposed by "the English heretics" who, in Ireland, "have stripped us of all our goods, and at present treat us like brutes, herding us around like wild beasts" all "for no other cause than their excessive hatred of our Religion." That cruelty had moved "all the people to rebellion in Ireland." In Barbados they not only had been denied "liberty of Religion" but also had been prevented from returning home to Ireland. The "sick and wretched" Irish begged the Spanish governor for "Refuge," explaining how the English took their rosaries away and denied them "the hours of prayer, among many other evils." Unfortunately, the Spanish still opposed the idea of having foreigners establish a colony in their empire, even if they were good Roman Catholics. When Hackett then suggested he could raise a regiment of a thousand Caribbean Irish refugees if he were appointed commander, they instead encouraged him to serve as a captain in the European army. As for the Irish still on Santo Domingo, the Spanish tried to disperse them by either having them either work on Spanish farms or sending them to Spain.[27]

In England, the Irish revolt added to the mutual mistrust between Parliament and king. Radicals like John Pym were convinced that there was "a malignant and pernicious design of subverting the fundamental laws of government, upon which the religion and justice of this kingdom are firmly established," as the "Grand Remonstrance," drafted by Pym and a small committee of fellow puritans described it. This long and detailed petition placed "Jesuited papists" together with the "bishops, and the corrupt part of the clergy, who cherish formality and superstition" at the top of its list of 204 separate complaints to the king. Presented on behalf of Parliament in December 1641, the Grand Remonstrance represented, in hindsight, the last effort at peaceful Parliamentary reform. It was not promising.[28]

The House of Commons had only approved the Grand Remonstrance by a narrow majority. Parliament was becoming more divided as it became more radical. Heartened by the growing split among MPs, Charles thought he could end his problems by arresting a few ringleaders. In January 1642, he broke legal protocol and Parliamentary privilege by invading Parliament with armed men to capture them. Forewarned, they managed to escape. This drastic action convinced those who were already suspicious about the king's motives that he could not be trusted. Faced with palpable hostility in Parliament and London, Charles abandoned his capital a few days later.[29]

Over the winter and spring of 1642 England steadily drifted toward civil war. Each side rallied support for its cause while blaming the other for undermining peace. Charles sought support in the countryside while Parliament passed a revolutionary spate of acts in London. In February it banned bishops from sitting in the House of Lords. In March it passed a Militia Ordinance granting itself the power to raise an army to protect the kingdom from "the bloody counsels of papists and other ill-affected persons, who have already raised a rebellion in the kingdom of Ireland." This increasing radicalism persuaded a growing number of MPs to leave London and join the king. While both sides raised armies over the summer, they established a Royalist Parliament at Oxford. The fighting began in September.[30]

Only one significant battle took place in the fall of 1642: the bloody but inconclusive encounter at Edgehill. After the battle, royalist and Parliamentarian forces would battle each other to a draw by the autumn of 1643. Royalist forces advanced to the edge of London. A massive turnout by the city's militiamen persuaded them to turn back. The rebels then fortified London while Parliament secured its control over London and much of the southeast. The royalists fortified Oxford while building up their strength in the north and west, including Wales. However, they were cut off from the sea—and the colonies—until July 1643, when royalist troops captured the key port city of Bristol.[31]

The king lost contact with the colonies at the outbreak of war, but his enemies still worked to found new colonies. Having purchased the Earl of Montgomery and Pembroke's patent to "Trinidado, Tobago, Barbados and Fonseca" in 1638, the Earl of Warwick was in the middle of a series of efforts to colonize these islands with colonists who seem to have been either puritans or amenable to puritanism. His first expedition colonized Trinidad, but ran into some trouble after the Trinidadian Kalinago killed its leader in 1639. The survivors refused to recognize the reinforcements Warwick sent out in 1640, saying "it would destroy the Privilleges graunted them from the Earle of Warwick which were the grownds of their Leaving their Native Countrie." Meanwhile, some three hundred English, including a future puritan minister, Nicholas Leverton, arrived to colonize Tobago in 1639, but were driven off by the Kalinago. In 1642 Warwick sponsored an expedition to Tobago from Barbados; the Kalinago drove them off as well. He then sent "300 Families of English" to colonize Guiana and Surinam in 1643. In 1645 this colony too was "cut of[f] by the natives." Warwick then granted "divers Liberties and Privilledges" to another group of "Sober Judicious" colonists in 1644. Sadly, they had all died of disease or fled by 1645. Soon thereafter the survivors of the 1639 Trinidad expedition ("the greater part Planters from St. Christophers, and other of the Islands in those parts," including Barbados) finally abandoned the island out of fear of a Spanish attack. Evidence for the religious character of these enterprises comes from Warwick's 1647 call for colonists. Motivated "out of a Godly Zeale for the promoteing of the Gospell in that Island," Warwick was also "desiourous and carefull to cause that Island to be planted and Peopled in such sort and manner with such People as may be (by Gods blessing) Instruments of Promoteing and publishing the true Protestant Religion there." Although in England he was generally a Presbyterian, Warwick took something of an Independent approach to overseas colonies, encouraging Baptists and possibly other Protestant radicals to join his expeditions.[32]

The one area where Warwick could claim some success was Barbados. The island's economy thrived as it entered the early stages of the sugar revolution that would transform the economy and society of the English Caribbean. Although the Church of England was established on the island, Barbados attracted its fair share of puritans, including Nicholas Leverton. Leverton served as a conformist minister on Barbados in the 1630s before going to Tobago and then Providence Island, where he became a Congregationalist. Puritan sympathies are also evident in Barbados's decision to request ministers from Massachusetts in 1642. However, Barbados also contained the full range of religious diversity in the English world: Catholics, Baptists, and other Protestant radicals. That unstable mix discouraged Massachusetts from sending any of its precious ministers there, having heard complaints "that these people were much infected with familism."[33]

When the fighting broke out, a number of colonists returned to fight on one or the side of the civil war. The colonies, however, initially strove to remain neutral. Colonial leaders feared an openly bellicose stance would alienate at least some of colonists. A number of colonists clearly sympathized with Parliament while others clearly favored the king. There was no fighting between the colonies, but most experienced at least some inner turmoil. Taking advantage of England's fall into chaos, those in charge of the different colonies strove to consolidate their hold over the territory and its church.[34]

In 1643, colonial neutrality began to break down. Virginia came out in favor of the royalist cause. Its governor, Sir William Berkeley, had fought for the king before arriving in 1642. Soon, three ministers arrived from New England and organized conventicles in the puritan-leaning counties of the southeast. Berkeley, the royalist conformist, was determined to reinforce the colony's commitment to the cause of the king and his church. In March 1643, the assembly reinforced its commitment to the Laudian church, ordering that "the litargie of the church of England for the administration of the word & sacrament, be duely performed according to the booke of common prayer, allowed by his Matie & confirmed by consent of parliament." For "the preservation of the puritie of doctrine & unity of the church," they added the command "that all ministers whatsoever which shall reside in the collony are to be conformable to the orders and constitutions of the church of England, and the laws therein established, and not otherwise to be admitted to teach or preach publickly or privately." Virginia's burgesses then bestowed upon Berkeley unprecedented power over the church. He was allowed to choose the minister for Jamestown as well as "any parish where the governor & his successors shall have a plantation (as long as they do it only in one parish at a time)." Furthermore, acting in concert with his council, Berkeley could punish any minister in the colony for "neglect or misbecoming behavior" based upon a complaint made by a vestry. Although only the assembly had the ultimate authority to remove a minister from his position, the governor and counsel were obliged to compel "all nonconformists . . . to depart the colony with all conveniencie." In June, Virginia's General Court ordered a letter from the king to be read out in all parish churches, commanding that those "speaking scandalous words of the king or queen" would be punished. At some point in the spring of 1643, the three New England ministers left Virginia.[35]

That summer, Maryland's governor, Leonard Calvert, made what could be called the first effort in American history to openly recruit immigrants with explicit offers of religious toleration. Turning to heavily populated New England, he commissioned Captain Edward Gibbons, then living in Boston, to offer colonists "free liberty of religion, and all other privileges which the place afforded." Unfortunately, the offer was not enough to overcome the New Englanders' hostility to popery. John Winthrop noted that Captain Gibbons "had no mind to further" the plans of the "papist" governor, "nor had any of our people temptation that way." They had not come to America to live in a colony "of protestants and papists." Calvert then turned to the puritans in Virginia. Their anti-Catholic qualms led them to hesitate for several years before accepting the offer. For the moment they still lived in relative peace, as Berkeley's ability to interfere with their religious lives remained limited.[36]

Massachusetts, on the other hand, took advantage of the distractions in Britain to reduce the religious diversity on its frontiers and extend its hegemony over its smaller neighbors. In June 1641, some New Hampshire colonists invited Massachusetts to annex the small colony, "whereby they may be ruled and ordered according unto God both in church & commonweal, and for the avoyding such insufferable disorders whereby God hath been much dishonoered amongst them." Although incorporated into Massachusetts until 1679, New Hampshire's distinctive origins merited some toleration for its less than perfectly godly population. In 1642, the General Court ruled that those who had been freemen before the annexation could "send a deputy to the General Court though they be not at present Church members." It also allowed non-Congregational church members to serve on local courts. Overall, the Massachusetts system of local town and church autonomy helped absorb New Hampshire's diversity while keeping it within acceptable bounds. Massachusetts's capacity for tolerance had clear limits, however. John Wheelwright and his followers had to seek refuge across the border in Maine. Not until 1647, and after a carefully worded apology, was Wheelwright permitted to return to Massachusetts.[37]

Massachusetts was less tender toward Rhode Island. In March of 1643, Roger Williams, sensing trouble, sailed for London to procure a charter to protect his little colony. While he was away, Massachusetts had the leader of the Narragansetts, Williams's crucial ally, killed. Then, in October 1643, troops from Massachusetts attacked Samuel Gorton's village of Shawomet in an effort to prevent their unconventional religious views from infecting Massachusetts. The Gortonists were so controversial that even in Rhode Island no one was willing to stand up for them. When they had first arrived, a group at Pawtuxet actually decided to submit themselves to Massachusetts rather than welcome the Gortonists. Like Roger Williams, the Gortonists had purchased the land at Shawomet directly from the Narragansetts, but they did it without the support of Williams or William Coddington, Rhode Island's other important leader. Without friends or allies, the Gortonists were defeated after a short firefight and brought back to Boston. Put on trial, they were almost condemned to death for their religious views. In the end, they were sentenced to virtual slavery instead. Released from his sentence of hard labor in the spring of 1644, Gorton followed Williams's example and returned to England to secure a patent to protect his tiny colony from further assaults.[38]

*

The breakdown of monarchical authority in Britain and Ireland was a decisive moment in early American religious history. It gave the colonies the chance to go their own way without fear of interference from England. Almost none of them used that opportunity to promote religious liberty or offer religious refuge to persecuted minorities. On the contrary, most colonial rulers doubled down on their religious establishment, insisting on full conformity to it while trying to reduce the range of available religious alternatives. In New England, Massachusetts began to take over its smaller, weaker neighbors. Imposing the Congregational church order, it threatened Rhode Island with extinction. Small, weak, Catholic-ruled Maryland was the great exception, with its willingness to offer toleration to puritans. Madras in India was another exception. There, a handful of English East India Company agents tolerated a local Roman Catholic majority in order to secure their labor, business, and trade contacts, without which the colony would be worthless. Even Rhode Islanders would have had trouble accepting such a radical religious difference. Their colony's generous religious liberty was deeply Protestant and gave no clear toleration for Catholics. Since puritans had no interest in toleration as a principle if it forced them to coexist with, and respect the religious privileges of, Roman Catholics, Maryland's pioneering offer of colonial toleration went nowhere. It remained a small, poor, vulnerable colony, as was Rhode Island. Religious liberty was not enough of an appeal on its own, as a number of Rhode Island's original colonists, including Anne Hutchinson, demonstrated. They eventually moved to the more economically promising colony of New Netherland even though its religious liberty was narrower.

Religious liberty and tolerance remained unpopular tools for colonization. Religious unity was still the goal for most. However, while Massachusetts and Virginia became increasingly homogenous within their borders, they became increasingly different from each other. Colonial religious life was fragmenting, mirroring the fragmentation happening in Charles's European territories. Congregationalism came to prevail in New England just as Presbyterianism prevailed in Scotland. In Ireland, Catholics successfully claimed large portions of their country, driving out Protestants and restoring Roman Catholicism. Catholics reminaed in control of Maryland. England, meanwhile, fell into a divisive civil war between different schools of Protestants, divided between those who supported a church with bishops and those who supported a church without bishops. A few individuals hoped to resolve or escape those tensions by joining new colonial projects, but the conflict was steadily spreading to all corners of the English world. America offered no safe refuge from the revolution.

ELEVEN

Toleration: New England, Bermuda, Madagascar, 1643–1646

In England, while procuring a patent from the revolutionary Parliament to protect Rhode Island from being swallowed up by Massachusetts, Roger Williams became both a hero of religious liberty and a thorn in the side of Massachusetts, using his experience of persecution in Massachusetts to inflame England's great toleration debate. Williams's advocacy of religious freedom is a cornerstone of accounts of early American religious liberty. Less discussed are the views of his former neighbors back in Massachusetts, like Nathaniel Ward, who proclaimed that "all Familists, Antinomians, Anabaptists, and other Enthusiasts, shall have free Liberty to keep away from us, and such as will come to be gone as fast as they can, the sooner the better." For, Ward averred, "God doth no where in his word tolerate Christian States, to give Toleration to such adversaries of his Truth, if they have power in their hands to suppresse them." Far more of the English in America agreed with Ward than Williams.[1]

Outside of Rhode Island, colonial America showed few signs of becoming a pioneer of religious pluralism. Colonization remained a religiously conservative endeavor. While the chaos of the English Civil War tended to discourage efforts to establish a new colony, the few attempts that were made, focused on Madagascar, showed no more willingness to advance the cause of religious pluralism than Massachusetts. As Roger Williams discovered, the real support for religious toleration lay in England, not America. Without the support Williams secured from England's revolutionary government, Rhode Island's experiment in religious liberty likely would have been absorbed into Massachusetts along with New Hampshire and Maine. As England's civil war expanded, few colonists embraced religious toleration as a solution to their dilemmas. Instead, they tended to align with the other side that favored their church order. New England favored Parliament while Virginia and several Caribbean islands proclaimed their allegiance to the monarchy and the Church of England. Maryland was unusual in its effort to balance out the growing tensions with a policy of religious tolerance. It was also unsuccessful. A band of Protestants attacked the colony, plundered the estates of its Catholic community, rounded up its Jesuits, and sent them back to Europe. Thus was the most successful English mission to Native Americans brought to an end along with Maryland's special role as a Catholic-run enclave in a world dominated by Protestants.

Even in England, though, only a minority favored religious toleration, even among the Parliamentarians. Most favored some sort of presbyterian religious settlement. The toleration debate broke out after an assembly of churchmen gathered at Westminster to discuss the comprehensive religious reform of England's church and a handful of individuals leaning toward Congregationalism threw a wrench into the process by insisting that they not be incorporated into a national church without some form of toleration. In Massachusetts, Congregationalists refused to tolerate others, but in England they insisted on toleration for themselves. In both word and deed, the colonies thus figured on both sides of the debate. While Roger Williams made one of the most influential arguments in favor of tolerance and disestablishment, the rest of New England supported religious unity and a strong establishment. Parliament stayed aloof until the religious strife on Bermuda provoked it to finally articulate an official colonial religious policy. While on its face it was a statement in favor of tolerance, it simply confirmed the de facto devolution of ecclesiastical authority to the individual colonies. Most colonists took advantage of Parliament's hands-off stance to shore up their religious establishments rather than open them up to toleration.

*

While Roger Williams was in England, Massachusetts joined with New Plymouth, Connecticut, and New Haven in the summer of 1643 to form a confederation, the United Colonies of New England. Rhode Island was conspicuous by its absence. Ostensibly designed for defense against the Dutch and Native Americans, the United Colonies also bolstered the regional hegemony of Congregationalism. As the Articles of Confederation proclaimed, "in Nation and Religion so in other respects we bee and continue One." The articles had a transatlantic purpose as well. As historian

Harry Ward has argued, a "unified policy in ecclesiastical matters was deemed necessary because of the fear that if Presbyterianism triumphed in England, the churches of New England . . . might be brought under the tight control of the English Presbyterians." Congregational unity would also help protect New England's church order from the increasing calls "for a broader base of toleration" coming out of England—and Rhode Island.[2]

Strengthened by the confederation, Massachusetts began taking measures against the religious diversity beginning to appear in the colonies. The first and most serious threat came from the Baptists. In November 1644 the General Court passed a law banishing Anabaptists from Massachusetts if they openly and obstinately asserted their views or went "about secretly to seduce othrs." The law labeled Baptists "ye incendiaries of common wealths, & ye infectors of persons in maine mattrs of religion, & ye troublers of churches in all places where they have bene." Although some colonists questioned the law, the following year it was "voted yt ye laws mentioned should not be altered at all, nor explained." In May 1646, a petition "for ye continuance of such ordrs, wthout abrogation or weakening, as are in force agst Anabaptists, & othr erronios prsons, whereby to hindr ye spreading or divulging of their errors," was granted. The authorities likely insisted on discriminating between religious confessions in this fashion because, for a significant share of the laity, those divisions were not always so stark or clear. A range of New Englanders were sympathetic to Baptists and their arguments.[3]

The seat of colonial America's Baptist community in Rhode Island survived thanks to Roger Williams's campaign for a colonial patent. He succeeded for two main reasons. First, Parliament controlled London and most of the major ports, allowing it to control colonial policy in a way King Charles, who had limited access to the seas, could not. Second, Williams personally knew the man with the most influence over Parliament's emerging colonial policy: Robert Rich, the Earl of Warwick. When Williams first arrived in London, Parliament did not have a colonial policy. Only in December 1643 did it begin to contemplate colonial religious issues after it replaced the commission that had been in charge of the navy with the Earl of Warwick as lord high admiral and governor-in-chief of all the English plantations "upon the islands and coasts of America." Warwick was seconded by a commission for colonies and trade that included an array of other leading puritans, many of them so-called Independents, like Viscount Saye and Sele, John Pym, and Oliver Cromwell. A new committee replaced Warwick in October 1645, but his influence over Parliamentary colonial policies continued, only terminating with his death in 1658. Overseas, he favored ecclesiastical tolerance among anti-episcopal Protestants and encouraged radical puritans to go to the colonies. John Featley, the Laudian minister of Saint Christopher, encountered the fruit of this trend. His ship on his voyage back to the Caribbean in 1643 was, he complained, "pestered with Brownists, Anabaptists, Antinomians, etc."[4]

Warwick's commission granted Rhode Island its charter in March 1644. It was the first colonial charter not granted by the monarchy and, unlike the royal charters, said nothing about religion or church order. It simply conferred to the inhabitants of Providence, Portsmouth, and Newport the corporate power to form a civil government. The sole restriction was that its "Laws, Constitutions, and Punishments . . . be conformable to the Laws of England, so far as the Nature and Constitution of the place will admit," suggesting matters could be handled somewhat differently overseas.[5]

Roger Williams's capacity for religious tolerance is legendary. However, it had its limits and his Gortonist neighbors in Shawomet exceeded them. He did not include them in his patent, forcing them to secure one on their own. Warwick, on the other hand, who did not have to live with Samuel Gorton as his neighbor, happily granted Gorton's petition. He even gave Gorton and his followers a safe conduct pass when they returned to New England in 1646. The Massachusetts authorities were ordered not to disturb the Gortonists "in their Consciences or Civill peace" as they passed through the colony on their way back to Shawomet, so long as they were "demeaninge themselves Civilly." Once they were safely home, the Gortonists promptly renamed their village Warwick. The name both honored and proclaimed their powerful transatlantic patron.[6]

Still in England, Roger Williams became caught up in the great debate over toleration that has been a cornerstone of Anglo-American discussions of tolerance ever since. Stoked by the end of print censorship, it took place amidst a flood of publications on religion and reform attempting to influence the future of England's church, currently under discussion at a special assembly meeting in Westminster. The Westminster Assembly had not been part of the revolutionaries' original plan. They had wanted to defer the question of church reform until the war's end. However, by the spring of 1643, the failure of either the royalists or Parliamentarians to win a quick victory led members of the Long Parliament to think that an alliance with the Scots was necessary. The Scots insisted that church reform be part of the alliance, hoping that England would adopt a presbyterian system similar to theirs.

Rather than resort to Convocation, the church's traditional assembly for deciding church matters, the Long Parliament turned to a revolutionary invention: an elected assembly of ministers and laity who would draft a plan for church reform to be approved by Parliament, not the king. Responding to Parliament's call to reform the "present Church government by archbishops, bishops," which was "evil, and justly offensive and burdensome to the kingdom," local constituencies of laypeople elected the 121 clergymen and thirty-one lords and MPs who served as representatives to the Westminster Assembly. They took their seats in July 1643. After the Scottish alliance was cemented that fall, they were joined by five Scottish representatives, four prominent ministers (Alexander Henderson, Samuel Rutherford, George Gillespie, and Robert Ballie) and one layman (John Maitland, later Earl of Lauderdale). The assembly's major accomplishments include the Directory for Public Worship (1645), designed to replace the *Book of Common Prayer*; the allowing of informal and extempore prayers in worship rather than just rote prayers; and the Westminster Confession of Faith (1647), designed to be the creed of the reformed national church. It finished its most important work by the spring of 1648, but continued to sit for several more years since there was no other entity able to exercise authority over the church. Until it was dissolved in 1653, the Westminster Assembly also took on some of the work bishops had done before the civil war, especially by approving and rejecting ministers for service in the national church. In the end, the Westminster Assembly was unable to transform the Church of England, but it became a crucial reference point for Reformed Protestantism. The Westminster Confession became the official doctrine of Scottish and English Presbyterians. A modified version adopted at the Savoy Assembly in 1658 became the official doctrine of Congregationalists.[7]

Parliament had decided on an alliance with the Scots Presbyterians because it feared that King Charles would strike an alliance with the Irish Catholic Confederates. Charles did in fact negotiate a truce with the Confederates in September 1643, but he never managed to conclude an alliance with them nor secure a lasting peace for Ireland. Nevertheless, that possibility spurred the Long Parliament's alliance with the Scots or, as it was officially known, the "Solemn League and Covenant for reformation and defence of religion, the honour and happiness of the King, and the peace and safety of the three kingdoms of England, Scotland and Ireland." Aspiring to reform and harmonize the religious life of all three kingdoms, its members pledged to preserve "the reformed religion in the Church of Scotland, in doctrine, worship, discipline and government, against our common enemies" and promote "the reformation of religion in the kingdoms of England and Ireland in doctrine, worship, discipline, and government." Dedicated to "endeavour the extirpation of popery, prelacy (that is, Church government by archbishops, bishops, etc.)," they also opposed "superstition, heresy, schism, profaneness, and whatsoever shall be found to be contrary to sound doctrine and the power of godliness, lest we partake in other men's sins, and thereby be in danger to receive of their plagues." While the Scots were, as one historian points out, "scrupulous in trying to avoid the impression that they were attempting to impose their own reformation upon England" (as hostile English commentators claimed), they clearly hoped and expected the English to favor some sort of presbyterian system: but so did the majority of English delegates to the Westminster Assembly.[8]

While it lasted (1643–47), the Solemn League and Covenant marked the high point of presbyterian power in the English world. Unfortunately, it was not militarily decisive. Sure, fear of the Scottish army tied down Royalist forces in the north, allowing Parliament's armies to gain some small victories in the south during the fall of 1643. They relieved Gloucester from siege, and bested Royalist forces at Newbury and Winceby. However, the royalist position remained strong. Charles rejected efforts to negotiate a peace. The fighting continued.[9]

As the war dragged on, Parliamentarians began splintering into factions defined by a mix of religious and political priorities that reflected different hopes and strategies for ending the war and reforming the church. They generally boiled down into two groups, commonly known as Presbyterians and Independents. Although each faction contained a mix of religious and political stances and was not as coherent as the names suggest, the terms nevertheless are useful. Individuals' relationship to the Solemn League and Covenant provides a good index of their factional loyalties. Presbyterians represented the majority of puritan revolutionaries. They took the oath of the Solemn League and Covenant quickly and without personal qualms. Generally conservative and favoring a quick, negotiated peace with the king, they hoped to secure some sort of presbyterian church system but were willing to compromise with the king along the way. Unfortunately, they did not entirely agree on what sort of presbyterianism they wanted to establish. Should the church be reformed into a divine right Presbyterianism that separated it completely from governmental control? Should there be an Erastian solution, where the government presided over church affairs? If so, to what degree should secular authorities be involved in the running of the church? And which ones?[10]

"Independents," as the Presbyterians termed their rivals, wanted to win the war first then negotiate peace and religious reform from a position of strength. Independent ministers complained the term was a "proud and insolent title" suggesting "an exemption of all Churches from all subjection and dependence"—which they claimed not to want. Nevertheless, the term stuck because it was not entirely inaccurate. Independents never quite explained just how much subjection they would accept. Like the Presbyterians, they were generally Calvinist, but Independents favored congregational autonomy over a strong centralized church system. One of their most important leaders was Sir Henry Vane, the former Massachusetts governor and supporter of Anne Hutchinson. As one of the negotiators for the Solemn League and Covenant, Vane worked to make sure the English had room within it to reform the church as they, not the Scots, saw fit. However, his fellow Independents generally put off swearing it as long as they could. Their most prominent figure, Oliver Cromwell, who served as both a general in the field and an MP in Parliament, hesitated for almost five months before taking it.[11]

The Scots claimed the Independents supported "the New England Way," a term they coined. It was not a compliment. English Independents did in fact have much in common with New Englanders. Many had been friends and neighbors before the exodus to America. Both favored gathered churches of the elect. However, there were also crucial differences. Where Massachusetts, Connecticut, and New Haven adopted Congregationalism and persecuted the Baptists and the various sorts of spiritual Seekers huddling in Rhode Island, English Independency included them. Independents questioned the wisdom of strictly imposing any particular confession or ecclesiastical system. Only from the broadest perspective was the "New England Way" an apt description of their priorities, for English Independents included the full range of opinions within all of New England, including Rhode Island. Facing the greater immediate threats of both Presbyterians and Royalists, they found it more important to cooperate than quibble as the New Englanders were doing. When push came to shove, what the Independents really had in common was a roughly shared "godly" religious sensibility and a desire for liberty of conscience to pursue what for many was a spiritual journey they had just begun.[12]

When these different viewpoints met in the Westminster Assembly, they set off the great toleration debate. Theologically, the assembly represented a strong consensus on matters of faith. Ecclesiastically, however, it was divided. The assembly had little trouble revising the Thirty-Nine Articles, the Church of England's definition of orthodoxy. Problems began when it confronted questions of church structure, power, discipline, and the church's relationship to the state. Many in Parliament preferred an Erastian system that gave the government a significant role in church affairs and found the arguments about *adiaphora* useful in defending this position. Many in the Westminster Assembly, on the other hand, preferred a strong, virtually autonomous church like that of Scotland. Only five Independent ministers sitting in the assembly disagreed. Thomas Goodwin, Philip Nye, Sidrach Simpson, Jeremiah Burroughs, and William Bridge were all former exiles that had been deprived of their positions by Laud. Calling themselves "Dissenting Brethren," they requested a looser church system that would protect the autonomy of individual congregations. Their request, made at the end of December 1643, ignited a debate over whether, how, and how much religious difference the church could tolerate.[13]

The Independent ministers became worried after the Westminster Assembly passed a resolution endorsing "the rights of particular congregations, according to the Word; and to bear with such whose consciences cannot in all things conform to the public rule, as far as the Word of God would have them borne withal." True, it was an endorsement of congregational rights. However, by qualifying it as something to be determined by Scripture, the assembly's presbyterian majority could decide that Scripture did not in fact permit the concessions the Independents wanted. They submitted a text to Parliament pleading their case then published it to make their dilemma public. Their *Apologeticall Narration* claimed their position was "a middle way betwixt that which is falsly charged on us, Brownisme; and that which is the contention of these times, the authoritative Presbyteriall Government in all the subordinations and proceedings of it." They stressed their affinity with the Reformed Churches abroad and the churches in the "Wilderness" (i.e., New England), but refused to fully endorse any of them. Instead, they insisted that they were still sorting out a system of church government through trial, error, and the searching of Scripture. They desired the assembly and Parliament to grant them a "happy latitude and agreement" to continue their quest. They did not want to be locked into an official ecclesiology before discovering the right path.[14]

Although the Dissenting Brethren insisted they simply wanted to create a compromise position between congregational independence and subjection to presbyterian synods, Scots and English Presbyterians immediately denounced them for demanding religious toleration. Starting in January 1644, they began publishing tracts objecting to toleration in principle. After all, "god in the Old Testament granted no toleration of divers Religions, or Disciplines," as Adam Stuert pointed out. Toleration was "dangerous for the State" as "it may breed factions and divisions betwixt all persons of whatsoever relation." English Presbyterians like Thomas Edwards not only shared the hostility of Scots Presbyterians to toleration but took matters a step further. Edwards used sexual innuendo to discredit the Independents, salaciously claiming, "there is no end of errours that the Independent principles and practices lead unto." It was a growing threat, for "daily the Independent Churches like Africa doe breed and bring forth the Monsters of Anabaptism, Antinomianism, Familisme." Toleration, even of theologically closely related Protestants, would open up the floodgates of religious error by submerging the fragile truth in a muddle of misguided beliefs. It would also encourage a faith-destroying skepticism about revealed truth. Presbyterians insisted they wanted to reach an accommodation with the Independents, but also insisted that the Independents submit to the national church establishment. As a Scottish delegate proclaimed, "for that toleration they aime at we cannot consent."[15]

Roger Williams made his famous pronouncement on religious liberty in response to these presbyterian arguments. He first penned a quick response in February, then elaborated it over the next several months. In July he published his famous and influential rejection of coercive authority over religious matters, *The Bloudy Tenent, of Persecution, for Cause of Conscience*. This large tome claimed "inforced uniformity of Religion" was "the greatest occasion of civill Warre, ravishing of conscience, persecution of Jesus Christ in his servants, and of the hypocrisie and destruction of millions of souls." Williams's arguments would be echoed in many subsequent defenses of tolerance or, as many called it, religious liberty.[16]

Significantly, Williams was the only defender of religious liberty who had colonial experience. Generally, Englishmen who had gone overseas opposed religious toleration and favored religious unity. For example, Edward Terry had served as a chaplain to the East India Company before returning to serve for two decades as a minister in Middlesex. He had personally benefited from the religious toleration of the Moghul Empire, but that did not stop him from joining the chorus against toleration. In a 1646 sermon at Paul's Cross, Terry proclaimed that the "Church of God in this Kingdome, at this time, is in very much danger," for liberty of religion "will undoubtedly undoe us." People were using religious liberty "to doe what they please, not what they should." Religious dissent was like a mental illness: "he that hath a Phrensie must be bound; He that hath a Lethargy must be prickt up; And they which strengthen themselves in error or schisme, & diffuse them amongst others, to the prejudice of Church or State, must be violently pull'd out of them." If "allurements and perswasions will not serve the turne," compulsion was acceptable. They "must not alwaies be entreated."[17]

Most of the advocates of religious liberty, like William Walwyn, had neither gone overseas nor did they want to leave England. On the contrary, Walwyn lamented it was "a shame to our profession, and scandall to our cause that well affected men, reall and irreconcileable enemies to tyranny and our common adversaries should be necessitated to leave their native Countrey." He blamed "our Divines" who preferred to imprison and punish people "for exercising their consciences." He also reminded them that it was "by their helpe you should be settled in your liberties." Addressing the Westminster Assembly in 1644, he asked, would "you . . . rather be slaves to the King and hazard the freedome of the whole Nation then that these men should have freedome with you?" Walwyn concluded by warning against "a most pestilent and dangerous designe" to divide "the honest party amongst themselves" by discrediting "the difference of judgement in matters of Religion amongst conscientious well minded people." No doubt with men like Thomas Edwards in mind, he claimed instigators would propound "some grosse and foolish errours," then attribute them to "all those that are called Anabaptists, Antinomians, Brownists, Separatists or Independents," and then advise people "to flye from them as from Serpents, and not to heare them or discourse with them, as they tender the safety of their souls." In consequence, they would be "glad & rejoyce when they heare any of them are imprisoned or silenced; or their bookes (though slightly and absurdly) answered." Indeed, "when they heare that many of" the Independents "are forsaking the Kingdome, and betaking themselves to the West Indies and other places for Liberty of their Consciences (as void of all remorse) they cry out, Let them goe, a good riddance." Like Archbishop Laud they would say, "it will never bee well in England . . . so long as these Sects are permitted to live amongst us." They would urge Parliament to "set up one expresse way for exercise of Religion, and compell all men to submit thereunto, and most severely to punish all such as will not." Walwyn's warning that this was "the very voice of Prelacie, and the authours thereof to bee the very same in heart," was echoed by John Milton in his 1646 poem "On the New Forcers of Conscience under the Long Parliament." Milton complained that, having "thrown off your Prelate Lord," the English and Scots Presbyterians wanted to use "the Civil Sword to force our Consciences that Christ set free." He concluded with the famous line, "New Presbyter is but Old Priest writ Large."[18]

There was a curious transatlantic discrepancy to the debate. In England, Congregationalists advocated liberty of conscience. In New England, they adopted the Presbyterian arguments against toleration as they defended their church order—and their treatment of Roger Williams. John Cotton affirmed in 1652 that "wee have tolerated in our church some Anabaptists, some Antinomians, and some Seekers, and do still," as long as they could "continue in church fellowship" or at least "carry their dissent more privately and inoffensively." They were "borne withall in much meeknesse." As for those who could not do so without going "against their owne judgment and conscience," they were allowed to leave the colony. Massachusetts was "farr from arrogating infallibility of judgement to ourselves or affecting uniformity," Cotton claimed. On the contrary, "wee have here presbyterian churches as well as congregationall" (a few churches favored presbyterian ways, but there was no presbyterian structure beyond an individual congregation). Within this (rather limited) ambit, the people of Massachusetts had "learned (through grace) to keepe the unity of the spirit in the bond of peace" while avoiding being "blowne up and downe (like chaff) by every winde or new notions." This Massachusetts minister was clearly not impressed by the toleration debate.[19]

Bermuda came to figure directly in the toleration debate. Here, an influential Congregationalist minority struggled against the majority that preferred an inclusive, parish-based church. Congregationalism had likely entered the island through a mix of contacts with the Massachusetts Bay colony and the ministry of John Oxenbridge, a Cambridge tutor deprived by Laud who served on Bermuda between 1635 and 1641. In 1641, he and the colony's three other ministers (Nathaniel White, Patrick Copland, and William Golding [or Goulding]) joined with a minority of Bermudans to endorse the New England Way. However, Bermudans did not set up a congregational-style church until January 31, 1644. By then, Oxenbridge was long gone, but the Congregationalists had the support of the new governor, William Sayle. Sayle never became a member of their church, but his wife did. In fact, only about thirty-five men and women (including all the minsters) out of the roughly two thousand colonists on the island qualified for membership in the new church. The ministers now refused to administer sacraments to the rest, claiming to be "private men" only able to serve the congregation that called them, not the colony as a whole. Suddenly, the vast majority of the colonists found themselves deprived of basic religious services. The ministers would preach to them, but would not baptize their children, offer them communion, or even marry them. The colonists' complaints reached England soon after the toleration took off.[20]

In October 1644, the Earl of Warwick, acting on behalf of the Bermuda Company, responded to the colonists' petition by issuing a proclamation calling for moderation. He wanted to slow the pace of religious change until Parliament approved the Directory of Worship. For the time being, the religious and political leadership of the colony would continue in place. Emphasizing the company's desire "to approve ourselves to every mans conscience in the sight of God," Warwick would not compel the ministers to administer the sacraments to all the colonists. However, he requested they preach "the Word of God" in "every church" until the company could send out a minister who would. Praying that the controversy would not destroy the island's piety, Warwick urged the magistrates to "be as a Sanctuary, and City of refuge to all such as love the Lord Jesus Christ in sincerity" by "promoting the power of Godliness in all places" and "suppressing all manner of sinne and wickednesse," such as "Tipling Houses, Idelnesse, and ill Company."[21]

Not everyone shared Warwick's tolerance for Bermuda's Congregationalists. English Presbyterians criticized them as hypocrites. Did they not deny to others in Bermuda and New England what they insisted on for themselves in England, that is, toleration? This hypocrisy illustrated the fundamental dangers of Independency, according to the Presbyterian MP William Prynne. They were "schismatical, Tyrannicall, and Seditious" and the creators of a "faction." The Scot Robert Ballie saw their actions as proof that "the Independents avowd and cleare intention when they have power" was "to dissolve and annull all the Churches of England, yea of the world." Concerned about the future of their church, Nathaniel White and William Goulding returned to London to defend it. They were not crazy sectaries, they insisted, just godly men whose church was the same as New England's.[22]

The controversy over Bermuda's church prompted Parliament's first statement on colonial religious policy. The October 1645 Act "for the establishment of freedom of worship in the American Plantations and especially in Bermuda" ordered that colonists were not to suffer "trouble & molestation by & for any ceremony or imposition in the matters of Gods worship" as long as they obeyed the civil authority. They were to be allowed "quietly, freely, & peaceably to worship God accordingly in those Islands, and also in all other parts & through out the coasts of America" and to settle where they desired. It was both an endorsement of the godly pluralism emerging in the colonies loyal to Parliament and a possible model for England's church. As historian Rachel Schnepper notes, it represented "a moderate, limited, accommodation" that many Parliamentary Presbyterians and Independents could support. Indeed, it "was also precisely the sort of settlement the political independents hoped to achieve in England," namely, "an Erastian national church, reformed in both doctrine and practice, but with a moderate accommodation for the godly who differed from the national church, not in matters of theology, but only in a few minor points of church government." It was, in short, more about England than America.[23]

Most colonists remained either unaware or deliberately ignorant of the Parliamentary ordinance. Faced with similar dilemmas, they had come to rather different conclusions. That same October, for example, Plymouth colony debated the idea of allowing "full and free tollerance of religion to all men that would preserve the Civill peace, and submit unto Goverment." It would have been extremely generous, imposing "no limitacion or excepcion against Turke Jew Papist Arian Socinian Nicholaytan Familist or any other" sect. The mover of the motion was the merchant William Vassall. Like his brother Samuel, who had recently tried to colonize Carolana, William had been involved in colonial projects for years. Samuel was now serving in the revolutionary Parliament and, as a commissioner for plantations alongside Warwick, he likely had a hand in drafting the act for the establishment of freedom of worship in the American plantations. Still, that did not give William Vassall enough clout to overthrow the New England Way. Governor William Bradford, Edward Winslow, and other prominent colonists who had long been resident in Plymouth prevented his proposal from even coming to a vote, "having expressed the sad consequences" that "would follow." It "would eate out the power of Godlines," Bradford insisted. Vassall, proclaiming his intent to "injoy gods ordinancis," said "if through persecution we bee debarred in New England we must waite till the lord remidie it heare or till we can returne to the land of our nativitie again." Not long afterward he returned to England before moving to Barbados, whose economy was booming.[24]

England's toleration debate was never resolved, largely because it took place against a background of continuing warfare and political revolution. Another year of campaigning during 1644 failed to achieve either victory or a negotiated peace. The Scots had improved Parliament's military position, but not enough to win. Their main military contribution came at Marston Moor in July, where they joined with a Parliamentary army to defeat a royalist force trying to relieve the siege of York. The victory brought the north of England under Parliamentary control and secured the reputation of its victorious general, Oliver Cromwell. However, in August the army sent to conquer the West Country was completely defeated at the Battle of Lostwithiel, Cornwall. Surrounded, it surrendered while its commanders made a humiliating escape by boat.[25]

Meanwhile, the colonies were gradually pulled into the conflict as their initial efforts at neutrality wore thin. Virginia went royalist for several reasons, including its opposition to Parliamentary plans to control the colony's trade. In the spring of 1644, Governor Berkeley was able to get an oath of loyalty to the king passed. Those who refused to take it were to be fined and imprisoned. Before it could be imposed, however, the Powhatans, thinking they could take advantage of the English while they were divided, rose up in a second revolt that killed about four hundred colonists. The ensuing war temporarily prevented Berkeley from suppressing the colony's puritans.[26]

Massachusetts made its Parliamentarian sympathies public in a May 1644 proclamation accusing "evill affected prsons" of fomenting "divisions in many places of government in America." Gesturing at neutrality, it noted that some profess "themselves for the king, & othrs for the Parliament," but pointed out "that the Parliament themselves professe that they stand for the king & Parliament against the malignant Papists & delinquents in that kingdome." Anyone who tried to rally people "under pretence that he is for the King of England, & such as adioyne wth him, against the Parliament, shalbe accounted as an offender of an high nature against this common wealth," subject to severe, even capital, punishment. However, as Massachusetts was still dependent on trade with England, "this shall not be extended against any marchant, strangers, & shipmen that come hither merly for matter of trade and marchandize." Even if they came from ports "that are in the hands of the king," they would be left alone, as long as they behave "quietly, & free from raising or nurishing any faction, mutiny, or sedition among us."[27]

In Maryland, the attempt to maintain a religious and political balance between Catholics and Protestants broke down completely. What Catholics would call the "plundering time" began in 1644, when Richard Ingle, a ship captain who traded regularly with the colony, and his crew began plundering the homes of all Marylanders who would not swear loyalty to Parliament. Posing as Protestant heroes, they targeted Catholics, expelled the Jesuits, and shut down their mission. William Claiborne took advantage of the chaos to reclaim Kent Island for Virginia. On the other hand, royalist Virginia gave Maryland's governor Leonard Calvert and other Catholics refuge until the spring of 1647. Calvert was then able to regain control of the colony with the help of troops he hired in Virginia. Unfortunately for the cause of Maryland's Catholics, he suddenly died that summer, probably from a snakebite.[28]

Warwick and his commission supported Ingle's aggression against the Catholic Marylanders. Responding to what it claimed were the petitions of "many of the Inhabitants of Maryland in America," in the fall of 1645 the Commissioners for Foreign Plantations described to Parliament "the oppressions" colonists had "undergone under the Tyrannicall goverment of that Province, since its first setling by Recusants, who have not only seduced but forced many of his Mats subiects from their religion." Claiming that Lord Baltimore had thus "wickedly broken the trust reposed in him," it recommended revoking his patent. It then ordered the commissioners "to nominate and appoint an able Governor and other fitt Officers of the Protestant Religion and well affected to the Parlyament" to govern Maryland in Leonard Calvert's stead. In the event, it took until 1647 for Parliament to get to the brink of actually revoking the patent, at which point Baltimore, having carefully preserved his neutrality during the war, was able to step in and, it seems, get it dismissed. There is no more record of the ordinance after March 1647.[29]

The firm anti-Catholicism of Warwick's commission reflected the increasing power of the Independent faction. Also known as the war party, they gained the upper hand in 1644 after the combination of Cromwellian victory at Marston Moor and the embarrassing defeat in the West Country. In December they inaugurated a new war policy. First, Parliament passed a self-denying ordinance prohibiting MPs from serving as officers. Then, a new officer corps was appointed. The overall result was to replace political Presbyterians with more aggressive, Independent commanders. Cromwell, the victorious commander, was not only exempted from the self-denying ordinance: he was promoted to second-in-command of the New Model Army, the select and highly trained force assembled over the winter. Flush with determination and material support, the New Model Army proceeded to trounce the king's armies in 1645. By the end of summer, Charles had no more armies left, nor the resources to raise a new one. In Ireland, meanwhile, the truce broke down. The Catholic Confederates gained control of almost all of Ireland outside Dublin and Ulster, but they were not strong enough to save their king. With his back to the wall, Charles decided against retreating to Ireland: the Confederates, on the advice of a papal nuncio, were insisting on the restoration of the Catholic Church as a condition for cooperating with him. Instead, in May 1646 he surrendered to the Scots.[30]

A long, frustrating round of peace negotiations ensued. Charles, rather than capitulate or cooperate, preferred to play the many factions among the rebels against one another. He repeatedly considered then refused their demands. Eventually, in January 1647, the exasperated Scots, in need of money, despaired of reaching a satisfactory conclusion. Eager to maintain good relations with Parliament, they exchanged control of the king's person for £400,000 to reimburse their wartime expenses.[31]

In the meantime, religious and political change was becoming evermore closely linked. Well before the Westminster Assembly had come to any conclusions, Parliament began taking an active role in altering the character of the national church. First, in August 1643, it had acted on complaints about scandalous, popish, persecuting, innovating, or openly royalist ministers by setting up committees for "plundered ministers." If suspect ministers were found guilty, they could be ejected from their pulpits. A purge of the clergy followed. While most were accused of immorality, it is clear that ministers associated with the Laudian program were targeted for their religious and political allegiances. Most of these deposed ministers would not regain their old positions until after the Restoration of the monarchy in 1660. Since a number had already fled to royalist territory, the committees were able to give their posts to loyal Parliamentarian ministers, some of whom had fled royalist territory. Over time, these committees gained more power over church policy.[32]

In the fall 1646, with the king now a prisoner, Parliament took a powerful step in the direction of Presbyterianism. It abolished the institution of bishops, forbade the use of the *Book of Common Prayer*, and seized and sold off episcopal lands: largely to pay off the Scottish army. In a pattern recalling that of the Reformation's dissolution of the monasteries, wealthy laymen—in particular London merchants—bought up much of the lands. Since most of them also supported presbyterianism, they had now literally invested in, and were profiting from, the new, Parliamentary church order. While these elites' attachment to the presbyterian cause remained strong, London was also becoming the most religiously diverse part of the English world. All sorts of new sects and congregations began appearing in its streets, fueling presbyterian hostility toward tolerance.[33]

Nevertheless, Parliament's treatment of individual bishops was, in practice, fairly lenient. Only two bishops, both notorious for their hostility to puritans, suffered imprisonment. Archbishop William Laud and Matthew Wren, bishop of Ely, were arrested as the war broke out. In 1643, Laud heard a rumor that a recently arrived delegation from New England led by Hugh Peters had suggested that Parliament send the two imprisoned bishops to Massachusetts. The "plot," as Laud called it, was rejected. Instead, at the insistence of the Scots, Parliament impeached and executed the aged Laud in January 1645, who thereby became a martyr for episcopacy. Understanding the power of martyrdom, the revolutionary regime was reluctant to create any more and held Wren a prisoner without trial for eighteen years, until March 1660. The rest of the bishops were allowed to live in peace under varying degrees of supervision. Some managed to continue the episcopal traditions of the church, most importantly by ordaining ministers. Their greatest foe was time. The bishops grew old and sick and died until, by 1658, only eleven of the original twenty-three were still alive. Boasting an average age of seventy-three, it seemed likely that a hard winter could extinguish England's episcopate. Fortunately for them, the revolution ended first. When episcopacy was restored in 1662, the Restoration Church would be able to maintain a tenuous but unbroken continuity with the prerevolutionary church.[34]

Even though it was now prohibited, devotion to the religion represented by the bishops and the *Book of Common Prayer*—what might be called episcopalianism—persisted among a sizeable portion of the population. Driven underground, episcopalians used the techniques of a clandestine sect, including secret ordinations of ministers, to survive. Still, a significant number of ministers conformed to the revolutionary church even as they respected the old ways. Only a dedicated few absolutely refused to conform to the new order. Had the revolution managed to survive for another generation or so, episcopalianism might have faded away along with its bishops. As it was, there were plenty of episcopal loyalists among clergy and laypeople to smooth the return to an episcopal church after 1660. In a number of instances, their experience of persecution under the revolutionary regime only increased their attachment to bishops and the *Book of Common Prayer*.[35]

In the midst of this religious strife, projectors of new colonies hoped expansion could provide a path back to religious unity. The Courteen Association revived its royal patent to Madagascar, sponsoring two efforts to colonize that distant land. The first expedition, led by William Courteen Jr., set out in August 1644. Its 140 men, women, and children did not realize until after they arrived that the soil was too poor to grow food. That quickly put them in a relationship of dependence on the indigenous inhabitants. When those relations deteriorated into violence, the

English lost access to their principal source of sustenance and began to die of starvation. In May 1646 the sixty survivors abandoned the colony for the Comoros islands, hoping to eventually return to England. In the end, twenty-four managed to sail across the Indian Ocean to the East India Company outpost in Aceh, Indonesia. A passing ship carried the rest to India, where a few joined the Portuguese in Goa and others joined the East India Company in Surat. Only about twelve of the colonists ever made it back to England. A second expedition in 1649 also failed due to indigenous resistance. This attempt to create a Barbados-style plantation colony in northwestern Madagascar provoked the Madagascans, who killed the governor and several of other colonists shortly after they landed. The survivors fled.[36]

While little is known about the religious provisions for the Madagascar expeditions, it is clear that they were not envisioned as havens for tolerance and diversity. The godly ambitions of its leading early promoter, Richard Boothby, a former East India Company merchant and councilor, were clear. At the company's outpost in Surat in the 1630s, he had been regarded as "a Puritan" because he objected to attending to "the Custome-House affairs on the Sabbath days" and reproved the "wicked President" of the council and "his lewd Favourite" for their "Bachanalian Sabbath-breakings, and lewd discourse" when they "feasted, and drunk themselves drunk with Dutch, French, Italians, Arminians." In a 1646 promotional tract, Richard Boothby had urged his divided country to unite around efforts to plant colonies. He prayed for religious unity, "that the Lord Jesus would please to break in peeces the most hurtfull Cords of Contention with the spirit of truth and concord . . . that we may be joyned together in one minde, in truth love and Christian Charity, to the praise honour and glory of God Almighty." Looking from Virginia to Madagascar, he anticipated the colonies would be "speciall receptacles and succours to truly religious English Protestants," fleeing an England punished by God "for the crying sinnes thereof, by the prevalence of Malignants tirranous Papists." To relieve one current cause of strife, he suggested England's bishops could "goe and plant a Colony in Madagascar . . . and indeavour to reduce those ignorant soules to Christianity." A Madagascar colony would contribute to the honor and happiness of "a pious Christian protestant Nation, unspotted and undefiled with Idolatry, Atheisme, Papisme, Anabaptisme, Brownisme, Antinomianisme, or otherwise heresie or error." Its geographic isolation would guarantee that "neither Heathen, nor Idolatrous superstitious or Malignant Christians can come to hurt or annoy them (being once settled therein)." Finally, what "an addition will it be to Gods glory to reduce and convert so many" of those "brave personable affable people (poore ignorant soules) to christianity." If "the English, Scotch, and Dutch all of one Religion, could perfectly and Christianly agree together in the enterprize," it would "make them a terrour, to all atheisticall heathen and Idolatrous Christians." His deepest hope was that the Dutch and British, as well as Britains Protestants, could live "in Peace, Unity, and Amity together."[37]

A similar vision of colonies as instruments for religious unity was proposed in the winter of 1645 by some of the same Huguenots who had earlier proposed a colony in Carolana. Resurrecting their former plan, they petitioned Parliament for a patent with the backing of the influential Hartlib circle. Led by Samuel Hartlib and John Dury, this circle of correspondents connected learned Protestants across Europe with a shared commitment to social, economic, and other reforms in the hopes of creating an improved society that fostered ecumenical unity within the greater cause of international Protestantism. Although based in London, Dury, a Scot, and Hartlib, son of a wealthy German merchant in Poland and an English gentlewoman, actively cultivated the international dimension of their reform program and took an interest in colonization. As before, the Huguenot colony was imagined as a sort of transplanted La Rochelle, the Huguenots' once mighty fortress-port city. Strict religious purity and Reformed unity would prevail in this bastion against Spanish power. France and Spain were now at war with each other, and the colony might also help liberate the Palatinate from Spanish occupation. Unfortunately, neither the Huguenots nor the Hartlib circle were able to persuade Parliament to accept the conditions they insisted on. This second attempt to bring an international Protestant dimension to English America sputtered and was forgotten.[38]

As for the official religion of the English revolutionaries, it remained rather vague apart from its firmly anti-Catholic and anti-episcopal character. There were many different opinions within the Westminster Assembly and Parliament. Had the war been won sooner, the majority within the Westminster Assembly might have had their way when they recommended a presbyterian church settlement. However, by the time they made that recommendation, Cromwell and the Independents were in power. They supported a church that was largely Calvinist in theology, but a mixed bag ecclesiastically: part Presbyterian, part Independent, and very Erastian.[39]

With secular authorities continuing to play a significant role in church affairs, Congregationalists had difficulty holding their own outside of New England. The Bermudan case is exemplary. The colony remained under the control of the Somers Isles Company in London, whose directors decided to send out a new governor, Thomas Turner, and two more ministers, William Vilner and Thomas Hooper, all of presbyterian inclinations in 1646. Soon after they arrived, Turner turned the previous ministers out of office. Then a jury questioned whether the company could permit them to create a separate Congregational church. After all, it had hired the ministers to serve the whole community. Surely liberty of conscience did not mean that they could abandon their contractual responsibilities? That fall, former governor Sayle and the congregational minister Golding sailed back to England to petition for help. The company refused to take a firm stance in favor of either party, effectively supporting the current presbyterian status quo on the island.[40]

Oddly, Sayle's struggle for the religious liberty of Independents on Bermuda intersected with a similar struggle by presbyterians in Massachusetts. His journey back to England took him to Massachusetts, where his ship picked up the presbyterian Robert Child. Child was carrying a Remonstrance demanding liberty of conscience for presbyterians in New England. He, Samuel Maverick, and several other colonists had demanded civil and religious liberties for non–church members, but the Confederation of New England had ignored their demands for liberty of conscience just as it did those of the Baptists. After the Massachusetts General Court refused their petition, they decided to take their case to Parliament. The unfortunate Maverick, who stayed behind, was imprisoned and fined £150. Alas, Child found no more support for his cause in England than Sayle did, thanks to the efforts of Edward Winslow, who had returned to England to defend the right of Plymouth and Massachusetts to continue on their godly way, without toleration.[41]

*

Had the majority of colonists had their way, America would have emerged from the era of the English Civil War as less religiously diverse than before. However, the changes in religious attitudes and policies taking place in England put limits on their ambitions, most importantly by allowing Rhode Island to survive. The Earl of Warwick deserves as much credit as, if not more than, Roger Williams for keeping the colony—and its Baptist influence—alive at a time when its neighbors were eager to devour it. Warwick even went beyond Williams to support the rights of the Gortonists to religious liberty. Although the colonial periphery generally disagreed, there was little it could do to prevent the revolutionary Parliament from moving further down the road of religious liberty than most of them were willing to go. Unfortunately, once it abolished the Church of England, the revolutionary Parliament discovered that there was no clear consensus on where to go next. Those proposing new colonies in Madagascar and Carolana tended to affirm a Reformed Protestant religious unity, but no one in England could agree more particularly on how such a Reformed Church should be organized. In the meantime, colonies pursued their own policies with little interference from England.

Apart from Rhode Island and Maryland, the North American colonies largely achieved religious unity at the local level. However, the consolidation of regional church orders contributed to the overall fragmentation of colonial religious life, as the different regions moved in different directions. Massachusetts's church order set the tone for New England outside of Rhode Island. Virginia and Saint Christopher reinforced their support for the king's church. Bermuda attempted to imitate the New England way, but could not because it was still subject to directors in England. These mixed results explain the colonies' contradictory role in the great debate over toleration. On the one hand, some of the most outspoken voices on both sides—for and against toleration—came from the colonies. On the other, the colonies offered no coherent religious vision for the future of the English world, just a range of options that were becoming increasingly difficult to reconcile. Colonial religious pluralism was emerging despite—or even because of—the efforts of most colonists to combat it.

TWELVE

Revolution: New England, the Bahamas, Barbados, the Leewards, 1647–1649

From his perch in Massachusetts, John Winthrop gloated over the failure of the first Bahamas colony. There, with great promises of "Libertye of Conscience," English radicals had launched the colony of Eleutheria in late summer 1647. Unfortunately, as they arrived in the Bahamas several months later, one of the colonists, "Captain Butler a yonge man who came in the Shiuppe from England," took things too far and "made use of his Libertye to disturbe all the Company." Apparently, "he could not endure any ordinances, or worshipp, etc." Too independent for the Independents who had launched the colony, Butler "made suche a Faction," that he forced the leader of the colony "to remove to an other Ilande." On the way over, the ship wrecked, stranding the colonists. For the next several years, they scratched out a miserable existence before they finally abandoned the island. The Eleutheria disaster seemed to confirm the righteousness of Massachusetts's rejection of religious liberty.[1]

In England, on the other hand, the cause of religious liberty began moving closer to the position of Eleutheria just weeks after the colonists left its shores. Led by the New Model Army, a stunning series of events transformed England's civil war into a revolution. The army overawed a reluctant Parliament with its military power and advanced revolutionary arguments for political and religious liberties in the name of promoting a more just, godly, and equitable society. Rather than support them, a number of conservative Presbyterians and their Scottish allies joined with royalists in 1648 in a desperate attempt to reinstate the king. This second civil war was a terrible miscalculation. The New Model Army won handily, but its sense of betrayal accelerated the revolutionary process. The culmination came in January 1649 with the execution of the king. The monarchy was abolished. England was declared a republic. The world of religious and political possibilities was radically transformed.

The year 1649 saw a broad swath of religious liberties enshrined on both sides of the Atlantic. Presiding over an increasingly polarized religious and political order, England's republican government set the outer bounds of acceptable religious belief with a new blasphemy act that was far more liberal than the one passed by Massachusetts. Maryland, meanwhile, passed an extraordinary piece of tolerationist legislation: the 1649 Act concerning Religion. Unfortunately, Maryland, like Eleutheria, discovered that religious toleration was no guarantee of political stability, especially if it required Protestants tolerating Catholics. A quick comparison of the fates of Massachusetts with Eleutheria and Maryland demonstrates that toleration, especially as an abstract, universal principle applying to a wide range of occasionally antagonistic beliefs, was no guarantee of political stability or economic prosperity.

Elsewhere, Royalists, who had little more interest in toleration than Massachusetts, continued to resist the revolutionaries on both sides of the ocean. Although they had lost England, they still controlled Scotland, much of Ireland, and most of the colonies outside of New England. Virginia and several Caribbean islands reinforced their support for the old Church of England by suppressing or expelling the puritans and Catholics within their borders. Nevertheless, Irish and English Catholics persisted in both regions despite the repression from royalists in the Caribbean and Parliamentarians in Maryland. In the Leewards, Irish Catholics even gained a new lease on life thanks to an enterprising French Jesuit mission.

*

It was not immediately clear if the revolutionary Republic's religious liberty would affect colonial religious establishments. It was certainly not what most New Englanders favored. From New Haven to Maine, they were busily consolidating the Congregational order. Massachusetts had begun setting the outer boundaries of Congregational orthodoxy in May 1646 with a Blasphemy Act, the first of a series of laws punishing religious deviancy. It was directed at Christians as well as "such pagan Indians as have submitted themselves to" our government. Admitting that they could not compel faith "either by force of armes or by poenall laws," it argued that "common reason requireth every state & society of men to be more carefull of prventing ye dishonor & contempt of ye most high God (in whom we all consist)" in "any mortall princes & magistrates." Therefore, "no prson wthn ys iurisdiction, whethr Christian or pagan, shall wittingly & willingly prsume to blaspheme his holy name, eithr by wilfull or obstinate deniing ye true God, or his creation or govermt of ye world, or shall curse God, or reprach ye holy religion of God, as if it were but a politic device to keepe ignorant men in awe, nor shall uttr any other eminent kind of blasphemy, of ye like nature & degree," on pain of death.[2]

Other, less sanguinary, laws followed, forbidding alternative religious practices and suppressing criticisms of the Congregational order. Indigenous New Englanders could not "at any time pawwaw, or prforme outward worship to their false gods, or to ye devill, in any prt of our iurisdiction, whethr they be such as dwell here, or shall come hithr," on pain of a fine for the powwow (the religious leader) and everyone attending the ceremony. A series of heresies were also condemned, including "dening ye immortality of ye soule, or ye resurrection of ye body, or any sinn to be repented of in ye regenrate, or any evill done by ye outward man to be accounted sinn, or deniing yt Christ gave himselfe a ransome for our sinns, or yt we are iustified by his death & righteousness, but by ye prfection of our owne works, or deniing ye morallity of ye 4th commandment" (commanding Sabbath observance). Any "Christian wthin this iurisdiction" who attempted "to subvert & destroy ye Christian faith & religion, by broaching or maintaining" such heresies, was subject to fines. A much steeper fine would be applied to those who "shall endeavor to seduce others to ye like heresy & apostacy from ye faith & religion of or Lord Jesus Christ." Six years later, in May 1652, a new law ordered imprisonment and whipping, or a fine, for any adult who denied "either by word or writing, any of the bookes of the Old Testament or New . . . to be the written & infallable word of God." The punishment would be withheld if the offender recanted. However, if the individual again were to "publish & obstinatly & pertinanciously mayntaye the said wicked opinion, he shall be banished or put to death."[3]

The raft of laws intended to secure respect and obedience for Massachusetts's official religion continued. The General Court admitted that it refused "to compell any to enter into ye fellowship of ye church, nor force ym to prtake in ye ordinance peculier to ye church"; however, it did require everyone within its jurisdiction to attend "ye ministery of ye word . . . upon ye Lords dayes, & upon such publike fasts dayes & dayes of thanskgiving as are to be genrally held by ye appointment of authority." As with England's recusancy laws, those who failed to attend "wthout iust & necessary cause" could be fined. Also subject to fine were those who did attend but then criticized "the ordr of ye churches established in ys country, by open renouncing their church estate, or their ministery, or othr ordinances dispenced in ym, eithr upon pretence yt ye churches were not planted by any new apostles, or yt ordinances are for carnall Christians; or babes in Christ, & not for spirituall or illuminated prsons, or upon any othr such like groundles conceite." Additional offenses liable to punishment included, swearing "rashly & vainely, eithr by ye holy name of God, or any othr oath," interrupting a minister "in his preaching, or . . . charging him falsely wth any error wch he hath not taught, (in ye open face of ye church)." Concluding this spate of legislation was a law commanding the death penalty for any child over sixteen that "shall curse or smite their naturall fathr or mother." Another prescribed the same punishment for "a stubborne or rebellious sonne" who would "not obey ye voyce of his fathr or ye voyce of his mothr."[4]

In May 1647, the Massachusetts General Court capped off this line of religious legislation with several anti-Catholic acts. One law banished any "Jesuite or spirituall or ecclesiasticall prson (as they are termed) ordained by ye authority of ye pope or sea of Rome," who might "at any time repair to or come wthin this iurisdiction." Blaming the "great warrs, combustions, & divisions wch are this day in Europe" on the "secret undrminings & solicitations of those of ye jesuiticall order, men brought up & devoted to ye religion & corte of Rome," the General Court claimed it was simply following the precedent of other states who had expelled the Jesuits from their territories. Should any such expelled priest return to Massachusetts, they would, "upon lawful tryall and conviction, be put to death." Provision was made for Jesuits who might be shipwrecked on their shore: they would be permitted to stay in peace until they could organize a voyage out of the colony.[5]

In 1648, Massachusetts turned its attention to witchcraft. These laws were prompted by events in England where, between 1644 and 1647, the puritan-dominated region of East Anglia experienced a major witch hunt. Some three hundred people died, most of them women. Many New Englanders, including John Winthrop, had emigrated from East Anglia. They paid close attention to the actions of the notorious instigator of the trials, the so-called witch finder general, Matthew Hopkins. The young son of a local puritan minister, Hopkins outlined his techniques for procuring confessions from suspected witches in his published defense, *The Discovery of Witches* (1647). New Englanders had clearly read it, for in May 1648, the General Court ordered that "the course wch hath bene taken in England for discovry of witches, by watching them a certeine time" be used in a suspected case of witchcraft, ordering the investigation "to begin this night if it may be." Between 1648 and 1663, about eighty people in Massachusetts and Connecticut were accused and seventeen executed in New England's first witch hunt.[6]

The consolidation of Congregationalism was capped off with a synod bringing together all the New England colonies outside of Rhode Island. Held in Cambridge, Massachusetts, between 1646 and 1648, it produced the "Cambridge Platform," which laid out the essentials of New England Congregational belief and church order. The platform accepted the Confession of Faith drawn up by the Westminster Assembly, but rejected its proposal for a presbyterian church. The synod reflected Massachusetts's domination of the region's religious order. When some of its neighbors were less than rigorous in their suppression of religious dissent, Massachusetts urged greater severity. For example, the Massachusetts General Court admonished the Plymouth General Court in October 1649 for conniving at "diverse Annabaptists, arison up in your jurisdiction." The men of Plymouth should have "reduced such erring men againe into the right way." Alas, "your patient bearing wth such men hath produced another effect, namely, the multiplying and encreasing of the same errors," especially in the town of Seekonk, on the border of Rhode Island. The magistrates of Massachusetts pointed out that the "infeccion of such diseases, being so neere us, are likely to spread into our jurisdiccion." They concluded with the hope, "that wee shall both so aequally and zealously uphold all the truths of God revealed, that wee may render a comfortable accompt to Him that hath sett us in our places, and betrusted us wth the keeping of both tables."[7]

In England, by contrast, the rising power of the New Model Army and Oliver Cromwell forced the revolutionary government to abandon strict religious uniformity. Armies were not a major factor in colonial religious history, but they were in Britain and Ireland. All the armies fighting the Wars of the Three Kingdoms were religious as well as political and military institutions. Each left some sort of religious legacy. Scottish Covenanters advanced the cause of Presbyterianism wherever they went, including Ulster. Their army's strategy of recruiting directly from the country's parishes reinforced the Presbyterian ethos from the top to the bottom of Scotland's social scale. The Irish Catholic Confederate army, by contrast, restored the Catholic Church where it could. It divided over the question of tolerating Protestantism, however, splitting along the broader Irish Catholic ethnoreligious divide. The Gaelic Old Irish tended to support a strong connection to the papacy and be the least inclined to tolerate Protestants. The Old English tended to be less enthusiastic about the pope's role in Irish politics and more open to cooperation with Protestant royalists. In turn, royalist forces in all three kingdoms had to make some sort of accommodation with Roman Catholics. This need was most obvious in Ireland, but even in England a disproportionate number of Catholics fought as royalist officers and soldiers. Some English Catholics, like Lord Baltimore, tried to remain neutral in hopes of preserving their lives and property, but none risked their lives in the armies of Parliament or the Covenanters, whose anti-Catholicism extended to the architecture of the Church of England. Whenever possible, they tore down railings and other Laudian renovations. Their royalist opponents in Ireland and England meanwhile strove to protect churches from being taken over by Catholics or devastated by Calvinist iconoclasts.[8]

Nevertheless, the religious influence of the New Model Army had no peer. It was, in the words of one historian, "a privileged enclave in that it enjoyed complete freedom of preaching and theological speculation, immune from interference by magistrates, county committees, presbyterian clerics, even parliament; and the continuance of this *de facto* toleration was always high on its list or priorities, for officers as well as men." Where presbyterians tended to be favored in appointments to parish churches, Independent-minded ministers took up a disproportionate number of chaplaincies within the army. Their influence over its soldiers and officers, including Cromwell, encouraged its support of the Independents' cause. Hugh Peters from New England was especially influential as an army chaplain. By 1647, the New Model Army had become the most powerful institutional advocate for religious tolerance in the English world, carrying its mix of faiths on campaign across England, Ireland, Scotland, and, eventually, the Americas.[9]

Oliver Cromwell's religious evolution is a good illustration of how the pressure of events could strengthen an individual's support for Independency and religious tolerance. Cromwell began very much like John Winthrop, as a puritan country gentleman. They came from the same region and had similar backgrounds. Cromwell even had contemplated migrating to New England. However, experience set them on different tracks. In his fledgling colony, Winthrop's support for established religion became rigid and unshakeable. Cromwell's wartime experience taught him a very different lesson. Where Winthrop saw religious liberty undermining the foundations of society, Cromwell saw how godly people with a variety of religious views made excellent soldiers and concluded that the real danger to the godly cause was the persecution of these valuable allies. His endorsement of liberty of conscience only became firmer with each military victory.[10]

The New Model Army's rise to power was not inevitable, but England's political elite proved too divided to resolve the country's political and religious crisis without it. Presbyterians wanted a moderate peace, but could not secure it because King Charles refused to commit to a specific plan. Meanwhile, Parliament's refusal to pay off the army led many soldiers to realize that their best interests lay in collaborating with the Independents to have a say in the peace process. Soldiers began mobilizing in April 1647, when regiments elected representatives to express their grievances to their commanding officers as well as Parliament. In June, some of these representatives, or "agitators," joined with a group of radical officers to kidnap the king and bring him under the control of the army. Perhaps then the slippery monarch would make a satisfactory peace. Their commanding general, Sir Thomas Fairfax, responded by forming a General Council of the Army consisting of himself, Cromwell, Henry Ireton (Cromwell's friend and son-in-law as well as a fellow cavalry commander), and four representatives from each regiment. They made a Solemn Engagement not to disband until the army's demands were met. On June 14, from the army's camp at Saint Albans, the General Council presented Parliament with a declaration proclaiming that they "were not a mere mercenary army" but defenders of "the people's just rights and liberties." After listing their demands for a peace settlement, they claimed that they did not intend "to overthrow Presbytery or hinder the settlement thereof, and to have the Independent Government set up." However, like the Dissenting Brethren within the Westminster Assembly, they insisted that church reform include "a provision of tender consciences" so that those who differ in matters of religion "may not for that be debarred from the common rights, liberties or benefits belonging equally to all . . . while they live soberly and inoffensively towards others, and peaceably and faithfully towards the state."[11]

The religious principles set forth in the Saint Albans declaration remained a consistent demand of the New Model Army. Parliament's refusal to accept them pushed the soldiers toward ever more radical action. In July, the Council of the Army drew up the Heads of the Proposals: suggestions for a constitutional settlement involving a series of legal, political, and constitutional reforms. Regarding religion, they demanded the abolition of episcopal power, along with the laws "enjoining the use of the Book of Common Prayer" and acts imposing penalties for not using it or "for not coming to church, or for meetings elsewhere for prayer or other religious duties, exercises or ordinances." They also insisted that no man be forced to swear the Solemn League and Covenant "against their judgments or consciences." They even wanted to reconsider the use of oaths, "so far as they may extend or be construed to the molestation or ensnaring of religious and peaceable people merely for nonconformity in religion." However, their ideal of liberty of conscience did not extend to Roman Catholics. They urged for "some other provision to be made for discovering of papists and popish recusants, and for disabling them, and of all Jesuits or priests, from disturbing the state."[12]

This religious agenda did not have much support in the colonies. While few wanted a Presbyterian church, most supported the presbyterian vision of religious unity. Colonists like Edward Winslow lobbied on both sides of the Atlantic against radical religious liberty. Results varied from colony to colony and region to region. New England Congregationalists effectively defended their gains everywhere outside of Rhode Island. Their colleagues on Bermuda, however, were treated as an unwelcome sect. First, Governor Turner's regime forbade them from using any of the churches, forcing them to worship in a mill. Then, in June 1647, Bermuda's assembly passed an act that effectively called for conformity to the presbyterian system favored by the governor and his ministers. Everyone (except bastards and the children of "negroes") was to be baptized within two weeks and receive the Lord's Supper from one of the presbyterian ministers who had accompanied the governor. The assembly excused the act by claiming that the Congregationalist ministers had abandoned their responsibility to the colonists. Governor Turner then demanded the Congregationalists cease meeting separately and insisted everyone use Parliament's Directory of Worship. Those who refused could be fined or imprisoned.[13]

Soon, Bermuda's struggles fed back once again into England's toleration debate. This time, it led to the creation of a new colony. Named Eleutheria, after the Greek word for liberty, it might have become a Caribbean Rhode Island had it survived. Like Rhode Island, it was a religious refuge from another colony, in this case Bermuda. While its pioneers were more favorable to Congregationalism than Roger Williams, some had a more revolutionary edge. Eleutheria was the brainchild of a mix of Parliamentary radicals and Bermudan Congregationalists represented by former governor William Sayle. After receiving a Parliamentary patent in the summer of 1647, they publicly announced the colony in hopes of recruiting more investors. Eleutheria would be open to all who were "of the body of Jesus Christ" (i.e., Protestant Christians). The announcement bemoaned the disastrous effects of "a rigid imposing on all an uniformity and conformity in matters of judgement and practice in the things of Religion." In Eleutheria, differences "of judgement, under whatsoever other names conveyed" would not be cause for discrimination, as long as the colonists behaved "with justice and sobriety" and lived "peaceably and quietly as Members of the Re-publick." Furthermore, "there shall be no names of distinction or reproach, as Independents, Antinomians, Anabaptist, or any other." Those who used them would be accounted "as enemies of the publick peace." No one would be allowed to "speak reproachfully of any person for his opinion, or of the opinion itself, otherwise than in the Scripture language."[14]

Curiously, Eleutheria's sentiments were strikingly similar to a defense of tolerance published around the same time by a protégé of Archbishop Laud. Jeremy Taylor was a former royalist chaplain and deposed Anglican minister writing from semi-exile in Wales. He too was troubled by the "infinite variety of Opinions in matters of Religion" and the way "they have troubled Christendome, with interests, factions, and partialities," causing "great divisions of the heart, and variety of thoughts and designes amongst pious and prudent men." However, his interest in, and approach to, tolerance was entirely at odds with the Eleutheria project. While Taylor opposed coercion in matters of religion, believing churchmen should avoid "weapons . . . carnal" and restrict themselves to those that were "spiritual" and "gentle," he was skeptical of the ability of "foolish men" to arrive at true Christianity simply by finding a "warrant" for their "opinion" in "a place of Scripture." Far from encouraging a "variety of Sects," his toleration simply responded to a situation where they were "already in being." It would allow people to argue for their beliefs—which in his case would include Laudian episcopalianism—free "from tyranny." In the spirit of *concordia*, Taylor favored this freedom of debate because he believed truth and reason were on his side. A determined Arminian who publicly questioned the doctrine of original sin, Taylor was also a religious polemicist who had denounced Roman Catholicism and Protestant sectarianism. Later, after becoming a bishop in the Church of Ireland in 1660, he would take a firm stand against both Presbyterians and Catholics. In the meantime, he was willing to set the boundaries of tolerance at "whatsoever is against the foundation of Faith, or contrary to good life and the lawes of obedience, or destructive to humane society, and the public and just interests of bodies politick." Beyond the pale were "Religions whose principles destroy Government" or "teach ill life."[15]

Despite the superficial resemblance of his tolerance to that of Eleutheria, Taylor would have delighted in its dismal fate. The colony was the fruit of exactly the sort of sectarianism he despised—and several of its backers would later support the regicide. The expedition to Eleutheria left England at the end of summer 1647, picked up about seventy more individuals on Bermuda, including the aging Scottish minister Copland. Shortly after arriving in the Bahamas in early 1648, disaster struck. Captain Butler divided the colonists into two factions over the question of religious liberty and "enforced Capt. Sayle to remove to an other Ilande." On its way into harbor, Sayle's ship was wrecked. The colonists were stranded. After several months, Sayle built a small boat and sailed to Virginia for help. Meanwhile, Butler and his compatriots abandoned the Bahamas. Sayle, his family, and a few dozen others stayed on in miserable conditions for several years. Fortunately for them, Eleutheria's high-profile puritan connections encouraged some in Massachusetts to send the occasional relief ship.[16]

For Winthrop, Eleutheria's fate exemplified the dangers of religious liberty, especially in a fragile, new colony. Many on Bermuda no doubt interpreted it similarly, albeit it to anti-Independent ends. In 1649 Bermuda declared for the king and began to exile criminals and dissidents to Eleutheria. Eleutheria's role as a place of banishment only changed when the Bermuda Company finally warmed to Congregationalists a few years later. The Eleutherians were allowed to return, and Sayle, arriving in 1656, became governor of Bermuda again from 1658 to 1662. Meanwhile, since Copland had died and the other Congregational ministers had moved on, Bermuda's church order did not have to accommodate them. The Eleutheria experience had essentially eliminated the Congregational challenge. The few colonists remaining in the Bahamas showed little interest in continuing its radical religious experiment.[17]

Back in England, on the other had, the situation had become dramatically radicalized right after the expedition to Eleutheria had departed. In the autumn of 1647, a new group of political actors appeared in the New Model Army: the Levellers. A product of London's growing community of religious, political, and social radicals, they presented the so-called Agreement of the People to the army council at the end of October. It urged a more dramatic set of social, political, and economic reforms than the army council's Heads of the Proposals. Among them was universal manhood suffrage and the insistence that "matters of religion and the ways of God's worship are not at all entrusted by us to any human power, because therein we cannot remit or exceed a tittle of what our consciences dictate to be the mind of God without wilful sin." At the same time, the

Levellers supported "the public way of instructing the nation (so it be not compulsive)." Like their other demands, these were declared "to be our native rights" to be defended "against all opposition whatsoever." On October 28, the Council for the Army met with civilian representatives of the Levellers at Putney Church just beyond Westminster to debate the agreement along with other proposals for action. A number of the officers and MPs dismissed the Levellers' proposal as too radical, but their ideals would persist for years afterward.[18]

In November, a dramatic shift in political circumstances distracted attention from the Agreement of the People. King Charles tried to flee his prison. He failed and was confined to Carisbrooke Castle on the Isle of Wight. There, in December, he signed a secret treaty with the Scots. This Engagement provided that in exchange for liberating the king and restoring him to the throne, Charles would make the Church of England Presbyterian for a provisional three-year test period. The Scots believed that only if they could make England's church Presbyterian would the Presbyterian churches in Scotland and Ireland be safe.[19]

The Scots had become fatally disillusioned with England's Parliament. The rise of the Independents was disquieting, and their presbyterian allies disappointing. The recommendations of the Westminster Assembly were less than satisfactory, the failure to implement them even worse. Deciding that the Parliamentarians had become too radical, the Scots Covenantors turned to their former royalists enemies. The result was a second civil war. In the winter of 1648, royalist uprisings took place across England. In July the Scots invaded. Unfortunately for the royalists, their resistance was uncoordinated, and the Parliamentarian veterans more effective than ever. After several months of bitter fighting, the New Model Army handily defeated them by the fall of 1648.[20]

Even as the second civil war raged, many presbyterians and conservative Independents in the Long Parliament still hoped to create a strong, Erastian, national church with limited toleration. In May 1648, Parliament defined the limits of orthodoxy with an ordinance against blasphemy and heresy. The ordinance threatened execution to those who in speech or print "maintain and publish that there is no God, or that God is not present in all places, doth not know and foreknow all things, or that he is not Almighty," unless they recanted. In other words, atheists and those, like Socinians, Jews, and other non-Christians who claimed "Jesus Christ is not the Son of God" were beyond the pale. As for those who claimed that "all men shall be saved, or that man by nature hath free will to turn to God, or that God may be worshipped in Pictures or Images, of the Soul of any man after death goeth neither to Heaven or hell, but to Purgatory"—in other words, Arminians, Roman Catholics, Greek Orthodox, and other non-Calvinist Christians—they were liable to imprisonment unless they recanted in their parish church. Compared to Massachusetts, these rules were actually fairly mild.[21]

Combined with the Directory of Worship, this ordinance was the closest the revolutionary Parliament got to creating a new church order. The second civil war destroyed hopes for a peaceful restoration of the monarchy. The army, furious that Charles had started yet another war, was radicalized. It rejected a negotiated settlement. Even the comparatively conservative General Fairfax felt that the king needed to "be speedily brought to justice for the treason, blood and mischief he" was guilty of. The November 1648 Remonstrance of the Army containing this demand also insisted that the Long Parliament disband and arrange for elections to create a new, reformed Parliament. When it did not, the army moved into the capital. On December 6, with Cromwell's approval, Colonel Thomas Pride, backed by a troop of soldiers, arrested or turned away a majority of the MPs attempting to enter the House of Commons. "Pride's Purge" only allowed the Independents and radicals to sit in what critics called the Rump of the Long Parliament. The Rump voted to put the king on trial. Convicted by a special court, Charles was executed on January 30, 1649. A month and a half later, the Rump Parliament abolished "the kingly office" along with the House of Lords and declared England to be a Commonwealth. The civil war had become a revolution.[22]

The revolution did not discourage colonial schemes. Just two weeks after the execution of the king, a new proposal for a colony was made by Balthazar Gerbier, a Dutch-born Huguenot connected to the Hartlib circle, who submitted it to the son of the assassinated Duke of Buckingham. Gerbier had known the man's father, having drawn up a "Project for Establishing a New State in America" for him in 1628. Like Utopia, it had mostly been an ideal, but Buckingham considered supporting it as an anti-Spanish Huguenot outpost in America. Gerbier's new plan, like the Huguenot Carolana proposal of 1629, contained a fascinating social-political vision that also allowed no room for religious pluralism. In this American state, there "will only be a single religion," and (while not specified) it would certainly not be Roman Catholic or episcopal. It was radically Erastian, subordinating the church and clergy to lay elites. The church was forbidden from owning property, and no churchman could "through that position possess lands or inheritances." No one would be able to will any property to the church, for church property was "the source of all the corruption that has been introduced into it in the past thousand or twelve hundred years." Instead, the colony's aristocrats would preside over the rights and property of the church and its clergy "will be supported through pensions by the Lords of the Lands, who will be obliged to do so according to his position." The king could be deposed as a tyrant (but not executed) for four reasons, one of which was "changing the religion, and forcing consciences." Although nothing came of the project, Gerbier's interest in colonization was not purely philosophical. He later tried to found a colony in Dutch Guiana.[23]

With the notable exception of Maryland, the revolution marked by the execution of the king had little effect on the colonies' religious policies. Lord Baltimore, busy fending off the efforts by Warwick and the Commission on Foreign Plantations to have Parliament revoke his patent, took advantage of the untimely death of his younger brother Leonard Calvert to appoint a governor of acceptably puritan sensibilities. William Stone was a Virginian planter with family connections to London tobacco merchants. After becoming Maryland's governor in 1648, he persuaded about fifty families of Virginia puritans to move to Maryland. Between 1649 and 1652, as many as seven hundred new colonists arrived, mostly from the puritan counties in southeast Virginia. Traveling north well past the Catholic-dominated Saint Mary's County, they created a second county and named it Providence. They gave the same very puritan name to its main town as well. Their arrival more than doubled the population of the colony.[24]

In April 1649, in anticipation of this migration, and barely two months after the king's execution, Maryland passed its extraordinary Act concerning Religion. The act has long been seen as one of the most important endorsements of religious liberty in colonial American history, giving Maryland boasting rights alongside Rhode Island as an inspiration for American religious freedom. When restored to its contemporary context, however, the act appears to be both more and less than what historians have claimed it was. It was not a direct response to the colonial situation, resembling instead similar legislation and proposals circulating in England, like Parliament's 1648 Blasphemy Act. It also was not a stand-alone law, but part of a bundle of legislation that Baltimore drew up for his assembly to pass in the wake of the abolition of the monarchy. He was adapting more to the English than the American context.[25]

The Act concerning Religion was a proclamation of religious liberty, but with a distinctly pro-Catholic twist. It represented less an embrace of the English revolution than a desire to protect its Catholics from aggressive Protestants. Asserting that "in a well governed Xpian [Christian] Comon Wealth matters concerning Religion and the honor of God ought in the first place to bee taken into serious consideracon and endeavoured to bee settled," it ordered that any inhabitant who blasphemes God, "that is Curse him, or deny our Saviour Jesus Christ to bee the sonne of God, or the Godhead of any of the said Three psons of the Trinity or the Unity of the Godhead," or anyone who uttered "reproachfull Speeches, words, or language concerning the said Holy Trinity or any of the said three psons thereof, shalbe punished with death and confiscation or forfeiture of all his or her lands and goods to the Lord Proprietary and his heires." Agreeing with Protestant radicals that "the inforcing of the conscience in matters of Religion hath frequently fallen out to be of dangerous Consequence in those commonwealths where it hath been practised," it commanded that no Marylander could "bee any waies troubled, Molested or discountenanced for or in respect of his or her religion nor in the free exercise thereof," or "compelled to the beliefe or exercise of any other Religion against his or her consent." Offenders would be fined twenty shillings sterling, or whipped and imprisoned. However, colonists must also "be not unfaithfull to the Lord Proprietary or molest or conspire against the civill" government of the province. Catholics were not mentioned by name, but were clearly included within these provisions, which extended to all those "professing to believe in Jesus Christ." While this excluded Jews and pagans, it included Catholics.[26]

For all its similarities to other proposals for religious liberty, Maryland's Act concerning Religion departed from them in its explicit inclusion of Roman Catholics and their religion. Those who "utter any reproachfull words or Speeches concerning the blessed Virgin Mary the Mother of our Saviour or any Apostles or Evangelists" were subject to the heavy fine of five pounds sterling, or a public whipping and imprisonment. Three-time offenders would be banished from the province forever. Protestant sectarians were protected at a lesser rate. Those who dared "call or denominate any" person "an heretick, Scismatick, Idolator, puritan, Independant, Prespiterian popish priest, Jesuite, Jesuited papist, Lutheran Calvenist, Anabaptist, Brownist, Antinomian, Barrowist, Roundhead, Separatist, or any other name or terme in a reproachfull manner relating to matter of Religion" were liable to a fine of ten shillings sterling. Ironically, this effort to dampen religious conflict in his colony may have inadvertently brought the colonists up to speed on the range of religious slurs then common in England. They passed the act, but requested him "to send us no more such Bodies of Laws which serve to little other end then to fill our heads with suspicious Jealousies and dislikes of that which verily we understand not" but rather to send "short heads of what is desired" for them to implement as best they could. Finally, the Act concerning Religion contained Sabbatarian provisions that Protestants and Catholics alike could support. Those who profaned "the Sabbath or Lords day called Sunday by frequent swearing, drunkennes or by any uncivill or disorderly recreacon, or by working on that day when absolute necessity doth not require it" would receive a lesser fine.[27]

Elsewhere, colonies from Newfoundland to Virginia and the Leewards remained loyal to the king and his church. In the Caribbean, efforts to balance support for the old church with the new revolutionary pressures produced several noticeably different arrangements. On Barbados, the governor had the final say in the selection or rejection of parish ministers, but much of the decision-making power about local religious practice remained in the hands of the vestry, allowing for some local nuance. In 1641 it had ten clergymen to serve roughly ten thousand colonists. That number rose to seventeen by 1648 thanks mostly, it seems, to the arrival of royalist exiles. The church of Laud had significant support, but Barbados's role as the dynamic center of the English Caribbean made it the most religiously diverse of all the colonies. Henry Whistler, visiting in 1655, found it to be "inhabited with all sortes: with English, French, Dutch, Scotes, Irish, Spaniards they being Iues [Jews]: with Ingones [Indians] and miserabell Negors borne to perpetuall sluery thay and thayer seed." Protestant religious inclinations ran the gamut from conservative conformists to radicals, and there were reports of "many sects" holding conventicles. In the early 1640s, rumors of "familism" on the island had reached Massachusetts. Baptists and others arrived later, some of them survivors of Warwick's failed Trinidad colony. There was also a surreptitious Roman Catholic community, most of them Irish. Individual Jews began arriving in the 1640s.[28]

Presiding over this jumble of religious inclinations, as well as the island's neutrality between king and Parliament from 1641 to 1650, was governor Philip Bell. A former governor of Bermuda and Providence Island, Bell was a conservative puritan with connections to Warwick and a commission from the Earl of Carlisle. His first instinct was to strengthen Barbados's church establishment. Parishes were created, churches built, vestries elected, and attendance at services mandated. Indeed, Bell seems to have done all he could to keep the island's religious diversity in check. In 1648–49, his assembly passed two acts regarding religion. The first denounced "divers opinionated and self-conceited persons" who had "declared an absolute dislike of the Government and Church of England" and were neglecting or refusing "the prayers, sermons or administration of the sacraments and other rites and ordinances thereof, used in their several parish churches." Without official approval, they were "holding conventicles in private houses and other places; scandalizing ministers and endeavouring to seduce others to their erroneous opinions, upon pretence of an alteration of Church-government in England." It ordered all colonists to "give due obedience, and conform themselves unto the government and discipline of the Church of England as the same hath been established by several Acts of Parliament." The second act upheld religious priorities that would not seem out of place in Massachusetts. Masters of households were required to hold family prayers every morning and evening under penalty of a fine. Parish ministers had to hold two services each Sunday, preaching at least once, and catechizing youths and other persons on Sunday afternoons. All free people living within two miles of a church had to attend both services each Sunday; those living between two and four miles had to attend once. Constables and churchwardens were to patrol taverns and alehouses during times of divine service. Those found drinking, swearing, or gaming would be put in the stocks. A graduated table of fines for swearing was established. Bell was not a Congregationalist, but it is not hard to see how he could get along so well with the New Englanders who were becoming increasingly important to the island's economy.[29]

On the Leeward Islands, conditions were different. Unfortunately, the situation is even less well documented than Barbados. We know the islands had been divided into parishes, but they had trouble recruiting sufficient numbers of ministers, leaving much religious practice in the hands of the laity. Conformist Protestants could always read from the *Book of Common Prayer* and other approved texts, but the religious situation seems to have varied significantly from island to island along a spectrum running from the rather Reformed Protestant flavor of Nevis to the Catholic majority on Montserrat even before the civil war exacerbated matters. The Leewards had been included in the Earl of Carlisle's Caribee grant, but in July 1645, the embattled Charles had replaced Carlisle's patent with a new proprietary colony. Carliola was entrusted to John Ley, the second Earl of Marlborough. Barbados refused to recognize his authority, but Saint Christopher, Montserrat, and Santa Cruz (Saint Croix) accepted him. Marlborough returned the favor by leaving local government in the hands of the existing authorities.[30]

Officially, the Leewards continued to conform to the old Church of

England until Parliament gained control of them in 1652. Exactly what that meant was full of local nuance and struggle, as elsewhere in the English Atlantic. Intra-Protestant conflicts were strongest on Saint Christopher, where the antipuritan royalist Sir Thomas Warner remained in charge until his death in March 1649. John Featley, his Laudian minister, returned to the island in 1643, and, together, they quickly managed to alienate about half of the island's population. Whether puritans, Parliamentarians, or just economic competitors, roughly two thousand people fled to other islands or left the Caribbean altogether. About eight hundred of the hotter Protestants reputedly left for Santa Cruz, a similar number to Nevis. Around five hundred went further afield.[31]

Saint Christopher became a bastion of Laudian conformism and pressured its Irish Catholics into conformity. An Irish Jesuit priest who visited the island in 1650 reported a number of them had fallen into "heresy." Here, the Laudian dream of bringing Catholics into the Protestant fold evidently had some success. The Jesuit soon undid it. To revive the Irish Catholic community, he set up a chapel on the French part of the island near the quarter where most of the Irish lived. As soon as they heard that "a Father of their nation had come," the Irish flocked to greet him, forgetting "the danger they exposed themselves to." The Jesuit claimed "they looked at him as a man sent by God for their relief." Certainly, the unbounded joy and fervor with which they received him, kissing his hands and throwing themselves at his feet to be blessed, says much about the repression and deprivation they had been suffering. For three months the Irish Jesuit administered the sacraments, heard confession, dispensed communion, instructed, and baptized children. To deprive their masters of "all pretext for mistreating them," he did this early in the morning, from the break of day until midday. The Jesuit proudly reported that he brought a number of his countrymen who had become Protestant "back into the good path." Indeed, he claimed to have gathered a "flock" of "three thousand people" before moving on (in disguise) to revive Montserrat's Catholic Irish community.[32]

Returning to Saint Christopher in late 1650 or perhaps 1651, the Irish Jesuit found his flock facing a new wave of persecution. Warner's successor as governor, Clement Everard, evidently shared his prejudices and was determined to suppress the Catholic community the Jesuit had just revitalized. He forbade Irish Catholics from traveling to the French zone, ostensibly for fear the French would recruit them into a conspiracy against the English colony. Guards were placed on the main road, forcing those intent on attending the Jesuits' services to travel surreptitiously. Defying stiff penalties, dedicated Catholics snuck out Saturday night, traveling along byways and cliffs to attend Mass Sunday morning. Everard's campaign for conformity could be rough: one young woman was dragged to church by her hair. The cruelty with which she was treated "intimidated" many of the Irish to "obey at least externally and attend the services of the heretics." Then, 925 of the most committed and prominent Irish Catholics were rounded up one night and shipped to Crab Island (today's Vieques). Left to starve to death on this desolate, uninhabited strip of sand, a number were rescued by a passing ship that carried them, after several ordeals, to Tortuga Island, where the French received them well. The rest eventually built a raft but died "miserably at sea." In 1653, to save his Irish flock, the Irish Jesuit took as many of them as he could with him to the French colony of Guadeloupe. Once again, the French extended more hospitality to the Irish than the Spanish. Nevertheless, judging by the Jesuit's account, Everard's harsh campaign for conformity was not a complete success. The Jesuit continued to return over the next two years, working in disguise with the Irish "among the English." By the time he finished, he claimed to have won over "various heretics, English as well as Irish."[33]

Judging by the fact that Everard had the same enemies as Warner, he evidently maintained antipuritan policies as well. In 1655, a Cromwellian commissioner called him "a covetuos and grevious opresser, not carring what will become of his people, soe [long as] hee thrives." In 1659, Everard turned out John Price, "a godly minister" from his living, appointing instead "notoriously debauched persons . . . to the chief places in the magistracy and ministry." England's revolutionary government decided to replace him, but they lost power before they could do so. Everard held on to his post and in 1667, along with other members of the island's council and assembly, boasted of how Saint Christopher had been a center of royalist loyalism during the civil wars. They had "maintained the government of the Church of England" and denied a foothold to any "factious person, as Independent, Anabaptist, Quaker, or rigid Presbyterian."[34]

Catholics on English Saint Christopher and Montserrat benefited from their proximity to the French, who erected a Jesuit college to support the efforts of the Irish Jesuit "Jean Destriche" and later missionaries. A series of local laws passed from 1646 to 1668 barred Catholic priests from living on Montserrat, visiting it, celebrating the Mass, or dispensing any of the other sacraments, but after the New English Irishman Roger Osborne of county Cork became governor in 1650, the Irish Catholic majority seems to have enjoyed a certain degree of indulgence. An English colonist later denounced Osborne for working closely with "Papist" colonists and keeping "the Barbarous Irish and their Abetters in arms." Worse, Osborne allegedly tolerated the presence of a Catholic priest and certain Catholic rituals, such as allowing a cross to be carried before a woman's coffin as it was carried out for burial. Nonetheless, Osborne was a Protestant and capable of cooperating with puritans as well. When the Cromwellian fleet arrived in 1655, he entertained its commissioners with "all sevellitye."[35]

Antigua and Nevis, on the other hand, seem to have leaned toward puritan norms. Nevis appears to have resembled Massachusetts. Luke Stokes, its aged governor, judged a "most sober, godley and discrete person" by a visiting Cromwellian commissioner in 1654, was no more a friend of sectarians than John Winthrop. The commissioner noted Stokes was "perplexed with some annebaptest." Meanwhile, Antigua was puritan friendly enough to attract John Winthrop's son Samuel. In 1644 it passed an act against incest, followed by another act "against carnal copulation between Christian and heathen." Christopher Kaynell (or Kennell), the man serving as governor in 1655, had once served under Philip Skippon, one of Cromwell's major-generals.[36]

*

The English revolution widened the gap between metropolitan and colonial religious policies. In some colonies, royalists continued to defend the old church order, clamping down on both puritans and Catholics. In the Leeward Islands, this led to a sort of religious Balkanization, as each island followed a somewhat different path. Royalist conformists reigned in Saint Christopher. Puritans gained the upper hand on Nevis and Antigua. Irish Catholics had less room for maneuver, but with a new Jesuit mission on the neighboring French colonies offering support, they kept their community alive, especially on Montserrat, which was virtually a Roman Catholic enclave. Although ruled by Protestants, it rejected the fierce anti-Catholic approach of Saint Christopher. Barbados, meanwhile, balanced all of these elements within a somewhat flexible church establishment that reflected its political neutrality.

In most of New England, on the other hand, Congregationalists reinforced their church establishment using methods that their Independent colleagues in England resented. Rulers on both sides of the puritan Atlantic shared similar godly goals, but supported different methods. In England, Independents encouraged the acceptance of precisely the sort of broad liberty of conscience that New Englanders (outside of Rhode Island) denied. Confronting a much more complex and fraught situation, they came up with a blasphemy law that was noticeably less strict than its Massachusetts counterpart and criminalized fewer heresies. However, both groups shared the same desire to spread true religion and assert political control over their neighbors. Massachusetts was able to annex its neighbors in a largely peaceful and consensual process. England's Independents had to resort to conquest. Massachusetts managed to incorporate its new territories fairly smoothly into its Congregational church system; England's revolutionary army, by contrast, imposed religious liberty.

PART 5

Commonwealth, 1649–1660

THIRTEEN

Republic: New England, the Caribbean, Acadia, 1649–1654

During the civil war, Barbados's booming economy attracted a mix of royalists and Parliamentarians hoping to profit off of its sugar revolution. Unfortunately, they also imported England's political and religious divisions, making it harder to maintain the official neutrality. In 1649, the assembly passed an act to appease colonists who, "under pretence of tendernesse of conscience and differing in Religion" might cause trouble. Inaugurating a new era of tolerance, it ordered "that coercive Ecclesiastical Lawes, and the penalties thereof, and every clause and particle in any former, shall be and are hereby fully, absolutely, and totally repealed." However, it did not sanction alternative gatherings for worship, for fear they might become a political threat. Those who attended conventicles "or shall labour to seduce any person or persons from repairing to the publick Congregation, or receiving of the holy Sacrament" would be punished. A special oath was drawn up requiring all colonists to swear loyalty and profess "that civill Government is a necessary Ordinance of God, and ought as well for conscience sake, as fear, to be obeyed by all Christians, how different soever in opinion concerning matters of Religion." These concessions failed to preserve the government. Some felt the act was gratuitously oppressive. Royalists, claiming they needed to protect Governor Bell from the island's "Independents," then staged a coup in the spring of 1650. Breaking with the island's neutrality, they declared for King Charles II and ordered "all the Independent party, non-conformists to the antient Discipline of the Church of England, and all other Sectaries" together with anyone else who supported "the late endeavour to suppresse the reformed Religion formerly Established, in the Raigne of our late Queene Elizabeth; within the Kingdome of England, and such as are disloyally affected to his Majesty" to turn in their arms and leave Barbados within three months. Governor Bell was among those who left. Back in England, the exiles convinced Parliament to attack.[1]

The conquest of Barbados in 1652 was one of the last campaigns by the revolutionary republic. It had already brought the rest of the English world under its obedience and was transforming its constitutional makeup by uniting Scotland and Ireland to England. As republican religion replaced royalist worship, the Directory for Public Worship replaced the *Book of Common Prayer*, and a new blasphemy law readjusted the boundaries of acceptable religion, extending liberty of conscience even further. Within England, liberty of conscience was designed to cope with the growing religious diversity among revolutionary Protestants. In Scotland and Ireland, however, it inaugurated a religious diversity far beyond what either country had been accustomed to.

In the colonies too, the arrival of revolutionary authority increased religious pluralism. The greatest measure of this change is the expansion of Baptist communities. Baptists, as loyal Independents, benefited greatly from the extension of the republican church order around the English world and successfully carved out new homes almost everywhere except Massachusetts. Massachusetts could fend off Baptist efforts to expand into its territory because the English republicans treated it as a partner in empire rather than a subordinate, letting it sort out its own religious affairs. Accordingly, the New England Way remained noticeably stricter and less tolerant than the rest of the English world. Meanwhile, Massachusetts expanded north, taking in New Hampshire, Maine, and even French Acadia. With the ever-present, but small, exception of Rhode Island, New England became the least religiously tolerant part of the English world thanks to its close affinity with Oliver Cromwell.

*

The early 1650s were the high point for the New England Way. Massachusetts expanded to acquire territory that would remain part of the province until the nineteenth century. In 1651 it annexed the last remaining town in New Hampshire. Between 1652 and 1658, it swallowed up Maine, establishing a civil and religious union that lasted until 1820. With Plymouth, New Haven, and Connecticut following essentially the same Congregational church order, it was now effectively the Church of New England—with the exception of most of Rhode Island.[2]

Rhode Island in the 1650s resembled England much more than its neighbors. Had Massachusetts been more like England, where Baptists and Congregationalists coexisted and cooperated within the broad category of Independents, Rhode Island's Baptists would have had a good chance of making inroads across the region. After all, apart from a few key issues like infant baptism and ministerial authority, they had a good deal in common. A number of the puritans who migrated to Massachusetts in the 1630s had Baptist sympathies, including Roger Williams. A few stayed in Massachusetts, even though they were not allowed to worship separately. A number of their neighbors not only tolerated but also respected their Baptist views. Those Baptist intent on worshipping publicly moved on, either to Rhode Island, where the first Baptist congregation in the Americas had been established in 1639, or New Netherland, where the town of Gravesend became an unofficial Baptist congregation around 1642. From Rhode Island, Baptists missionaries fanned out across the region but with indifferent success. Some converts were made in Flushing, New Netherland, but when John Clarke and others tried to evangelize in Massachusetts in 1651, they were quickly arrested and banished.[3]

Meanwhile, Baptists gained ground in other colonies. They were on Barbados and Nevis and, in November 1657, even tried to gain access to India. The governing court of the East India Company was confronted with the demand by a group of "Anabaptists" to drop the use of oaths. They wanted merchants trading to India to be able to take "an Engagement, without Swearing," saying they would still respect the company's rules about private trading. The court, which had just received a new charter, was able to uphold the use of oaths and keep Protestant sectarianism away from India.[4]

Maryland, by contrast, drew less interest from Baptists, notwithstanding its public endorsement of religious toleration, in part because it was widely recognized as favoring Catholics. Around 1650, one observer described Maryland as a place where the "English inhabitants are few, and those of different Religions, for some amongst them are Papist, but most Protestants. There hath always been toleration in Religion, and is this present." Trans-Atlantic English Catholic networks seem to have kept the widowed Queen Henrietta Maria apprised of the colony's situation. From her exile in France, she urged the head of the Capuchin order in Paris "to send missionaries to New England, called Virginia, where live more than fifty thousand people, the greater part of whom are heathen, many are English heretics and a few are Catholics deprived of every sort of spiritual assistance." The French nuncio supported the plan, as did the provincial of the Capuchins. Both sought the support of the papal Congregatio de Propaganda Fide, but it seems nothing ever got off the ground.[5]

Maryland's radical act of toleration failed to save Lord Baltimore's government. The regicide soon provoked a political crisis that took the colony out of his hands for most of the next decade. Governor Stone was out of the colony on business when the news arrived. Although Baltimore had accepted the revolutionary regime, Stone's lieutenant, ignorant of the proprietor's wishes, opted to follow Virginia's lead and declare for King Charles II. Baltimore rejected the proclamation and affirmed his loyalty to the Commonwealth, but the actions of Stone's lieutenant rendered the colony suspect to both the Commonwealth in England and the Protestants of Providence County. They began objecting to the way the Act concerning Religion forced them to tolerate Roman Catholicism and finally challenged Lord Baltimore's right to rule them in 1654. They refused to swear an oath of loyalty to the lord proprietor because it would require them to "countenance and defend the Roman Popish Religion," something they could not in good conscience do. In 1655, Governor Stone led a loyalist militia to bring them in line. They fought back and defeated Stone's expedition in a fight near Providence. In this so-called Battle of the Severn River, Stone was wounded and captured. Some of his compatriots were executed. Lord Baltimore's government had been overthrown again. Baltimore did not fully regain control of his colony until November 1657. Even then, he did so only after accepting most of the rebels' demands, including that they did not have to swear an oath of fealty to him. They merely submitted to his government. Their one concession was to finally accept the Act concerning Religion.[6]

In the meantime, the New Model Army conquered Ireland and Scotland, stamping out the last embers of royalist resistance in a rapid series of campaigns from 1649 to 1651. Cromwell, who had been investing in and advocating for the conquest of Ireland since 1641, personally led the massive invasion of 1649. In several months of intense campaigning, he dealt the Irish armies a decisive defeat. Returning to Britain at the end of the year, he left the final stages of conquest to his second-in-command and son-in-law, Henry Ireton. Although Irish Confederates managed to sustain a drawn-out campaign of desperate resistance, by 1652 they were thoroughly defeated. For the first time in history, English dominance over Ireland was complete. With its army stationed in garrisons across the entire desolated island, the English Republic then annexed Ireland and its church, urged on by anti-Catholic Irish Protestant "Independents" who wanted to integrate Ireland into England's "empire."[7]

Cromwell set very narrow boundaries for Ireland's Roman Catholic majority. Firmly denying their requests for toleration, he had explained to one rebel commander, "if by liberty of conscience you mean a liberty to exercise the mass, I judge it best to plain dealing, and to let you know, where the Parliament of England have power, that will not be allowed of." A 1650 declaration against "the Popish Prelates and Clergy" clarified the republic's Irish policy. Blaming the Catholic clergy for the "unprovoked . . . most unheard of & most barbarous massacre" of the English, it called them "a part of Antichrist, whose Kingdome the Scripture so expressly speakes should be layed in blood, yea in the blood of the Saints." Denying the claims of priests that the English intended to massacre the "Catholique Inhabitants," it insisted that only "Papists" caught "seducing" the people or violating the laws would be punished. Those who kept "matters of Religion in their owne breasts" would be left alone "if they walke honestly and peaceably." Those who "shall headily run on after the Councells of their Prelates and Clergy and other Leaders," on the other hand, were threatened with "misery and desolation, blood and ruine." Full of the anti-Catholicism that had been stoked by the hostile accounts of the Irish uprising, Cromwell and his troops treated their Irish opponents harshly, most notoriously by killing some two thousand civilians in Drogheda and Wexford. Irish Catholic priests, whom Cromwell denounced for their covenant with "death and hell," suffered especially. Some were executed during the fighting. The rest were banished.[8]

After a decade of relentless warfare, Ireland was devastated. War, disease, and starvation had killed some four hundred thousand people, about 15–20 percent of its population. Before the rebellion had broken out in 1641, it had seemed like Ireland might become a partner in England's colonization of America. Now it was reduced to little more than a source of labor. The kingdom's economy was gutted. Its people were destitute, oppressed, and suffering. The occupying regime began to ship them out to work as servants in the colonies.[9]

Cromwell was bloodthirsty when it came to Catholic rebels and clergy, but he could be fairly tolerant of Roman Catholics as individuals. His regime did not persecute them as severely as the Elizabethan regime. Of course, Cromwell hoped for their eventual conversion, just as he hoped for the conversion of Native Americans and Jews, but in the meantime he recognized their secular rights. This attitude lay behind his restoration of

Maryland to its Catholic proprietor in 1657. In doing so, he defied the will of the colony's Protestants, but they respected his decision—as long as he lived. After Cromwell died in 1658, they staged another rebellion that kept the colony out of Baltimore's hands until 1660.[10]

Scotland succumbed even quicker than Ireland to Cromwell's armies. However, its encounter with Cromwellian tolerance was rather different. Scots Presbyterians might have avoided war if they had been able to accept the demands of English Independents. They could not. Their 1648 invasion in support of King Charles I had failed, but after the regicide they nevertheless proclaimed Charles II as their king. In 1650 they invaded again, only to be defeated even more severely. Virtually their entire army was killed or captured at the Battle of Worcester in September 1651. Charles II was one of the few individuals to escape. After famously hiding in an oak tree, he was smuggled back into exile in France with the help of an underground network of Catholics and royalists. The New Model Army then conquered and quickly occupied Scotland in 1652.[11]

The stress of over a decade of war and civil conflict had begun to divide the Covenanters even before the Cromwellian conquest. The first cracks appeared in 1647, when the "Engagers" signed the secret treaty with Charles I that brought Scotland into the second civil war. For the so-called Kirk Party, the Engagement's promise of a trial run of English Presbyterianism was not enough. They insisted the king take the Solemn League and Covenant and swear to establish Presbyterianism in England and Ireland. When the Scottish invasion failed, the Kirk Party turned on the Engagers. Scotland's Parliament passed the 1649 Act of Classes, which banned Engagers from holding office in the government or army. A year later, to attract royalist support and encourage Charles II to uphold the covenant, the Scottish Parliament repealed this act with a public resolution approved by the General Assembly. Engagers could again serve in the army. Nevertheless, some members of the Kirk Party thought the "Resolutioners" had acted too hastily and even sinfully in their eagerness to please Charles II. After all, he showed no genuine desire to support the covenant or its church. In 1651, these "Protestors" were barred from the General Assembly for placing their Presbyterianism before their royalism. A schism had appeared in the Kirk. Charles II swore to uphold the covenant, but could not repair this split, which mirrored Scotland's long-standing divide over religious policy that tended to pit the firmly Reformed Protestant south and west against the more religiously conservative north and east. These divisions produced a range of theological disputes that were only exasperated by the Cromwellian conquest. Forbidding the General Assembly of the Kirk from meeting, imposing liberty of conscience, and then, in April 1654, annexing Scotland, the Cromwellians prevented the Socts from resolving the disputes and securing their beloved church order.[12]

With the annexation of Ireland and Scotland, the Atlantic isles of Britain and Ireland were united under one government and one ecclesiastical order for the first time in history. The parameters for this new religious order had been legislated by the Rump Parliament in 1650, through a series of acts defining the limits of acceptable religious belief and behavior. First, all adult males eighteen and over were required to swear an Engagement to "give assurance of their living quietly and peaceably" and loyally under "the Commonwealth of England as it is now established, without a king or House of Lords." This loyalty oath pointedly separated political loyalty from religious affiliation. There was no Act of Uniformity, nor was there a demand to conform to a particular church order. However, additional acts set up certain basic religious obligations that were enforced by the regime. Resembling the laws passed in Massachusetts a few years before, they ordered better observance of the Christian Sabbath, made incest and adultery punishable by death, and set up fines for swearing and cursing. This campaign of moral reform and Sabbatarianism was the most consistent aspect of the regime's religious demands. It did not, in the end, win over the bulk of the population.[13]

The revolutionary regime's ultimate statement on doctrinal orthodoxy was the new blasphemy act passed in the summer of 1650. A response in part to the radical preaching of Laurence Clarkson, a one-time Antinomian, current Ranter, and later Muggletonian, it reflected the disinclination of Independents to punish religious dissent as long as it was conceivably godly. The act targeted those "who should abuse and turn into Licentiousness the liberty given in matters of Conscience," a distinction not made in the Long Parliament's 1648 Blasphemy Act. Exempting those "distempered with sickness, or distracted in brain," it set a six-month prison sentence for those who denied that swearing, "lying, stealing . . . murther, adultery, incest, fornication, uncleanness, sodomy, drunkenness," and so on were "things in themselves shameful, wicked, sinful, impious and detestable in any person." However, in contrast to the detailed list of "atheistical, blasphemous or execrable opinions" outlawed by the Long Parliament (and Massachusetts), the only opinions explicitly punished by the Rump's act were those claiming that an individual either denied "the holiness and righteousness of God" or claimed that he or someone else was God, "or in honor, excellency, majesty to be equal, and the same with the true God." Those who dared affirm the proscribed opinions did not, however, face the death penalty, only the lighter punishment of banishment. These provisions, aimed at Antinomians and Ranters, set the bar for unacceptable belief so high that much of the existing range of religious speculation could continue with little fear of persecution. Even the small, new community of Jews in London could breath easier: there was no longer a demand to acknowledge the divinity of Jesus Christ.[14]

Protestant liberty of conscience was now effectively the religious establishment of the English world. Some individuals still managed to exceed it. In London that June, Mary Usher was indicted by the Middlesex sessions for being a common swearer. A former royalist officer accused her of swearing a hundred oaths at several different times, among them "By God," "God's blood," and "God's wounds." At the same court sessions, Thomas Kirbie confessed that he believed that John Robins alias Roberts was God and father of Jesus Christ. For these and other "blasphemous opinions," he was jailed for six months without bail according to the "late Act of Parliament against several atheistical, blasphemous and execrable opinions."[15]

Such individuals did not discourage the Rump from its commitment to religious liberty. In September 1650, to protect the "divers Religious and peaceable people, well-affected to the prosperity of the Commonwealth," it repealed much of the coercive church apparatus created by the Elizabethan Act of Uniformity and subsequent penal laws. The laws repealed included those that had punished "Recusants not coming to church" or enjoined "the use of Common-Prayer, the keeping and observing of holydays" and other manifestations of religious conformity. Individuals could no longer be punished for "not repairing to their parish church," not keeping religious holidays like Christmas, or failing to use the *Book of Common Prayer* or "inveighing against" it. With recent history in mind, including the migration to New England, the act lamented that "religious people . . . have not onely been molested and imprisoned, but also brought into danger of abjuring their country, or in case of return, to suffer death as felons, to the great disquiet, and utter ruine of such good and godly people, and to the detriment of the Commonwealth."[16]

The Rump Parliament still insisted that its subjects had a duty to worship regularly. Individuals were expressly forbidden from taking advantage of the *Act for relief of religious and peaceable people* "to neglect the performance of Religious duties." Another law required the observance of the Christian Sabbath and official "Days of Publique Fasting and Humiliation" by "diligently resorting to some publique place where the service and worship of God is exercised." If the officially available venues did not appeal to people, then they had to "be present at some other place in the practice of some Religious Duty, either of prayer, preaching, reading or expounding the Scriptures, or conferring upon the same." Individuals did not have to attend their local church, conform to a particular theology, or worship according to a prescribed liturgy, but they still had to be, or at least behave like, some sort Protestant Christian.[17]

In both Scotland and Ireland, this religious liberty fostered unprecedented degrees of religious diversity. In Scotland, the division between Resolutioners and Protestors split Calvinists into liberal and militant camps. Through these cracks entered the new forms of Protestantism that accompanied the Cromwellian conquest. With the military regime encouraging sectarians to preach and worship across the country, Scots—often for the first time—encountered the views of Baptists, Congregationalists, and, later, Quakers. Some Scots, perhaps discouraged by the bitter contentions among their countrymen, took advantage of the new liberty of conscience to explore these spiritual alternatives. A number of them converted. By 1660 there were Scottish Baptists, Congregationalists, and Quakers. However, most depended on the support of the military regime. The few Scots who became Baptists and Congregationalists failed to establish lasting congregations. The most enduring religious legacy of the occupation was the Scottish Quaker community that took root in the northeast, especially around Aberdeen.[18]

In Ireland, the New Model Army's impact on religious life was even more dramatic. Catholics remained the bulk of the population, but they were split between the generally Ultra-Montagne Gaels and the generally more pragmatic Old English. These affiliations mattered little in practice, for the Cromwellian army suppressed Roman Catholicism more thoroughly than any Protestant regime before or since. Catholic religious services were prohibited. Priests were banished. The lands of the elites who funded the priests and missionaries were seized. The 1652 Act for the Settlement of Ireland was especially severe. It refused pardon to a potentially significant portion of the population: the leaders of the revolt or "all and every Jesuit priest, and other person or persons who have received orders from the Pope or See of Rome or any authority derived from the same." Parliament then proposed to "transplant" most of the Catholic population to the poor western province of Connacht. The fertile east and south would be turned over to Protestant colonization. All

Catholic priests were formally banished from the island in January 1653. Irish Catholics were not compelled to convert to Protestantism, but they were deprived of the priestly services essential to their faith.[19]

As for Irish Protestants, their episcopal loyalties had eroded during the long years of war. To preserve their church, clergymen had adopted a variety of mechanisms, some of which resembled presbyterian methods of cooperation through councils. These methods muffled some of the blow when, after the union with England, the *Book of Common Prayer* was prohibited, bishops abolished, and the Church of Ireland replaced by an Erastian settlement whereby the English governors set the religious tone for the country. In Ulster, the Presbyterian church set up by the Scottish army prospered, while the English army brought in a range of new sects, most notably Baptists. Over the next several years, the official religious tone shifted several times depending on who was in charge. Henry Ireton, commander-in-chief of the army and lord deputy of Ireland, had died in 1651. Charles Fleetwood, who replaced him, was, like Ireton, a staunch Independent, friend of Cromwell, cavalry officer (men from his regiment had seized the king in 1647), and (after he married Ireton's widow), Cromwell's son-in-law. Fleetwood indulged radical Independents, Baptists in particular, and supported a firm anti-Catholic policy that included the dispossession of Irish Catholics and their transplantation to Connacht. Oliver's son Henry Cromwell replaced Fleetwood in 1654. A man of more moderate sentiments, Henry Cromwell curbed the radicalism Fleetwood had encouraged. With an eye toward restoring civilian rule, he reined in the Baptists, who he suspected resented his father's authority, improved relations with former royalist Protestants, and cooperated with the Scots Presbyterians. Henry Cromwell's willingness to allow their ministers to preach beyond Ulster suggests he favored a presbyterian-style religious order. Those same conservative instincts led him to treat the Quakers harshly when they first arrived in 1656. Less fiercely anti-Catholic than Fleetwood, he nonetheless oversaw the policies of land seizures and transplantation. He even supported sending Catholic girls and boys to Jamaica in hopes of making them Protestant. His ultimate intentions are unknown, as he was dismissed from office in 1659 before he could reorganize Ireland's church.[20]

By then, Ireland was more religiously pluralistic than ever. Although few Irish Catholics converted to Protestantism, Ireland's Protestants would never again fit into a single church. Presbyterian influences were strong, from the associations governing much of the former Church of Ireland, especially in Munster, to the actual Presbyterian church among the Scots in Ulster. The major ports and garrison towns harbored Baptist, Congregational, and Quaker communities. It was at a Quaker meeting in Cork that William Penn became a Quaker in 1667. The countryside remained heavily Catholic, but without priests or bishops Irish Catholics existed in a spiritual limbo. Dublin, the capital, was the most religiously diverse place in the country, containing representatives of the full range of the country's Christianity.[21]

Having consolidated control of its European territories, the revolutionary Parliament turned its attention overseas. After the execution of King Charles I, Newfoundland, Virginia, Antigua, Barbados, and Bermuda had all declared for his son. Two fleets were sent out in 1651 to bring them to heel. Only Barbados put up a real fight. In Virginia, Governor Berkeley made a show of resistance but quickly surrendered. Newfoundland's royalist governor Sir David Kirke was deposed without a struggle and the colony abandoned, reverting to a mere fishing station. The Leewards also accepted Parliamentary sovereignty peacefully. The commissioners accompanying the conquering fleets appointed new governors and, in Maryland, supported the Protestant rebels against Baltimore's government. Between 1652 and 1657, they, not the Calvert family, ruled. One of Baltimore's supporters denounced them as "inhuman, ingratefull, and blood-sucking Sectaries, which mention God in their lips, but their hearts are farre from him," suggesting the Act concerning Religion had not suppressed religious bitterness.[22]

By the end of 1652, the entire English world was under the authority of the revolutionary Commonwealth. Overseas, in the religious transition to republican rule New England was left alone. Bermuda, which had come around of its own accord, was also allowed to continue governing itself and made few changes to its roughly presbyterian church order, apart from readmitting the Eleutheria exiles. On Newfoundland, the few fishing families who remained in residence had no choice but to revert to private worship. They hearkened to the occasional sermon by passing puritan preachers, but the puritan message did not seem to have much appeal for them. Neither did that of the Quaker missionaries who arrived in 1656.[23]

In Virginia, the transition to the republican church order was gradual. Before surrendering, Berkeley had negotiated several points that allowed for some short-term continuity. If a majority of members within a parish wished, they could continue using the *Book of Common Prayer* for one year, "provided that those things which relate to kingship or that government be not used publicly." In addition, Virginia's ministers were permitted to continue in their positions: a stark contrast to England, where hundreds

FIGURE 11. Manuscript map of Virgo Triumphans owned by Farrar, Rare Books Division, New York Public Library

of royalist ministers had been ejected. In general, apart from imposing allegiance and the new Navigation Acts, the Commonwealth government continued most of Virginia's laws and policies in hopes of keeping the colony prosperous and profitable. Only a few royalist sympathizers, like Berkeley, lost their posts. The republican governors preserved Virginia's parish system and encouraged the laying out of new parishes. The assembly, concerned that "many places" were "destitute of ministers," also sought to strengthen the church's institutional foundations. It not only collected funds to allow local vestries to build churches and purchase "a gleab and stock for the next minister that shall be settled there," it even offered to reimburse colonists who brought in ministers at their own cost. The ministers and up to six members of their household were exempted from paying taxes.[24]

In sum, despite preserving the parish system, the tenor of Virginia's religious life began to approach that of New England. The laws that had permitted Berkeley to lord over the colony's religious life were replaced with acts that enhanced the authority of parish vestries. A series of laws reinforced Sabbath observance and punished immorality. Attendance at

"Meetings" on "the Lords day" was required. Travel, working, "shootinge in guns," or any other activities "tending to the profanation" of the Sabbath were prohibited. Likewise "the frequent practice of sheriffs and officers" serving "executions, warrants, and other writs," at "the churches on Sabboth days and other public meetings" was ended, because Sabbath "duties are neglected by such who are in danger of arrests." The Commonwealth government wanted there to be no excuse for fulfilling one's religious obligations. County courts were commanded to suppress "the odious Sinns of Common Drunkeness, Blasphemous swearing, and Cursinge, Scandalous Liveings in Adultery, and fornication" with a series of fines. Finally, Virginia's relations with its Indigenous neighbors were shifted onto a more Christian path. Worried that dishonest individuals were enslaving Indigenous children "to the great Scandall of christianitye, and of the English nation . . . Renderinge Religion Contemptible, and the name of Englishmen odious to them," the assembly made it illegal "to buy any Indian, or Indians" and set aside reservation land for several Indigenous groups "for theire Reducemnt to Civillitye, and a hopefull progresse there to theire Conversion to Christianitye."[25]

The most dramatic changes took place in the colonies that had fought hardest for the Church of England. On Saint Christopher, the prevailing Laudian style came to an end as a number of those who had been exiled or moved away because of their puritan sensibilities returned. Others joined them, including Samuel Winthrop. Judging by his account, it seems that Saint Christopher adapted to the revolutionary religious order with less than complete enthusiasm. It lacked, in Winthrop's words, "the cheif good, a powerfull ministery." In the winter of 1660, the minister who presided over the island's principal parish, Middle Parish, for the previous several years was dismissed "in regard of some great scandols in life discovered," as Samuel explained to his brother John Winthrop Jr., the governor of Connecticut. Perhaps he was an immoral man, but similar complaints were commonly used to dismiss Laudians and other royalist conformists. Samuel asked his brother to find a replacement, saying the "Benefice is the Best in the Island, and might content a reasonable minister, and the people are verry desirous, if possible to be supplyed from New-England." It would "much farther the worke of the Lord if you doe incourage any godly able grave minister to accept thereof." Suggesting something of what the local religious atmosphere was like, Samuel insisted the new minister "must not be a young man . . . nor ane that will seem to winke at" the "madnesse" of "this people." He should be "a verry seveer reprover of their vices." He should also be able to "teach them by his example, to walke soberly as in the daye." He wrote at the request of members of the parish who wanted their new minister to "also bring his Certificates with him from some of the churches and persons of quality." Repeating his request a few weeks later, he noted that the island's governor had also written the governor of Massachusetts asking "assistance in inviting to us a good minister." It is not clear if a minister ever was sent, but the incident suggests how the Commonwealth era permitted New England's religious influence to extend into the Caribbean.[26]

The most dramatic religious change was on Barbados. Its proprietor, the second Earl of Carlisle, had served as a royalist officer during the civil wars. When peace came, he received no Parliamentary support for his proprietary claims. Making the best of a bad deal, he had leased his rights to Francis Lord Willoughby for twenty-one years. A presbyterian for whom the revolution had gotten too radical, Willoughby had switched to the royalist side at the end of the wars and seems to have decided it would be best to leave England. Arriving on Barbados in May 1650, shortly after the royalist coup, he once again found himself resisting the revolution.[27]

Parliament's fleet arrived at Barbados in the fall of 1651. Meeting strong resistance, it could not land. Only after several months of skirmishes and a certain amount of intrigue did the Parliamentary commanders persuade leading planters to accept their authority. After gaining control of the island in the winter of 1652, they banished Lord Willoughby and several of the most active royalists. Willoughby was supposed to go to Surinam, where he had sent some colonists shortly before the fleet arrived. He went to England instead, where he spent the next several years occasionally suffering imprisonment for his royalist sympathies.[28]

On Barbados, as in Virginia, the republican government preserved the parish system. However, its articles of surrender forbade use of the *Book of Common Prayer*. They also explicitly guaranteed "a libertie of Conscience in matters of Religion" for all except those "whose tenents, are inconsistant to a Civill government," a statement that could include outspoken royalist episcopalians. Meanwhile, no minister was to "bee deprived except upon scandalous livinge, seditious Preaching or unsound Doctrine sufficiently proved against him." The surrender agreement also insisted laws be put in place "against Atheisme, Blasphemy, and open scandalous livinge." The assembly fulfilled this requirement in October 1652, when it passed an act granting "free enjoyment of Religion" to "all the inhabitants" as long as it remained consistent with the laws of England. The following month, justices of the peace went around collecting the books of common prayer. One minister, a royalist formerly attached to Salisbury

Cathedral, protested, inspiring a surrounding crowd of "many hundreds" to raise "swords, canes and cudgels" in his defense. The justices of the peace adjourned their court session, determined to punish the instigators later. One of them, writing to Parliament, pointed to the incident as an example of "how these prelatical crew with serpentine subtlely win themselves into the affection, and so ensare their blindfolded followers, of which sort our Island is supplied." The conquest and submission of Barbados would not be complete, they said, until "a Gospel Ministry be settled to win the people (which are pliable and apt to receive impression) to a Gospel submission." Barbados's religious and political loyalties remained decidedly mixed.[29]

Having secured the revolution, the republic turned its attention to expanding England's trade, which it believed would help consolidate its economic control over the colonies. Turning to the newly independent Dutch Republic, the Rump Parliament suggested a union into a single Protestant Republic. The Dutch rejected the idea. The Rump responded by passing the Navigation Act of 1651, ordering that all trade with the colonies had to be done in English ships. Since the Dutch currently carried much of that trade, it was clearly a deliberate provocation. By the summer of 1652, the two countries were at war. Fighting primarily in the North Sea, the combatants more or less reached a draw by the spring of 1653. Then came another political coup in England.

The inconclusive war with a fellow Protestant Republic had upset Oliver Cromwell. The powerful general worried that the two nations were wasting their blood and treasure fighting against each other rather than the greater Catholic enemy. He was not the only person who felt that a new, elected assembly should replace the Rump and its aggressive stance against the Dutch mercantile empire. In April, Cromwell dismissed the Rump in a sudden coup. Establishing a Council of State to take over the executive functions of the government, Cromwell then coordinated with the army and Independent churches in England, Scotland, and Ireland to nominate members for a new assembly. This Nominated Parliament was also known as the assembly of saints, or Barebone's Parliament, after one of the London nominees, Praisegod Barebone (although his name is more accurately rendered Barnbone or Barbon). A leather-seller and one-time member of Henry Jacobs's London Congregational church, Barebone had become leader of half of Jacobs's old congregation after it split in 1640. His reputation for political and religious Independency, his less than gentlemanly origins, and his colorful name made him a convenient namesake for an institution so closely associated with the

Independent cause. Alas, this mix of radicals was unable to agree on a coherent agenda. The Nominated Parliament was dissolved in December 1653 and replaced by a new constitution. This "Instrument of Government" made Cromwell the chief executive as Lord Protector for life. A Council of State advised him and helped him to govern. Legislation was handled by regularly elected Parliaments—for which neither royalists nor Roman Catholics could vote.[30]

The Cromwellian coup against the Rump also saw the Westminster Assembly dissolved. Cromwellian religious policy was now governed by the Instrument of Government, which endorsed "the Christian religion" but only "as contained in the Scriptures." While it forbade punishing those who did not attend the "Public Profession," the Instrument urged members of the official church to "endeavour" to win them "by sound doctrine and the example of a good conversation." Although, in the long-standing debate about whether persuasion or persecution was the best method for expanding the faith, Cromwell's Commonwealth came down firmly on the side of persuasion, it laid down important qualifications to its liberty of conscience. The ideal of a single official church remained. And, while a bit vague on exactly what the national religion was, the Instrument was clear on what it was not. It explicitly forbade the toleration of "popery" or "Prelacy," that is Roman Catholics and episcopalians. Furthermore, by allowing freedom and protection to "such as profess faith in God by Jesus Christ (though differing in judgment from the doctrine, worship, or discipline publicly held forth)," the revolutionary government implicitly left certain faiths out of the mix, especially Jews and Socinians. In 1657 they would be explicitly excluded. Moreover, even those tolerated were not to abuse "this liberty to the civil injury of others, and to the actual disturbance of the public peace on their parts." This proviso eventually justified harsh action against sectarians like the radical Baptist Fifth Monarchists and the Quaker leader James Nayler.[31]

One unexpected offshoot of the Anglo-Dutch War was the conquest of Acadia. Shortly before Cromwell made peace with the Dutch in the spring of 1654, the Massachusetts colonist Robert Sedgwick had persuaded Cromwell to support an expedition to capture New Netherland. When the fleet arrived in Boston that June, Sedgwick learned that peace had just been concluded. Rather than disband his force, Sedgwick decided to divert it to conquer the French colony of Acadia, which occupied the territory once claimed by Nova Scotia. Long coveted by Massachusetts, Acadia was thinly populated and currently divided between rival factions. It proved an easy conquest.

Acadia covered an enormous amount of territory. Its few European inhabitants were mostly concentrated in and around the capital at Port Royal. The rest were scattered around a handful of outlying trading outposts where soldiers protected traders bargaining for fur with the Micmac natives of the region. The English conquerors compelled the French to sign a registry saying they would not bear arms against the English. Those who refused were sent back to France. The little evidence on the religious life of English Nova Scotia suggests an uneasy coexistence between the French Catholic majority and their English rulers. English colonists were few and mostly transient: fishermen, merchants, soldiers, and fur traders. The surrender treaty had granted the French toleration for Roman Catholic worship, but the arrangement did not last.[32]

In August 1656, the Cromwellian government named Sir Thomas Temple proprietor of Nova Scotia along with two partners. A former Parliamentarian soldier and relative of the revolutionary peer Lord Saye and Sele, Temple had acquired property rights to the colony by helping its original French proprietor pay off his debts. To govern the colony, Temple moved to Boston in 1657, where he became a respected member of its Congregational church. His government required that all soldiers stationed in Nova Scotia and "any person or persons whatsoever" allowed "to plant or inhabit within the said Countries" be "such onely as are of the protestant Religion." In November 1658 the French ambassador complained that Temple's government had "pulled down the church and fort at Port Royal" and forbidden the French from engaging in the fur trade. Temple "has no power to do this," the ambassador complained, "nor to deprive the French of the exercise of their religion; the civil and spiritual liberties having been confirmed by an order of the late Protector" (Cromwell had just died). His complaints had little effect. Probably sometime in 1659 Temple's agent on the ground, Captain Thomas Breedon, drew up proposals for a trading company to help Temple better profit from his colony. Breedon's plan included a treaty to resolve the ongoing contest for control of the region with the French. Those at Port Royal should agree to live there "in due submission to" Temple's government, or to "quitt their farmes and bee transported to any other Plantations, out of that jurisdiction," suggesting that their Roman Catholic religion was seen as a potential act of political defiance. More direct evidence of religious regulations for the colony comes from a 1662 proclamation ordering "corporal punishment" for a variety of penalties, including "profaning the Lord's day, cursing or swearing, drinking to excess," and other offenses. It is unclear if or how these regulations were enforced. There were clear limits on Temple's power in Nova Scotia. His authority did not reach far beyond the forts. He only made occasional visits. Preferring to spend most of his time in Boston, he delegated much of the colony's trade to merchants from Massachusetts who profited more from his colony than he did. The French Catholic community moved away from Port Royal to lands less immediately under English oversight. With the help of visiting missionary priests, they preserved their religion until Temple finally lost his colony in 1670. In accordance with the 1667 Treaty of Breda, he was compelled to return it to France.[33]

*

By 1652, the entire English world was living under the same, revolutionary, religious order. In a breathtaking series of political and military events, the entire English world from the Shetlands to Barbados had been brought under the authority of the regime led by Oliver Cromwell. The last holdouts for King Charles's church in Newfoundland, Virginia, and the Caribbean had been subjugated by Parliamentary fleets. From Ireland to the Caribbean, Roman Catholicism was more effectively suppressed than ever before. Maryland's Catholic-led experiment in toleration had collapsed again. New England Congregationalism thrived everywhere outside of Rhode Island, where Baptists schemed in vain to challenge it. In the end, Baptists fared better in Ireland.

Despite some variety, this religious order had an unprecedented commonality of laws and purpose. Ancient distinctions between kingdoms and provinces were broken down by the annexation of Scotland and Ireland. A loose but consistent Republican church order prevailed. Both Roman Catholicism and episcopalianism were banned and effectively suppressed. The church was Erastian, with enough liberty of conscience to permit a range of different Protestant opinions and practices, but it had a fundamentally Reformed Protestant character. It agreed rather well with what the New England colonies had accomplished, even if New Englanders (with the perennial exception of Rhode Island) rejected its broad liberty of conscience. It was a godly church order reflecting the evangelical Protestant priorities of the Independents who made up the Rump Parliament and the military, especially Oliver Cromwell. By repealing the laws enjoining religious conformity, the Rump allowed Congregationalist, Presbyterian, and Baptist churches to flourish, albeit to different degrees in different places. The Rump also set the bar for unacceptable heresy so high that a wide range of religious Seekers—including men like Roger Williams and his Gortonist neighbors—could worship without fear. A degree of religious pluralism was becoming the norm, but nevertheless a loosely united religious system was being created that could have provided the foundation for a unified transatlantic religious order. However, challenges from within—especially the rise of the Quakers—and without—especially the conquest of more Catholic territory, starting with Acadia in 1654—soon threatened the Reformed Protestant hopes of its rulers.

FOURTEEN

Empire: Surinam, Barbados, Jamaica, Dunkirk, 1654–1660

In the late 1650s, a new religious group emerged and rapidly spread across the English world. Determined and dauntless missionaries endured all sorts of pain and indignity to spread the vital message of the Society of Friends. They seemed unstoppable. Occasionally, however, they hit a roadblock as Henry Fell did in Surinam in the winter of 1659. After a successful visit to Barbados, he and a fellow missionary went to Surinam where, during a stay of two and a half months, they made several converts. Fell believed Surinamers to be horrible Christians. They "exceed in wickedness; more than any I have bene among of ye English." He worried whether the new Quaker community would survive, as "the crosse will bee hard for many of them to take up it being great as to ye outward." That judgment was soon confirmed when he and his companion confronted "a rage against the Truth." Surinam's governor, William Byam, and council ordered the arrest of the Quakers. They were put "into the stocks part of that day and all ye night in ye raine and wett, which was much, being about 16 or 17 houres." The "next day they tooke our bookes and papers from us to burne them." Released, the missionaries persisted in organizing Quaker meetings. Two weeks later, Byam had them arrested again. According to Fell, they were imprisoned for sixteen days on the basis of a warrant "full of lyes and slanders and their own imaginations." Byam then insisted that the Quakers depart on a ship ready to sail for Barbados. Fell refused, presenting instead his written response to the warrant's accusations. Byam refused to read it, threatened to whip the Quakers, and uttered "many evill & wicked speeches against us, & the truth with scorne." He then had the Quakers forcibly carried aboard the ship. Surinam did not become a center of Quakerism. Barbados did.[1]

Quakers were only the most dynamic and largest of several new Protestant sects operating in the late 1650s. With Independents setting the terms of religious and political life, this era represents a distinct period in the history of early America and the English world. Oliver Cromwell was Protector of the Commonwealth. New England was no longer a refuge but the cutting edge of an aggressively expansionistic Reformed Protestant empire stretching from Canada to South America. Religiously diverse, it nevertheless operated under a Reformed religious establishment that—more than any time before or since—promised to unite the expanding English world within a single church system. It was admittedly loose and fuzzy at points, sometimes lacked popular support, and was unevenly enforced from place to place, as Henry Fell learned. The governor of Barbados treated Quakers in a manner similar to Oliver Cromwell. Surinam's governor treated them more like New Haven did. However, had this system survived another decade or so, it could have provided the foundation for a broad Protestant unity.

Instead, the Cromwellian era ended up entrenching religious pluralism, thanks in large part to the consequences of Cromwell's war against the Spanish. The war added the new territories of Jamaica and Dunkirk, increased the presence of Roman Catholicism within the English world, and opened it up to Jewish settlement. Protestant policies within these territories fit within the Cromwellian spectrum. Surinam's conservative Protestantism was not unlike the conservative New England regimes. Jamaica's radical approach resembled that of Rhode Island. Dunkirk, where a British Protestant army occupied a Roman Catholic territory, had a clear parallel in Ireland. However, the international context undermined the Cromwellian Protestant hegemony. Dunkirk became the first place Roman Catholicism was officially tolerated in the English world since the Reformation. Jews in Jamaica, Barbados, and Surinam contributed to the creation of the first openly Jewish community England had seen in three and a half centuries. Locally, conditions continued to vary from jurisdiction to jurisdiction, as the contrasting experience of Quakers in Barbados and Surinam or Roman Catholics in Jamaica and Dunkirk illustrates. Still, the Cromwellian regime generally managed to subordinate this expanding religious diversity to Reformed Protestant hegemony. Alas, that dominance depended on the uncertain health and vigor of Oliver Cromwell, who soon proved all too mortal.

*

In most respects, the Cromwellian church remained consistent with that of the republic. Reformed Protestant priorities continued to predominate. Liberty of conscience remained the language of power. A group of French and Dutch immigrants took advantage of this when pleading for support against unruly peasants. They had moved to Hatfield Chase in Lincolnshire in the 1630s as part of a project to drain the fenlands. While they profited off the rich new farmlands, the locals lost their traditional access to the free resources of the fenlands. Resentful, they destroyed the grain, homes, and mills of the immigrants. Petitioning for relief in 1656, the French and Dutch emphasized the threat to their religious liberty over that to their property. After all, they had "fled hither that they might have the free exercise of the Protestant Religion." With the locals interrupting their religious services and defacing "the places of their publique meeting," they needed protection so as "not to be debarred of their liberty for the free exercise of their religious worship."[2]

Cromwellian liberty of conscience was not a general religious freedom. It restricted itself to Protestant Christians of generally reformed tastes and Calvinist beliefs: those whom Cromwell recognized as "godly," regardless of their ethnicity. These godly did not entirely agree on church matters. Some, especially presbyterians, wanted more independence for the church and less tolerance for sectarians. Still, the regime's Erastian approach allowed it to accommodate much of the era's religious diversity, within certain bounds. Presbyterians often cooperated with Congregationalists and Baptists while Quakers hovered on the edge of acceptability. Cromwell was ambivalent about the new sects but showed them more indulgence than many of his contemporaries. Two famous cases illustrate how he negotiated the outer boundaries of acceptable religion with his Parliaments. In 1655, John Biddle, an outspoken Socinian, was convicted of heresy for denying the Trinity. Rather than pardon Biddle or execute him as some in Parliament wanted to do, Cromwell banished him to the isolated Scilly Isles off the coast of Cornwall. In 1656, the Quaker James Nayler came in for more brutal treatment. He had ridden into Bristol on the back of a donkey while his followers (many of them women) praised him in the words applied to Jesus when he had entered Jerusalem. Again, many in Parliament wanted an execution. Cromwell kept Nayler alive but imposed a harsh sentence. After being severely whipped through London and Bristol and having his tongue bored through with a hot iron, Nayler was locked in prison.[3]

It is difficult to describe the content of Cromwellian religion more specifically because Cromwell's own religious views have proven remarkably difficult to categorize. Having begun as a Calvinist much like his puritan friends who migrated to New England, Cromwell drifted toward a godly antiformalism, believing that more, not less tolerance was needed, at least for the time being. Still, he admired New Englanders and guided his policy with them in mind. In a 1654 speech to the first Protectorate Parliament, he maintained that the absolute power of the state had to be tempered with "allowances and exceptions from the rule." Otherwise, "we shall have our people driven into the wilderness, as they were when those poor and afflicted people . . . were necessitated to go into a vast howling wilderness in New England." He believed they had gone for "for liberty's sake." Having "stripped themselves of all their comfort," they chose "loss of friends and want than to be so ensnared in bondage."[4]

Beyond this general affinity for godliness, the Cromwellian church system had no specific set of doctrines or liturgical practices that everyone was expected to adhere to. There was an evangelical ambition to bring everyone in the English world into some sort of Reformed Protestant religion, and the deep respect for liberty of conscience allowed a wide range of individuals, including the majority of prerevolutionary clergy (about three-fourths), to fit into the official church in one way or another. For large swaths of the laity, this immersion in a world of reformed priorities shifted their religious tastes away from the ritual and ceremony of prewar Laudian parish life in favor of a compelling sermon. People also cared less whether their local minister or a visitor preached the sermon. Only a few die-hard episcopalian royalists preferred to remain a persecuted minority rather than cooperate with this system.[5]

The ability of conservative Protestants to accept the Cromwellian church system was crucial to its success. A good illustration of this acceptance comes from a minister in Essex, Dr. John Gauden, who teetered on the edge between presbyterianism and moderate episcopalianism. His views are suggestive of what was likely the case in the many colonies from Virginia to Barbados where similar calculations must have been made, although we lack similar evidence. Gauden had been a chaplain to the Earl of Warwick and remained close to Warwick's family. He also had links to the Cromwells. His brother-in-law Sir Francis Russell was Oliver Cromwell's friend and comrade. His wife was the aunt of Henry Cromwell's wife. However, after the Restoration he became a bishop in the Church of England. In a 1656 letter to Nicholas Bernard, chaplain to the Irish archbishop James Ussher (who straddled the same ecclesiastical line), Gauden expressed optimism that, under Cromwell, ministers were "moving toward a fraternall accord." If "Presbyterians and Independents" as well as "episcopall men" could coexist in "a calme temper," he had hopes that England's "reformed church" could "be restored and preserved" with "sound doctrine, holy lifes, brotherly love, sanctity of dutys." Gauden regretted the "scattered and confused state it hath beene in and still is," but nonetheless believed that a revival of "the beauty, solemnity, and unity of religion, which is not only its honor, but its safety against popery and other enemies of the reformed religion" would "oblige men to civill peace and willing subjection."[6]

While Quakers and other sectarians could sometimes fit under this umbrella, they also posed a dramatic challenge to its conservative hopes. They took ideas about divine inspiration that had long been circulating in puritan circles and developed them into a belief in individuals' connection to God through an "Inner Light." Anyone willing to repent and convert could discover within them this piece of the divine. Around 1650, this powerful message had coalesced around the person of George Fox. With the support of influential and charismatic allies, Fox then oversaw the rapid spread of Quakerism, first across the north of England by 1653, then to the south in 1654, beyond England in 1655, and to the colonies in 1656, where Quakers took their message everywhere from Barbados to Massachusetts. They made converts in New England, New Netherland, and the Caribbean from Bermuda to Barbados. In the Leewards one of their converts was Samuel Winthrop. Along the way, their beliefs in the fundamental spiritual equality of all persons challenged social conventions as well as the church establishment. They ignored traditional ideas about dress and honor; let uneducated laypeople become preachers; and appealed to young people. They even allowed women to preach and sent them on missions to distant places. Many of the first Quaker missionaries to the colonies were women.[7]

There was no limit to where Quakers would go. In December 1656 the English resident in Hamburg complained that he had "much truble with them" before shipping them back to England. A year later, the English agent at Leghorn, Italy, saw "four, cald Quakers" arrive with hopes of going on missions to "Egipt, and thence to Jerusalem," or to "Smirna and Constantinople." The Grand Duke of Tuscany would not let them stay "abov three dayes." Several made it to Constantinople, where the English ambassador complained in July 1658 about the troubles "occasioned by a generation of people crept in unawares, called Quakers." He initially "suffered" their presence "with tenderness, so long as theer comportment was offencelesse." However, he worried that their behavior was "scandalous to our nation and religion, (which upon this occasion was censured and scoffed at, by Papist, Jew, and others of a strange faith).” Moreover, the Quakers were becoming “insufferable . . . by reason of their disturbances of our divine exercises, and severall notorious contempts of mee and my authority.” When one of them refused to leave after the ambassador “friendly warned them to returne,” the tolerance ended. The ambassador shipped the Quaker back to England.[8]

In the American colonies, the Quaker experience was more varied. In Maryland, after Lord Baltimore regained control in November 1657 the (mostly Catholic) Proprietary party found common ground with many of the puritans in persecuting Quakers. They justified this persecution by pointing out that Quakers did not even exist at the time Maryland’s Act of Religion was passed, so how could it apply to them? Nonetheless, Quakers converted a number of the former puritans and established a permanent community, especially on the Eastern Shore, where Quakers formed an enclave protected by the geographical shield of the Chesapeake Bay. Maryland may have been predicated on toleration, but its religious coexistence was largely premised on segregation into widely separated counties: Catholics in the south, puritans in the north, Quakers in the east.[9]

With a few exceptions, persecution generally failed to deter Quakers. Despite their efforts to suppress the movement, New Plymouth, Massachusetts, and New Netherland all developed Quaker communities. Massachusetts’s campaign of repression was the fiercest of all. In 1658 it passed a law banishing Quakers under pain of death if they returned. In 1659, two missionaries were executed under this law’s provisions. Two more were executed in 1661. Nevertheless, a Quaker community took root. Surinam, Connecticut, and New Haven, on the other hand, managed to keep Quakers out by the less lethal means of humiliation and banishment. John Davenport refused to debate the Quakers in print or person, but publicly denounced Humphrey Norton just before he was branded on the hand “with the Letter H. for Heresie,” fined, and “conveyed out of their Colonie.” Other Quaker missionaries to New Haven colony were not even permitted to “discharge and unburthen their Consciences” before they were “forced away with the burthen of that Word upon them.” The Quaker message was squashed without creating Quaker martyrs, as Massachusetts did.[10]

Almost all of the colonies, with the notable exceptions of Barbados and Rhode Island, persecuted Quakers to some degree. Even in Barbados, where the governor tolerated Quakers, he had to protect them from hostile colonists. Rhode Island simply had no mechanism for persecuting them. Called “the *caeca latrina* of New England” in the words of the Dutch ministers of New Netherland, Rhode Island was the "one place in New England where they are tolerated." Roger Williams might publicly denounce their doctrine, but he would not and could not stop them from converting a significant number of Rhode Islanders. Nor did he stop them from using his colony as a base to send out missionaries across the region, as the Baptists did. The Dutch ministers complained that from Rhode Island the Quakers "swarm to and fro sowing their tares."[11]

Barbados's approach was a more deliberate, magisterial toleration that resembled Cromwell's approach in England. Like Cromwell, Daniel Searle, the governor appointed by the Parliamentary forces in 1652, presided over an increasingly diverse society. Among the free European population, there were, in addition to a wide array of British Protestants, some Dutch Reformed Protestants, Jews, and Catholics (mostly Irish servants). There was also a rapidly growing population of Africans. Searle set the terms for what was religiously acceptable. Reformed Protestantism was the official religion, but within the privacy of their own homes and on their plantations, colonists could worship as they wished, as the French Catholic priest Antoine Biet discovered in 1654. Biet arrived on Barbados, in disguise, as part of a group of French people escaping from Cayenne, where their efforts to plant a colony had failed. Searle greeted the French colonists pleasantly, saying they "were very welcome, and that they could land and live in the island as if they were in France." That welcome was not extended to the public exercise of their faith, however. As a young Irish man informed Biet, "If they discover he is a priest . . . they will handle him pretty roughly." Indeed, when three Irish Catholic priests arrived in the spring of 1656, they were prohibited from settling on the island and given fifteen days to leave. Nevertheless, as Biet was pleased to discover, a number of French and Irish Catholic laypeople lived on the island. Buying a plantation near one of their French acquaintances, his company discovered that within its confines they could live peacefully "in the practice of our Holy Religion." Biet "said mass on holidays and Sundays, above all Sundays, when each one is free to do as he wants on the plantation, and to live with whatever religion he wants," including Judaism. As long as they did not "carry out religious exercises in public, no one bothers with what one is doing." Later, Biet visited a room in Bridgetown used by Catholics for religious gatherings.[12]

For this Catholic priest, Barbados showed "no sign of religion . . . except for the observance of Sunday which is inviolably kept." Describing the public religion as "Calvinism," Biet noted that each parish had a minister "who is not hindered from preaching any kind of sermon." He was impressed that Sabbath-breakers who frequented taverns were "severely punished," but he was not impressed by the quality of their Christian faith, calling it "almost no religion." The majority of the population, he noticed, seemed to prefer to spend the Sabbath on their plantations, which may account for their lack of instruction. To his dismay, one old man told him, "It is enough to believe that there is a God, and that Jesus Christ died for us."[13]

A more dynamic illustration of Governor Searle's toleration at work comes from Henry Fell. Arriving in 1656 as one of the first Quaker missionaries to Barbados, Fell described his struggles with the island's "priests" (the Protestant ministers) and "ye people that follow ye priests." Like Father Biet, Fell had little respect for the common Anglo-Barbadian. They "are for ye most part exceeding rude & brutish." Yet he also encountered an impressive religious diversity, curiosity, and evangelical fervor. For example, the Ranter Joseph Salmon had recently arrived and was also looking to make converts. Fell also encountered Baptists and managed to convert "some" who became "convinced of the truth, and have denyed the rest." The "others" however, "are enemyes in their minds ag[ains]t the truth." Finally, there were individuals who were "high in their wisdomes by reason of w[hi]ch & ye love & hon[o]r of ye world doe not owne truth."[14]

Searle's tolerance mattered because the people of Barbados did not welcome Quakers with open arms. On the contrary, soon after Fell arrived, the assembly passed a classical piece of anti-Quaker legislation to fine Quakers for not doing militia service. Fell reacted by presenting Governor Searle with a pamphlet protesting the act. To his surprise, Searle not only read Fell's pamphlet but "sayed it was good counsell." Moreover, "he tooke noe offence att my hatt or thouinge of him." Most authority figures reacted angrily to the Quakers' refusal to remove their hats, a traditional sign of respect, as well as their policy of addressing everyone by the archaic "thou" to emphasize their spiritual equality. Still, Fell thought Searle rather "conceited of himselfe" when he insisted on engaging the Quaker in a theological discussion. For half an hour, they discussed "perfection and such like." Searle concluded by telling Fell that he thought the Quakers lived "inoffencive or unblamable" lives. However, their "Judging of others, he could not beare," suggesting something of his own tolerant attitudes. Fell responded by presenting the governor with more Quaker pamphlets, speaking "some few words," and leaving.[15]

Like Cromwell, Searle was more tolerant than many of the people he governed. A few weeks after meeting the governor, Fell was attacked by several Barbadians while on his way to visit a prominent Quaker plantation owner. They left him "much abused & beaten." The planter told him he would have the assailants brought before the governor and "was sure" that Searle "would punish them & would not suffer any to abuse me if he knew of it." Indeed, not long afterward, Fell learned that the men had been "bound over to their sessions as they call them." It is not known if anything more happened, but Searle was clearly indicating that unauthorized violence would not be tolerated. Fell acknowledged Searle to be "pretty moderate" and recognized that, with his influence, "persecution is somethinge restrayned" on Barbados. This protective attitude made the island a major base for Quakerism. By 1680 several hundred of its planters were organized in six separate Quaker meetings.[16]

Surinam's governor, by stark contrast, chose to resist the Quakers. Land-hungry Barbadians had colonized Surinam in 1650–51. While it is unclear if Lord Willoughby was responsible for the first group of colonists who went there, he quickly sent out 150 men in two separate expeditions. After the Parliamentary fleet forced him out of Barbados, Willoughby stopped briefly in Surinam on his way back to England, where he persuaded the Cromwellian government to grant him a patent for the new colony in 1657. Willoughby said nothing specific about religion when he published inducements to attract colonists. However, he explicitly encouraged ministers to go to Surinam, including them alongside other professionals, or "all considerable persons & ingenuous Artists or Students, as able preachers, schoolmasters, Physitians, Chyrurgions, midwives, Surveyors, Architectors, Chymists & other persons singularly improveable for ye good of ye Colonye." He promised that their "books instruments or tooles needful in ye exercise of their ingenuity, shalbe fraight free, & any other reasonable foods indulged."[17]

The available evidence indicates Surinam was considerably less religiously diverse and less tolerant than Barbados. In 1660 Willoughby claimed he had founded Surinam as "an English Protestant Colonie." His choice of governor suggests the sort of Protestantism he had in mind was the conservative Protestant mix advocated by men like John Gauden. William Byam was the son of a Church of England clergyman and member of a royalist family from Somerset. He had two uncles who were conformist clergymen. One of them, Henry, was an outspoken anti-puritan Laudian. Byam may have sympathized with the moderate episcopalianism associated with Prayer Book worship. At least, he does not seem to have actively suppressed it. An Independent minister who arrived in early 1662 discovered colonists "were much offended" by his refusal to use "the Common Prayer and the Cross in Baptism." Nevertheless,

Byam supported Willoughby's policy of recruiting ministers even if they were Independents. Although we know little of religious life in the colony during the 1650s, several important Independent ministers served there after 1660. One was John Oxenbridge, the man who had helped pioneer Congregationalism on Bermuda. Another, Nicholas Leverton, had served on Barbados before the civil war and been converted to the Congregational cause while serving on Providence Island in the 1630s. He found Byam "to be a man of learning, ingenuity and of great civility, the famous non-conformist beyond all others." Either way, Byam clearly believed religious tolerance was necessary to make his colony thrive. In 1662, he had the assembly "send out a declaration for liberty of conscience to all that shall live peaceably under government in the land," evidently hoping to attract Jewish sugar planters, among others. They came and set up what became one of the most important Jewish communities in America. Alas, a few years later, Byam had to surrender the colony to the Dutch during the second Anglo-Dutch War.[18]

While Surinam espoused liberty of conscience, it did not do so to the same degree as Barbados, as the Quaker Henry Fell discovered. Arriving in the winter of 1659, he and his fellow missionary moved about freely for two months, during which time they made some converts. Then Byam and his council turned on the Quaker missionaries. First, they put them "into the stocks," and then seized and burneded their papers. When the missionaries continued to proselytize after their release, Bryan had them packed onto a ship back to Barbados. There, Governor Searle was once again "pritty moderate and noble and loveing to Friendes." Indeed, he had recently released two Quakers imprisoned for refusing to bear arms after having paid their fine himself. Searle even suggested to Fell that he would get the anti-Quaker militia act repealed, "soe that the enemyes will not have their wills."[19]

In the meantime, a new war against Spain allowed the English world to expand through conquest. Cromwell had begun planning this Anglo-Spanish War soon after coming to power. It proved much more successful than the previous two. Spain was now weaker, England stronger. And trickier: Cromwell initiated the conflict with a secret invasion of the Spanish Caribbean. By 1660, his armies had added Jamaica and Dunkirk to his empire. However, while it was larger and more militantly Protestant than ever, these conquests, together with Acadia, also made it less thoroughly Protestant—less Christian even.[20]

Jamaica joined the English world first. The Western Design that captured the island in 1655 was supposed to conquer the island of Santo

Domingo. The massive amphibious expedition combined a fleet commanded by Admiral William Penn, father of the famous Quaker, with an army commanded by General Robert Venables, a veteran of Cromwell's expedition to Ireland, where he had been particularly brutal to Catholics. Venables's appointment did not bode well for any Spanish Catholics who fell into his clutches. Santo Domingo was lucky. It drove the English off. Jamaica, poorly fortified and less populous, was picked up as a consolation prize.[21]

Credit for inspiring the Western Design is often given to Thomas Gage. A Protestant minister who had previously been a Roman Catholic priest, in 1648 he had published *The English American*, an account of his travels through Spanish America—the first English account of daily life there. In it, Gage claimed that Spanish ambitions combined with "Jesuiticall policy" to meet "with Antichrists policy and Ambition" of filling "the Infantile Church of Asia and America with troopes of" missionaries who, "under pretence of salvation," brought "damnation and misery to their poor and wretched souls." Indigenous Americans needed to be brought into the Protestant faith instead. Fortunately, Gage could attest that the Spanish were now weak and divided by tensions between Europeans and American Creoles. What godly imperialist could resist such a plumb?[22]

Gage's popular text was music to Cromwell's ears. It was also a testament to Gage's conversion from Catholicism. His Spanish American adventure had only been possible because he came from a militant Catholic background. His father and mother, Margaret Copley, were members of prominent recusant families in Surrey who had harbored priests and been condemned to death for it, but reprieved. A less lucky uncle was executed in connection with the Babington Plot. The Jesuit martyr Robert Southwell was a cousin. Sir Henry Gage, Thomas's eldest brother, had been a royalist commander in the civil war. Several other brothers became Catholic priests. Gage himself, after being educated at Saint Omer and then in Spain, became a Dominican. Defying the expectation that he would serve in England, he made his way to Mexico around 1625, then spent over a decade as a priest and missionary in Central America. He made his way back to England in 1637, where religious misgivings prompted his conversion to the Church of England just as the civil war broke out. A year later, in 1643, Parliament granted him a pulpit in Kent. There, he composed his book, married, betrayed several Catholic priests (who were then executed), and, in 1654, vigorously defended the Cromwellian church order of "Parochial Churches and Parish Officiating Ministers" from the criticisms of the minister of a "Separated Congregation." He also developed a plan for invading the Spanish Caribbean.[23]

Joining the Western Design as chaplain to General Venables, Gage never had a chance to proselytize among Spanish Catholics or Native Americans. Instead he became one of the hundreds of Englishmen who died, mostly from disease, on Jamaica. Although the Spanish had surrendered shortly after the English arrived in May 1655, the island was not so easily subdued. As they had in Ireland, the English immediately banned Catholic worship. A Spanish account recorded that "No priest nor book might remain in the island," but it mattered little, for almost all of the Jamaican Spanish relocated to Cuba or retreated into the interior to fight a drawn-out guerilla war. Only "some negroes and Portuguese," according to a Spanish account, "submitted to the English." The peculiar nature of the conquest spared the English of any need to develop a more extensive policy of repression since they had virtually no Catholics to govern.[24]

Very little is known about religious life on Cromwellian Jamaica, but it doubtlessly reflected the Independent sensibilities of the expedition's leaders: a mix of presbyterians, Baptists, Congregationalists, and others. These included two New England men, Robert Sedgwick and Edward Winslow, who both followed Gage in quickly succumbing to disease. New England served as something of a model for English Jamaica. Like New England, the island was not divided up into parishes. The Cromwellian regime also sought to recruit colonists for Jamaica from among the puritan colonists of New England, Bermuda, and Eleutheria, but with little success. Only a few New Englanders dared make the move, joined by a handful from Bermuda and Eleutheria. However, Luke Stokes, the "most sober, godley and discrete" governor of Nevis, led a migration of some 1,500 colonists to Jamaica in 1656. Soon thereafter, Quakers arrived. They easily gained a foothold because, unlike New England, ministers seem to have been in short supply on Jamaica. For years, religious leadership was restricted to a handful of military chaplains, about whom we know very little. One of the few to survive the difficult early years was George Johns, referred to in 1664 as "an old army preacher not yet in orders," that is, not episcopally ordained.[25]

Despite having chased out the Spanish, English Jamaica was never a purely Protestant society. The desperate need for labor and inhabitants soon drew in Irish Catholic servants. It even led the regime to consider sending over two thousand Irish boys and girls to work as servants in Protestant households: in theory, this would also facilitate their conversion to Protestantism. More important for the development of colonial pluralism were the several "Portuguese" who stayed behind when the rest of the Spanish fled. At least some of these people were likely of Jewish ancestry. Persecuted in Spain and Portugal, they had survived by hiding their ancestral religion under a veil of conformity to the Roman Catholic Church. For them, the Cromwellian conquest offered both religious liberation and new trade opportunities. It was not long before they connected to the small Jewish community developing across the English world.[26]

The intersection of Caribbean and European developments in the 1650s allowed an openly Jewish community to return to England for the first time since Jews had been expelled in 1290. Before the 1640s, there had been no sign the English would reverse that policy. In 1498, while negotiating with Spain for the marriage of Catherine of Aragon to his son Arthur, Henry VII had promised the Spanish envoy that "he would prosecute without mercy any Jewish renegade or fugitive from the Inquisition who could be discovered in his dominions." The occasional Jewish person made his way (it was almost always a he) into England, but usually just for a brief sojourn. Official repression prevented the establishment of a community. Still, a number of Sephardi from Iberia or Italy, often skilled specialists, rabbis, doctors, financiers, soldiers, and diplomats, had spent time in England before the 1650s. A few were converts to Protestantism. Mostly they were so-called conversos operating under the guise of being Roman Catholic. At several different moments, wealthy conversos managed to sustain a small clandestine Jewish community by holding worship services in their London homes: in the 1540s, the 1590s, and again around 1609. Each time, the community was quickly dispersed after being discovered. More Jewish individuals appeared in the 1630s, but not enough to form a community. Then, in the 1640s, a few Jews from Amsterdam were allowed in to help protect the trade of English merchants during the civil war. By that point, a new doorway into the English world was opening up in the Caribbean, first in Barbados, then in Jamaica and Surinam.[27]

In the meantime, British attitudes toward Jews were changing. Jews came to coexist in English Protestant minds alongside Native Americans and Africans as people who should and could be converted through colonization. Puritans in New England believed their religious example would bring on the conversion of the Jews—and the millennium. This hope derived from the wave of Philo-Semitism washing across England in the first half of the seventeenth century. Protestants became fascinated with Judaism and Hebraic studies. A couple even claimed to be, or to have become, Jewish. For example, in December 1648, Anne Curtyn had been committed to the New Prison at Clerkenwell for denying "Jesus Christ to be a prophet, and His prophetical office," and "for being a professed Jew and causing children to be circumcised." The following January, at the urging of the Middlesex sessions, several ministers "conferenced" with her about her opinions. They found that her opinion of Christ being not a prophet only differed from them in terms but not in substance. However, she was obstinate in her profession and practice as a Jew. It is unclear where she got her ideas from, but in the 1640s and 1650s, the learned and respected rabbi of the Jewish congregation in Amsterdam, Menasseh ben Israel, was attracting admiration and curiosity as reports circulated that Jewish tribes had been discovered in America. The idea that all Native Americans were actually descendants of the Lost Tribes of Israel was one aspect of millenarian hopes in these years, reflecting the Protestant hope that both groups would soon convert. These hopes echoed various apocalyptic prophesies circulating around Europe.[28]

These religious-millenarian hopes combined with a peculiar mix of economic desires and the shifting international political scene to persuade the Cromwellian regime to reconsider the country's ancient policies toward Jews. A small but growing number of overseas merchants of Jewish origin were becoming involved in the English trade in munitions as well as sugar and other colonial products as England fought first the Dutch then the Spanish for commercial and colonial supremacy. These merchants generally presented themselves as Iberian Catholics, but their Jewish roots were not entirely hidden. Menasseh ben Israel was encouraged to visit England and consider whether some sort of broader Jewish resettlement was possible. Cromwell then opened the question of a formal readmission up to a public debate involving religious leaders and members of the Council of State. In the end, it provoked more hostility than amity, on both economic and religious grounds. Cromwell decided against a formal pronouncement of readmission. However, the Jews already living in London—now living openly as Jews rather than Catholics—were allowed to stay and worship quietly in their homes. London merchants would complain about their presence after the Restoration, but King Charles II continued Cromwell's policy of letting the Jewish community stay on as long as it remained quiet and obedient. In 1673, he finally gave them formal recognition and publicly tolerated them.[29]

The scholarship on the readmission of Jews to England tends to overlook the Caribbean, but it was a crucial part of this story. Several Jews—men who were recognized and accepted as such, not men presenting themselves as Iberian Catholics—were living on Barbados by the 1650s.

Most likely they were a mix of refugees from Dutch Brazil and European entrepreneurs taking advantage of Barbados's sugar boom. Some Jews then moved to Surinam and possibly Nevis. If those on Jamaica weren't already part of this transatlantic network, they quickly joined it.[30]

The Western Design's religious consequences were multiple. In addition to facilitating the return of Jews to the English world, it also revived Huguenot interest in colonization. In 1657, René Augier, Esq., submitted a petition for another anti-Catholic Huguenot colony. Recalling the earlier Huguenot dreams for Carolana, Augier proposed that his colony could be "either att Jamaica or else where in the West Indies." He wanted the colony to challenge "the Jesuits fondamentall designe," which was "to settle their Empire by their commerce in the one and in the others Indies." Augier was not interested in toleration. Instead, he insisted that "all the Strangers whome the Society he propounds will imploye" in the colony "shall professe the Protestant Reformed Religion." To ensure they were religiously qualified, the colonists would have to confirm their faith by "attestations and certificats of the ministers or consistorys of those places where they shall have been inroled." Augier also would have all prospective colonists swear to exclude Jesuits, Catholic missionaries, and monks from the colony.[31]

Augier's colony did not come to pass. Indeed, no new English colonies would be founded until Carolina was chartered in 1663. Instead, English expansion took place in Europe, where an army captured Dunkirk from the Spanish in June 1658. A mighty fortress perched on the border with France, Dunkirk was also an import port from which Spanish privateers harassed their enemies. English planners had high hopes it could become their alternative to Amsterdam. To achieve that goal, some were willing to make major religious concessions. One suggested that if "ther mae bee a tolleration of a sinagoge for the Jewes they will give 60,000 or 80,000 pound for that freedom: it will bring all the Portugal marchants from Amsterdam." Moreover, if "the Catholick shall have freedom of consciens and liberty to goe to ther naboring plases to church, it will bring many French and Duch marchant dealers." The majority of the surrounding population, from northern France to the southern provinces of the Dutch Republic was Catholic. Protestant French and Dutch merchants also would be encouraged, "especially if ther be a prodistant church of those 2 nations ordayned in the towne." With toleration, Dunkirk could become a "flurrishing commonwealth of it selfe." This particular proposal was optimistic that within five years the economic benefits of this pluralism would render Dunkirk "nott much inferior to Amsterdam as Amsterdam is nowe."[32]

Cromwell, however, wanted Dunkirk to be a Protestant bulwark, a base for supporting the Huguenots in France as well as aiding the Dutch Republic against its Catholic enemies. Immediately after the conquest, his government resolved to send over "a Bible to each file of soldiers, and to consider of an able minister to be sent thither." Reliable chaplains were appointed for the garrison including, briefly, the New England revolutionary Hugh Peters. At least one minister had an appointment as both regimental chaplain and minister to the Flemish community, a few of whom were Protestants. Andrew Forbes, a Scot from a family with possible Dutch trading connections, spoke the language and could potentially make more converts.[33]

In the event, Dunkirk became neither an alternate Amsterdam nor a Protestant bulwark. Instead, strategic and diplomatic considerations forced Cromwell to make it a Roman Catholic enclave with an official grant of toleration. The English had only managed to capture the fortress city with the help of a recently signed alliance with France. It was a Franco-English army that had defeated the Spanish forces, who had been backed by British royalist exiles, including Charles II and his brother James, Duke of York. As per the terms of the alliance, the young French king Louis XIV accepted the keys to the city then turned them over to the Cromwellian commander, Sir William Lockhart. King Louis likely (and correctly) anticipated that in the long run the English would be no more able to hold on to Dunkirk then they had been to Boulogne and Calais. In the meantime, he insisted the English tolerate the city's Roman Catholicism. Dunkirk's population of roughly five thousand was allowed to retain its fifty-nine priests and monks and fifty-three nuns. The English tried to reduce Catholicism's public profile. For a time they banned public processions. They required priests as well as magistrates to swear an oath of allegiance (like the Engagement, it was silent on questions of religion). The few incidents of harassment by the Protestant soldiery, such as the soldier who lit his pipe with an altar candle, were petty. In general, Roman Catholicism continued much as before. Only one priest who refused to swear the oath of allegiance was banished. Indeed, apart from his case, the English occupation is virtually undetectable in the Catholic records. A Catholic deacon inspecting Dunkirk's church in 1659 found a thriving community. Mass was celebrated, confessions heard, the church bells, ornaments, and relics were in good condition. Three lay confraternities were active. Monasteries belonging to the Recollets, Capuchins, Jesuits, Carmelites, and several other religious orders—including a group of English Benedictines nuns—operated smoothly. Religious processions were made for Corpus Christi and the feast of Saint John the Baptist. The cemetery, south of town, had not been profaned. Priests collected their tithes. The English did not interfere with the church's property rights, including a new chantry established by a noted sea captain. Indeed, the deacon detected "no adversary to the precepts of the Church" within the parish. On the contrary, the church was confident enough to request the return of the one precious item it had sent abroad for safety during the siege.[34]

While Dunkirk's Catholics thrived, the Protestant cause suffered. It took a great deal of effort to maintain a Protestant outpost in the Spanish Low Countries. Lockhart, the commander, struggled to procure ministers. He wanted a total of three for his six regiments and promised "to procure them 180" pounds sterling a year "a-piece, which, I think, is encouragement enoff to any honest man, who hath zeal for his master's service, or the propagation of his gospel." Yet his appeals met with little success. He glumly compared the failure of Protestant ministers even "upon reasonable terms" of employment "to preach the gladd tydings of salvatione to their poor countrimen" to the "Popish priests" who were willing to "go a begging to vent their errours." Unable to find "not one minister," he sent his personal chaplain to serve the soldiers "out of charity." They "need much to be both dehorted from evil, and exhorted to good." Several years later, a pamphlet reminded readers of the fragile condition of Protestantism in Dunkirk, asking "Whether it be not a shame to the Protestant Religion, that the English in Dunkirk must be forced to send their children to the Papists to baptize, or keep them unchristened, as above 30 are at this time in that garrison? And whether an able Orthodox ministery there is not more requisite then in any part of the three Nations?" In this respect, Dunkirk resembled the English outpost at Madras, where a small cluster of English Protestants ruling over a larger and more vigorous Roman Catholic community occasionally relied on the basic religious services of Catholic priests.[35]

Notwithstanding the toleration in Dunkirk, everywhere else Oliver Cromwell's empire did more to suppress Roman Catholicism than any English government before or since. Far more often than not, his regime seemed to be irresistibly expanding the godly cause. New Englanders, benefiting from their close connection to England's ruler, were delighted. Unfortunately for this "good old cause," the constant wars, struggles, and stress wore Cromwell out. In September 1658 he passed away at the age of fifty-nine. He would not be easily replaced.

At first, after some political jostling, Cromwell's son Richard succeeded him as Protector. Richard seems to have wanted to stabilize his father's religious policy. Much like his brother Henry in Ireland, he favored a conservative Calvinist hegemony over the blossoming of sectarian religious freedom. In October, the Congregational ministers meeting at the Savoy Palace presented him with their Declaration of Faith. He gladly accepted it. Calling Congregationalists "the choicest part" of the Nation and "next my heart," he professed the same affection to them "which my Father had." He hoped "wee may study peace and unity one to another" to "incorporate the interest of the people of God" and promote "the beating downe of superstition."[36]

Unfortunately, Richard lacked his father's influence over the army. Resuming its political role, the army soon dismissed him and reinstated the Rump Parliament. The Rump then called for a Convention Parliament to create a stable government and church system. It was a fatal mistake. The army was no longer united. Neither it nor the Rump made a concerted effort to restrict the Convention to reliable Republicans. Consequently, many men who resented the revolutionary regime were able to participate. Rather than repair the republic, they chose to restore monarchical rule. Coups and factional struggles in Ireland and Scotland ensured those kingdoms likewise supported a Restoration. In the spring of 1660, King Charles II peacefully reclaimed his kingdoms. Puritans lost their hegemony and became a minority.[37]

*

The Cromwellian period was brief, but it is instructive for those considering the religious history of colonial America and the budding British Empire. Cromwell's fairly liberal approach to religious diversity arguably had more potential to reunite the English world within a single church system than any policy before or after. This possibility is especially important when considering colonial America. In the 1650s, the religious establishments of Massachusetts and Virginia were closer than any time before or since, and even Rhode Island fit within the spectrum of legitimate possibilities, with Jamaica's religious order a close relative. Guided by Protestant liberty of conscience, this system had an adaptability and fluidity that was key to its hegemony. It offered a Reformed Protestant consensus able (more or less) to unite Presbyterians, Independents, and moderate episcopalians. Baptists, Quakers, and other sectarians proved harder to digest, but they were not completely beyond the pale. As the contrast between the Quakers' early experience of Barbados and Surinam demonstrates, Cromwellian liberty of conscience could sometimes grant them a space. While not everyone in authority shared Oliver Cromwell's idiosyncratic understanding of who was godly and worthy of tolerance, on the whole, the system provided a more than superficial religious unity. Who knows what it would have produced had Cromwell lived longer or his succession been more stable?

Overseas, the Cromwellian religious system bumped up against distinct limits, as evidenced by its relationship to Roman Catholics. The remarkably effective suppression of Roman Catholic worship in Ireland showed what the regime was capable of; only on Jamaica did it manage to completely obliterate a preexisting Catholic community. They deserve little credit for that feat, however, which was primarily the choice of the Spanish to withdraw and fight. In Nova Scotia, the English struggled to enforce their religious supremacy over a widely scattered and entrenched French Catholic population. In Madras, on the other hand, they could not prosper without the aide of neighboring Roman Catholics, and so they developed a semiofficial policy of toleration. Finally, in Dunkirk the English were constrained by both the demands and influence of other European nations and a certain lack of missionary zeal. Here, Roman Catholics enjoyed the sort of formal toleration British and Irish Catholics had long hoped for but never yet attained.

Finally, a similar mix of forces—expansion, the need for labor, and a desire for more profitable trade—combined with aspects of Protestant millennialism to undermine the Christian character of the English world. From the beginning of English overseas exploration, the professed intention had been to expand Christendom by incorporating foreign lands and peoples into the English church, be they Native Americans, Africans, or Jews. Indeed, legally, there was still no formal space for non-Christian religion while missionary efforts in Massachusetts were beginning to make strides in the conversion of Native Americans. However, the vast majority of English colonists preferred to leave Native Americans and Africans to their traditional beliefs if only because religious difference conveniently reinforced the social distance that made their exploitation easier. Jews fit in a somewhat different category. As Europeans who were not Christian but whose religion was closely related to Christianity, they played a special role in Protestant eschatological and millennial schemes and dreams—

virtually all of which imagined their ultimate conversion to Christianity. As skilled merchants, they also played an important role in the developing Atlantic economy. Nevertheless, no legal or institutional mechanism existed to procure their conversion. When a small but noticeable number of Jews began extending their trade connections to the English world and settling there in the 1640–50s, the same traditions of household worship and practice that had long allowed Roman Catholics and Protestant dissidents to survive, and allowed Africans enslaved on English plantations to also preserve something of their own beliefs, worked to help Judaism gain a toehold in the English world as well.

Thus, in a number of small ways in various corners of the English world, religious pluralism was taking root long before it was officially recognized and tolerated. The Cromwellian regime's championing of liberty of conscience facilitated this coexistence, even though its ultimate aim was to create a unified Protestant world. That was not an impossible goal, but its time in power was too brief to achieve it. After 1660, a new political and religious settlement would add yet another religious twist to the English world. Cromwell's failure to live to a ripe old age condemned New Englanders and their friends to enter this new era of pluralism as one of its constituent religious minorities rather than the hegemonic religion governing it.

Conclusion

On May 29, 1660, Charles II entered London and became king of the English world. It was his thirtieth birthday. The era of puritan hegemony was over, to the delight of many on both sides of the Atlantic. John Featley, formerly the minister of Saint Christopher and now a chaplain to Charles II, celebrated the return of "your Subjects safest Liberty" by publishing a manuscript his uncle Daniel Featley had written "Proving, that the Protestant Church (and not the Romish) is the onely Catholick and true Church." Daniel, famous for his polemics against Roman Catholics and Arminians, had been a moderate Calvinist and conformist who remained loyal to the established church during the civil war. Dismissed and imprisoned for his loyalties by the revolutionary Parliament, he died under house arrest in 1645, making him a royalist martyr for the episcopal church. Urging the king to "restore the true Reformed Protestant Church," his nephew John invoked the well-worn language of moderation, situating "her Purity, and pristine Glory" between "the Papists on the one side; and the Sectaries and Schismatics on the other." For the moment, though, Featley advised "a moderate Complyance, and a discreet Condescension in things indifferent, even on both sides," as it would "be a Work of time . . . to repair al our breaches; and to build again the waste places of [God's] Church among us."[1]

Politically, the restoration went fairly smoothly, culminating with the summoning of a new Parliament. Later known as the "Cavalier Parliament" for its fierce royalism, it quickly voided the acts of the revolutionary regime. Religiously, however, the restoration was more convoluted. The Cavalier Parliament restored the acts that had regulated religious life before 1640, including the Elizabethan recusancy laws. However, it abandoned the unpopular High Commission, and for a couple of years, the exact composition of the restored church remained up for negotiation. Perhaps some sort of compromise, or "comprehension" as it was termed, could be reached to include at least those who preferred presbyterianism to episcopalianism? Then, in January 1661, a group of Fifth Monarchists, the most politically radical of the revolutionary sects, staged an uprising in London. Though quickly suppressed, it strengthened popular support for bringing back the bishops as a symbol of royalist loyalty. Several months later Parliament voted to let them sit in the House of Lords again. Over the next year, the bishops negotiated with leading Reformed ministers over "comprehension" to create a less rigorously episcopal church, perhaps by having bishops govern alongside a council of ministers. Known as the Savoy Conference, it ultimately failed, and in 1662 a new Uniformity Act formally restored the Church of England along much the same lines as before 1640. Moreover, the Church of Ireland was remade as an extension of the Church of England, and bishops were reinstalled in the Church of Scotland as well. The foundation of modern Anglicanism had been laid. It was now the official religion of the English world—but not of all the king's subjects.[2]

The colonies' religious response to the Restoration was starkly divided. Several colonies had actually preceded England in restoring the old Church of England. Virginia took the lead after its Cromwellian governor died in March 1660. Sir William Berkeley and the colony's royalist sympathizers regained control of the government and in October petitioned the king for pardon for their "Apostacy" from "their dutie and Allegiance" to him. They then restored the prerevolutionary church in March 1661 with an order that everyone elected to serve on a parish vestry, "shall take the oaths of allegiance and supremacy and subscribe to the conformable doctrine and discipline of the church of England, and if any person elected shall deny to take the said oaths or make such subscriptions he shall not be admitted." Vestries were ordered to collect the funds necessary to maintain their parish churches and offer "able and Orthodox Ministers" decent salaries to encourage ministers to serve, especially in parishes currently "destitute of Ministers." Each parish also had to provide "at their own cost a great church bible and two books of common prayer," as well as "communion plate, pulpit cloth and cushion that all things may be done orderly and decently in the church." Another law, requiring readers to be appointed "to read the prayers and homilies of the church . . . and to catechise children and servants," explicitly invoked the model of "the church of England . . . in the times of Queen Elizabeth" and the methods "used . . . when there was a scarcity of orthodox reformed ministers to supply the congregations." The assembly petitioned the king for help in setting up schools and colleges and recruiting ministers from the universities of Oxford and Cambridge. It then dismissed Major John Bond from his position as magistrate because of his "factious and schismatical demeanors."[3]

In March 1662—several months before it became the law in England—Virginia required its ministers to have received "ordination from some Bishop in England" and "subscribe to be conformable to the orders and constitutions of the church of England." Neither they nor the readers were to teach their parishioners "any other catechisme than that by the canons appointed and inserted in the book of common prayer." Ministers were to "expound no other" doctrine, "that our fundamentals at least may be well laid." Any who claimed to be ministers without such ordination and presumed "to teach or preach publicly or privately" would be suspended and silenced by the governor and council. If they continued to preach with "obstinate persistence," they would be compelled "to depart the country with the first conveniency." Virtually all of the dozen ministers currently in Virginia conformed, some very gladly. The presbyterian Francis Doughty, on the other hand, could not and left for Maryland. Virginia's church was now on a separate trajectory from the religious order prevailing in New England. The aspiration of generations for colonial religious unity was destroyed.[4]

Virginia not only anticipated the metropolitan restoration of the prerevolutionary church. It also anticipated the suppression of religious dissent, especially of Quakers. Shortly after Berkeley returned to power in March 1660, Virginia's House of Burgesses passed "An Act for the suppressing the Quakers . . . an unreasonable and turbulent sort of people." Two years later Berkeley oversaw passage of another law singling out Quakers for special punishment. Requiring attendance at church on Sundays and declared holidays, it imposed a fine of fifty pounds of tobacco on those who could not "diligently resort to their parish church or chapel accustomed" and "abide orderly and soberly during the time of common prayers preaching or other service of God." However, "Quakers or other recusants who out of nonconformity to the church totally absent themselves" were to be punished more severely. Reviving the harshest of the Elizabethan recusancy statutes, the burgesses decreed a fine of twenty pounds sterling for every month an individual did not attend church. Moreover, Quakers who gathered "in unlawful assemblies and conventicles" would be fined £200 for each time they met. Then it required church attendance for two new holy days: the thirtieth of January, the anniversary of Charles I being "bloodyly massacred," when Virginians would "expiate our crimes" for having submitted to the revolutionary government that beheaded him, and the twenty-ninth of May, the anniversary of the Restoration.[5]

With their proactive restoration of the church, Virginians displayed the confidence of many other English people that the restoration of the monarchy would entail the restoration of the prerevolutionary church. During what royalists now began referring to as the Interregnum between the reigns of Charles I and Charles II, a number of churchmen had clandestinely continued to receive episcopal ordinations and otherwise kept alive practices and habits of the prewar church. Intriguingly, those most active in this movement tended to favor a moderate interpretation of episcopacy. Laudians, with more radical views on the power and dignity of bishops, did little to keep episcopacy alive once they lost power. However, even though they represented just a minority of active episcopalians in 1660, the Laudians exercised significant influence over the Restoration church settlement precisely because they had refused compromise.[6]

The 1662 Act of Uniformity brought back the bishops and the *Book of Common Prayer*, alienating the many Protestants who had rejected both over the previous twenty years. Some, especially conservative Presbyterians, adopted techniques of partial or occasional conformity to maintain a relationship with the national church. Like many contemporaries, they found it difficult to accept a schism in England's Protestant community. For years afterward, they would continue to work and hope for a reunion through some sort of comprehension. Others refused to conform at all to parish religion, forcing the government and the church to recognize the category of "Dissent." With a number of Protestants along with the Roman Catholic recusants now outside of the church, the question of toleration would come to dominate Restoration era religious politics.[7]

Initially, the church acknowledged the revolution's legacy of pluralism by legislating against it. The Uniformity Act proclaimed its aspiration to "a universal agreement in the public worship of Almighty God." Religious unity would be conducive both "to the settling of the peace of this nation" and to "the honour of our religion and the propagation thereof." Unfortunately, "great numbers of people in divers parts of this realm" followed "their own sensuality and living without knowledge and due fear of God." They were "wilfully and schismatically" abstaining from conformity and refusing "to come to their parish churches" thanks to the "scandalous neglect of ministers" who were leading them "into factions and schisms, to the great decay and scandal of the reformed religion of the Church of England, and to the hazard of many souls." Restoring the Elizabethan requirements for church attendance, the Uniformity Act hoped to ensure "that every person within this realm may certainly know the rule to which he is to conform in public worship" by compelling the ministers to conform and follow the prescribed liturgy. The Act of Uniformity required that all church ministers be ordained by a bishop and accept the *Book of Common Prayer* and the Thirty-Nine Articles by the time it went into effect on August 24, 1662. That was Saint Bartholomew's Day. On this ominous anniversary of the notorious massacre of Huguenots in France, the roughly one thousand ministers who could not conform lost their posts. Altogether, for one reason or another (including the 1660 Act for Settling Ministers, which restored ministers ejected by the revolutionary government to their old posts, forcing 695 parish ministers to find new positions), about 1,900 clergy in England and Wales were forced out of their parishes between 1660 and 1663, together with an additional two hundred university lecturers, dons, and schoolmasters. It was a day of great drama. Many of the ministers preaching poignant farewell sermons went on to become leaders of Restoration nonconformity—Dissenters.[8]

Subsequent acts suppressed Dissenters' religious and political privileges. Known as the Clarendon Code after King Charles II's chief minister, the Earl of Clarendon (misleadingly so, as he did not think they were wise), this series of laws established a framework for actively discriminating against Protestant nonconformists alongside the penal laws against Roman Catholics. First came the Corporation Act of December 1661. It aimed to exclude presbyterians and other former radicals from positions of power by requiring all officeholders elected to a position within a city or other corporate government to receive the sacrament with the Church of England, take the Oaths of Allegiance and Supremacy, swear belief in the Doctrine of Passive Obedience, and renounce the Solemn League and Covenant. In 1662, the "Act for preventing the Mischiefs and Dangers that may arise by certaine Persons called Quakers and others refusing to take lawfull Oaths" made it illegal to refuse to swear the oath of allegiance if demanded. Anyone who was convicted of refusing three times could be "transported in any Ship or Ships to any of His Majesties Plantations beyond the Seas." Quakers, who had rejected oath swearing on scriptural grounds, began to experience unprecedented levels of harassment.[9]

While the Restoration did its best to erase the religious legacy of the revolutionary years, the colonies did their best to revert to their pre-Cromwellian arrangements. Maryland was restored to the Catholic Lord

Baltimore. Its Act concerning Religion, revoked under the revolutionary government, became law again. Everywhere south of Maryland established the Church of England. For Virginia and the old Caribbean colonies, this was an act of restoration. For Jamaica, it involved imposing the parish system of conformity for the first time. Some tolerance was extended to the island's many different Protestants, but oaths of loyalty and supremacy were demanded of those in authority. Rhode Island, once again, found itself petitioning for an English charter to preserve its experiment in disestablishment.[10]

Although Anglicanism was gaining the upper hand, colonial America was religiously fractured beyond repair. New England continued to defend its Congregational religious order, sometimes quite ruthlessly. The open dissent of Quakers and Baptists was punished. It would be years before the Church of England dared to confront this defiant region. Nevertheless, while toleration remained an unpopular and controversial policy almost everywhere outside of Maryland and Rhode Island, pluralism was now the reality for the colonies as a whole if only because New England and the Chesapeake would never fit within the same church again.[11]

*

America did not begin as a religious refuge. On the contrary, from the time England first officially encountered America, the expansion of established Christendom was universally affirmed as a motive for colonization. It was assumed that colonies would foster and strengthen the Christian unity of the English world by extending the official church overseas and converting new peoples to it. It was an ancient ideal. England's first historian, the eighth-century monk Bede, had celebrated Christianity's ability to unite Britain, divided at the time into "four nations—English, British, Irish, and Picts." Each had its own language and religion. Unity came through "their study of God's truth" in a fifth language, "Latin—which has become a common medium through the study of the scriptures." As the Spanish Empire demonstrated, religious unity could help overcome ethnic diversity by uniting a wide variety of peoples within a single church. Had England's Reformation failed or turned out differently, the religious history of its empire could have been very similar. That is, after all, how it had begun.[12]

Toleration and pluralism were not foreseen as colonial America's destiny. Early modern Europeans were familiar with toleration and debated them throughout the first century and a half of colonial expeditions. There were historical and biblical precedents. There were contemporary examples such as the Holy Roman Empire, the bustling port city of Amsterdam, and, further afield, the empires of the Ottomans and Mughals. However, until political and religious chaos broke out in the 1640s, the English almost universally rejected them as a model for colonizing America. The 1662 Act of Uniformity confirmed this preference for religious unity. Religious unity was seen as an essential strength. The outposts that tolerated religious pluralism were few, rare, small, weak, and discordant: Maryland, Rhode Island, New Albion, and Eleutheria. Even then, it is vital to remember that their ability to practice toleration depended on the support of authorities in England. Their colonial neighbors would, and occasionally did, suppress them if they could.

Nevertheless, religious pluralism worked its way into the early colonies. There was no formal plan or logic to its willy-nilly progress. Instead, the emergence of pluralism in the first Anglo-American colonies reflected their close connection to the shifting religious politics of the early modern English world. Early American religion was a moving target, not just geographically from one expanding colony to another, but also institutionally, in the ways the official religion kept changing, sometimes dramatically, sometimes subtly, and even individually, in the variable spiritual journeys undertaken by the people involved with the colonies, from those securing the patents in England to those digging into the American soil: all at a time when everyone was supposed to be conforming to the one official religion. This multifaceted religious instability at the heart of the budding empire at the very same time its first colonies were being established was the key factor in rendering the American colonies pluralistic in spite of themselves. This convoluted story is foundational to the religious history of England, the British Empire, and the United States, yet it has not yet been told in anything other than fragments because it falls through the historiographical cracks of each historical tradition. It is too complex for the usual narratives of imperial history, which depend on the politics and religion of the home country being fairly stable so that its institutions and ideas can be constructed and projected overseas. For historians of England, the early colonies seem too small and tentative to have much relevance to the main action at home. American historians, meanwhile, tend to overlook the big picture in favor of local perspectives rooted in the future boundaries of the United States. Even the currently popular framework of the Atlantic world reproduces this rather provincial mindset by marginalizing the European core and emphasizing the American periphery. Crafting this history has required taking a whole series of national and imperial narratives and weaving them together into a new narrative that gives equal billing to early modern England and colonial America in a story that is not beholden to the framework of either but rather situates them both in a bigger story of the emerging empire and its future fragments. Only then can we properly analyze what was, after all, a shared experience.

The answer given here to the origins of America's distinctive religious pluralism and freedom goes against two and a half centuries worth of theories that have sought the answer within the borders of the United States. Perhaps most influential has been one of the earliest theories, proposed by J. Hector St. John de Crèvecoeur, who famously proposed that in America the religious hostility that plagued Europe simply "evaporates in the great distance it has to travel . . . it burns away in the open air, and consumes without effect." Crèvecoeur was struck by how Americans seemed indifferent to religious difference. He marveled at how "the daughter of the Catholic will marry the son of the seceder, and settle by themselves at a distance from their parents." In America, there seemed to be a "very perceptible indifference, even in the first generation," to the religious conflicts that vexed Europe. If people ran into religious trouble in one colony, they could simply move away to another. Or even just over the hills and out of sight.[13]

Sheer physical geography remains a popular explanation for the religious pluralism of the United States: it's simply too big to fit into a single church. However, if religious pluralism is simply a function of space, then why did other European colonies not produce similar if not greater results? The Spanish comparison is especially revealing. Its colonies covered a vaster, much more rugged and challenging terrain stretching from California to the southern cone of South America. Yet, Spain nevertheless managed to keep it all within one church. Sure, there was religious diversity under the surface, but no actual pluralism and no plans to even think of toleration until the dawn of the nineteenth century. Comparison with the colonies of other European empires, which likewise succeeded in integrating their colonies within a stable metropolitan religious system, indicates that what really set the Anglo-America's experience apart was its tie to England, not America.[14]

Crèvecoeur based his analysis on his experience of life in the middle colonies of New York and Pennsylvania—colonies that did not yet exist in 1662. Had he lived in Connecticut or Virginia he surely would have told a very different story. The religious pluralism that seemed so natural to the eighteenth century was, it turns out, far from inevitable. It was the long-contested and contingent outcome of events and ambitions that played out on both local and transatlantic scales over several generations. The role of the North American environment was minimal. Indeed, in 1662 there was more religious diversity on the small Caribbean island of Barbados than in all of New England. Colonial America was not exceptional but rather part of the broader spectrum of the English world: and often it was the more religiously conservative part. We lose this sort of insight when we only analyze early American religious history within the anachronistic framework of the future United States.

As with the rest of the English world, there was no single path to pluralism in early America. Every colony followed its own trajectory. Although each worked with similar and closely related elements, the particular combination of individuals, ideas, and influences could vary. Even when religious liberty appeared, it had different guises depending on its source. Roger Williams's Rhode Island and Lord Baltimore's Maryland came to similar conclusions, but for very different reasons. The histories of Avalon, New Albion, and Eleutheria demonstrate they were not alone, but also that religious liberty was no guarantee of colonial success. The strongest, wealthiest, and most powerful colonies tended to be the least tolerant, but even they could take different paths, as Massachusetts and Virginia illustrate. Early American pluralism is the cumulative result of all of these stories and more, not any one example. Moreover, within the global English context, American religious pluralism turns out to be neither exceptional nor even particularly radical. It is much more impressive in the aggregate than at the local level.

American religious pluralism was not the expression of a distinctive colonial or national destiny. Instead, it was one fragment of the failure of England's rulers to unite their subjects in one religion. That process began years before Virginia gave the English a permanent American foothold and continued for decades thereafter, notwithstanding several different attempts at religious unity by both the early Stuart monarchs and puritan revolutionaries. Pluralism grew up in the gap between what was legally permissible and practically possible in a variety of different jurisdictions around the English world, threading its way between what was supposed to be happening and what actually did happen. By time of the American Revolution, Americans had forgotten the details and uncertainty of those struggles, but were happy to take credit for the result. The religious pluralism they celebrated as their own was, however, merely an accident or, better, a long series of accidents mostly driven by English people and events. How Anglo-America became more, rather than less, pluralistic after 1662, is a rather different story, but one that once again depends more on England than America.

Acknowledgments

Well, this book came as something of a surprise. It began as the opening chapter of another book, and might have stayed that way without my wonderful year as the Gilder Lehrman Fellow at the Dorothy and Lewis B. Cullman Center for Scholars and Writers at the New York Public Library. There, from the fall of 2011 to the spring of 2012, in the company of an engaging group of fellows, I took the time to expand my intellectual and cultural horizons at a point in one's academic career where they usually tend to narrow. I am grateful for the support of the center's staff, especially the director, Jean Strouse, who inspired me to spend more time reading than writing and even indulge in the occasional game of table tennis in the park. I am also grateful for an earlier semester spent attending the English Caribbean workshop at the Folger Shakespeare Library run by Carla Pestana and David Shields, which convinced me I could no longer write or think about colonial North America without including the Caribbean.

A difficult life transition almost killed off this project. Columbia University saw fit to deny me tenure in the spring of 2013, throwing me on the tender mercies of an increasingly unforgiving job market. Luckily, Texas A&M University stepped in at quite literally the very last moment and saved this historian's career. Texas treated this refugee New Yorker well, giving me the job security of tenure and leave to write undisturbed over three different semesters between the fall of 2014 and spring of 2018. I could not have completed this book without that support or the funds provided by the Texas A&M University History Department travel and research budget, the Melbern G. Glasscock Center for Humanities Research's Faculty Research Fellowship, Texas A&M University's Division of Research PESCA grant, and the Texas A&M Arts and Humanities Fellowship. A teaching release in the last months of my time at Columbia also helped, as has the continuing friendship and encouragement of a number of my former Columbia colleagues.

The support of my new colleagues in Texas has been indispensable. Cyndy Bouton smoothed my entry into Texas. David Vaught, as head of the department, supported my research ambitions. The chance to be colleagues with April Hatfield is one of my favorite things about being here. I very much appreciate her feedback on my writing as well as our random discussions about researching, teaching, and living with colonial America. Cyndy and April, together with Rebecca Schloss, have been terrific colleagues in the research cluster on Caribbean and Atlantic Studies (CAST), helping to complete my transition out of the traditional North American framework of colonial American history. Adam Seipp's enthusiasm and advice have been invaluable. The RouleaUntermans, Brian Rouleau (another CAST colleague) and Kate Unterman, have been irreplaceable colleagues and, along with their rescue dog, Hudson, the closest thing to family I have had in the Brazos Valley. I'm not sure I could have made it through these last five years without them. Their friendship and that of other new Texas colleagues, including Trent MacNamara, Side Emre, Dan Schwartz, Felipe Hinojosa, Jason Parker, Brian Linn, Andy Kirkendall, and Angela Hudson, is deeply appreciated. Finally, the comments on an earlier draft of this book by the Texas A&M graduate students in my fall 2018 Early American Readings class brought some essential clarity.

Along the way, this book also has benefited from the generous feedback and encouragement of many different individuals. Intellectually, it reflects my effort to reconcile what I learned in graduate school at Princeton University from John Murrin about colonial America and Peter Lake about early modern England. Mark Petersen gave me the book contract at a crucial moment. Along with my editor at Chicago, Tim Mennel, the other series editors, and the two anonymous reviewers, he has been instrumental in shaping the final product. I thank them for their patience. Early on, the manuscript was improved by the erudite input of Stephen Foster and Michael P. Winship. Winship's support has been vital in several other ways, including his generosity in sharing the prepublication manuscript of his masterpiece on Puritanism. David R. Como also kindly shared his unpublished scholarship and offered valuable encouragement. I am grateful to Scott Sowerby for his critical feedback on an earlier draft, and to him and Owen Stanwood for their support in various ways, tangible and intangible, over the years. I have also discovered the new pleasure of getting informed critical feedback from former students: my deepest thanks to Peter Walker, Sonia Tycko, and Deborah Hamer. In England, Charles Walton was a kind host and good friend, John Arnold made me take the Middle Ages more seriously, and Jason Peacey and Simon Middleton strengthened my connection to the world of early modern English historians. Simon's feedback on several chapters at an important point late in the game, along with (Cameron) Alasdair MacFarlane's enthusiastic feedback on the Scottish bits, helped get me to the finish. Finally, Adam Bright and D. Foy gave excellent editorial advice on my writing, which is now better than it was if not as good as I wish it were.

Over the past decade, aspects of this work has also benefited from the feedback received at presentations at a variety of international venues. These include Texas A&M University, its Glasscock Center for Humanities Research, the University of Chicago Divinity School, Utah Valley University, Sheffield University, the Université de Montréal, the Université de Paris 7 Denis-Diderot, the University of Hamburg, the Herbert H. Lehman Center for American History at Columbia University, the Early Americanists of Texas seminar, the Institute for Historical Research's Seventeenth-Century Britain seminar, the Early American Studies seminar at the University of Chicago, and the seminars at the American Antiquarian Society. I also have given papers relevant to this project at conferences including "The Spectacle of Toleration" at Salve Regina University in Newport, Rhode Island, "New Worlds, New Philosophies" at Princeton University, "Rethinking Religion in India: Secularism" in New Delhi, India, and the "International Conference on Tolerance" organized by the USC-Huntington Library Early Modern Studies Institute and USC Shoah Foundation Institute for Visual History and Education. I was fortunate to be invited to participate in a number of special workshops, including the International Law, Human Rights, and the Politics of Religious Difference workshop at Princeton University; the Politics of Religious Freedom at Home and Abroad workshop at Northwestern University; the Independence, Freedom and Religion in the Early Modern World workshop at Monticello; the Early Modern Research Colloquium of the University of Bayreuth; the Colonisation et Confessionalisation en Amerique du Nord, xviie–xviiie siècles workshop at the Maison Descartes in Amsterdam; and the Religion and the Law workshop at Harvard University. Additionally, I have benefited from presentations at institutions open to the wider public, including Historic Saint Mary's City, Maryland, and the New Netherland Institute Annual Conference.

The research and writing of this book enjoyed the assistance of a number of other individuals and institutions. The National Endowment for the Humanities has been a great supporter over the years. Portions of the manuscript were written with the help of one of its summer stipends in 2017; it was finalized while I held one of its yearlong fellowships in 2019–20. Naturally, any views, findings, conclusions, or recommendations expressed in this publication do not necessarily reflect those of the National Endowment for the Humanities. Additional help came in the summer of 2016 from the Ruth R. and Alyson R. Miller Fellowship at the Massachusetts Historical Society and in the summer of 2018 from a Jamestown Rediscovery Foundation–Omohundro Institute short-term visiting fellowship. I must also thank the staff of the Columbia University Libraries, the Texas A&M Libraries, the Folger Shakespeare Library, the Massachusetts Historical Society, the Bodleian Library, the Friends House Library, the London Metropolitan Archives, and the National Archives in Kew. The New York Public Library, the John Carter Brown Library, the British Library, and the Huntington Library deserve additional thanks for their assistance in supplying the images included in this book. I also thank Craig Irving, archivist at Arundel Castle, and the staff at Bridgeman Images for their help in securing a picture of the Madagascar portrait. I'm especially grateful to my cartographer friend Kate Blackmer for drawing the maps. A special thanks goes to the staff and libraries of the Universidad Internaciónal Menendez Pelayo's Santander campus, the Biblioteca Central de Cantabria in Santander, and the Biblioteca de Castilla y León in Valladolid, where the final revisions to this book were completed in the fall of 2019.

Finally, the unquestioning support of my parents, Richard T. and Nancy Crowell Haefeli, has been as crucial as ever. I dedicate this book to the special German who got me to hike up the Austrian Alps and take in the view from the top: not something I would have dared to do on my own at age fifty.

Abbreviations

AHR *American Historical Review*

AOM William Hand Browne, et al., *Archives of Maryland*, 72 vols. (Baltimore: Maryland Historical Society, 1883–1972)

APCC W. L. Grant, James Munro, and Almeric W. Fitzroy, eds., *Acts of the Privy Council, Colonial Series*, 6 vols. (London: H.M.S.O., 1908–12)

BL British Library

BODL. Bodleian Library, University of Oxford

CBI Michael A. Mullet, *Catholics in Britain and Ireland, 1558–1829* (London: MacMillan, 1998)

CDPR Samuel Rawson Gardiner, ed., *The Constitutional Documents of the Puritan Revolution, 1625–1660* (Oxford: Clarendon Press, 1968)

CH *Church History*

CHR *Catholic Historical Review*

CO Records of the Colonial Office, TNA

C&O *Conformity and Orthodoxy in the English Church, c. 1560–1660*, ed. Peter Lake and Michael Questier (Rochester, NY: Boydell Press, 2000)

COLONISING Vincent T. Harlow, ed., *Colonising Expeditions to the West Indies and Guiana, 1623–1667* (London: Hakluyt Society, 1925; reprint, 1967)

COMPANION John Coffey and Paul C. H. Lim, eds., *The Cambridge Companion to Puritanism* (Cambridge: Cambridge University Press, 2008)

CSPCA W. Noel Sainsbury et al., eds., *Calendar of State Papers, Colonial Series, America and West Indies*, 44 vols. (London: H.M.S.O., 1860–1963)

CSPD Mary A. E. Green et al., eds., *Calendar of State Papers, Domestic Series* (London: Longman, Brown, Green, Longmans & Roberts, 1856–1947)

CSPI H. C. Hamilton et al., eds., *Calendar of the State Papers relating to Ireland*, 24 vols. (London: Longman, 1860–1910)

DCB *Dictionary of Canadian Biography*, vol. 1, University of Toronto/Université Laval, online ed., 2003–16

EHR *English Historical Review*

ESC Kenneth Fincham, ed., *The Early Stuart Church* (London: Macmillan, 1993)

HENING, ED., *STATUTES* William Waller Hening, ed., *The Statutes at Large: Being a Collection of all the Laws of Virginia from the first session of the Legislature in the year 1619*, 13 vols. (Richmond, VA, 1809–23)

HR *Historical Research*

HJ *Historical Journal*

HORN, ED., *SMITH* *Captain John Smith: Writings with other Narratives of Roanoke, Jamestown, and the First English Settlement of America*, ed. James Horn (New York: Library of America, 2007)

IWI Aubrey Gwynn, "Documents Relating to the Irish in the West Indies," *Analecta Hibernica* 4 (1932), 139–286

JBS *Journal of British Studies*

JEH *Journal of Ecclesiastical History*

LEFROY, *MEMORIALS* John Henry Lefroy, *Memorials of the Discovery and Early Settlement of the Bermudas or Somers Islands, 1515–1685*, 2 vols. (Toronto: University of Toronto Press, for the Bermuda Historical Society and the Bermuda National Trust, 1981)

LMA London Metropolitan Archives

NAW David B. Quinn, ed., *New American World: A Documentary History of North America to 1612*, 5 vols. (New York, 1979).

NEM Clayton Coleman Hall, ed., *Narratives of Early Maryland, 1633–1684* (New York: Charles Scribner's Sons, 1925)

NEQ *New England Quarterly*

ODNB *Oxford Dictionary of National Biography*, Oxford University Press, online ed., 2006–16

OHA *The Oxford History of Anglicanism*, ed. Rowan Strong, 5 vols. (Oxford: Oxford University Press, 2017), vol. 1, *Reformation and Identity, c. 1520–1662*, ed. Anthony Milton

OPP William Bradford, *Of Plymouth Plantation, 1620–1647*, ed. Samuel Eliot Morison (New York: Knopf, 1952)

PAAS *Proceedings of the American Antiquarian Society*

PC Records of the Privy Council and other records collected by the Privy Council Office, TNA

P&C Crawford Gribben and R. Scott Spurlock, eds., *Puritans and Catholics in the Trans-Atlantic World, 1600–1800* (Basingstoke: Palgrave MacMillan, 2015)

P&P *Past & Present*

RMB Nathaniel Shurtleff, ed., *Records of the Governor and Company of Massachusetts Bay in New England*, 5 vols. (Boston: William White, 1853–54)

RRE Christopher Durston and Judith Maltby, eds., *Religion in Revolutionary England* (Manchester: Manchester University Press, 2006)

RVC Susan Mary Kingsbury, ed., *Records of the Virginia Company*, 4 vols. (Washington, DC: Government Printing Office, 1906–35)

RW Glenn W. LaFantasie et al., eds., *The Correspondence of Roger Williams*, 2 vols. (Hanover and London: University Press of New England)

SC J. P. Kenyon, ed., *The Stuart Constitution: Documents and Commentary* (Cambridge, 1986)

SCJ *Sixteenth Century Journal*

SDEH Newton Key and Robert Bucholz, eds., *Sources and Debates in English History, 1485–1714* (Oxford: Blackwell, 2004)

SP State Papers, TNA

TNA The National Archives, Kew, Richmond, Surrey

TSP Thomas Birch, ed., *A Collection of the State Papers of John Thurloe*, 7 vols. (London, 1742)

VMHB *Virginia Magazine of History and Biography*

WINSHIP, *GODLY* Michael P. Winship, *Godly Republicanism: Puritans, Pilgrims, and a City on a Hill* (Cambridge, MA: Harvard University Press, 2012)

WJ Richard S. Dunn, James Savage, and Laetitia Yeandle, eds., *The Journal of John Winthrop, 1630–1649* (Cambridge, MA: Harvard University Press, 1996)

WMQ *William and Mary Quarterly*

WP Worthington C. Ford, Stewart Mitchell, Allyn Bailey Forbes, and Malcolm Freiberg, eds., *The Winthrop Papers*, 6 vols. (Boston: Massachusetts Historical Society, 1925–92)

Note on Transcriptions, Dates, Sources, and Terminology

When transcribing seventeenth-century English, I have generally preserved the existing spelling. However, where an *i* functions as a *j* or a *u* as a *v* (or *v* as a *u*), I have silently corrected it to modern usage. The resulting confusion to readers unfamiliar with the older conventions does not seem worthy of the literalness in transcription.

The English did not switch to our modern calendar until the mid-eighteenth century. Consequently, dates are in Old Style, but with the new year beginning January 1 rather than March.

For books published before 1800, place of publication is London unless otherwise indicated. Finally, references to secondary literature have been kept to a minimum for reasons of length.

Following current English scholarly conventions, I keep "puritans" and "presbyterians" in the lowercase when talking about them as movements within the churches of England, Ireland, and Scotland. Puritans in New England may seem a coherent group, but from this wider perspective they wound up in too many different churches and sects to merit the uppercase, which implies a more unified cause. "Presbyterian" becomes uppercase when it takes over an official church, as with the Scots in the 1640s. Otherwise it is avoided to emphasize that there were several different possible forms of presbyterianism in play. "Separatist," "Congregationalist," and "Independent," on the other hand, retain the uppercase. While Separatists and Independents also had a variety of ideas, the basic fact conveyed by their moniker remained. Congregationalists may have had some different ideas, but like Presbyterians, they merit the uppercase when they have clearly established an institutional presence distinct from other church orders. "Anglican" is an anachronistic term before 1662 and is largely absent here. "Dissenter" merits the uppercase once it becomes a distinct category in 1662, but not before when "dissenter" simply means disagreement within a religious community but not a separate church order.

Notes

Introduction

1. Thomas Paine, *Common Sense Addressed to the Inhabitants of America* (Philadelphia, 1776), 22; Anna Su, *Exporting Freedom: Religious Liberty and American Power* (Cambridge, MA: Harvard University Press, 2016).
2. Ezra Stiles, *The United States Elevated to Glory and Honor: A Sermon* (New Haven, CT, 1783), 52–54; Sam Haselby, *The Origins of American Religious Nationalism* (New York: Oxford University Press, 2015), chap. 2.
3. David Sehat, *The Myth of American Religious Freedom* (New York: Oxford University Press, 2011); Winnifred Fallers Sullivan, Elizabeth Shakman Hurd, Saba Mahmood, and Peter G. Danchin, eds., *The Politics of Religious Freedom* (Chicago: University of Chicago Press, 2015); John Fea, *Was America Founded as a Christian Nation? A Historical Introduction* (Louisville, KY: Westminster John Knox Press, 2011); Carl H. Esbeck and Jonathan Den Hartog, eds., *Disestablishment and Religious Dissent: Church-State Relations in the New American States, 1776–1833* (Columbia: University of Missouri Press, 2019).
4. Sydney E. Ahlstrom, *A Religious History of the American People* (New Haven, CT: Yale University Press, 1972); Carla Gardina Pestana, *Liberty of Conscience and the Growth of Religious Diversity in Early America, 1636–1786* (Providence, RI: John Carter Brown Library, 1986); Thomas J. Curry, *The First Freedoms: Church and State in America to the Passage of the First Amendment* (New York: Oxford University Press, 1986); Jon Butler, *New World Faiths: Religion in Colonial America* (New York: Oxford University Press, 2000); Chris Beneke, *Beyond Toleration: The Religious Origins of American Pluralism* (New York: Oxford University Press, 2006); James H. Hutson, *Church and State in America: The First Two Centuries* (Cambridge: Cambridge University Press, 2008); Rebecca Anne Goetz, "Religious Diversity and the Coming of Christianity in the Prerevolutionary South," *Journal of Southern Religion* 14 (2012): http://jsr.fsu.edu/issues/vol14/goetz.html.
5. John M. Lenhart, "An Important Chapter in American Church History

(1625–1650)," *CHR* 14, no. 4 (January 1929): 505–6; Edmund S. Morgan, *Roger Williams: The Church and the State* (New York: Harcourt, Brace, and World, 1967); William G. McLoughlin, *New England Dissent, 1630–1833: The Baptists and the Separation of Church and State* (Cambridge, MA: Harvard University Press, 1971); Paul Finkleman, "The Soul and the State: Religious Freedom in New York and the Origin of the First Amendment," in *New York and the Union*, ed. Stephen L. Shechter and Richard B. Bernstein (Albany: New York State Commission on the Bicentennial of the United States Constitution, 1990), 78–105; J. William Frost, *A Perfect Freedom: Religious Liberty in Pennsylvania* (New York: Cambridge University Press, 1990), 1–9; James Lowell Underwood and W. Lewis Burke, eds., *The Dawn of Religious Freedom in South Carolina* (Columbia: University of South Carolina Press, 2006); Paul Rasor and Richard E. Bond, *From Jamestown to Jefferson: The Evolution of Religious Freedom in Virginia* (Charlottesville: University of Virginia Press, 2011); Scott D. Gerber, "Law and Catholicism in Colonial Maryland," *CHR* 103, no. 3 (Summer 2017): 465–90.

6. Carla Gardina Pestana, *Protestant Empire: Religion and the Making of the British Atlantic World* (Philadelphia: University of Pennsylvania Press, 2009), 11, 13; James B. Bell, *The Imperial Origins of the King's Church in Early America, 1607–1783* (Houndmills, Basingstoke, Hampshire: Palgrave MacMillan, 2004); Rowan Strong, *Anglicanism and the British Empire, c. 1700–1850* (New York: Oxford University Press, 2007); Andrew Porter, *Religion versus Empire? British Protestant Missionaries and Overseas Expansion, 1700–1914* (Manchester: Manchester University Press, 2004); Ulrike Kirchberger, *Konversion zur Moderne? Die Britische Indianermission in der atlantischen Welt des 18. Jahrhunderts* (Wiesbaden: Harrassowitz Verlag, 2008); Travis Glasson, *Mastering Christianity: Missionary Anglicanism and Slavery in the Atlantic World* (Oxford: Oxford University Press, 2012).
7. Ian K. Steel, *The English Atlantic: An Exploration of Communication and Community* (New York: Oxford University Press, 1986), 50, 91, 295.
8. See Michael J. Braddick, *State Formation in Early Modern England, c. 1550–1700* (Cambridge: Cambridge University Press, 2000), where chap. 9 treats the colonies, albeit not in great detail nor with their religious history in mind.
9. István Bejczy, "*Tolerantia*: A Medieval Concept," *Journal of the History of Ideas* 58, no. 3 (July 1997): 365–84; John Coffey, *Persecution and Toleration in Protestant England, 1558–1689* (London: Longmans, 2000), esp. 51–68; Joseph Lecler, *Toleration and the Reformation*, 2 vols., trans. T. L. Westow (London: Longmans, 1960), 1:65–106, 114–33; Rainer Forst, *Toleration in Conflict: Past and Present* (Cambridge: Cambridge University Press, 2013), 103–9; Teresa M. Bejan, *Mere Civility: Disagreement and the Limits of Toleration* (Cambridge, MA: Harvard University Press, 2017); Alexandra Walsham, *Charitable Hatred: Tolerance and Intolerance in England, 1500–1700* (Manchester: Manchester University Press, 2006); Benjamin J. Kaplan, *Divided by Faith: Religious Conflict and the Practice of Toleration in Early Modern Europe* (Cambridge, MA: Belknap Press of Harvard University Press, 2007).

10. Courtney Bender and Pamela E. Klassen, eds., *After Pluralism: Reimagining Religious Enlightenment* (New York: Columbia University Press, 2010), quote on 2; William R. Hutchinson, *Religious Pluralism in America: The Contentious History of a Founding Ideal* (New Haven, CT: Yale University Press, 2003).
11. Michael Questier, *Conversion, Politics and Religion in England, 1580–1625* (Cambridge: Cambridge University Press, 1996); Alexandra Walsham, *Church Papists: Catholicism, Conformity and Confessional Polemic in Early Modern England* (Woodbridge, Suffolk: Boydell & Brewer, 1999); Patrick Collinson, *Richard Bancroft and Anti-Puritanism in Elizabethan England* (Cambridge: Cambridge University Press, 2013).
12. Peter Lake, "'Puritans' and 'Anglicans' in the History of the Post-Reformation English Church," in *OHA*, 352–79, quote on 377; Peter Lake, "Serving God and the Times: The Calvinist Conformity of Robert Sanderson," *JBS* 27, no. 2 (April 1988): 81–116; Peter Lake, "Defining Puritanism—Again?," in *Puritanism: Transatlantic Perspectives on a 17th-Century Anglo-American Faith*, ed. Frank Bremer (Boston: Massachusetts Historical Society, 1993), 3–29; Michael P. Winship, "Were There Any Puritans in New England?," *NEQ*, 74, no. 1 (March 2001): 118–38, and the essays in *Companion.*
13. Michael P. Winship, *Hot Protestants: A History of Puritanism in England and America* (New Haven, CT: Yale University Press, 2019); David D. Hall, *The Puritans: A Trans-Atlantic History* (Princeton, NJ: Princeton University Press, 2019).

Chapter One

1. NAW 1:98; James A. Williamson, ed., *The Cabot Voyages and Bristol Discovery under Henry VII* (Cambridge: Hakluyt Society, 1962), 208, 212.
2. Kenneth R. Andrews, *Trade, Plunder, and Settlement: Maritime Enterprise and the Genesis of the British Empire, 1480–1630* (Cambridge: Cambridge University Press, 1984); Karen Ordahl Kupperman, *The Jamestown Project* (Cambridge, MA: Harvard University Press, 2009); Peter C. Mancall, "The Raw and the Cold: Five English Sailors in Sixteenth-Century Nunavut," *WMQ* 70, no. 1 (January 2013): 3–40.
3. David Armitage, *The Ideological Origins of the British Empire* (Cambridge: Cambridge University Press, 2000); Andrew Fitzmaurice, *Humanism and America: An Intellectual History of English Colonisation, 1500–1625* (Cambridge: Cambridge University Press, 2003); Ken MacMillan, *Sovereignty and Possession in the English New World: The Legal Foundations of Empire, 1576–1640* (Cambridge: Cambridge University Press, 2006); Alexander B. Haskell, *For God, King, and People: Forging Commonwealth Bonds in Renaissance Virginia* (Chapel Hill: University of North Carolina Press for OIEHC, 2017).
4. Heather Dalton, "Negotiating Fortune: English Merchants in Early Sixteenth-Century Seville," in *Bridging the Early Modern Atlantic World: People, Products, and Practices on the Move*, ed. Caroline A. Williams (Farnham, Surrey: Ashgate, 2009), 57–73; Evan T. Jones, "Bristol, Cabot and the New Found Land, 1496–1500," in *Exploring Atlantic Transitions: Archaeologies of*

Transience and Permanence in New Found Lands, ed. Peter Pope and Shannon Lewis-Simpson (Woodbridge: Boydell Press, 2013), 25–34.

5. Williamson, ed., *Cabot Voyages*, 214–15; NAW 1:104, 117, 159–60; Richard Hakluyt, *Principal Navigations, Voyages, Traffiques and Discoveries of the English Nation*, 12 vols. (New York: Augustus M. Kelley, 1969), 11:24; R. G. Marsden, "Voyage of the 'Barbara,' of London, to Brazil in 1540," *EHR* 24, no. 93 (January 1909): 96–100; Andrews, *Trade, Plunder*, 48–55.
6. Thomas More, *Utopia*, ed. George M. Logan (New York: W. W. Norton, 2011), 84–93.
7. Bejczy, "*Tolerantia*," 365–84, quotes on 381; Bejan, *Mere Civility*, chap. 1; Forst, *Toleration*, 109–12; Lecler, *Toleration*, 1:134–41; Thomas F. Mayer, "'Heretics be not in all things Heretics': Cardinal Pole, His Circle, and the Potential for Toleration," in *Beyond the Persecuting Society: Religious Toleration before the Enlightenment*, ed. John Christian Laursen and Cary J. Nederman (Philadelphia: University of Pennsylvania Press, 1998), 107–24.
8. Richard Eden, *A Treatyse of the Newe India* (1553), Sigs. aai, aaiiii, aaiiiii; Richard Eden, *The decades of the newe worlde or West India* (1555), Sigs. B4v–C1v; Andrew Hadfield, "Eden, Richard (*c.* 1520–1576)," *ODNB*.
9. Sir G. Birdwood and W. Foster, eds., *The First Letter Book of the East India Company, 1600–1619* (London, 1893), 53; David Beers Quinn, "Notes by a Pious Colonial Investor, 1608–1610," in *Explorers and Colonies: America, 1500–1625* (London: Hambledon Press, 1990), 415–19; John Mason, *A Briefe Discourse of the Newfound-land . . .* (Edinburgh, 1620), n.p., [B2v]; TNA CO 1/2/207; TNA CO 1/13/189–90; Louis B. Wright, *Religion and Empire: The Alliance between Piety and Commerce in English Expansion, 1558–1625* (Chapel Hill: University of North Carolina Press, 1943), chap. 3; Alison Games, *Web of Empire: English Cosmopolitans in an Age of Expansion, 1560–1660* (Oxford: Oxford University Press, 2009), chaps. 2–3, 5, 7; Philip J. Stern, *The Company-State: Corporate Sovereignty and the Early Modern Foundations of the British Empire in India* (Oxford: Oxford University Press, 2011), chap. 5; Daniel O'Connor, *The Chaplains of the East India Company, 1601–1858* (London: Continuum International Publishing Group, 2012).
10. Richard Hakluyt, *Voyages and Discoveries: The Principal Navigations, Voyages, and Discoveries of the English Nation*, ed. Jack Beeching (New York: Penguin, 1985), 204; Andrews, *Trade, Plunder*, 71–279. P. E. H. Hair, "Protestants as Pirates, Slavers and Proto-Missionaries: Sierra Leone 1568 and 1582," *JEH* 21, no. 3 (July 1970): 203–24.
11. David B. Quinn, ed., *The Roanoke Voyages, 1584–1590: Documents to Illustrate the English Voyages to North America under the Patent Granted to Walter Ralegh*, 2 vols. (London: Hakluyt Society, 1955), 1:126–27, 531n3; 2:531–32. David Beers Quinn, *Set Fair for Roanoke: Voyages and Colonies, 1584–1606* (Chapel Hill: University of North Carolina Press, 1985), 96, 260, proposes that Thomas Luddington, who had been a "Fellow of Lincoln College, Oxford and thus possibly in Holy Orders," might have been chaplain to the first expedition, but this has not been proven.
12. John Brereton, *A Briefe and True Relation of the Discoveries of the North Part of*

Virginia (1602), in *The English New England Voyages, 1602–1608*, ed. David B. Quinn and Alison M. Quinn (London: Hakluyt Society, 1983), Ser. II, no. 161, 168, 174, 181, 186; David Harris Sacks, "Richard Hakluyt's Navigations in Time: History, Epic, and Empire," *Modern Language Quarterly* 67, no. 1 (March 2006): 31–62.

13. Hening, ed., *Statutes*, 1:68–69.
14. Joyce Lorimer, ed., *English and Irish Settlement on the River Amazon, 1550–1646* (London: Hakluyt Society, 1989), 11–26, 37–84; James A. Williamson, *English Colonies in Guiana and on the Amazon, 1604–1668* (Oxford: Clarendon Press, 1924), 52–59, chap. 5; Mark Nicholls and Penry Williams, "Ralegh, Sir Walter (1554–1618)," *ODNB*; Michael Strachan and Joyce Lorimer, "Ley, John (1549?–1604)," *ODNB*.
15. *CSPCA, 1574–1660*, 5; Leigh had connections to the Separatists, but seems to have been a puritan. Joyce Lorimer, "Leigh, Charles (*bap.* 1572, *d.* 1605)," and "Sir Oliph Leigh (1559–1612)," *ODNB*; L. H. Roper, *Advancing Empire: English Interests and Overseas Expansion, 1613–1688* (Cambridge: Cambridge University Press, 2017), 18–19.
16. *Acts of the Privy Council of England*, ed. John Roche Dasent et al., 46 vols. (London: H.M.S.O., 1890–1964), 33:135–36; Lorimer, ed., *Amazon*, 39–50.
17. Robert Harcourt, *A relation of a voyage to Guiana* (1613), [A3r], [A4v], Br-v, B2r-v, 59, 60, 70–71.
18. "Ralegh, Sir Walter," *ODNB*; "Roe, Sir Thomas (1581–1644)," *ODNB*; Aubrey Gwynn, "An Irish Settlement on the Amazon (1612–1629)," *Proceedings of the Royal Irish Academy: Archaeology, Culture, History, Literature* 41 (1932–34): 1–54; Roper, *Advancing*, 26–29.
19. John Day, *A Publication of Guiana's Plantation . . .* (1632), 1, 2, 3, 6, 11, 13, 14, 17, 23–24.
20. William Alexander, *Doomes-Day, or, the great day of the Lords judgement* (Edinburgh, 1614), second hour, stanza 30; Sir William Alexander, *An encouragement to colonies* (1624), 6, 13–14; George Pratt Insh, *Scottish Colonial Schemes, 1620–1686* (Glasgow: Maclehouse, Jackson & Co., 1922), 49, 60–62.
21. Sir Robert Gordon, *Encouragements. For Such as shall have intention to bee under-takers in the plantation of Cape Briton, now New Galloway in America* (Edinburgh, 1625), Sigs. Br, B2r, B3r-v, [B4v], C2v.
22. T.C., *A Short Discourse of the New-Found-Land* (Dublin, 1623), [A4r-v], C3v; Alexander, *An encouragement*, 25.
23. John Donne, "A Sermon . . . preached to the Honourable Company of the Virginia Plantation," in John Donne, *Five Sermons upon Speciall Occasions* (1626), 22, 25, 36, 42, 44.
24. "A Report of the Colony of the Lord Baron of Baltimore, in Maryland, near Virginia, in which the quality, nature, and condition of the region and its manifold advantages and riches are described," in *Tracts and other papers, relating principally to the Origin, Settlement, and Progress of the Colonies in North America from the Discovery of the Country to the Year 1776*, ed. Peter Force, vol. 4, no. 12 (Washington, DC: Wm. Q. Force, 1846), 3–7.
25. *A True and Sincere declaration of the purpose and ends of the Plantation begun*

in Virginia (1610), reprinted in Sarson, *American Colonies*, 1:79; *Laws Divine, Morall and Martiall* (1612), n.p.; *CSPCA, 1574–1660*, 22–23; TNA CO 1/2/173; Rebecca Anne Goetz, *The Baptism of Early Virginia: How Christianity Created Race* (Baltimore: Johns Hopkins University Press, 2012), chaps. 1–2.

26. White, "Narrative," in *Tracts and other papers*, 29–39; James Axtell, "White Legend: The Jesuit Missions in Maryland," in *After Columbus: Essays in the Ethnohistory of Colonial North America* (New York: Oxford University Press, 1988), 73–85; James H. Merrell, "Cultural Continuity among the Piscataway Indians of Colonial Maryland," *WMQ* 36, no. 4 (October 1979), 548–70; Ralph Pastore, "The Collapse of the Beothuk World," *Acadiensis* 19, no. 1 (Autumn 1989), 52–71; Donald H. Holly Jr., "The Beothuk on the Eve of Their Extinction," *Arctic Anthropology*, 37, no. 1 (2000): 79–95.
27. RMB 2:178–79.
28. *RW*, 2:409–10; Teresa Bejan, "'When the Word of the Lord Runs Freely': Roger Williams and Evangelical Toleration," in *The Lively Experiment: Religious Toleration in America from Roger Williams to the Present*, ed. Chris Beneke and Christopher S. Grenda (Lanham, MD: Rowman & Littlefield, 2015), 65–84; Jeremy Dupertuis Bangs, *Pilgrim Edward Winslow, New England's First International Diplomat: A Documentary Biography* (Boston: New England Genealogical Society, 2004), 251–61; Richard W. Cogley, *John Eliot's Mission to the Indians before King Philip's War* (Cambridge, MA: Harvard University Press, 1999); David J. Silverman, *Faith and Boundaries: Colonists, Christianity, and Community among the Wampanoag Indians, 1600–1871* (New York: Cambridge University Press, 2005); William Kellaway, *The New England Company, 1649–1776: Missionary Society to the American Indians* (Westport, CT: Greenwood Press, 1961).
29. Emmanuel Downing to John Winthrop, August 1645, *WP* 5:38–9; Douglas Bradburn, "The Eschatological Origins of the English Empire," in *Early Modern Virginia: Reconsidering the Old Dominion*, ed. Douglas Bradburn and John C. Coombs (Charlottesville: University of Virginia Press, 2011), 40.
30. *CSPCA, 1574–1660*, 148; Karen Ordahl Kupperman, *Providence Island, 1630–1641: The Other Puritan Colony* (Cambridge: Cambridge University Press, 1995), 166–73, quotes on 166 and 168; Larry Gragg, "'To procure negroes': The English Slave Trade to Barbados, 1627–60," *Slavery and Abolition* 16, no. 1 (April 1995): 65–84; William A. Green, "Supply versus Demand in the Barbadian Sugar Revolution," *Journal of Interdisciplinary History* 18, no. 3 (Winter 1988): 403–18; John C. Coombs, "The Phases of Conversion: A New Chronology for the Rise of Slavery in Early Virginia," *WMQ* 68, no. 3 (July 2011): 332–60.
31. Robert E. Moody, ed., *The Letters of Thomas Gorges: Deputy Governor of the Province of Main, 1640–1643* (Portland: Maine Historical Society, 1978), 98; Michael Guasco, *Slaves and Englishmen: Human Bondage in the Early Modern Atlantic World* (Philadelphia: University of Pennsylvania Press, 2014).
32. Jerome S. Handler, ed. and trans., "Father Antoine Biet's Visit to Barbados in 1654," *Journal of the Barbados Museum and Historical Society* 32 (1967): 56–76, quotes on 67. See also Heather Miyano Kopelson, "'One Indian and

a Negroe, the first thes Ilands ever had': Imagining the Archive in Early Bermuda," *Early American Studies* 11, no. 2 (Spring 2013): 272–313.

33. "A Briefe Discription of the Ilande of Barbadoes," in *Colonising*, 45; George Warren, *An Impartial Description of Surinam upon the Continent of Guiana in America* (1667), 19–20; White Kennett, mss. History of the propagation of the gospel, BL Landsdowne MS 1032, fol. 19/235.
34. Marcellus Rivers and Oxenbridge Foyle, *England's Slavery, Or Barbados Merchandise* (1659), 5–8, 17.
35. TNA CO 1/2/115–16; *WP*, 1:361–62; List written by Marchmont (n.d.), GD158/1222, papers of Hume of Polwarth Earls of Marchmont (1173–1928), National Archives of Scotland; Hening, ed., *Statutes*, 1:539; Evan Haefeli, "Breaking the Christian Atlantic: The Legacy of Dutch Tolerance in Brazil," in *The Legacies of Dutch Brazil*, ed. Michiel van Groesen (Cambridge: Cambridge University Press, 2014), 124–45; Edward B. Rugemer, "The Development of Mastery and Race in the Comprehensive Slave Codes of the Greater Caribbean during the Seventeenth Century," *WMQ* 70, no. 3 (July 2013), 429–58.
36. Katherine Gerbner, *Christian Slavery: Conversion and Race in the Protestant Atlantic World* (Philadelphia: University of Pennsylvania Press, 2018); Goetz, *Baptism*, chaps. 3–6.
37. Jon Sensbach, "Slaves to Intolerance: African American Christianity and Religious Freedom in Early America," in *The First Prejudice: Religious Tolerance and Intolerance in Early America*, ed. Chris Beneke and Christopher S. Grenda (Philadelphia: University of Pennsylvania Press, 2011), 206.

Chapter Two

1. Hakluyt, *Voyages and Discoveries*, ed. Beeching, 235; George Peckham, *True report of the late discoveries, and possession . . . of the Newfoundland* (1583), Sigs. Bi–Bii; David B. Quinn, ed., *The Voyages and Colonizing Enterprises of Sir Humphrey Gilbert*, 2 vols. (London: Hakluyt Society, 1940), 1:192, 2:270, 277–78.
2. Hening, ed., *Statutes*, 1:68–69, 97, 114, 120, 123; Virginia Council, "Instructions, Orders and constitucions . . . To . . . Sir Thomas West, Knight, Lord La Warr," in *The Three Charters of the Virginia Company of London with Seven Related Documents, 1606–1621*, ed. Samuel M. Bemiss (Williamsburg: Virginia 350th Anniversary Celebration Corporation, 1957), 57, 73; Horn, ed., *Smith*, 809.
3. SDEH, 46–47; Richard Rex, *The Lollards* (New York: Palgrave, 2002); Walsham, *Charitable Hatred*, 39–105, quote on 39; Lecler, *Toleration*, 1:107–13, 134–46.
4. Roger L'Estrange, *Toleration Discuss'd* (1663), 100. Key statements by early Christian advocates of coercion in David George Mullan, ed., *Religious Pluralism in the West: An Anthology* (Oxford: Blackwell, 1998), 32–50, 55–73. For their influence, see Walsham, *Charitable Hatred*, 5, 40–49; Forst, *Toleration*, 3, 18–20, 50–55, 64–68, 117–23; Lecler, *Toleration*, 1:147–64, 224–69; John

Marshall, *John Locke, Toleration and Early Enlightenment Culture* (Cambridge: Cambridge University Press, 2006), 197–466, 593–612.

5. Coffey, *Persecution*, 22–38, 78, 99, 114–15.
6. G. R. Elton, ed., *The Tudor Constitution: Documents and Commentary* (Cambridge: Cambridge University Press, 1960), 353; SDEH, 48–50; Diarmaid MacCulloch, "England," in *The Early Reformation in Europe*, ed. Andrew Pettegree (Cambridge: Cambridge University Press, 1992), 166–87.
7. Coffey, *Persecution*, 28–29, 71, 79, quote on 28; Lecler, *Toleration*, 1:107–13, 134–46; Charles W. A. Prior, *Confusion of Tongues: Britain's Wars of Reformation, 1625–1642* (Oxford: Oxford University Press, 2012), 20–29.
8. Kenneth Fincham, *Prelate as Pastor: The Episcopate of James I* (Oxford: Oxford University Press, 1990), esp. 22–34; Martin Ingram, *Church Courts, Sex and Marriage in England, 1570–1640* (Cambridge: Cambridge University Press, 1980); Ethan H. Shagan, "The English Inquisition: Constitutional Conflict and Ecclesiastical Law in the 1590s," *HJ* 47 (September 2004): 541–65.
9. Robert O. Bucholz and Joseph P. Ward, *London: A Social and Cultural History, 1550–1750* (Cambridge: Cambridge University Press, 2012), 126; Jane F. Merritt, "Religion and the English Parish," in *OHA*, 1:122–47.
10. Forst, *Tolerations*, 117–23; Lecler, *Toleration*, 1:147–64, 224–69. On the evolving assumption that conscience was something for adults, see Holly Brewer, *By Birth or Consent: Children, Law, and the Anglo-American Revolution in Authority* (Chapel Hill: University of North Carolina Press for the Institute of Early American History and Culture, 2005).
11. SDEH, 64–65; Peter Lake, "The Significance of the Elizabethan Identification of the Pope as Antichrist," *JEH* 31, no. 2 (April 1980): 161–78.
12. Walsham, *Charitable Hatred*, 251; Diarmaid MacCulloch, *The Boy King: Edward VI and the Protestant Reformation* (Berkeley: University of California Press, 2002).
13. Diarmaid McCulloch, *The Later Reformation in England, 1547–1603* (London: MacMillan, 1990), 19–26. On the fragility of Lady Jane Grey's reign, see David M. Loades, *The Reign of Mary Tudor: Politics, Government, and Religion in England, 1553–1558* (London: Ernest Benn, Ltd, 1979), 62–64, 71–73, 148–50.
14. C. S. Knighton, ed., *CSPD, Mary I, 1553–1558*, rev. ed. (London: Public Record Office, 1998), 1 #1, 5–6 #9; Elton, ed., *Tudor Constitution*, 400–401; Coffey, *Persecution*, 80–81.
15. Eamon Duffy, *Fires of Faith: Catholic England under Mary Tudor* (New Haven, CT: Yale University Press, 2009), provides the geography of executions and argues they were part of a broader, positive effort to rebuild and reform Roman Catholicism. David Loades, *The Religious Culture of Marian England* (London: Pickering and Chatto, 2010), emphasizes English Catholic ambivalence about the killings. On the brutality and potential effectiveness of the campaign, see Thomas S. Freeman, "Burning Zeal: Mary Tudor and the Marian Persecution," in *Mary Tudor: Old and New Perspectives*, ed. Susan Doran and Thomas S. Freeman (New York: Palgrave MacMillan, 2011), 171–205.

16. "The Thirty-Nine Articles, 1563, 1571," in *Religion in Tudor England: An Anthology of Primary Sources*, ed. Ethan H. Shagan and Debora Singer (Waco, TX: Baylor University Press, 2016), 103–10, for the controversial articles.
17. Elizabeth's religiosity is notoriously difficult to pin down, but see Patrick Collinson, "Windows in a Woman's Soul: Questions about the Religion of Queen Elizabeth I," in his *Elizabethan Essays* (London: Hambledon Press, 1994), 87–118; Susan Doran, *Elizabeth I and Religion, 1558–1603* (London: Routledge, 1994), esp. 6–10; Susan Doran, "Elizabeth I's Religion: The Evidence of Her Letters," *JEH* 51 (October 2000): 699–720; Katherine Butler, "'By Instruments her Powers Appeare': Music and Authority in the Reign of Queen Elizabeth I," *Renaissance Quarterly* 65 (Summer 2012): 353–84.
18. Horn, ed., *Smith*, 809; John E. Booty, "History of the 1559 Book of Common Prayer," in *The Book of Common Prayer, 1559: The Elizabethan Prayer Book*, ed. John E. Booty (Charlottesville: University of Virginia Press, 2005), 327–82; Judith Maltby, *Prayer Book and People in Elizabethan and Early Stuart England* (Cambridge, 1998).
19. Bernard J. Verkamp, *The Indifferent Mean: Adiaphorism in the English Reformation to 1554* (Athens: Ohio University Press, 1977), quotes on 158.
20. On the idea of *via media* and its politics, see Diarmaid Macculloch, "The Myth of the English Reformation," *JBS* 30 (January 1991), 1–19.
21. "Richard Hooker (1554–1600), *Of the laws of ecclesiastical polity*," in *Religion in Tudor England*, ed. Shagan and Shuger, 201–30, quote on 203; Peter McCullough, "'Avant-Garde Conformity' in the 1590s," in *OHA*, 380–94.
22. "The Lambeth Articles (1595) and Glosses (1595–c. 1605)," in *Religion in Tudor England*, ed. Shagan and Shuger, 330–46, quotes on 333, 334. On Oxford versus Cambridge, see Francis J. Bremer, *Congregational Communion: Clerical Friendship in the Anglo-American Puritan Community, 1610–1692* (Boston: Northeastern University Press, 1994), chap. 1.
23. Peter Lake, "Lancelot Andrews, John Buckeridge, and Avant-Garde Conformity at the Court of James I," in *The Mental World of the Jacobean Court*, ed. Linda Levy Peck (Cambridge: Cambridge University Press, 1991), 113–33; Nicholas Tyacke, "Lancelot Andrewes and the Myth of Anglicanism," in *C&O*, 5–33.
24. William Craig, "Hampton Court Again: The Millenary Petition and the Calling of the Conference," *Anglican and Episcopal History* 77, no. 1 (March 2008): 46–70, argues that there is no evidence James called the conference in response to a petition and was only trying to get ministers to support his agenda.
25. William Barlow, *The Summe and Substance of the conference . . . at Hampton Court* (1604), F2v, Mv; David Harris Wilson, *King James VI and I* (London: Jonathan Cape, 1956), chap. 12; Winship, *Godly*, 67–85.
26. Andrew Foster, "Neile, Richard (1562–1640)," *ODNB*; Andrew Foster, "Archbishop Richard Neile Revisited," in *C&O*, 159–78.
27. Anthony Milton, "Laud, William (1573–1645)," *ODNB*, contains a nuanced account of Laud's murky religious allegiances.
28. Peter Lake, "The Laudians and the Argument from Authority," in *Court,*

Country and Culture: Essays on Early Modern British History in the Honor of Perez Zagorin, ed. Bonnelyn Young Kunze and Dwight D. Brautigam (Rochester, NY: University of Rochester Press, 1992). On the more popular dimensions of Laudianism, see Alexandra Walsham, "The Parochial Roots of Laudianism Revisited: Catholics, Anti-Calvinists and 'Parish Anglicans' in Early Stuart England," *JEH* 49, no. 4 (October 1998): 620–51.

29. On Arminianism, see Nicholas Tyacke, *Anti-Calvinists: The Rise of English Arminianism, c. 1590–1640* (Oxford: Oxford University Press, 1987). For a useful approach that importantly separates out the attitudes and actions of individuals from the polemical power of the categories, see Michael Questier, "Arminianism, Catholicism, and Puritanism in England during the 1630s," *HJ* 49 (March 2006): 53–78.
30. Peter Heylyn, *Cyprianus Anglicus . . .* (1668), 67.
31. Peter Lake, "The Laudian Style: Order, Uniformity and the Pursuit of the Beauty of Holiness in the 1630s," Anthony Milton, "The Church of England, Rome, and the True Church: The Demise of a Jacobean Consensus," in *The Early Stuart Church, 1603–1642*, ed. Kenneth Fincham (London: MacMillan, 1993), 161–85, and 187–210; Kenneth Fincham, "The Restoration of Altars in the 1630s," *HJ* 44, no. 4 (December 2001): 919–40; Polly Ha, "Spiritual Treason and the Politics of Intercession: Presbyterians, Laudians and the Church of England," in *Puritans and Catholics in the Trans-Atlantic World, 1600–1800*, ed. Crawford Gribben and R. Scott Spurlock (Basingstoke: Palgrave MacMillan, 2015), 66–88.
32. Lake, "Argument from Authority"; Anthony Milton, *Catholic and Reformed: The Roman and Protestant Churches in English Protestant Thought, 1600–1640* (Cambridge: Cambridge University Press, 1995).
33. Pauline Croft, "The Religion of Robert Cecil," *HJ* 34, no. 4 (December 1991): 773–96, quotes on 787, 794.
34. Anon., *The Arminian Nunnery* (1641); David R. Ransome, "Ferrar, John (*c.* 1588–1657)," *ODNB*; Nicholas W. S. Cranfield, "Ferrar, Nicholas (1593–1637)," *ODNB*; Croft, "Religion of Robert Cecil," 788–89.
35. Roger Williams, *The Bloudy tenent of persecution for cause of conscience discussed in a conference between truth and peace* (1644), 185.

Chapter Three

1. Hakluyt, *Principal Navigations*, 8:6–7; 5:68; 11:25; Andrews, *Trade, Plunder*, 54–56, 59–62; Francis Bremer, *Building a New Jerusalem: John Davenport, a Puritan in Three Worlds* (New Haven, CT: Yale University Press, 2012), 198, 220–25, 236; Francis Bremer, "Families and Religious Conflict in the Early Modern Atlantic World," in *P&C*.
2. Christopher Hill, *Economic Problems of the Church from Archbishop Whitgift to the Long Parliament* (Oxford: Clarendon Press, 1956). For two very different cases of patronage, compare Barbara Donagan, "The Clerical Patronage of Robert Rich, Second Earl of Warwick, 1619–1642," *Proceedings of the American Philosophical Society* 120, no. 5 (October 1976): 388–419, with Kenneth

Fincham, "William Laud and the Exercise of Caroline Ecclesiastical Patronage," *JEH* 51, no. 1 (January 2000): 69–93.

3. Kenneth Fincham, "Clerical Conformity from Whitgift to Laud," in *C&O*, 125–58, quote on 127. For a model local study, see Diarmaid MacCulloch, *Suffolk and the Tudors: Politics and Religion in an English County, 1500–1600* (Oxford: Clarendon Press, 1986), chaps. 4–6.
4. Hakluyt, *Principal Navigations*, 2:198–99. For a glimpse of a shipboard religious service, and the lack of tolerance for religious difference among the crew, see Harry Kelsey, *Sir John Hawkins: Queen Elizabeth's Slave Trader* (New Haven, CT: Yale University Press, 2003), 41–42, 68.
5. "Voyage to Guinea in the Year 1554," in Hakluyt, *Voyages and Discoveries*, ed. Beeching, 68; P. E. H. Hair and J. D. Alsop, eds., *English Seamen and Traders in Guinea, 1553–1565: The New Evidence of Their Wills*, Studies in British History, vol. 31 (Lewiston, NY: Edwin Mellen Press, 1992), 2–3, 96, 174–75, 205, 224, 235, 264, 286, 325. Alison Sandman and Eric Ash, "Trading Expertise: Sebastian Cabot between Spain and England," *Renaissance Quarterly* 57, no. 3 (Autumn 2004): 813–46, provides an excellent overview of Cabot's career and technical skills without ever mentioning his religion. Nor is there reference to his religion in David Loades, "Cabot, Sebastian (*c.* 1481/2–1557)," *ODNB*. On the ambiguous religious affiliation of William Hawkins and his son John, which carried over to their voyages, see Kelsey, *Sir John Hawkins*, 8–9, 12, 58–59, 60, 257–58.
6. Travis G. Parno and Brent Fortenberry, "Catholic Artefacts in a Protestant Landscape: A Multi-Vocal Approach to the Religiosity of Jamestown's Colonists," in *Historical Archaeologies of Cognition: Explorations into Faith, Hope and Charity*, ed. James Symonds, Anna Badcock, and Jeff Oliver (Sheffield: Equinox, 2013), 15–27.
7. Susan Rose, *Calais: An English Town in France, 1347–1558* (Woodbridge, Suffolk: Boydell Press, 2008), 127–33, 165.
8. J. S. Brewer et al., eds., *Letters and Papers, Foreign and Domestic, of the Reign of Henry VIII*, 21 vols. (1864–32), vol. 19, part 2, 269; Neil Murphy, *The Tudor Occupation of Boulogne* (Cambridge: Cambridge University Press, 2019), 160–66.
9. C. S. L. Davies, "International Politics and the Establishment of Presbyterianism in the Channel Islands: The Coutances Connection," *JEH* 50, no. 3 (July 1999): 498–522, quote on 521; Tim Thornton, *The Channel Islands, 1370–1640: Between England and Normandy* (Woodbridge, Suffolk: Boydell Press, 2012), chaps. 3–5; Helen Mary Elizabeth Evans, "The Religious History of Jersey, 1558–1640" (PhD thesis, Cambridge University, 1991); Darryl M. Ogier, *Reformation and Society in Guernsey* (Woodbridge, Suffolk: Boydell Press, 1996).
10. D. G. Newcombe, "Tunstal, Cuthbert (1474–1559)," *ODNB*; Tim Thornton, "The Palatinate of Durham and the Maryland Charter," *American Journal of Legal History* 45, no. 3 (July 2001): 235–55.
11. *CBI*, 27–32; J. Gwynfor Jones, *Wales and the Tudor State: Government, Religious Change and the Social Order, 1534–1603* (Cardiff: University of Wales Press, 1989), chap. 3.

12. David W. Moore, *The Other British Isles: A History of Shetland, Orkney, the Hebrides, Isle of Man, Anglesey, Scilly, Isle of Wight and the Channel Islands* (London: McFarland & Company, Inc., 2005), chap. 4.
13. Colm Lennon, *Sixteenth-Century Ireland: The Incomplete Conquest* (Dublin: Gill and Macmillan, 1994), chaps. 1–6.
14. *CSPI, 1509–1573*, 265, #1; Aidan Clarke, "Varieties of Uniformity: The First Century of the Church of Ireland," in *The Churches, Ireland and the Irish*, ed. W. J. Sheils and Diana Wood (Oxford: Blackwell, 1989), 105–22; Lennon, *Incomplete Conquest*, chap. 11; Alan Ford, *James Ussher: Theology, History, and Politics in Early-Modern Ireland and England* (Oxford: Oxford University Press, 2007), esp. chap. 1; Crawford Gribben, "Puritanism in Ireland and Wales," in *Companion*, 159–73.
15. Alan Ford, *The Protestant Reformation in Ireland*, 2nd ed. (Dublin: Four Courts Press, 1997); Nicholas Canny, *Making Ireland British, 1580–1650* (Oxford: Oxford University Press, 2001), chaps. 1–5; Alan Ford, "Dependent or Independent: The Church of Ireland and Its Colonial Contexts, 1536–1647," *Seventeenth Century* 10 (January 1995): 163–87.
16. *Calendar of the Salisbury (Cecil) Manuscripts Papers*, 24 vols. (London: Historical Manuscripts Commission, 1883–1976), 14:240, 314; Lennon, *Incomplete Conquest*, 299–302.
17. Jenny Wormald, "The 'British' Crown, the Earls and the Plantation of Ulster," Martin MacGregor, "Civilizing Gaelic Scotland: The Scottish Isles and the Steward Empire," and Colin Breen, "Randal MacDonnell and Early Seventeenth-Century Settlement in Northeast Ulster, 1603–1630," in *The Plantation of Ulster: Ideology and Practice*, ed. Éamonn Ó Ciardha and Micheál Ó Siochrú (Manchester: Manchester University Press, 2012), 18–32, 33–54, 143–57; *CBI*, 30–50, 100–120.
18. "Luke Gernon's Discourse of Ireland, 1620," in *Illustrations of Irish History and Topography, Mainly in the Seventeenth Century*, ed. Caesar Litton Falkiner (London: Longmans, 1904), 353; D. L. Edwards, "A Haven of Popery: English Catholic Migration to Ireland in the Age of Plantations," in *The Origins of Sectarianism in Early-Modern Ireland*, ed. Allan Ford and John McCafferty (Cambridge: Cambridge University Press, 2005), 105–26; Alan Ford, "'Force and Fear of Punishment': Protestants and Religious Coercion in Ireland, 1603–33," in *Enforcing Reformation in Ireland and Scotland, 1550–1700*, ed. Elizabethanne Boran and Crawford Gribben (Aldershot: Ashgate, 2006), 91–130; Ford, *Ussher*, chaps. 4–5; Alan Ford, "The Church of Ireland, 1558–1634: A Puritan Church?," in *As by Law Established: The Church of Ireland since the Reformation*, ed. Alan Ford, James McGuire, and Kenneth Milne (Dublin: Lilliput Press, 1995), 52–68.
19. IWI, 157–59; *OPP*, 191–92; Kristen Block and Jenny Shaw, "Subjects without an Empire: The Irish in the Early Modern Caribbean," *P&P* 210, no. 1 (February 2011): 41–42.
20. IWI, 160–69, quote on 167.
21. George Pratt Insh, *Scottish Colonial Schemes, 1620–1686* (Glasgow: Maclehouse, Jackson & Co., 1922), 27–30.

22. Gordon Donaldson, "Scotland's Conservative North in the Sixteenth and Seventeenth Centuries," and "The Emergence of Schism in Seventeenth-Century Scotland," in *Scottish Church History* (Edinburgh: Scottish Academic Press, 1985), 191–219.
23. John McCallum, *Reforming the Scottish Parish: The Reformation in Fife, 1560–1640* (Burlington, VT: Ashgate, 2010), quote on 9; Margo Todd, "The Problem of Scotland's Puritans," in *Companion*, 174–88.
24. *CBI*, chap. 2; Jane H. Ohlmeyer, "'Civilizinge of those Rude Partes': Colonization within Britain and Ireland, 1580s–1640s," in *The Origins of Empire: British Overseas Enterprise to the Close of the Seventeenth Century*, ed. Nicholas Canny (Oxford: Oxford University Press, 1998), 124–47.
25. Pauline Croft, *King James* (Basingstoke: Palgrave MacMillan, 2003), 1–47.
26. Alan R. Macdonald, *The Jacobean Kirk, 1567–1625: Sovereignty, Polity and Liturgy* (Ashgate: Aldershot, 1998), 89; David George Mullan, *Episcopacy in Scotland: The History of an Idea, 1560–1638* (Edinburgh: John Donald, 1986).
27. Peter Lake, "The King (the Queen) and the Jesuit: James Stuart's *True Law of Free Monarchies* in Context/s," *Transactions of the Royal Historical Society* 14 (2004): 243–60; Jenny Wormald, "James VI and I (1566–1625)," *ODNB*; Maureen M. Meikle and Helen Payne, "Anne (1574–1619)," *ODNB*; Mark Dilworth, "Ogilvie, John [St John Ogilvie] (1578/9–1615)," *ODNB*.
28. Macdonald, *Jacobean Kirk*, 101–87; Alan R. MacDonald, "James VI and I, the Church of Scotland, and British Ecclesiastical Convergence," *Historical Journal* 48 (2005): 885–903.

Chapter Four

1. Roger Williams, *The Bloudy tenent of persecution for cause of conscience discussed in a conference between truth and peace* (1644), 185; Francis J. Bremer, "Williams, Roger (c. 1606–1683)," *ODNB*.
2. Michael Questier, "Conformity, Catholicism and the Law," in *C&O*, 237–61, quote on 261; Carlos M. M. Eire, "Calvin and Nicodemism: A Reappraisal," *SCJ* 10, no. 1 (Spring 1979): 44–69; Alexandra Walsham, *Church Papists: Catholicism, Conformity and Confessional Polemic in Early Modern England* (Woodbridge, Suffolk: Boydell & Brewer, 1999); Michael Questier, "Sermons, Separatists, and Succession Politics in Late Elizabethan England," *JBS* 52 (April 2013): 290–316.
3. SDEH, 76–77.
4. Elton, ed., *Tudor Constitution*, 363–68, 401–4; Diarmaid MacCulloch, *The Later Reformation in England, 1547–1603* (London, 1990), 27–31; Eamon Duffy, "William Allen, 1532–1594," *Recusant History* (April 1995): 265–90; Mary Rowlands, "English Catholics in the Reign of Elizabeth," *History Review* no. 59 (December 2007): 7–9.
5. SDEH, 81; Ginevra Crosignani, Thomas M. McCoog, and Michael Questier, eds., *Recusancy and Conformity in Early Modern England: Manuscript and Printed Sources in Translation* (Toronto: Pontifical Institute of Mediaeval Studies, 2010); Michael Questier, *Conversion, Politics and Religion in England,*

1580–1625 (Cambridge: Cambridge University Press, 1996); Peter Lake and Michael Questier, "Margaret Clitherow, Catholic Nonconformity, Martyrology and the Politics of Religious Change in Elizabethan England," *P&P* 185 (November 2004): 43–90.

6. Elton, ed., *Tudor Constitution*, 418–32; Coffey, *Persecution*, 85–90; Peter Lake, "A Tale of Two Episcopal Surveys: The Strange Fates of Edmund Grindal and Cuthebert Mayne Revisited: The Prothero Lecture," *Transactions of the Royal Historical Society*, 6th ser., 18 (2008): 129–63.
7. Peter Lake and Michael Questier, "Puritans, Papists, and the 'Public Sphere' in Early Modern England: The Edmund Campion Affair in Context," *Journal of Modern History* 72, no. 3 (September 2000): 587–627, quote on 616; Robert Persons, *A Brief Discours Contayning Certayne Reasons Why Catholiques Refuse to Goe to Church* ("Doway" [English secret press], 1580), Sigs. 3–3v.
8. Michael A. R. Graves, "Campion, Edmund [St Edmund Campion] (1540–1581)," *ODNB*; Lake and Questier, "Edmund Campion Affair."
9. David B. Quinn, "The English Catholics and America," in *England and the Discovery of America, 1481–1620: From the Bristol Voyages of the Fifteenth Century to the Pilgrim Settlement at Plymouth; The Exploration, Exploitation, and Trial-and-Error Colonization of North America by the English* (London: George Allen & Unwin, Ltd, 1974), 364–82; Glyn Parry, *The Arch-Conjuror of England: John Dee* (New Haven, CT: Yale University Press, 2011), 28–29, 94–113.
10. Quinn, ed., *Gilbert*, 1:57–62, 71–76, 81, 90–93, 2:255, 278, 344.
11. Parry, *John Dee*, 94–113, 184–89; Walter Trattner, "God and Expansion in Elizabethan England: John Dee, 1527–1583," *Journal of the History of Ideas* 25, no. 1 (January–March. 1964): 17–34.
12. John Dee, *A True and Faithful Relation of What passed for many years between Dr. John Dee and Some Spirits*, ed. Meric Casaubon (1659), 28; Quinn, ed., *Gilbert*, 96–100; 485.
13. [William Allen], *A Briefe Historie of the Glorious Martyrdom of XII. Reverend Priests . . .* ([Rheims?], 1582), 41–42.
14. Patrick Collinson, *Archbishop Grindal, 1519–1583: The Struggle for a Reformed Church* (Berkeley: University of California Press, 1979), chap. 9; Winship, *Godly*, 41–42.
15. Winship, *Godly*, 41–44; Patrick Collinson, *The Elizabethan Puritan Movement* (Berkeley: University of California Press, 1967), parts 1–2.
16. Collinson, *Movement*, part 3; Winship, *Godly*, 13–38.
17. SDEH, 100–102; Collinson, *Movement*, part 4; Collinson, *Grindal*, 12–15; Coffey, *Persecution*, 96–98; Brett Usher, "Aylmer, John (1520/21–1594)," *ODNB*; Lake, "Episcopal Surveys."
18. Elton, ed., *Tudor Constitution*, 418–32; Geoffrey P. Nuttall, "The English Martyrs, 1535–1680: A Statistical Review," *JEH* 22 (July 1971): 191–97; Rowlands, "English Catholics"; Coffey, *Persecution*, 86–92.
19. J. Hurstfield, "Church and State, 1558–1612: The Task of the Cecils," in G. J. Cuming, ed., *Studies in Church History* 2 (1965), 123; Collinson, *Movement*, part 5.
20. Edward Gee, ed., *The Jesuit's Memorial . . .* (1690), 12–14, 32–34, 43–44.

21. Quinn, ed., *Roanoke Voyages*, 1:203; James Horn, *A Kingdom Strange: The Brief and Tragic History of the Lost Colony of Roanoke* (New York: Basic Books, 2010), 131–34.
22. SDEH, 83; J. Gwynfor Jones, *Wales and the Tudor State: Government, Religious Change and the Social Order, 1534–1603* (Cardiff: University of Wales Press, 1989), 111–14, 251–53, quote on 252; Claire Cross, "Penry, John (1562/3–1593)," *ODNB*; Collinson, *Movement*, parts 6–8.
23. Patrick Collinson, "Cartwright, Thomas (1534/5–1603)," *ODNB* (quote); Polly Ha, *English Presbyterianism, 1590–1640* (Stanford, CA: Stanford University Press, 2010).
24. Thomas Freeman, "Demons, Deviance and Defiance: John Darrell and the Politics of Exorcism in Late Elizabethan England," in *C&O*, 34–63.
25. Peter Lake, "Moving the Goal Posts? Modified Subscription and the Construction of Conformity in the Early Stuart Church," in *C&O*, 179–205; Charles E. Hambrick-Stowe, "Practical Divinity and Spirituality," Dewey D. Wallace, "Puritan Polemical Divinity and Doctrinal Controversy," and Alexandra Walsham, "The Godly and Popular Culture," in *Companion*; John Spurr, *English Puritanism, 1603–1689* (New York: Palgrave MacMillan, 1998); Francis Bremer, *Lay Empowerment and the Development of Puritanism* (New York: Palgrave MacMillan, 2015), chaps. 1–3.
26. Karl Gunther, *Reformation Unbound: Protestant Visions of Reform in England, 1525–1590* (Cambridge: Cambridge University Press, 2014), chap. 3. Karl Gunther and Ethan Shagan, "Protestant Radicalism and Political Thought in the Reign of Henry VIII," *P&P* 194 (February 2007): 35–74, esp. 63–69, where John Frith's arguments for toleration in the 1530s foreshadow Roger Williams's claim that conscience cannot be coerced or controlled by the state.
27. Stephen Wright, *The Early English Baptists, 1603–1649* (Woodbridge, Suffolk: Boydell Press, 2006), 13–44; Coffey, *Persecution*, 99–102, 114–15; Christopher Marsh, *The Family of Love in English Society, 1550–1630* (Cambridge: Cambridge University Press, 1994); David R. Como, *Blown by the Spirit: Puritanism and the Emergence of an Antinomian Underground in Pre-Civil-War England* (Stanford, CA: Stanford University Press, 2004), esp. 4–9, 38–53; Michael P. Winship, *Making Heretics: Militant Protestantism and Free Grace in Massachusetts, 1636–1641* (Princeton, NJ: Princeton University Press, 2002), 188–93 and passim.
28. B. R. White, *The English Separatist Tradition: From the Marian Martyrs to the Pilgrim Fathers* (Oxford: Oxford University Press, 1971); Wright, *English Baptists*, chap. 1. On differences between puritans and Separatists, see Spurr, *Puritanism*, 1–58. Winship, *Godly*, esp. 39–66, emphasizes the common origins of Separatists and puritans and the importance of their continuing relationship to the creation of Congregationalism.
29. *CSPI, 1598–1599*, 428–31; Quinn, "First Pilgrims," 338–39; Keith L. Sprunger, *Dutch Puritanism: A History of English and Scottish Churches of the Netherlands in the Sixteenth and Seventeenth Centuries* (Leiden: Brill, 1982); Michael Moody, "The Apostasy of Henry Ainsworth: A Case Study in Early Separat-

ist Historiography," *Proceedings of the American Philosophical Society* 131 (March 1987): 15–31.

30. Elton, ed., *Tudor Constitution*, 427–32, 447–50; Coffey, *Persecution*, 88, 98; David Beers Quinn, "The First Pilgrims," in *Discovery of America*, 337–63.
31. John Brereton, *A briefe and true relation of the discoverie of the north part of Virginia* (1602); David R. Ransome, "Gosnold, Bartholomew (*d.* 1607)," *ODNB*.
32. Andrew J. Hopper, "Arundell, Thomas, first Baron Arundell of Wardour," *ODNB*; David R. Ransome, "Waymouth [Weymouth], George (fl. 1587–1611)," *ODNB*.
33. Thomas Hughes, ed., *History of the Society of Jesus in North America, Colonial and Federal: Documents*, 2 parts (London: Longmans, Green, and Co., 1908–10), 1:3–5.
34. James Rosier, *A true relation of . . . Captain George Waymouth . . .* (1605), A2v; *The English New England Voyages, 1602–1608*, ed. David B. Quinn and Alison M. Quinn (London: Hakluyt Society, 1983), Ser. II, no. 161, 62–64; Donald F. X. Connolly, "A Chronology of New England Catholicism before the Mayflower Landing," *Records of the American Catholic Historical Society of Philadelphia* 70, no. 3/4 (September, December, 1959): 94–97.
35. Quinn, "The Voyage of *Triall*, 1606–1607: An Abortive Virginia Venture," in *Explorers and Colonies*, 363–81.

Chapter Five

1. Horn, ed., *Smith*, 965–66; [Silvester Jourdain], *A plaine description of the Barmudas, now called the Sommer Ilands* (1613), Sig. G; Peter Lake, "Joseph Hall, Robert Skinner and the Rhetoric of Moderation at the Early Stuart Court," in *The English Sermon Revised: Religion, Literature and History, 1500–1700*, ed. Lori Ann Ferrell and Peter McCullough (Manchester: Manchester University Press, 2000), 167–85.
2. Clements R. Markham, ed., *A Tract on the Succession to the Crown (A.D. 1602) by Sir John Harington, Kt. of Kelston* (1880; New York: Burt Franklin, 1970), 3, 95–96; Jason Scott-Warren, "Harington, Sir John (*bap.* 1560, *d.* 1612)," *ODNB*.
3. W. B. Patterson, *James VI and I and the Reunion of Christendom* (Cambridge: Cambridge University Press, 1997).
4. Charles Howard McIlwain, ed., *The Political Works of James I* (Cambridge, MA: Harvard University Press, 1918), 276; Arthur Wilson, *The History of Great Britain, Being the Life and Reign of King James the First* (1653), 18–19; Kevin Sharpe, "Private Conscience and Public Duty in the Writings of James VI and I," in *Public Duty and Private Conscience in Seventeenth-Century England: Essays Presented to G. E. Aylmer*, ed. John Morrill, Paul Slack, and Daniel Woolf (Oxford: Clarendon Press, 1993), 77–100.
5. Kenneth Fincham and Peter Lake, "The Ecclesiastical Policies of James I and Charles I," in *The Early Stuart Church, 1603–1642*, ed. Kenneth Fincham (London: MacMillan, 1993), 23–49.
6. Croft, "Religion of Robert Cecil," 773–76.
7. Alexandra Gajda, *The Earl of Essex and Late Elizabethan Political Culture*

(Oxford: Oxford University Press, 2012); Elizabeth Gilliam and W. J. Tighe, "To 'Run with the Time': Archbishop Whitgift, the Lambeth Articles, and the Politics of Theological Ambiguity in Late Elizabethan England," *SCJ* 23, no. 2 (Summer 1992): 325–40.

8. Robert Parsons, *A Conference about the next succession to the crowne of Ingland* (1595), Sig. B; Francis Bacon, *A Declaration of the Practises and Treasons attempted and committed by Robert late Earle of Essex* (1601), Sig. D3v; Lake, "'True Law of Free Monarchies' in Context/s," 243–60.
9. Richard Bancroft, *A Sermon Preached at Paules Crosse the 9. of Februarie . . . 1588* (1588), 3; [Richard Bancroft], *Dangerous Positions and Proceedings, published and practices within this Iland of Brytaine, under pretence of Reformation, and for the Presbiteriall Discipline* (1593), 1–3; Patrick Collinson, *Richard Bancroft and Elizabethan Anti-Puritanism* (New York: Cambridge University Press, 2013).
10. Winship, *Godly*, 67–85.
11. Andrew Willet, *Hexapla in Genesin* (Cambridge, 1605), Sigs. [ii–iii], KK1v–KK2r; Anthony Milton, "Willet, Andrew (1561/2–1621)," *ODNB*; Robert C. Ritchie, "Willet, Thomas (1610/11–1674)," *ODNB*; Tom Webster, "Early Stuart Puritanism," in *Companion*, 48–66.
12. Rawdon Brown et al., eds., *Calendar of State Papers and Manuscripts . . . Venice*, 38 vols. (London: Her Majesty's Stationer's Office, 1864–1947) 10:9–10, 21–22; Michael Questier, "Sermons, Separatists, and Succession Politics in Late Elizabethan England," *JBS* 52 (April 2013): 290–316; John J. LaRocca, "'Who Can't Pray with Me, Can't Love Me': Toleration and the Early Jacobean Recusant Policy," *JBS* 23, no. 2 (Spring 1984): 22–36; Coffey, *Persecution*, 117.
13. Park Honan, "Wriothesley, Henry, third earl of Southampton (1573–1624)," *ODNB*. Southampton also may have been involved with Gosnold's 1602 voyage, but that is disputed; Quinn, "English Catholics and America."
14. Mark Nicholls, "Fawkes, Guy (*bap.* 1570, *d.* 1606)," *ODNB*; Mark Nichols, "The Gunpowder Plot," *ODNB*; Jennifer Wormald, "Gunpowder, Treason and Scots," *JBS* 24 (April 1985): 141–68.
15. *SC*, 170; Questier, *Catholicism and Community*, 355–72. For more on the connections between the Gunpowder Plot and early Jacobean colonization, see Cynthia van Zandt, "The Gunpowder Plot, Antipopery, and the Establishment of Virginia," in *Against Popery: Britain, Empire, and Anti-Catholicism*, ed. Evan Haefeli (Charlottesville: University of Virginia Press, 2020).
16. R[obert] J[ohnson], *Nova Britannia: Offering Most Excellent Fruits by Planting in Virginia* (1609), D2r; Hening, ed., *Statutes*, 1:69, 73, 97–98; Susan M. Kingsbury, ed., *The Records of the Virginia Company of London*, 4 vols. (1906–35), 3:4–5.
17. Gillian T. Cell, ed., *Newfoundland Discovered: English Attempts at Colonisation, 1610–1630* (London: Hakluyt Society, 1982), 49; TNA CO 1/5/28v; TNA CO 1/5/101 Governor John Pott et al. to Privy Council, November, 30, 1629, reprinted in "Virginia in 1629 and 1630," *VMHB* 7 (1900): 373–74.
18. Wright, *English Baptists*, 1–44; Winship, *Godly*, 85–88; Bremer, *Lay*

Empowerment, chap. 4; Keith L. Sprunger, "Robinson, John (1575/6?–1625)," *ODNB*.

19. Henry Jacob, *To the Right High and Mightie prince, James . . . An humble supplication for toleration* (1609), 6, 8; Stephen Wright, "Jacob, Henry (1562/3–1624)," *ODNB*.
20. Wright, *Baptists*, 13–74; Winship, *Godly*, 99–102.
21. Winship, *Godly*, 85–88.
22. Horn, ed., *Smith*, 965–66; Kevin Butterfield, "Puritans and Religious Strife in the Early Chesapeake," *VMHB* 109, no. 1 (2001): 8; Ralph Hamor, *A True Discourse of the Present Estate of Virginia* (1615), 60.
23. Harry Culverwell Porter, "Alexander Whitaker: Cambridge Apostle to Virginia," *WMQ* 14, no. 3 (July 1957): 317–43; C. S. Knighton, "Whitaker, William (1547/8–1595)," *ODNB*.
24. George Benson, *A Sermon Preached at Paules Crosse* (1609), reprinted in *The American Colonies and the British Empire, 1607–1783*, ed. Steven Sarson, 8 vols. (London: Pickering & Chatto, 2010), 1:16, 26, 28. For similar views from another Virginia Company supporter, see W[illiam] Crasha[we], *The Sermon Preached at the Crosse . . . Both against Papist and Brownist . . .* (1609), esp. 26, 32–34.
25. Robert Hayman, *Quodlibets lately come over from New Britaniola, old Newfound-land. Epigrams and other small parcels, both morall and divine . . .* (1628), 4, 5, 8; William Barker, "Hayman, Robert (*bap*. 1575, *d*. 1629)," *ODNB*.
26. Sir William Vaughan, *The Golden Fleece divided into three parts, under which are discovered the errours of religion, the vices and decayes of the Kingdom, and lastly the wayes to get wealth, and to restore trading so much complayned of* (1626); Sir William Vaughan, *The Church Militant, historically continued from the yeare of our Saviours incarnation 33 until this present 1640* (1640); Ceri Davies, "Vaughan, Sir William (*c*. 1575–1641)," *ODNB*; Hans Rollman, "Anglicans, Puritans and Quakers in Seventeenth Century Newfoundland," *Avalon Chronicles* 2 (1997): 43–55; Gillian T. Cell, ed., *Newfoundland Discovered: English Attempts at Colonisation, 1610–1630* (London: Hakluyt Society, 1982), 1–250.
27. Jean Kennedy, *Isle of Devils: Bermuda under the Somers Island Company, 1609–1685* (London: William Collins Sons & Co., 1971), chaps. 1–6; William Sears Zuill, "Somers, Sir George (1554–1610)," *ODNB*. On the population, see A. C. Hollis Hallett, *Chronicle of a Colonial Church: Bermuda, 1612–1826* (Pembroke, Bermuda: Juniperhill Press, 1993), 15.
28. Lefroy, *Memorials*, 1:83–100, quotes on 59, 95, 96.
29. [Silvester Jourdain], *A plaine description of the Barmudas, now called the Sommer Ilands* (1613), Sigs. D[vii], G, G[ii].
30. Lewis Hughes, *To the right honourable, the Lords and others of His Majesties most Honourable priuie councell* (n.d., ca. 1625), A2v, A3v; Lewis Hughes, *A Letter sent into England from the Summer Islands* (1615), [B3v–B4]; Hallett, *Chronicle of a Colonial Church*, chaps. 1–2, quote on 20; Michael J. Jarvis, "Hughes, Lewis (*b*. *c*. 1570, *d*. in or after 1646)," *ODNB*; Polly Ha, "Godly Globalization: Calvinism in Bermuda," *JEH* 66, no. 3 (July 2015): 543–61.

31. Michael Questier, "Loyalty, Religion, and State Power in Early Modern England: English Romanism and the Jacobean Oath of Allegiance," *HJ* 40 (June 1997): 311–29; Pauline Croft, "The Catholic Gentry, the Earl of Salisbury and the Baronets of 1611," *C&O*, 262–81, quote on 281.
32. Quinn and Quinn, eds., *English New England Voyages, 1602–1608*, 318, 319.
33. Questier, "English Romanism," 311–29.

Chapter Six

1. *RVC* 4:194–95; SP 105/102, fol. 64r, TNA; Conrad Russell, "The Parliamentary Career of John Pym, 1621–1629," in *Unrevolutionary England, 1603–1642* (London, 1990), 216.
2. *CSPI, 1615–1625*, 451–53 #1123; Michael C. Questier, ed., *Stuart Dynastic Policy and Religious Politics, 1621–1625* (Cambridge: Cambridge University Press for the Royal Historical Society, 2009).
3. Kenneth Fincham, "Abbot, George (1562–1633)," *ODNB*; Kenneth Fincham, "Prelacy and Politics: Archbishop Abbot's Defense of Protestant Orthodoxy," *HR* 61, no. 144 (1988): 36–64; Fincham, "Caroline Ecclesiastical Patronage," 82. David Como and Ian Atherton, "The Burning of Edward Wightman: Puritanism, Prelacy and the Politics of Heresy in Early Modern England," *EHR* 120 (December 2005): 1247–49, reveal the acute combination of national and international concerns about religious orthodoxy behind the two heresy cases.
4. L. A. Govett, *The King's Book of Sports: A History of the Declarations of King James I, and King Charles I, as to the Use of Lawful Sports on Sundays* (London: Elliot Stock, 1890), 36.
5. *OPP*, 356–59; Winship, *Godly*, 85–88; Babette M. Levy, "Puritanism in the Southern and Island Colonies," *PAAS* 70 (April 1960): 104–9; Quinn, "First Pilgrims," 361–63; Butterfield, "Puritans and Religious Strife," 8–10; Bond, *Damned Souls*, 110–16; Michael E. Moody, "Johnson, Francis (*bap.* 1562, *d.* 1617)," *ODNB*.
6. Jean Bodin, *The Six Bookes of a Commonweale*, trans. Richard Knolles (1606), 537; Christine Woodhead, "Knolles, Richard (Late 1540s–1610)," *ODNB*; Forst, *Toleration*, 143–52.
7. John Cartwright, *The preachers travels . . . and a brief rehersall of some gross absudities [sic] in the Turkish Alcoran* (1611), A2v–[A3]; Charles Robson, *News from Aleppo* (1628), 10, 14, 15, 19; Henry Blount, *A Voyage into the Levant* (1636), 110; Nabil Matar, *Islam in Britain, 1558–1685* (Cambridge: Cambridge University Press, 1998). Karen Barkey, *Empire of Difference: The Ottomans in Comparative Perspective* (Cambridge: Cambridge University Press, 2008), 109–53, urges the inclusion of Ottomans in the broader history of tolerance, but it was clearly more of a negative example than a model.
8. Theodore K. Rabb, *Jacobean Gentleman: Sir Edwin Sandys, 1561–1629* (Princeton, NJ: Princeton University Press, 1998), chaps. 2 and 12; Bond, *Damned Souls*, 110–16.
9. George Sandys, *A Relation of a Journey begun An: Dom: 1610 . . .* (1615), 14;

James Ellison, "Sandys, George (1578–1644)," *ODNB*; James Ellison, *George Sandys: Travel, Colonialism, and Tolerance in the Seventeenth Century* (Cambridge, 2002).

10. *RVC* 4:412–13, 420, and 408–35; Alexander B. Haskell, *For God, King, and People: Forging Commonwealth Bonds in Renaissance Virginia* (Chapel Hill: University of North Carolina Press for the Omohundro Institute of Early American History and Culture, 2017), 224–32. Bargrave wanted to avoid the sort of revolts currently plaguing the Spanish Hapsburg Empire.
11. Lewis Hughes, *A Plaine and True Relation of the Goodnes of God towards the Sommer Ilands* (1621), n.p. [12]; Ha, "Godly Globalization;" Hallett, *Chronicle*, chaps. 2–4.
12. Lewis Hughes, *To the right honourable, the Lords and others of His Majesties most Honourable priuie councell* (n.d., ca. 1625), n.p. [13–14].
13. Thomas Scott, *Vox populi, or News from Spayne* (1620), Sigs. B4–C; Peter Lake, "Constitutional Consensus and Puritan Opposition in the 1620s: Thomas Scott and the Spanish Match," *HJ* 25 (December 1982): 805–25; Cesare Cuttica, "Thomas Scott of Canterbury (1566–1635): Patriot, Civic Radical, Puritan," *History of European Ideas* 34 (December 2008): 475–89.
14. John Mason, *A Briefe Discourse of the Newfound-land . . .* (Edinburgh, 1620); Insh, *Schemes*, 30–39; Charles E. Clark, "Mason, John (1586–1635)," and David Stevenson, "Scot, Sir John, of Scotstarvit, Lord Scotstarvit (1585–1670)," *ODNB*.
15. Sir William Alexander, *An encouragement to colonies* (1624), 34–35; Insh, *Schemes*, 48–50, 57–80.
16. Insh, *Schemes*, 62–66, 82–83, 84; David Stevenson, "Gordon, Sir Robert, of Gordonstoun, first baronet (1580–1656)," *ODNB*.
17. Gordon, *Encouragements*, D3–[D4r]. The story of New Galloway is told in Insh, *Schemes*, 91–100, which, however, says virtually nothing about religion.
18. Nathaniel Bouton et al., eds., *Provincial Papers: Documents and Records Relating to the Province of New Hampshire, 1623–1686*, 7 vols. (Concord, NH: George E. Jenks, State Printer, 1867–73), 9; Charles E. Clark, "Gorges, Sir Ferdinando (1568–1647)," *ODNB*.
19. Charles M. Andrews, *The Colonial Period of American History: The Settlements* (New Haven, CT: Yale University Press, 1934), 320–37.
20. Andrews, 337–43.
21. Christopher Levett, *A Voyage into New England, Begun in 1623, and Ended in 1624* (1624), 18, 26, 35–37.
22. David Thompson to Earl of Arundel, in Mary F. S. Hervey, *The Life, Correspondence and Collections of Thomas Howard Earl of Arundel* (Cambridge: Cambridge University Press, 1921), 503, 505.
23. Winship, *Godly*, 93–107, 112–13. Edward Winslow, in a 1632 petition to the Privy Council, claimed "we procured a mocon to be made to his Matie of late & famous memory for liberty of conscience in America under his gratious proteccion, wch his Matie thinking very reasonable (as Sir Robert Naunton principall Secretary to the state in that time can testifie)," but

never produced written evidence of it; TNA CO 1/6/185. For Naunton, see Roy E. Schreiber, "Naunton, Sir Robert (1563–1635)," *ODNB*.

24. Winship, *Godly*, 117–19.
25. Charles Evans, "Oaths of Allegiance in Colonial New England," *PAAS*, 31, no. 2 (October 1921): 382–86.
26. Sir Ferdinando Gorges, *America Painted to the Life* (1658), 24–25.
27. *OPP*, 97.
28. *OPP*, 147–69, 179–80; Winship, *Godly*, 110–11, 120–33.
29. *Governor William Bradford's Letter Book*, intro. John C. Kemp (Bedford, MA: Applewood Books, 2001), 20–21.
30. Calvert to Buckingham, from Ferryland, August 25, 1628, TNA CO 1/4/141; Krugler, *English and Catholic: The Lords Baltimore in the Seventeenth Century* (Baltimore: Johns Hopkins University Press, 2004), chaps. 2 and 3.
31. TNA CO 1/2/140; Krugler, *English and Catholic*, 78–81, 88; Luca Codignola, *The Coldest Harbour of the Land: Simon Stock and Lord Baltimore's Colony in Newfoundland, 1621–1649*, trans. Anita Weston (Kingston and Montreal: McGill-Queen's University Press, 1988).
32. BL Sloane MS 3662, fol. 24; Cell, ed., *Newfoundland Discovered*, 49, 250; Debra A. Myers, "Calvert's Catholic Colony," in *Constructing Early Modern Empires: Proprietary Ventures in the Atlantic World, 1500–1750*, ed. Louis H. Roper and Bertrand van Ruymbeke (Leiden: Brill, 2007), 357–88. The charter granted the near vice-regal powers of the bishop of Durham, as well as "the Patronages and advousons of all churches which (as Christian Religion shall increase) within the sayd Region, Isles and Limittes shall happen thereafter to be erected"; Cell, ed., *Newfoundland Discovered*, 258–69, quote on 260.
33. Fernandeo Diaz-Plaja, ed., *Historia de España en sus documentos: El Siglo XVII* (Madrid: Instituto de Estudios Politicos, 1957), 118–19 (my translation); Thomas Cogswell, "England and the Spanish Match," in *Conflict in Early Stuart England*, ed. Cust and Hughes, 107–33.
34. Cell, ed., *Newfoundland Discovered*, 252; Krugler, *English and Catholic*, chap. 3.

Chapter Seven

1. John Featley, *A Sermon Preached to the Nobely-Deserving Gentelman, Sir Thomas Warner, and the rest of his Companie, bound to the West-Indies* (1629), 3, 9, 16, 21.
2. John C. Appleby, "An Association for the West Indies? English Plans for a West India Company, 1621–1629," *Journal of Imperial and Commonwealth History* 15, no. 3 (1987): 213–41; Thomas Cogswell, "'In the Power of the State': Mr Anys's Project and the Tobacco Colonies, 1626–1628," *EHR*, 123, no. 500 (February 2008): 35–64; Thomas Cogswell, "'The Warre of the Commons for the honour of King Charles': The Parliament-Men and the Reformation of the Lord Admiral in 1626," *HR* 84, no. 226 (April 2011): 618–36, esp. 624 for the proposal to attack Chile.

3. Anthony Milton, "Laud, William (1573–1645)," *ODNB.*
4. Caroline Hibbard, *Charles I and the Popish Plot* (Chapel Hill: University of North Carolina Press, 1983); John Fielding, "Arminianism in the Localities: Peterborough Diocese, 1603–1642," in *ESC*, 93–113. Richard Cust, "Anti-Puritanism and Urban Politics: Charles I and Great Yarmouth," *HJ* 35, no. 1 (March 1992): 1–26, shows Charles's court backing local efforts to suppress puritans out of a fear of "popularity," a term courtiers used to condemn puritans' use of popular politics.
5. SDEH, 149; Richard Cust, *Charles I: A Political Life* (Longman: Harlow, 2005), 13–16, 86–196, esp. 134–44.
6. Milton, "Laud"; John McCafferty, *The Reconstruction of the Church of Ireland: Bishop Bramhall and the Laudian Reforms, 1633–1641* (Cambridge: Cambridge University Press, 2007).
7. Horn, ed., *Smith*, 755–56.
8. Horn, ed., *Smith*, 921–22, 756–59; Roper, *Advancing*, 31–33, quote on 33; John Hilton, "Relation of the First Settlement of St. Christophers and Nevis," in *Colonising*, 1–4; *APCC*, 1:90–91; Michael A. LaCombe, "Warner, Sir Thomas (*c.* 1580–1649)," *ODNB.*
9. *Colonising*, 28; LaCombe, "Warner"; Natalie Zacek, *Settler Society in the English Leeward Islands, 1660–1776* (Cambridge: Cambridge University Press, 2010), 123–32; Arnold Hunt, "Featley, Daniel (1582–1645)," *ODNB.*
10. John Featley, "A succinct history of the life and death of the learned and famous divine, Daniel Featley," in *Featlaei . . . or, Doctor Daniel Featley revived* (1660), 38; Featley, *Sermon Preached*, A2–A3, 9, 11, 21–22, 32; Stephen Wright, "Featley [Fairclough], John (1604/5–1667)," *ODNB.*
11. John Featley, *Obedience and Submission* (1636), 4, 10, 19, 21, 22, 28–29.
12. Featley, 10; Horn, ed., *Smith*, 759; *WJ*, 329–30; *CSPCA, 1675–1676*, 500, 502; Peter Le Fevre, "Saltonstall, Charles (*bap.* 1607, *d.* 1665)," *ODNB.*
13. Featley, *Obedience*, 10; on Carolinism, see Julian Davies, *The Caroline Captivity of the Church* (Oxford: Oxford University Press, 1993), and Kevin Sharpe, *The Personal Rule of Charles I* (New Haven, CT: Yale University Press, 1992), esp. chap. 6. For Laudianism over Carolinism, see Amanda Capern, "The Caroline Church: James Ussher and the Irish Dimension," *HJ* 39, no. 1 (March 1996): 57–85, and Fincham, "Caroline Ecclesiastical Patronage."
14. Insh, *Schemes*, 100–104; TNA CO 1/4/77v–78, 107–8r; *CSPCA, 1574–1660*, 84, 87; Karen Ordahl Kupperman, *Providence Island, 1630–1641: The Other Puritan Colony* (New York: Cambridge University Press, 1995), 94; Paul E. Kopperman, "Profile of Failure: The Carolana Project, 1629–1640," *North Carolina Historical Review* 59, no. 1 (January 1982), 1–11.
15. Richard Cust, *Charles I and the Aristocracy, 1625–1642* (Cambridge: Cambridge University Press, 2013), does not discuss the colonies, but the colonial grants fit within the broader pattern he identifies.
16. *WJ*, 123; *OPP*, 384.
17. *CSPI, 1625–1632*, 305 #905.
18. E. Hunt, "Stourton, Erasmus," in *DCB*.
19. Cell, ed., *Newfoundland Discovered*, 36–57, suggests Newfoundland might

have been a refuge for Old English Catholics and describes the friendship and collaboration between Falkland and Calvert.

20. Lenhart, "Important Chapter," 501–2, 504, 505.
21. Bremer, *John Winthrop*, 140; Anon., *The Protestation of the Archbishops and Bishops of Ireland, against the Toleration of Poperie* (1641), Sig. A2r-v.
22. Thomas Cogswell, "Prelude to Ré: The Anglo-French Struggle over La Rochelle, 1624–1627," *History* 71, no. 231 (February 1986): 1–21; Thomas Cogswell, "Foreign Policy and Parliament: The Case of La Rochelle, 1625–1626," *EHR* 99, no. 391 (April 1984): 241–67.
23. Alastair Bellamy, "The Murder of John Lambe: Crowd Violence, Court Scandal and Popular Politics in Early Seventeenth-Century England," *P&P* 200 (August 2008): 37–76; Thomas Cogswell, "John Felton, Popular Political Culture, and the Assassination of the Duke of Buckingham," *HJ* 49, no. 2 (June 2006): 357–85.
24. Henry Powell, "The Humble Petition," in *Colonising*, 37–38; Williamson, *English Colonies in Guiana*, chap. 6; Carolyn Arena, "Indian Slaves from Guyana in Seventeenth Century Barbados," *Ethnohistory* 64, no. 1 (January 2017): 65–90.
25. P. F. Campbell, *The Church in Barbados in the Seventeenth Century* (Ellerton, St. George, Barbados: Barbados Museum and Historical Society, 1982), chaps. 1–3 and 5; Larry D. Gragg, *Englishmen Transplanted: The English Colonization of Barbados, 1627–1660* (Oxford: Oxford University Press, 2003), 69–87, 159–60. Recognizing the difficulty in gauging popular belief and religious knowledge from the scanty sources available, like wills, Gragg nevertheless argues that most colonists were conformists.
26. TNA CO 1/5/81–84, 138–51, 155–57; *CSPCA, 1574–1660*, 99, 102, 109; Kopperman, "Carolana Project," 1–13; Thomas Leng, "'A Potent Plantation Well Armed and Policeed': Huguenots, the Hartlib Circle, and British Colonization in the 1640s," *WMQ* 66, no. 1 (January 2009): 175–77.
27. Insh, *Schemes*, 67–69, 74–77, 225–26; Naomi E. S. Griffiths and John G. Reid, "New Evidence on New Scotland, 1629," *WMQ* 49, no. 3 (July 1992): 497. All the Kirkes became royalists during the 1640s, suggesting the family's antipuritan disposition, John S. Moir, "Kirke, Sir David (c. 1597–1654)," "Kirke, Sir Lewis, (c. 1599–ante 1683)," "Kirke, Thomas (c. 1603–post 1641)," all in *DCB*.
28. Insh, *Schemes*, 78–81, 83–84, 220–24; Griffiths and Reid, "New Evidence on New Scotland"; D. C. Harvey, "Alexander, Sr William, the Younger (1602–1638)," *DCB*.
29. Insh, *Schemes*, 104–12; Griffiths and Reid, "New Evidence on New Scotland, 1629," 503; "Stewart, James, Fourth Lord Ochiltree (1582?–1659)," *DCB*.
30. Quoted in Insh, *Schemes*, 83.
31. Insh, 81–83, 226.
32. Insh, 85–90; Griffiths and Reid, "New Evidence on New Scotland"; Lenhart, "Important Chapter," 519–20.
33. Insh, *Schemes*, 89–90.
34. Richard Broughton, *A new manual of old Christian Catholic meditations &*

praiers (Lancashire?: Birchley Hall Press?, 1617), 25–26; Lisa McClain, "Without Church, Cathedral, or Shrine: The Search for Religious Space among Catholics in England, 1559–1625," *SCJ* 33, no. 2 (Summer 2002): 383.

35. "Examination of Erasmus Stourton, late preacher to the colony of Ferryland in Newfoundland, October 9, 1628," TNA CO 1/4/144, reprinted in Cell, ed., *Newfoundland Discovered*, 284–85; Lenhart, "Important Chapter," 505.
36. Stourton remained Villiers's chaplain until Villiers's death in 1630, then quietly took up the rectorship of a village church in Lincolnshire bestowed on him by Lionel Cranfield, the Earl of Middlesex. This former minister of King James was an in-law of the Villiers; Rollman, "Anglicans, Puritans," 49–52; Hunt, "Stourton." On Buckingham's relationship with Calvert, see Krugler, *English and Catholic*, 44–65.
37. "Baltimore to King, Ferryland 19 August, 1629," TNA CO 1/5/75–76; "The King to George Lord Baltimore, 22 November, 1629," TNA CO 1/5/99; Ronald G. Asch, "Wentworth, Thomas, first earl of Strafford (1593–1641)," *ODNB*.
38. Aaron F. Miller, John D. Krugler, Barry C. Gaulton, and James I. Lyttleton, "'Over Shoes Over Boots': Lord Baltimore's Final Days in Ferryland, Newfoundland," *Journal of Early American History* 1, no. 2 (January 2011): 167–82; Krugler, *English and Catholic*, 108–18, 122–27; Francis J. Bremer, "Calvert, Cecil, second Baron Baltimore (1605–1675)," *ODNB*.
39. "The Charter of Maryland, 1632," Articles IV, VII, X, XXII, http://avalon.law.yale.edu/17th_century/ma01.asp.
40. BL, Sloane MS 3662, fols. 24–26; Antoinette Sutto, *Loyal Protestants and Dangerous Papists: Maryland and the Politics of Religion in the English Atlantic* (Charlottesville: University of Virginia Press, 2015), 33.
41. *SC*, 71.

Chapter Eight

1. Cotton Mather, *Eleutheria: or, An idea of the Reformation in England* (London, 1698), 75–76.
2. *SC*, 71–73; Cust, *Charles I*, 31–133; David R. Como, "Predestination and Political Conflict in Laud's London," *HJ* 46, no. 2 (June 2003): 263–94.
3. Susan Hardman Moore, *Pilgrims: New World Settlers and the Call of Home* (New Haven, CT: Yale University Press, 2007), 1.
4. Evans, "Oaths of Allegiance," 377–438, 383 (Plymouth), 393–95 and 405–8 (Massachusetts), 419 (Connecticut), 421–23 (New Haven), 427 (Rhode Island), 434 (Exeter, New Hampshire), 437 (Plymouth).
5. On the Feoffees, see Isabel M. Calder, "A Seventeenth Century Attempt to Purify the Anglican Church," *AHR* 53, no. 4 (July 1948): 760–77.
6. Winship, *Godly*, 132–36; David Underdown, *Fire from Heaven: Life in an English Town in the Seventeenth Century* (New Haven, CT: Yale University Press, 1994), 132–33.
7. Thomas Morton, *New English Canaan* (1637), 132–64, quote on 164; *OPP*, 204–10; William Heath, "Thomas Morton: From Merry Old England to New England," *Journal of American Studies* 41, no. 1 (April 2007): 135–68.

8. Bradford, *Letter Book*, 42, 57; *OPP*, 206; Winship, *Godly*, 135, 186.
9. Bradford, *Letter Book*, 46–48; *OPP*, 223–24.
10. TNA, CO 1/5/28v; RMB, 1:386, 394; Winship, *Godly*, chap. 6; Troy O. Bickham, "Cradock, Matthew (*c*. 1590–1641)," *ODNB*; Evans, "Oaths of Allegiance," 387–88.
11. Winship, *Godly*, chaps. 5 and 6; Bremer, *Lay Empowerment*, chap. 5.
12. James F. Cooper Jr., *Tenacious of their Liberties: The Congregationalists in Colonial Massachusetts* (New York: Oxford University Press, 1999), chaps. 1–2.
13. *OPP*, 213, 222–25, 257, 284–85, 292–93, 313–15; Winship, *Godly*, chap. 6; Bremer, *Lay Empowerment*, chap. 5; Mark A. Peterson, "The Plymouth Church and the Evolution of Puritan Religious Culture," *NEQ* 66, no. 4 (December 1993): 570–93.
14. Peter C. Mancall, *Envisioning America: English Plans for the Colonization of North America, 1580–1640* (Boston: Bedford/St. Martin's, 1995), 134; *OPP*, 214, 234–36, quote on 235; Jeremy Dupertuis Bangs, *Edward Winslow: New England's First International Diplomat; A Documentary Biography* (Boston: New England Genealogical Society, 2004), 123–27; Winship, *Godly*, chaps. 6–8; Bremer, *Lay Empowerment*, chap. 5.
15. RMB, 1:87, 140, 352; Stephen Foster, "The Godly in Transit: English Popular Protestantism and the Creation of a Puritan Establishment in America," in *Seventeenth Century New England*, ed. David Hall and David Grayson Allen (Boston: Colonial Society of Massachusetts, 1984), 185–238; Evans, "Oaths of Allegiance," 388–95.
16. Bremer, *Lay Empowerment*, chap. 4, esp. 65–67; Bremer, *Congregational Communion*, chaps. 4–5. Hunter Powell, *The Crisis of British Protestantism: Church Power in the Puritan Revolution, 1638–44* (Manchester: Manchester University Press, 2015), 248, points out that the Plymouth-Massachusetts model suggested by Michael Winship "does not explain how" contemporary Dutch, Scottish, and English theologians could "develop surprisingly similar views of church power reading a wide variety of reformed and post-reformation divines," without ever going to New England. On the break with "Big Tent" puritanism that included congregationalists and presbyterians, see Michael P. Winship, "Straining the Bonds of Puritanism: English Presbyterians and Massachusetts Congregationalists Debate Ecclesiology, 1636–1640," in *P&C*, 89–111.
17. Bremer, *John Winthrop*, chaps. 8–15; David D. Hall, *A Reforming People: Puritanism and the Transformation of Public Life in New England* (New York: Alfred A. Knopf, 2011).
18. *WJ*, 159–60; IWI, 171–72; Roger Thompson, "Gookin, Daniel (*bap*. 1612, *d*. 1687)," *ODNB*.
19. J. Hammond Trumbull et al., eds. *The Public Records of the Colony of Connecticut, 1636–1750*, 15 vols. (Hartford, CT, 1850–76), 1:20–21; Charles J. Hoadly, ed., *Records of the Colony and Plantation of New Haven, 1638–1664*, 2 vols. (Hartford, CT, 1857–58), 1:11–18; Bremer, *Building a New Jerusalem*, chaps. 11–18.
20. Karen Ordahl Kupperman, "Definitions of Liberty on the Eve of Civil War:

Lord Saye and Sele, Lord Brooke, and the American Puritan Colonies," *HJ* 32, no. 1 (March 1989): 17–33, quote on 21; Sargent Bush Jr., ed., *The Correspondence of John Cotton* (Chapel Hill: University of North Carolina Press, 2001), 523; Kupperman, *Providence Island*, 326–32, for Saybrook's church.

21. Bremer, *John Winthrop*, chap. 11.
22. Horn, ed., *Smith*, 808–11.
23. *APCC*, 1:199–202; Bremer, *John Winthrop*, 235–36; Alison Games, *Migration and the Origins of the English Atlantic World* (Cambridge, MA: Harvard University Press, 1999), 19–20.
24. Questier, "Arminianism, Catholicism, and Puritanism," 73–74; Bangs, *Edward Winslow*, 155; James Bliss, ed., *The Works of Archbishop Laud*, 7 vols. (1857; New York: AMS Press, 1975), 6:523.
25. *OPP*, 273–74.
26. Bremer, *John Winthrop*, 230–33, 240; Arthur Lyon Cross, *The Anglican Episcopate and the American Colonies* (New York: Longmans, Green, and Co., 1902), 13–18.
27. Lefroy, *Memorials*, 1:535–36; *APCC*, 1:241–42; September 4, 1639, *CSPCA, 1574–1660*, no. 36; Shona MacLean Vance, "Copland, Patrick (c. 1572—c. 1651)," *ODNB*. Richard Caswell, who passed on the information to Laud, was suspended from the company the following month; *CSPCA, 1574–1660*, no. 41.
28. Hallett, *Chronicle*, chaps. 1–3; Timko, "Puritans in Bermuda," 85–88; Ha, "Godly Globalization."
29. Kupperman, *Providence Island*, esp. 221–66; Charles Morton, "The Life and Death of Nicholas Leverton (1610–1661)," fols. 6–7, http://www.nickleverton.com/Site/Life_and_Death.html.
30. *TSP*, 3:754; J. H. Bennett, "The English Caribbees in the Period of the Civil War, 1642–1646," *WMQ* 24, no. 3 (July 1967): 359–77; Douglas Catterall, "Interlopers in an Intercultural Zone? Early Scots Ventures in the Atlantic World, 1630–1660," in *Bridging the Early Modern Atlantic World: People, Products, and Practices on the Move*, ed. Caroline A. Williams (Farnham, Surrey: Ashgate, 2009), 88–95.
31. *CSPCA, 1574–1660*, 241–43; Kupperman, *Providence Island*, 85, 94, 168–69, 197; S. A. G. Taylor, *The Western Design: An Account of Cromwell's Expedition to the Caribbean* (The Hague: Institute of Jamaica and the Jamaica Historical Society, 1965), 132; Pestana, *English Atlantic*, 47–8, 97, 111, 196–97.
32. TNA CO 1/12/156; Larry D. Gragg, "A Puritan in the West Indies: The Career of Samuel Winthrop," *WMQ* 50, no. 4 (October 1993): 768–86.
33. *APCC*, 1:127; Brent Tarter, "Sir John Harvey, Royal Governor of Virginia, 1628–1639," *VMHB* 125, no. 1 (January 2017): 3–37. For a good assessment of Harvey's tenure as governor that situates it within the context of contemporary English politics yet says virtually nothing about religion, see L. H. Roper, "Charles I, Virginia, and the Idea of Atlantic History," *Itinerario* 30, no. 2 (July 2006): 33–53.
34. "Virginia in 1629 and 1630," *VMHB* 7 (April 1900): 369; Hening, ed., *Statutes*, 1:149, 155–59, 208. For a rather different reading of Virginia's church in these

years, one that believes it was too busy struggling to get caught up in the "cauldron of religious hostility" plaguing the rest of the English world, and that "Virginia's religious history during the 1630s and early 1640s" was characterized by "relative peace and quiet . . . a quiet that did not extend to other elements of Virginia's existence," see Edward L. Bond, *Damned Souls in a Tobacco Colony: Religion in Seventeenth-Century Virginia* (Macon, GA: Mercer University Press, 2000), 136, 139, and chap. 3. Bond overlooks the ecclesiastical politics evident even in the surviving sources and unwittingly reproduces the Laudian *via media* vision in his portrayal of Virginia's church.

35. *CSPCA, 1675–1676, also Addenda, 1574–1674*, 78 #171.
36. Rollman, "Anglican, Puritans," 55–73; Peter E. Pope, *Fish into Wine: The Newfoundland Plantation in the Seventeenth Century* (Chapel Hill: University of North Carolina Press for the Omohundro Institute of Early American History and Culture, 2004), 288–95.
37. *OPP*, 236.

Chapter Nine

1. Carla Gardina Pestana, *The English Atlantic in an Age of Revolution, 1640–1661* (Cambridge, MA: Harvard University Press, 2004), 229–34.
2. R. Scott Spurlock, "Catholics in a Puritan Atlantic: The Liminality of Empire's Edge," in *P&C*, 21–46.
3. Aidan Clarke, "Sir Piers Crosby, 1590–1646: Wentworth's 'Tawney Ribbon,'" *Irish Historical Studies* 26, no. 102 (November 1988): 142–60.
4. CO 1/4/156–57; *CSPI, 1625–1632*, 555; Clarke, "Sir Piers Crosby." Unaware of the source in the Irish records, the summary in *CSPCA, 1574–1660*, 95, as well as a penciled note on the archival document misdate the petition to 1628.
5. *CSPI, 1625–1632*, 304 #902; Sean Kelsey, "Cary, Henry, first Viscount Falkland (*c.* 1575–1633)," *ODNB*.
6. *CSPI, 1647–1660, addenda 1625–1660*, 181–86; Andrew Hadfield, "Gookin, Sir Vincent (*d.* 1638)," *ODNB*.
7. *CSPI, 1647–1660, addenda 1625–1660*, 181–86.
8. Sir William Brereton, *Travels in Holland, the United Provinces, England, Scotland and Ireland, 1634–1635*, ed. Edward Hawkins ([Manchester]: Chetham Society, 1844), 141, 156; Jason McHugh, "'For our owne defence': Catholic Insurrection in Wexford, 1641–2," in *Reshaping Ireland, 1550–1700: Colonization and Its Consequences: Essays Presented to Nicholas Canny*), ed. Brian Mac Cuarta, SJ (Dublin: Four Courts Press, 2011), 214–40; Brian Mac Cuarta, SJ, "The Catholic Church in Ulster under the Plantation, 1609–42," in *The Plantation of Ulster: Ideology and Practice*, ed. Éamonn Ó Ciardha and Micheál Ó Siochrú (Manchester: Manchester University Press, 2012), 119–42.
9. Aidan Clarke, *The Old English in Ireland, 1625–42* (1966; Dublin: Four Courts Press, 2000); Canny, *Making Ireland British*, 276–88; Alan Ford, "'That Bugbear Arminianism': Archbishop Laud and Trinity College, Dublin," in *British*

Interventions in Early Modern Ireland, ed. Ciaran Brady and Jane Ohlmeyer (Cambridge: Cambridge University Press, 2005), 135–60.

10. Hilton, "Relation," in *Colonising*, 4–5, 11, 14, 20; Lorimer, ed., *Amazon*, 42–114; James A. Williamson, *English Colonies in Guiana and on the Amazon, 1604–1668* (Oxford: Clarendon Press, 1924), chaps. 1–6.

11. IWI, 184–85, 209 (quote, my translation), 225, 227, 242; Donald Harman Akenson, *If the Irish Ran the World: Montserrat, 1630–1730* (Montreal: McGill-Queen's University Press, 1997); Pestana, *English Atlantic*, 55, 125; Zacek, *Leeward Islands*, 71–99, 121–68; Block and Shaw, "Subjects without an Empire," 33–60. There is virtually no evidence for religious life on the island before the 1650s.

12. IWI, 172–82, quotes on 173, 179, 180, 181 (my translations), 183; Block and Shaw, "Subjects without an Empire," 36–38.

13. TNA CO 1/6/165; *CSPCA, 1574–1660*, 154; Beauchamp Plantagenet, *A Description of the Province of New Albion* (Middelburg?, 1648), 6, 13, 27–28; TNA CO 1/6/165; Louis H. Roper, "New Albion: Anatomy of an English Colonization Failure, 1632–1659," *Itinerario* 32, no. 1 (March 2008): 1–15.

14. Roper, "New Albion," 5–15; A. J. Loomie, "Matthew, Sir Toby (1577–1655)," *ODNB*.

15. MS Clarendon 102, fols. 231–32, Bodl.; Plantagenet, *Description*, 7, 8, 9–12.

16. Roper, "New Albion," 1–5. Discounting the idea that New Albion was intended as a "Catholic haven," Edward C. Carter and Clifford Lewis survey the history of the Plowden's claim in "Sir Edmund Plowden and the New Albion Charter, 1632–1785," *Pennsylvania Magazine of History and Biography* 83 (April 1959): 150–79, quote on 171.

17. Robert Evelin, *A direction for adventurers with small stock to get two for one, and good land freely* (1641), [n.p.]; Plantagenet, *A Description*, 6, 13, 27–28; Roper, "New Albion," 5–15.

18. *CSPCA, 1574–1660*, 190; *APCC*, 1:240. Antoinette Sutto connects Maryland's form of government to Charles's absolutist style in "Lord Baltimore, the Society of Jesus, and Caroline Absolutism in Maryland, 1630–1645," *JBS* 48 (July 2009): 631–52, and *Loyal Protestants*, chap. 2, "The Personal Rule of Lord Baltimore."

19. Krugler, *English and Catholic*, 119–21.

20. Krugler, 112–15, and chaps. 6–7; John D. Krugler, "Calvert, Leonard (1610?–1647)," *ODNB*; A. F. Allison, "Richard Smith, Richelieu and the French Marriage: The Political Context of Smith's Appointment as Bishop for England in 1624," *Recusant History* 7 (January 1964): 148–211; Michael C. Questier, ed., *Newsletters from the Caroline Court, 1631–1638: Catholicism and the Politics of the Personal Rule* (Cambridge: Cambridge University Press for the Royal Historical Society, 2005), introduction, esp. 4–5, 26–27, 242.

21. "Instructions to the Colonists by Lord Baltimore, 1633," NEM, 16; David B. Quinn, "Why They Came," John Bossy, "Reluctant Colonists: The English Catholics Confront the Atlantic," and Russell R. Menard and Lois Green Carr, "The Lords Baltimore and the Colonization of Maryland," in *Early*

Maryland in a Wider World, ed. David B. Quinn (Detroit: Wayne State University Press, 1982).

22. *APCC*, 1:192; Andrew White, "Narrative of a Voyage to Maryland," in *Tracts and other papers, relating principally to the Origin, Settlement, and Progress of the Colonies in North America from the Discovery of the Country to the Year 1776*, ed. Peter Force, vol. 4, no. 12 (Washington, DC: Wm. Q. Force, 1846), 8, 11, 14. The published account of the colony's beginnings, Andrew White, *A relation of the successefull beginnings of the Lord Baltemore's plantation in Mary-land* (1634), omits all references to Roman Catholicism.
23. White, "Voyage to Maryland," 17.
24. *Colonising*, 54–102, quotes on 57, 88, 94, 95–96.
25. White, "Voyage to Maryland," 18.
26. White, 19.
27. Thomas O'Brien Hanley, SJ, "Church and State in the Maryland Ordinance of 1639," *CH* 26, no. 4 (December 1957): 325–41; John D. Krugler, "Lord Baltimore, Roman Catholics, and Toleration: Religious Policy in Maryland during the Early Catholic Years, 1634–1649," *CHR* 65, no. 1 (January 1979): 49–75; Gerald Fogarty, SJ, "Property and Religious Liberty in Colonial Maryland Catholic Thought," *CHR* 72, no. 4 (October 1986): 573–600; Scott D. Gerber, "Law and Catholicism in Colonial Maryland," *CHR* 103, no. 3 (Summer 2017): 465–90.
28. Krugler, *English and Catholic*, chap. 7; Krugler, "Religious Policy in Maryland."
29. White, "Voyage to Maryland," 25, 26, 28, 34; *NEM*, 31, 118–23, 130, 133–34.
30. *CSPCA, 1574–1660*, 216; "Virginia in 1632-33-34," 161; Tarter, "Sir John Harvey," 3–37.

Chapter Ten

1. *OPP*, 317–18.
2. John Morrill, "The Religious Context of the English Civil War," in *The Nature of the English Revolution: Essays by John Morrill* (New York: Longman, 1993), 45–68, reviews the religious conflicts that led to what he calls the last of the Wars of Religion.
3. Michael P. Winship, *Making Heretics: Militant Protestantism and Free Grace in Massachusetts, 1636–1641* (Princeton, NJ: Princeton University Press, 2002); Edwin S. Gaustad, *Roger Williams* (Oxford: Oxford University Press, 2005).
4. Atherton and Como, "Burning of Edward Wightman"; Peter Lake and David Como "'Orthodoxy' and Its Discontents: Dispute Settlement and the Production of 'Consensus' in the London (Puritan) 'Underground,'" *JBS* 39, no. 1 (January 2000): 34–70.
5. Evans, "Oaths of Allegiance," 424–26; Theodore Dwight Bozeman, "Religious Liberty and the Problem of Order in Early Rhode Island," *NEQ* 45, no. 1 (March 1972): 54, 55, 60; Virginia DeJohn Anderson, "Coddington, William (1601?—1678)," *ODNB*.

6. Evans, "Oaths of Allegiance," 428; G. B. Warden, "The Rhode Island Civil Code of 1647," in *Saints and Revolutionaries: Essays in Early American History*, ed. David D. Hall et al. (New York: W. W. Norton, 1984), 138–51; Raymond D. Irwin, "Saints, Sinners, and Subjects: Rhode Island and Providence Plantations in Trans-Atlantic Perspective, 1636–1665," (PhD Diss., Ohio State University, 1996).
7. Evan Haefeli, *New Netherland and the Dutch Origins of American Religious Liberty* (Philadelphia: University of Pennsylvania Press, 2012), 95–98.
8. David E. Van Deventer, *The Emergence of Provincial New Hampshire, 1623–1741* (Baltimore: Johns Hopkins University Press, 1976), chap. 1.
9. Moody, ed., *Letters of Thomas Gorges*, 17; John G. Reid, *Acadia, Maine, and New Scotland: Marginal Colonies in the Seventeenth Century* (Toronto: University of Toronto Press, 1981), 90–91, 120–21.
10. Anon., *The Last and Heavenly Speeches, and Glorious Departure of John Viscount Kenmuir* (Edinburgh, 1649), 15, 18; Leigh Eric Schmidt, *Holy Fairs: Scottish Communions and American Revivals in the Early Modern Period* (Princeton, NJ: Princeton University Press, 1989), 21–32; John Coffey, *Politics, Religion and the British Revolutions: The Mind of Samuel Rutherford* (Cambridge: Cambridge University Press, 1997), 17–25, discusses the applicability of the term "puritan" to the Scottish case.
11. *CDPR*, 125, 131–32; *The Protestation of the Generall Assemblie of the Church of Scotland . . .* (1638), A2r-v; Michael Braddick, *God's Fury, England's Fire: A New History of the English Civil Wars* (London: Penguin, 2008), 33–39; Austin Woolrych, *Britain in Revolution, 1625–1660* (Oxford: Oxford University Press, 2012), 92–114; Allan I. Macinnes, *Charles I and the Making of the Covenanting Movement, 1625–1641* (Edinburgh: John Donald Publishers, Ltd., 1991), 49–213; John Morrill, "The Scottish National Covenant of 1638 in Its British Context," in *The Nature of the English Revolution: Essays by John Morrill* (New York: Longman, 1993), 91–117.
12. Braddick, *God's Fury*, 89–96.
13. Braddick, 116, 136; Woolrych, *Britain*, 117–18, 120; Mary F. S. Hervey, *The Life, Correspondence and Collections of Thomas Howard Earl of Arundel* (Cambridge: Cambridge University Press, 1921), 147–51; R. Malcolm Smuts, "Howard, Thomas, fourteenth earl of Arundel, fourth earl of Surrey, and first earl of Norfolk (1585–1646)," *ODNB*.
14. Hervey, *Earl of Arundel*, 508; W. Foster, "An English Settlement in Madagascar, 1645–6," *EHR* 27, no. 106 (April 1912): 239–50; Games, *Web of Empire*, 181–217. The little that has been written about English Madagascar says nothing about religion.
15. Hervey, *Earl of Arundel*, 508; William Davenant, *Madagascar, with other poems* (1638), 3, 16–17; Mary Edmond, "Davenant, Sir William (1606–1668)," *ODNB*; Anthony R. J. S. Adolph, "Jermyn, Henry, earl of St Albans (*bap.* 1605, *d.* 1684)," *ODNB*; Ronald G. Asch, "Porter, Endymion (1587–1649)," *ODNB*.
16. Hervey, *Earl of Arundel*, 416–20, 506.
17. TNA CO 1/5/86; *APCC*, 1:240; Kopperman, "Profile of Failure," 9, 14–19; Appleby, "An Association for the West Indies?," 234; Gordon Goodwin,

"Howard, Henry Frederick, fifteenth earl of Arundel, fifth earl of Surrey, and second earl of Norfolk (1608–1652)," rev. Jason T. Peacey, *ODNB*.

18. Frank Penny, *The Church in Madras*, 3 vols. (London: John Murray, 1904), vol. 1, chaps. 1–2, quote on 27–28; Jangkhoman Guite, "The English Company and the Catholics of Madras, in the Age of Religious Conflicts in England, 1640–1750," *Studies in History* 28, no. 2 (July 2012): 179–201, esp. 181–85.
19. *SC*, 185–86; John Morrill, "The Attack on the Church of England in the Long Parliament," in *The Nature of the English Revolution: Essays by John Morrill* (New York: Longman, 1993), 69–90.
20. *SC*, 191–92.
21. *SC*, 154, 157; Braddick, *God's Fury*, 81–155.
22. David Stevenson, "The Early Covenantors and the Federal Union of Britain," in *Scotland and England, 1286–1815*, ed. Roger A. Mason (Edinburgh: John Donald Publishers, 1987), 163–81.
23. William Castell, *A petition . . . for the propagating of the Gospel in America . . .* (1641), 6, 9, 11, 12, 14; Allan I. Macinnes, *The British Revolution, 1629–1660* (New York: Palgrave MacMillan, 2005), 18 and 271–72n18; David R. Ransome, "Castell, William (*d.* 1645)," *ODNB*.
24. Canny, *Making Ireland British*, 243–300.
25. Aidan Clarke, "The 1641 Rebellion and Anti-Popery in Ireland," in *Ulster 1641: Aspects of the Rising*, ed. Brian Maccuarta, SJ (Belfast: Queen's University Institution of Irish Studies, 1993), 139–57; Ethan Howard Shagan, "Constructing Discord: Ideology, Propaganda, and English Responses to the Irish Rebellion of 1641," *JBS* 36, no. 1 (January 1997): 4–34.
26. Raymond Gillespie, "Scotland and Ulster: A Presbyterian Perspective, 1603–1700," in *Scotland and the Ulster Plantations: Explorations in the British Settlements of Stuart Ireland*, ed. William P. Kelly and J. R. Young (Dublin: Four Courts Press, 2009), 84–107; Kathleen M. Noonan, "'The Cruell Pressure of an Enraged, Barbarous People': Irish and English Identity in Seventeenth-Century Policy and Propaganda," *HJ* 41, no. 1 (March 1998): 151–77.
27. Block and Shaw, "Subjects without an Empire," 38–44.
28. *SC*, 210.
29. Braddick, *God's Fury*, 169–80.
30. *SC*, 219; Braddick, *God's Fury*, 182–240; Woolrych, *Britain*, 115–233.
31. Braddick, *God's Fury*, chaps. 8–9.
32. *Colonising*, lv–lxv, 127–31, 115–19, 141; David R. Como, "Castles in the Ayre: Trinidad, Sectarian Puritanism, and the Caribbean in the English Revolution" (unpublished paper).
33. *WJ*, 406; Morton, "Nicholas Leverton."
34. Pestana, *English Atlantic*, chap. 2.
35. Warren M. Billings, *Sir William Berkeley and the Forging of Colonial Virginia* (Baton Rouge: Louisiana State University Press, 2004), 102–4; Hening, ed., *Statutes*, 1:241–42, 277; H. R. McIlwaine, ed., *Minutes of the Council and General Court of Colonial Virginia, 1622–1632, 1670–1676 with Notes and Excerpts from Original Council and General Court Records into 1683, Now Lost* (Richmond: Virginia State Library, 1924), 500.

36. *WJ*, 488–89; Butterfield, "Puritans and Religious Strife," 5–36; Eric John Malony, "Papists and Puritans in Early Maryland: Religion and the Forging of a Provincial Society, 1632–1665," (PhD diss., SUNY Stony Brook, 1996), chap. 3.
37. Nathaniel Bouton et al., eds., *Documents and Records Relating to the Province of New Hampshire, 1623–1686* (Concord, NH: George E. Jenks, State Printer, 1867–1943), 1:155, 161; Van Deventer, *New Hampshire*, chaps. 1 and 8; Michael P. Winship, "Wheelwright, John (1592?–1679)," *ODNB*.
38. John Donoghue, *Fire under the Ashes: An Atlantic History of the English Revolution* (Chicago: University of Chicago Press, 2013), 120–21, 144–58; Irwin, "Saints, Sinners, and Subjects," 130–73.

Chapter Eleven

1. Nathaniel Ward, *A Simple Cobler of Aggawam in America* (1647), A2 verso. No account yet has set the toleration debate within its full transatlantic context, but see Pestana, *English Atlantic*, chap. 2; Rachel N. Schnepper, "Qualified Toleration: Bermuda and the English Revolution," *Parliamentary History* 35, part 2 (June 2016): 132–51; and Polly Ha, "Religious Toleration and Ecclesiastical Independence in Revolutionary Britain, Bermuda, and the Bahamas," *CH* 84, no. 4 (December 2015): 807–27.
2. Harry M. Ward, *The United Colonies of New England, 1643–90* (New York: Vintage Press, 1961), 103, 384.
3. RMD 2:85, 141, 149; Bremer, *Congregational Communion*, 195–97; Bremer, *Lay Empowerment*, chaps. 8–9.
4. Featley, *Featlaei*, 39–40; D. E. Kennedy, "The Establishment and Settlement of Parliament's Admiralty, 1642–1648," *Mariner's Mirror* 48 (November 1962): 276–91; Schnepper, "Qualified Toleration," 147–48; Sean Kelsey, "Rich, Robert, second earl of Warwick (1587–1658)," *ODNB*. For connections between Baptists, the army, Warwick, and the Caribbean, see Como, "Castles." See also Wright, *English Baptists*, 75–142; Mark Bell, "Freedom to Form: The Development of Baptist Movements during the English Revolution," in *RRE*, 181–204.
5. http://avalon.law.yale.edu/17th_century/ri03.asp.
6. *WJ*, 652.
7. *SC*, 238; Powell, *Church Power*, chaps. 3–8; Chad van Dixhoorn, *Confessing the Faith: A Reader's Guide to the Westminster Confession of Faith* (Edinburgh: Banner of Truth Trust, 2014); Chad van Dixhoorn et al., eds., *The Minutes and Papers of the Westminster Assembly, 1643–1652*, 5 vols. (Oxford: Oxford University Press, 2012), vol. 1, chap. 2, "The Reformation at Westminster."
8. *SC*, 239–40; Edward J. Cowan, "The Solemn League and Covenant," in *Scotland and England, 1286–1815*, ed. Roger A. Mason (Edinburgh: John Donald Publishers, 1987), 182–202, quote on 191.
9. Braddick, *God's Fury*, chap 10.
10. Powell, *Church Power*, chaps. 5–8; David Underdown, *Pride's Purge: Politics in the Puritan Revolution* (Oxford: Clarendon Press, 1971), chaps. 1 and 3.

11. Goodwin et al., *An Apologeticall Narration*, 23; Powell, *Church Power*, chaps. 1–2; Lawrence Kaplan, "Presbyterians and Independents in 1643," *EHR* 84, no. 331 (April 1969), 244–56; Kirsteen M. MacKenzie, "Oliver Cromwell and the Solemn League and Covenant of the Three Kingdoms," in *Oliver Cromwell: New Perspectives*, ed. Patrick Little (New York: Palgrave MacMillan), 142–67; Ruth Meyers, "Vane, Sir Henry, the younger (1613–1662)," *ODNB*.
12. Ralph Young, "Breathing the 'Free Aire of the New World': The Influence of the New England Way on the Gathering of Churches in Old England, 1640–1660," *NEQ* 83, no. 1 (March 2010): 5–46.
13. The most thorough study remains W. K. Jordan, including *The Development of Religious Toleration in England: Attainment of the Theory and Accommodations in Thought and Institutions (1640–1660)* (Cambridge, MA: Harvard University Press, 1940). John Coffey provides a more recent account and insists on the importance of the debate to modern, liberal tolerance in "The Toleration Controversy during the English Revolution," in *RRE*, 42–68, and "Puritanism and Liberty Revisited: The Case for Toleration in the English Revolution," *HJ* 41 (December 1998): 961–85.
14. Thomas Goodwin et al., *An Apologeticall Narration humbly submitted to the Honourable Houses of Parliament* (1643), quotations on 5, 24, 26; Jordan, *Long Parliament to the Restoration*, 51–52. Hunter Powell argues the *Narration* was "a last attempt to keep the godly united and protect the unity that had been established in 1641," not "a call for religious toleration," even though scholars of the toleration debate customarily treat it as such; *Church Power*, chap. 4, quotes on 91. Ethan Shagan argues the Independents' language of moderation was revolutionary, "evidence of a fundamental conflict over the nature of governance, a conflict which could not yet be expressed in the modern idiom of transformative progress," in "Rethinking Moderation in the English Revolution: The Case of *An Apologetical Narration*," in *The Nature of the English Revolution Revisited: Essays in Honour of John Morrill*, ed. Stephen Taylor and Grant Tapsell (Woodbridge, Suffolk: Boydell Press, 2013), 27–52, quote on 51.
15. Adam Stuert, *Some Observations and Annotations upon the Apologeticall Narration* (1644), 61–63; Thomas Edwards, *Antaplogia, or a Full Answer to the Apologeticall Narration* (1644), L13v; Jordan, *Long Parliament to the Restoration*, 52; Crawford Gribben, "Samuel Rutherford and Liberty of Conscience," *Westminster Theological Journal* 71 no. 2 (Fall 2009): 355–73; Shaun De Freitas and Andries Raath, "Samuel Rutherford and the Protection of Religious Freedom in Early Seventeenth-Century Scotland," *Westminster Theological Journal* 78, no. 2 (Fall 2016): 231–48; Schnepper, "Qualified Toleration," 137–38.
16. Roger Williams, *The Bloudy Tenent, of Persecution, for Cause of Conscience, discussed* (1644), 3; Schnepper, "Jonas Cast up at London," 247–63.
17. Edward Terry, *Pseudeleutheria, or, Lawlesse Liberty* (1646), A2r, 26, 30.
18. William Walwyn, *The Compassionate Samaritane* (1644), 61–62, 79, 80, 83–84; John Milton, *Complete Poems and Major Prose*, ed. Merritt Y. Hughes (New

York: Macmillan Publishing Company, 1957), 144–45; Barbara Taft, "Walwyn, William, (bap. 1600, d. 1681)," *ODNB*.

19. *Correspondence of John Cotton*, 502–3.
20. Robert Bailie, *A Dissuasive from the errours of the time* (1646), 108; William Prynne, *A Fresh Discovery of some prodigious new wandring-blasing-stars . . .* (1645), Appendix, 1–26; Nathaniel White, *Truth Gloriously Appearing . . .* (1645); Timko, "Puritans in Bermuda," chap. 3; Ha, "Ecclesiastical Independence," 811–12; Michael P. Winship, "Oxenbridge, John (1608–1674)," *ODNB*.
21. Robert Rich, Earl of Warwick, *A Declaration of the Right Honourable Robert, Earle of Warwick, Lord High Admirall of England, and of all the plantations . . .* (1644), 2, 4; Schnepper, "Qualified Toleration," 132–33, 146, makes a convincing case that the tract was not published until 1645, although the original proclamation was made in 1644.
22. Prynne, *Fresh Discovery*, Appendix, 1; Robert Baillie, *A Dissuasive from the Errours of the Time* (1645), 108; Timko, "Puritans in Bermuda," 124–29; Ha, "Ecclesiastical Independence," 812–20; Schnepper, "Qualified Toleration," 145–47.
23. Lefroy, *Memorials*, 2:600–602; Schnepper, "Qualified Toleration," 148–50.
24. Bangs, *Edward Winslow*, 224–27.
25. Braddick, *God's Fury*, 304–55.
26. Joseph Frank, "News from Virginny, 1644," *VMHB* 65, no. 1 (1957): 84–87; Steven D. Crow, "'Your Majesty's Good Subjects': A Reconsideration of Royalism in Virginia, 1642–1652," *VMHB* 87, no. 2 (April 1979): 158–73.
27. RMB 2:69.
28. Timothy B. Riordan, *The Plundering Time: Maryland and the English Civil War, 1645–1646* (Baltimore: Maryland Historical Society, 2004); Sutto, *Loyal Protestants*, chap. 3.
29. AoM 3:173; Riordan, *Plundering Time*, 278–81. Schnepper, "Qualified Toleration," 147–48, mistakenly assumes it was revoked in February 1645.
30. Braddick, *God's Fury*, 347–55, 370–438.
31. Woolrych, *Britain*, 296–365.
32. Clive Holmes, ed., *The Suffolk Committees for Scandalous Ministers, 1644–1646*, (Ipswich: Suffolk Records Society, 1970); John Morrill, "The Church in England, 1642–1649," in *The Nature of the English Revolution: Essays by John Morrill* (New York: Longman, 1993), 148–75.
33. Braddick, *God's Fury*, 294, 477; Peter King, "The Episcopate during the Civil Wars," *EHR* 83, no. 1 328 (July 1968): 528–29.
34. Laud, *Works*, 3:250; W. Prynne, *A Breviate of the Life of William Laud* (1644), 27; King, "Episcopate," 526, 529–37.
35. Kenneth Fincham and Stephen Taylor, "Episcopalian Conformity and Nonconformity, 1646–60," in *Royalists and Royalism during the Interregnum*, ed. Jason McElligott and David L. Smith (Manchester: Manchester University Press, 2010), 18–43; Judith Maltby, "Suffering and Surviving: The Civil Wars, the Commonwealth and the Formation of 'Anglicanism,'" in *RRE*, 158–80; Kenneth Fincham and Stephen Taylor, "The Restoration of the Church of

England, 1660–1662: Ordination, Re-ordination and Conformity," in *The Nature of the English Revolution Revisited: Essays in Honour of John Morrill*, ed. Stephen Taylor and Grant Tapsell (Woodbridge, Suffolk: Boydell Press, 2013), 197–232.

36. The little written about these efforts has little discussion of religion; see Foster, "English Settlement in Madagascar," 239–50; Games, *Web of Empire*, 181–217.
37. Richard Boothby, *A True Declaration of the Intollerable Wrongs done to Richard Boothby . . .* (1644), 2; Richard Boothby, *A Briefe Discovery or Description of the most famous island of Madagascar . . .* (1646), Sig. A3v, 18, 65. 66.
38. Leng, "'A Potent Plantation,'" 173–94; John T. Young, "Durie, John (1596–1680)," *ODNB*; M. Greengrass, "Hartlib, Samuel (*c.* 1600–1662)," *ODNB*.
39. On the complex character of the English revolutionary church, see the following essays in *RRE*: Ann Hughes, "'The public profession of these nations': The National Church in Interregnum England," 93–114; Elliot Vernon, "A Ministry of the Gospel: The Presbyterians during the English Revolution," 115–36; Christopher Durston, "'Preaching and Sitting Still on Sundays': The Lord's Day during the English Revolution," 205–25.
40. Lefroy, *Memorials*, 1:612.
41. Robert Emmet Wall, Jr. *Massachusetts Bay: The Crucial Decade, 1640–1650* (New Haven, CT: Yale University Press, 1972), 93–120, 157–224; Bangs, *Edward Winslow*, 241–250.

Chapter Twelve

1. *WJ*, 720–21.
2. RMB 2:176–77. For a useful brief overview, see Francis J. Bremer, "The Puritan Experiment in New England, 1630–1660," in *Companion*, 27–142.
3. RMB 2:177; 3:259–60.
4. RMB 2:177–80.
5. RMB 2:193
6. RMB 2:242; 3:229, 273; Gaskill, *Witchfinders*, 272; Walter W. Woodward, *Prospero's America: John Winthrop, Jr., Alchemy, and the Creation of New England Culture* (Chapel Hill: University of North Carolina Press, 2010), chap. 7.
7. RMB 3:173–74.
8. Allan I. MacInnes, *Charles I and the Making of the Covenanting Movement, 1625–1641* (Edinburgh, 1991); Margaret Griffin, *Regulating Religion and Morality in the King's Armies, 1639–1646* (Leiden: Brill, 2004); William Sheils, "English Catholics at War and Peace," in RRE, 137–57.
9. *SC*, 247.
10. Blair Worden, *God's Instruments: Political Conduct in the England of Oliver Cromwell* (Oxford: Oxford University Press, 2012), 13–90. J. C. Davis, "Cromwell's Religion," in *Oliver Cromwell and the English Revolution*, ed. John Morrill (New York: Longman, 1990) 181–208, argues that the "denominational grid" cannot "measure the religious faith and sincerity of a man

who struggled to free himself and the godly in his society from formalistic declensions and paradigms," and that liberty of conscience (for those he recognized as godly) was his greatest achievement; quote on 208.

11. Kenyon, *Stuart Constitution*, 264, 268.
12. *SC*, 271, 274.
13. William Golding, *Servants on horse-back . . .* (1648), 12–14; Schnepper, "Jonas Cast up at London," 284–87; Timko, "Puritans in Bermuda," chap. 4.
14. *Articles and Orders, Made and Agreed upon the 9th Day of July, 1647 . . . By the Company of Adventurers for the Plantation of the Islands of Eleutheria* (1647) (broadsheet); Ha, "Ecclesiastical Independence," 820–22.
15. Jeremy Taylor, *Theologia eklektike: A discourse of the liberty of prophesying* (1647), 1, "The Epistle Dedicatory," 8–9, 11–12, 13, 14; John Spurr, "Jeremy Taylor (bap. 1613, *d.* 1667)," *ODNB*.
16. *WJ*, 720–21; W. Hubert Miller, "The Colonization of the Bahamas, 1647–1670," *WMQ* 2, no. 1 (January 1945): 33–46.
17. Timko, "Puritans in Bermuda," chaps. 5–6; Schnepper, "Jonas Cast up at London," 287–91; Virginia Bernhard, "Sayle, William (*d.* 1671)," *ODNB*.
18. Kenyon, ed., *Stuart Constitution*, 275, 276; Braddick, *God's Fury*, 508–19.
19. Braddick, *God's Fury*, 520–25.
20. Braddick, chap. 19.
21. *An Ordinance of the Lords & Commons Assembled in Parliament for the punishing of Blasphemies and Heresies* (1648), 3–8; Jordan, *Long Parliament to the Restoration*, 111–15.
22. *SC*, 289, 306; Braddick, *God's Fury*, 529–81.
23. Vera Keller, "The 'framing of a new world': Sir Balthazar Gerbier's 'Project for Establishing a New State in America,' ca. 1649," *WMQ* 70, no. 1 (January 2013): 147–76, quotes on 165, 169.
24. Years later the county would be renamed Anne Arundel, after the wife of Cecil Calvert, and the town rechristened Annapolis, after Anne Stuart. Lois Green Carr, "Stone, William (*c.* 1603–1659)," *ODNB*; Malony, "Papists and Puritans," chap. 4.
25. For discussions of the act see, Curry, *First Freedoms*, 38–42, and Patricia U. Bonomi, *Under the Cope of Heaven: Religion, Society, and Politics in Colonial America* (New York: Oxford University Press, 1986), 21–23.
26. AoM, 1:244–47.
27. AoM, 1: 243, 244–46.
28. Henry Whistler, "Extracts from Henry Whistler's Journal of the West India Expedition," appendix E, in *The Narrative of General Venables: With an Appendix of Papers Relating to the Expedition to the West Indies and the Conquest of Jamaica, 1654–1655*, ed. C. H. Firth (London, 1900), 14; *WJ*, 406; Campbell, *Church in Barbados*, chaps. 3–4; Como, "Castles."
29. Campbell, *Church in Barbados*, 50–56, quotes on 54–55; Natalie Zacek, "Bell, Philip (bap. 1590? d. in or after 1650)," *ODNB*.
30. J. H. Bennett, "The English Caribbees in the Period of the Civil War, 1642–1646," *WMQ* 24, no. 3 (July 1967): 359–77.
31. Bennett; LaCombe, "Warner." Pestana, *English Atlantic*, 229, calculates Saint

Christopher's 1640 population as 3,650, which would make the dissidents over half the population.

32. IWI, 209 (my translation).
33. IWI, 210–13 (my translations).
34. *TSP*, 3:754; *CSPCA, 1574–1660*, 473, 477; *CSPCA, 1661–1668*, 517.
35. IWI, 220–28; Pierre Pelleprat, *Relation des Missions des P.P. et de la Compagnie de Jésus dans les isles, et dans la terre ferme de l'Amerique meridionale* (Paris: Cramoisy, 1655), 19–20, 37–44; *A brief and true Remonstrance of the Illegall Proceedings of Roger Osburn (an Irish man born) Governor of Mount: Serrat . . .* (1654) (broadside); *TSP*, 3:754; Zacek, *Leeward Islands*, 71–78, 99–115, 123–25; Akenson, *Montserrat*, chap. 2; Johnston, "Papists in a Protestant World," chap. 1.
36. *TSP*, 3:754; *CSPCA, 1675–1676, also Addenda, 1574–1674*, 84–85 #194; Pestana, *English Atlantic*, 111, 170–71; Gragg, "Puritan in the West Indies."

Chapter Thirteen

1. Nicholas Foster, *A brief relation of the late horrid rebellion acted in the island Barbadas* (1650), 9–15, 40, 52; Zacek, "Bell, Philip," *ODNB*.
2. Bremer, *Congregational Communion*, chap. 7; Reid, *Acadia, Maine*, 130–35.
3. Haefeli, *New Netherland*, 146–47; Sydney V. James, *John Clarke and His Legacies: Religion and Law in Colonial Rhode Island, 1638–1750*, ed. Theodore Dwight Bozeman (University Park: Pennsylvania State University Press, 1999), chap. 3; Adrian Chastain Weimer, *Martyrs' Mirror: Persecution and Holiness in Early New England* (New York: Oxford University Press, 2011), chap. 4. On Congregational New England's greater affinity for Baptists than Quakers, see E. Brooks Hollifield, "Toleration in Massachusetts," *CH* 38, no. 2 (June 1969): 188–200.
4. E. S. De Beer, ed., *The Diary of John Evelyn*, 6 vols. (Oxford: Clarendon Press, 1955), 3:201–2.
5. George Gardyner, *A description of the new world, or, America, islands and continent* (1651), 103; Lenhart, "Important Chapter," 521–23, quote on 521.
6. NEM, 218–19; Malony, "Papists and Puritans," chaps. 6–7; Sutto, *Loyal Protestants*, chap. 4; Alison Gilbert Olson, *Anglo-American Politics, 1660–1775: The Relationship between Parties in England and Colonial America* (Oxford, 1973), 15–37.
7. Braddick, *God's Fury*, 439–581; Woolrych, *Britain*, 335–559; Patrick Little, "Cromwell and Ireland before 1649," in *Oliver Cromwell: New Perspectives*, ed. Patrick Little (New York: Palgrave MacMillan), 116–41; Patrick Little, "The Irish 'Independents' and Viscount Lisle's Lieutenancy of Ireland," *HJ* 44, no. 4 (December 2001): 941–61.
8. Micheál Ó Siochrú, *God's Executioner: Oliver Cromwell and the Conquest of Ireland* (London: Faber and Faber, 2008), quotes on 100 and 117; *A Declaration of the Lord Lieutenant of Ireland for the undeceiving of deluded and seduced people, which may be satisfactory to all that doe not willfully shut their eyes to the light* (Cork and London, 1650), [3], [6], [9–11], [15].

9. Simon P. Newman, *A New World of Labor: The Development of Plantation Slavery in the British Atlantic* (Philadelphia: University of Pennsylvania Press, 2013), 81–83; and Block and Shaw, "Subjects without an Empire," 33, 47–49.
10. Albert J. Loomie, SJ, "Oliver Cromwell's Policy toward the English Catholics: The Appraisal by Diplomats, 1654–1658," *CHR* 90 (January 2004): 29–44; Sutto, *Loyal Protestants*, 76.
11. David Stevenson, *Revolution and Counter Revolution in Scotland, 1644–51* (Edinburgh: John Donald, 2003).
12. Kirsteen M. MacKenzie, *The Solemn League and Covenant of the Three Kingdoms and the Cromwellian Union, 1643–1663* (London: Routledge, 2018), chaps. 1–3; R. Scott Spurlock, *Cromwell and Scotland: Conquest and Religion, 1650–1660* (Edinburgh: John Donald, 2007), chaps. 1–2.
13. *SC*, 296–98, 307–8; Christopher Durston, "'Preaching and sitting still on Sunday': The Lord's Day during the English Revolution," in *RRE*, 205–25.
14. *An Act against several Atheistical, Blasphemous and Execrable Opinions Derogatory to the Honor of God, and destructive to Humane Society* (1650), 980–83; Jordan, *From the Convention of the Long Parliament to the Restoration, 1640–1660*, 131–38; William Lamont, "Clarkson, Laurence (1615–1667)," *ODNB*.
15. Middlesex Sessions Books Calendar, October 1644 to April 1652, 146–47, LMA.
16. *An Act for relief of religious and peaceable people from the rigor of former acts of Parliament in matters of Religion* (1650), 1021.
17. *An Act for relief of religious and peaceable people*, 1024–25. For a case study of Cromwellian religious diversity at the county level, see Jacqueline Eales, "'So many sects and schisms': Religious Diversity in Revolutionary Kent, 1640–60," in *RRE*, 226–48.
18. Spurlock, *Cromwell and Scotland*, chaps. 3–5.
19. *CDPR*, 395, 399; Karl S. Bottigheimer, *English Money and Irish Land: The "Adventurers" in the Cromwellian Settlement of Ireland* (Oxford: Clarendon Press, 1971); John Cunningham, *Conquest and Land in Ireland: The Transplantation into Connacht, 1649–1680* (Woodbridge: Boydell, 2011).
20. *CSPCA, 1574–1660*, 429–30, 450, 453; Toby Barnard, "Fleetwood, Charles, appointed Lord Fleetwood under the protectorate (*c.* 1618–1692)," *ODNB*; Peter Gaunt, "Cromwell, Henry (1628–1674)," *ODNB*.
21. Toby Barnard, *Cromwellian Ireland: English Government and Reform in Ireland, 1649–1660* (Oxford: Clarendon Press, 2000), 90–182.
22. *Hammond versus Heamans . . .* (1655), 1; Pestana, *English Atlantic*, chaps. 3 and 5.
23. Peter E. Pope, *Fish into Wine: The Newfoundland Plantation in the Seventeenth Century* (Chapel Hill: University of North Carolina Press for the Omohundro Institute of Early American History and Culture, 2004), 288–95; Rollman, "Seventeenth-Century Newfoundland," 44–72.
24. Hening, ed., *Statutes*, 1:363, 399, 418, 424; Warren M. Billings, ed., "Some Acts Not in Hening's 'Statutes': The Acts of Assembly, April 1652, November 1652, and July 1652," *VMHB* 83, no. 1 (January 1975): 74.

25. Hening, ed., *Statutes*, 1:433, 457; Billings, ed., "Acts Not in Hening's 'Statutes,'" 24–25, 31–32, 64–65, 66, 68–69.
26. Samuel Winthrop to John Winthrop Jr., February 13, 1660; Samuel Winthrop to John Winthrop Jr., March 26, 1660; Box 4, Winthrop family papers [transcripts], 1630–1741, 10 boxes, Ms. N-2211, Massachusetts Historical Society.
27. Gragg, *Englishmen Transplanted*, chap. 3; Foster, *A brief relation.*
28. Michael A. LaCombe, "Willoughby, Francis, fifth Baron Willoughby of Parham (*bap.* 1614, *d.* 1666)," *ODNB.*
29. Zachary Grey, *An impartial examination of the fourth volume of Mr. Daniel Neal's History of the Puritans* (1739), 24–27; Gragg, *Englishmen Transplanted*, 75–78.
30. Austin Woolrych, *Commonwealth to Protectorate* (Oxford: Clarendon Press, 1982); Stephen Wright, "Barbon, Praisegod (*c.* 1598–1679/80)," *ODNB.*
31. *SC*, 312–13. Cromwellian religious policy has still not received a focused study, but see Barry Coward, *The Cromwellian Protectorate* (Manchester, 2002), 14–17, 39–47, 58–62, 80–85; Alan G. R. Smith, *The Emergence of a Nation State: The Commonwealth of England, 1529–1660* (London, 1997), 341–47; Jeffrey R. Collins, "The Church Settlement of Oliver Cromwell," *History* 57 (January 2002): 18–40; Ann Hughes, "'The public profession of these nations': The National Church in Interregnum England," in *RRE*, 93–114; Jordan, *Long Parliament to the Restoration*; Bernard S. Capp, *England's Culture Wars: Puritan Reformation and Its Enemies in the Interregnum, 1649–1660* (Oxford: Oxford University Press, 2012), chap. 6, "The Puritan Parish"; Ann Hughes, "The Cromwellian Church," in *OHA*, 444–56.
32. A. J. B. Johnston, "Borderland Worries: Loyalty Oaths in Acadie/Nova Scotia, 1654–1755," *French Colonial History* 4 (2003): 35–36.
33. *CSPCA, 1574–1660*, 470; TNA CO 1/13, No. 11, fol. 35v; *CSPCA, 1661–1668*, 39–41, #111; John G. Reid, "Temple, Sir Thomas (bap. 1614, d. 1674)," *ODNB*; Reid, *Acadia, Maine, and New Scotland*, 135–41; TNA CO 1/13, no. 64, fol. 156v; *CSPCA, 1661–1668*, 285 #952.

Chapter Fourteen

1. Caton MS, Vol. 3, 3/82, 228–35 Henry Fell to Margaret Fell, Barbadoes, the 8 of the third mo. [May], 1659, FHL.
2. SP 25/77/840, TNA.
3. Elliot Vernon, "A Ministry of the Gospel: The Presbyterians during the English Revolution," in *RRE*, 115–36; Worden, "Toleration and the Protectorate." On the Erastian nature of the Cromwellian church, and Thomas Hobbes's enthusiasm for it and resentment of it, see Jeffrey R. Collins, *The Allegiance of Thomas Hobbes* (Oxford: Oxford University Press, 2005).
4. *SC*, 321; John Morrill, "The Making of Oliver Cromwell," in *The Nature of the English Revolution: Essays by John Morrill* (New York: Longman, 1993), 118–47; J. C. Davis, "Cromwell's Religion," and Anthony Fletcher, "Oliver Cromwell and the Godly Nation," in *Oliver Cromwell and the English Revolution*, ed.

John Morrill (London: Longman, 1990), 181–208 and 209–33; David L. Smith, "Cromwell's Religious Attitudes," in his *Oliver Cromwell: Politics and Religion in the English Revolution, 1640–1658* (Cambridge: Cambridge University Press, 1991), 68–81; Blair Worden, "Toleration and the Protectorate," in his *God's Instruments: Political Conduct in the England of Oliver Cromwell* (Oxford: Oxford University Press, 2012), 63–90.

5. John Spurr, *The Restoration Church of England, 1646–1689* (New Haven, CT: Yale University Press, 1991), chap. 1; Judith Maltby, "From *Temple* to *Synagogue*: 'Old' Conformity in the 1640s–1650s and the Case of Christopher Harvey," *C&O*, 88–120; Kenneth Fincham and Stephen Taylor, "Episcopalian Conformity and Nonconformity, 1646–60," in *Royalists and Royalism during the Interregnum*, ed. Jason McElligott and David L. Smith (Manchester: Manchester University Press, 2010), 18–43; Kenneth Fincham and Stephen Taylor, "Episcopalian Identity, 1640–1662," in *OHA*, 457–76; John Spurr, "Religion in Restoration England," in *The Reigns of Charles II and James VII & II*, ed. Lionel K. J. Glassey (London: Palgrave Macmillan, 1997), 90–124.
6. *TSP*, 5:598; Bryan D. Spinks, "Gauden, John (1599/1600?–1663)," *ODNB*. On Gauden's affinity with important Cromwellian Protestants in Ireland as well as England, see Patrick Little, *Lord Broghill and the Cromwellian Union with Ireland and Scotland* (Woodbridge, Suffolk: Boydell Press, 2004), chap. 9, esp. 233–34.
7. Henry Fell to Margaret Fell, Barbados, December 19, 1656, Swarthmore MS 1/67, no. 345, Tr. 2:107–9, FHL; Richard Pinder to George Fox, Barbados, August 17, 1660, Swarthmore MS 4/39, Tr. 4:293–94; Gragg, "Puritan in the West Indies," 768–86; William C. Braithwaite, *The Beginnings of Quakerism to 1660* (Cambridge: Cambridge University Press, 1955), 402, 406–13.
8. *TSP* 5:693; 6:636; 7:287.
9. Graham, "Lord Baltimore's Pious Enterprise," 74–201; Kenneth Carroll, *Quakerism on the Eastern Shore* (Baltimore: Maryland Historical Society, 1970), 7–30.
10. Gandy, ed., *Sufferings of Early Quakers*, 181–82; Humphrey Norton and John Rous, *New-England's ensigne: it being the account of the cruelty, the professor's pride, and the articles of their faith . . .* (1659); 50–52; Carla Gardina Pestana, *Quakers and Baptists in Colonial Massachusetts* (Cambridge: Cambridge University Press, 1991), 25–43; Carla Gardina Pestana, "The Quaker Executions as Myth and History," *Journal of American History* 80, no. 2 (September 1993): 441–69; Weimer, *Martyrs' Mirror*, chap. 5; Worral, *Quakers in the Colonial Northeast*, 18–20; Haefeli, *New Netherland*, chap. 6 and 221–32.
11. Megapolensis and Drisius to Classis, September 24, 1658, Edward T. Corwin, ed., *Ecclesiastical Records: State of New York*, 7 vols. (Albany, NY: James B. Lyon, 1901–16), 1:433. On the hostility to Rhode Island, see Bozeman, "Problem of Order in Early Rhode Island," 52–54. For Roger Williams's rebuttal of Quaker doctrine in 1672, see Worral, *Quakers in the Colonial Northeast*, 31–41.
12. Handler, ed. and trans., "Biet's Visit," 56–76, quotes on 58, 61–63; Jerome S. Handler and Matthew C. Reilly, "Father Antoine Biet's Account Revisited: Perspectives on Irish Catholics in Mid-Seventeenth Century Barbados," in

Caribbean Irish Connections: Interdisciplinary Perspectives, ed. Alison Donnell, Maria McGarrity, and Evelyn O'Callaghan (Kingston: University of the West Indies Press, 2015), 33–46; Gragg, *Englishmen Transplanted*, 75–78.

13. Handler, ed., "Biet's Visit," 68.
14. Swarthmore MS 3/66, FHL, Transcription 2:101–5, Henry Fell to Margaret Fell, Barbados, November 3, 1656.
15. Swarthmore MS 3/66, FHL, Transcription 2:101–5, Henry Fell to Margaret Fell, Barbados, November 3, 1656.
16. Swarthmore MS 1/67, FHL, Transcription 2:107–9 Henry Fell to Margaret Fell, Barbados, December 19, 1656; Larry Gragg, *The Quaker Community on Barbados: Challenging the Culture of the Planter Class* (Columbia: University of Missouri Press, 2009), 32–37, argues for an "absence of religious enthusiasm on Barbados," 35.
17. "Certaine Overtures," in *Colonising*, 177; *CSPCA, 1574–1660*, 373–74 #922; CO 1/11; Sarah Barber, "Power in the English Caribbean: The Proprietorship of Lord Willoughby of Parham," in *Constructing Early Modern Empires: Proprietary Ventures in the Atlantic World, 1500–1750*, ed. Louis H. Roper and Bertrand van Ruymbeke (Leiden: Brill, 2007), 189–212.
18. Egerton MS 2395, fol. 279, BL; "Mr. Nicholas Leverton (1610–1661)," May 13, 1662, Leverton to Morton, fols. 18–19; J. Sears McGee, "Byam, Henry (1580–1669)," *ODNB*; Jacob Selwood, "Left Behind: Subjecthood, Nationality, and the Status of Jews after the Loss of English Surinam," *JBS* 54 no. 3 (July 2015): 578–601.
19. Caton MS, Vol. 3, 3/82, 228–35, Henry Fell to Margaret Fell, Barbadoes, the 8 of the third mo. [May], 1659, FHL.
20. Woolrych, *Britain*, chaps. 18–24.
21. Carla Gardina Pestana, *The English Conquest of Jamaica: Oliver Cromwell's Bid for Empire* (Cambridge, MA: Harvard University Press, 2017).
22. Thomas Gage, *The English-American his Travail by Sea and Land, or, A New Survey of the West Indias* (1648), 3. On Cromwell's anti-Catholic vision, see Karen Ordahl Kupperman, "Errand to the Indies: Puritan Colonization from Providence Island through the Western Design," *WMQ* 45, (January 1988): 70–99. Timothy Venning, *Cromwellian Foreign Policy* (New York: Saint Martin's Press, Inc., 1995), on the other hand, downplays Cromwell's anti-Catholic proclivities to insist on his "pragmatism."
23. *A Full Survey of Sion and Babylon* (1654) (title page); Allen D. Boyer, "Gage, Thomas (1603?–1656)," *ODNB*.
24. Julian de Castilla, *The English Conquest of Jamaica: An Account of What Happened in the Island of Jamaica, from May 20 of the Year 1655, when the English laid Siege to it, up to July 3 of the year 1656*, trans. Irene A. Wright, Camden Miscellany, 13 (London, 1924), 3rd ser., 35:12. For a recent discussion of the Western Design and religion, see Kristen Block, *Ordinary Lives in the Early Caribbean: Religion, Colonial Competition, and the Politics of Profit* (Athens: University of Georgia Press, 2012), chaps. 7–9.
25. *CSPA, 1574–1660*, 459; *TSP*, 3:754; Richard P. Gildrie, "Sedgwick, Robert (*bap.* 1619, d. 1656)," *ODNB*; Len Travers, "Winslow, Edward (1595–1655),"

ODNB. For the migration of the Nevis colonists, see Taylor, *Western Design*, chapter 11.

26. *CSPA, 1574–1660*, 429–30, 450, 453.
27. Cecil Roth, *A History of the Jews in England*, 2nd ed. (Oxford: Clarendon Press, 1949), chaps. 6–7, quote on 136; Ariel Hessayon, "Jews and Crypto-Jews in Sixteenth and Seventeenth Century England," *Cromohs* 16 (2011): 1–26.
28. Middlesex Sessions Books Calendar, October 1644 to April 1652, 126–27, LMA; David S. Katz, *Philo-Semitism and the Readmission of the Jews to England, 1603–1655* (Oxford: Oxford University Press, 1982); Richard W. Cogley, "The Ancestry of the American Indians: Thomas Thorowgood's *Iewes in America* (1650) and *Jews in America* (1660)," *English Literary Renaissance* 35, no. 2 (Spring 2005): 304–30; Andrew Crome, "The Jewish Indian Theory and Protestant Use of Catholic Thought in the Early Modern Atlantic," in *Puritans and Catholics*, ed. Gribben and Spurlock, 112–30; Andrew Crome, "Politics and Eschatology: Reassessing the Appeal of the 'Jewish Indian' Theory in England and New England in the 1650s," *Journal of Religious History* 40, no. 3 (September 2016): 326–46; [Thomas Brightman], *The Reverend Mr Brightmans Judgement or Prophesies, what shall befall England, and the hierarchy therein* (1642), and [R.W.], *An Information Concerning the Present State of the Jewish Nation in Europe and Judea* (1658). On puritan New Englanders' millennial hopes, which persisted into the 1640s, see Winship, *Godly*, 230–35, and Bremer, *John Davenport*, 168–80.
29. Roth, *History of the Jews*, 7. Katz, *Philo-Semitism*, emphasizes that those who favored Jews' readmission to England hoped that it would facilitate their conversion and thus hasten the arrival of the millennium.
30. The emergence of Jews in the Caribbean between the 1640s and 1660s has not yet been systematically studied, but see Jonathan I. Israel, "Menasseh Ben Israel and the Dutch Sephardic Colonization Movement of the Mid-Seventeenth Century (1645–1657)," in *Menasseh Ben Israel and his World*, ed. Yosef Kaplan, Henry Méchoulan, and Richard H. Popkin (Leiden, 1989), 139–63, and Nuala Zahedieh, "Defying Mercantilism: Illicit Trade, Trust, and the Jamaican Sephardim, 1660–1730," *HJ* 61, no. 1 (March 2018): 77–102.
31. Memorial of René Augier, Esq., July 25, 1657, CO 1/13/60–62.
32. Samuel R. Gardiner, "Cromwell and Mazarin in 1652," *EHR* 11, no. 43 (July 1896): 485.
33. *CSP Domestic, 1658–1659*, 78; *CSP Domestic, 1660–1661*, 228; Clyde L. Grose, "England and Dunkirk," *AHR* 39, no. 1 (October 1933): 5–17.
34. *TSP* 7:249; L. Lemaire, ed., *Inspections de l'Église Saint-Éloi de Dunkerque en 1659, 1662 et 1673* (Dunkirk: Imprimerie du Nord Maritime, 1935), 12–23, quote on 13; Grose, "England and Dunkirk"; L. Lemaire, *Dunkerque sous la domination anglaise: Correspondance de Mazarin et du père Canaye* (Lille, 1924).
35. *TSP*, 7:125–26; Theophilus Veraz, *Serious sober state-considerations, relating to the government of England and the garrison of Dunkirk in Flanders* (1660), 8; Timothy Venning, "Lockhart, William (1621?–1675)," *ODNB*.
36. C. H. Firth, "A Speech by Richard Cromwell, 14 October, 1658," *EHR* 23, no. 92

(October 1908): 734–36, quotes on 736. Jason Peacey, "'Fit for Public Services': The Upbringing of Richard Cromwell," in *Oliver Cromwell: New Perspectives*, ed. Patrick Little (New York: Palgrave MacMillan, 2009), 241–64, argues against the traditional image of Richard as incompetent "Tumble Down Dick," claiming he was an able ruler of moderate-conservative Presbyterian instincts.

37. Brian Manning, *Revolution and Counter-Revolution in England, Ireland and Scotland, 1658–60* (London: Bookmarks, 2003), argues against the usual sentiment that the Restoration was inevitable and insists on the persistence of revolutionary radicalism.

Conclusion

1. John Featley, *Featlaei . . . or, Doctor Daniel Featley revived* (1660), B3, B5r-v, B6r-v.
2. Woolrych, *Britain in Revolution*, chaps. 25–27; Spurr, *Restoration Church*, 29–41, and the following essays in N. H. Keeble, ed., *"Settling the Peace of the Church": 1662 Revisited* (New York: Oxford University Press, 2014): N. H. Keeble, "Introduction: Attempting Uniformity," 1–28; Jacqueline Rose, "The Debate over Authority: *Adiaphora*, the Civil Magistrate, and the Settlement of Religion," 29–56; Paul Seaward, "Circumstantial Temporary Concessions: Clarendon, Comprehension, and Uniformity," 57–84; Robert Armstrong, "The Bishops of Ireland and the Beasts at Ephesus: Reconstruction, Conformity, and the Presbyterian Knot, 1660–2," 114–43; Alasdair Raffe, "Presbyterian Politics and the Restoration of Scottish Episcopacy, 1660–2," 144–67.
3. Jon Kukla, ed., "Some Acts Not in Hening's 'Statues': The Acts of Assembly, October 1660," *VMHB* 83, no. 1 (January 1975): 87, 97; Hening, ed., *Statutes*, 2:25, 29–30, 31, 37.
4. Hening, ed., *Statutes*, 2:46–47; Bond, *Damned Souls*, chap. 4; Brydon, *Virginia's Mother Church*, 131–32.
5. Hening, ed., *Statutes*, 1:532–33, 2:47–49.
6. Kenneth Fincham and Stephen Taylor, "The Restoration of the Church of England, 1660–1662: Ordination, Re-ordination and Conformity," in *The Nature of the English Revolution Revisited: Essays in Honour of John Morrill*, ed. Stephen Taylor and Grant Tapsell (Woodbridge, Suffolk: Boydell Press, 2013), 197–232; Fincham and Taylor, "Episcopalian Identity," in *OHA*, 476–81.
7. John Spurr, "Schism and the Restoration Church," *JEH* 41 (July 1990): 108–24; John D. Ramsbottom, "Presbyterians and 'Partial Conformity' in the Restoration Church of England," *JEH* 43 (April 1992): 249–70.
8. Kenyon, ed., *Stuart Constitution*, 353–54; David J. Appleby, *Black Bartholomew's Day: Preaching, Polemic and Restoration Nonconformity* (Manchester: Manchester University Press, 2007); Michael Davies, "The Silencing of God's Dear Ministers: John Bunyan and His Church in 1662," in *"Settling the Peace of the Church,"* ed. Keeble, 85–113. For the anti-Dissenter position, see Mark Burden, "John Walker's *Sufferings of the Clergy* and the Church of England

Responses to the Ejections of 1660–2," in *"Settling the Peace of the Church,"* ed. Keeble, 233–62.

9. Kenyon, ed., *Stuart Constitution*, 335–39, 351–56; http://www.british-history.ac.uk/statutes-realm/vol5/pp350–351; John Spurr, *The Restoration Church of England, 1646–1689* (New Haven, CT: Yale University Press, 1991), 29–45; Barry Reay, "Popular Hostility Towards Quakers in Mid-Seventeenth-Century England," *Social History* 5, no. 3 (October 1980): 387–407.
10. Evan Haefeli, "How Special Was Rhode Island? The Global Context of the 1663 Charter," in *The Lively Experiment: Religious Toleration in America from Roger Williams to the Present*, ed. Chris Beneke and Chris Grenda (Lanham, MD: Rowman and Littlefield, 2015), 21–36.
11. Owen Stanwood, "Crisis and Opportunity: The Restoration Church Settlement and New England," in *"Settling the Peace of the Church,"* ed. Keeble, 190–208.
12. Bede, *Ecclesiastical History of the English People* (London: Penguin Books, 1990 ed.), 45; Henry Kamen, *Empire: How Spain Became a World Power, 1492–1763* (New York: Harper Collins, 2003), especially chap. 8; John H. Elliott, *Empires of the Atlantic World: Britain and Spain in America, 1492–1830* (New Haven, CT: Yale University Press, 2006), esp. chap. 7.
13. J. Hector St. John Crèvecoeur, *Letters from an American Farmer and Sketches of Eighteenth-Century America* (New York: Penguin, 1986), 75–76.
14. Comparative overviews are rare, but see Charles H. Lippy, Robert Choquette, and Stafford Poole, *Christianity Comes to the Americas, 1492–1776* (New York: Paragon House, 1992). For more specialized studies, see Cornelius J. Jaenen, *The Role of the Church in New France* (Toronto: McGraw-Hill Ryerson, 1976); Haefeli, *New Netherland*; Evan Haefeli, "The Pennsylvania Difference: Religious Diversity on the Delaware before 1683," *Early American Studies* 1, no. 1 (January 2003): 28–60. The vast literature on religion in Latin America suggests the diversity that was possible within the Roman Catholic establishment, but leaves no doubt that Catholicism was firmly established everywhere. Stuart Schwartz, *All Can Be Saved: Religious Tolerance and Salvation in the Iberian Atlantic World* (New Haven, CT: Yale University Press, 2008), only describes individual attitudes that defied that establishment. See also Javier Fernández Sebastián, "Toleration and Freedom of Expression in the Hispanic World between Enlightenment and Liberalism," *P&P* 211, no. 1 (2011): 159–97.

Index

Page numbers in italics refer to figures.

Abbot, George, 116, 119–20, 142–43
Abbot, Robert, 56
Aberdeen University, 69
Acadia, 280, 283
Act against Jesuits and Seminarists of 1585, 87
Act concerning Religion of 1649, 243, 254–56, 268, 289. *See also* Maryland
Act for preventing the Mischiefs and Dangers of 1662, 308
Act for relief of religious and peaceable people, 272
Act for Retaining the Queen's Subjects in their True Obedience of 1593, 92
Act for Settling Ministers of 1660, 308
Act for the Settlement of Ireland of 1652, 273
Act for the suppressing the Quakers of 1660, 306
Act of Classes of 1649, 270
Act of Supremacy: of 1536, 67; of 1559, 47–48; of 1560, 67
Act of Uniformity: of 1549, 47; of 1552, 48; of 1559, 49; of 1560, 67; of 1660, 307–8; of 1662, 305, 307, 310
Act to Retain the Queen's Majesty's Subjects in their Ture Obedience, 82
Acuña, Diego Sarmiento de, 125
adiaphora, 51–53, 228. *See also* liturgy
Admonition to Parliament, An, 86
advowson, 60–61
Africa, 8, 30, 34–35, 207–8, 296, 302
Agreement of the People, 251
Ainsworth, Henry, 91–92, 110
Albert, Archduke, 94
Albion, Earl of. *See* Plowden, Sir Edmund
Alexander, Sir William, 27, 126–28, 154–56, 168, 182. *See also* Stirling, Earl of
Alexander, Sir William, the Younger, 154–55
Allen, William (cardinal), 80, 84–85
altars, 53, 72
Amazon Company, 26
America, *19*; and England, 117, 205, 216; foundations of, 1, 25, 40, 60; as a refuge, 27, 78, 309; religious climate of, 4, 18, 95, 135, 195; and Scotland, 155; and separation of colonies, 124, 202; and Spain,

America (*continued*)
141–42. *See also* United States of America; *and specific colonies*
American Revolution, 1, 4, 195, 312
Ames, William, 109, 119
Amsterdam, 108
Anabaptists, 47, 90, 109, 201, 223, 267. *See also* Baptists
Andrewes, Lancelot, 53, 57
Anglo-Dutch War, 279–80, 293
Anglo-French War, 141, 152, 154, 182
Anglo-Spanish War, 84, 87–88, 92–93, 135, 141, 151, 293
Anjou Match, 82
Anne of Denmark, Queen, 207
anti-Calvinism, 40, 52–55, 119–20, 141. *See also* antipuritanism; Calvinism
anti-Catholicism, 23, 67–68, 84–87, 104, 107, 151–54, 197, 210–11, 235, 245–47, 269, 295. *See also* Catholicism
Antigua, 175, 185, 260, 275
Antinomian controversy of 1636–38, 202
Antinomians, 202, 272
anti-Popery, 47, 84, 101, 135. *See also* anti-Catholicism; popery
antipuritanism, 101–5, 146, 172. *See also* puritanism
anti-Semitism, 41. *See also* Judaism
Anti-Trinitarians, 91
Antrim, Earl of, 69, 83. *See also* MacDonnell, Randal
Antwerp, 89
Apologeticall Narration, 228
Aquinas, Thomas, 41
Arch-Conjuror of England, 83
Archer, Gabriel, 63
Arminians, 56, 58, 142, 146, 176
Arthur, King, 84, 134
Arthur, Prince of Wales, 296
Articles of Confederation, 222. *See also* United Colonies of New England
Articles of Perth, 71, 75, 205
Arundel, Earl of, 127, 129–30, 207–8, 210
Arundell, Sir Thomas, 93–94, 106, 159
Association Island, 175
atheism, 20
Augier, René, 298
Augustine (missionary), 30
Augustine, Saint, 41
Avalon, 3, 133–36, 142, 150, 156–60, 177, 180, 187, 195, 312
Aylmer, John, 87

Babington Plot of 1586, 80, 294
Bachiler, Stephen, 204
Bacon, Francis, 103
Bahamas, 242
Baillie, Robert, 232
Baltimore, Baron: and Avalon, 133–36, 142, 156–60, 177; and King James, 118, 189, 207; and Maryland, 148–50, 190–91, 195–96, 235, 254, 268, 275, 289, 308–9, 312. *See also* Avalon; Maryland
Bancroft, Richard, 103, 111, 116, 119
baptism, 22–25, 33–35, 49, 53, 110, 132, 158, 249
Baptist Fifth Monarchists, 280
Baptists: in the colonies, 60, 145, 223, 227, 240, 266; in England, 109, 203–4; and Presbyterians, 286; and puritanism, 12; and religious unity, 77–78, 282, 302; in Scotland, 273. *See also* Anabaptists
Barbados, 32–35, 142, 148, 153, 194, 214–15, 256–57, 265–67, 278–79, 284–85, 290–92, 298, 311–12
Barbados's 1661 slave code, 35
Barbados sugar revolution, 265
Barebone, Praisegod, 279–80
Barebone's Parliament, 279–80
Bargrave, Isaac, 123
Bargrave, John, 117, 123
Bargrave, Thomas, 123
Barrow, Henry, 91–92, 164
Barrowists, 91, 111. *See also* Brownists; Separatism

Battle of Edgehill, 216
Battle of Lostwithiel, 234
Battle of the Severn River, 268
Battle of Worcester, 270
Bede, 309
Bell, Philip, 256–57, 265
Beothuks, 31
Berkeley, Sir William, 216–17, 275, 305
Berkshire, Earl of, 26–27. *See also* Howard, Thomas
Bermuda, 99, 106, 112–16, 123–24, 149, 173–74, 178, 231–32, 239–41, 249–51, 275
Bermuda Company, 174, 232, 251
Bernard, Nicholas, 287
Bible, 53–54, 90, 228. *See also* Scripture
Biddle, John, 286
Biet, Antoine, 290
Bingley, Sir Ralph, 95
Bishops' Wars, 206–7, 211
Black Acts, 74
Blackwell, Francis, 120
blasphemy laws, 243, 254, 266, 271
Bloudy Tenent, The (Williams), 229
Blount, Charles, 68–69, 105
Blount, Henry, 122
Bodin, Jean, 122
Boleyn, Anne, 49
Bond, John, 306
Book of Common Prayer: and conformity, 47, 257; opposition to, 165, 172–75, 236, 278; requirement of, 177–78, 248–49, 272, 305–8; revisions to, 49, 206; selective use of, 85; translations of, 66; use of, 50, 63, 102, 114, 164, 195, 204, 275, 292. *See also* Directory for Public Worship
Book of Sports (James), 120, 132
Boothby, Richard, 238
Boulogne, 64
Bradford, William, 132, 166, 178, 233
Brewster, William, 132
Bridge, William, 228
Briskett, Anthony, 185
British Civil Wars. *See* English Civil War
British Empire, 4–5, 40, 84, 99–100, 134, 173, 179, 271, 310. *See also* English Empire
Brooke, Lord, 148–49, 169
Broughton, Richard, 157
Browne, Robert, 91
Brownists, 91, 111, 130, 155. *See also* Barrowists; Separatism
Bruce, Edmund, 105
Buchanan, George, 72
Buckingham, Duke of, 127–30, 134–35, 142–43, 148–53, 158–60, 182, 207, 253
Burroughs, Jeremiah, 228
Butler, Captain, 242–43, 251
Butler, James, 214
Butler, Nathaniel, 124
Buzzards Bay, Massachusetts, 92
Byam, William, 284, 292–93

Cabot, John, 17–18, 40, 62
Cabot, Sebastian, 62
Calais, 64
Calvert, Anne, 159, 207
Calvert, Cecil, 29, 127, 158, 190, 194, 207
Calvert, George. *See* Baltimore, Baron
Calvert, Leonard, 190, 194–95, 218, 235, 254
Calvert family, 275
Calvin, John, 46–47, 78
Calvinism: and the Church of England, 13, 91, 111; debates over, 49–50, 52–56, 119, 273, 286–87; doctrine of, 67, 69, 72, 205, 239; influence of, 40, 43, 99, 104, 145, 227, 301; and King James, 74–76, 101–2, 117–18; opposition to, 52–53, 172, 207. *See also* anti-Calvinism
"Cambridge Platform," 246
Cambridge University, 52, 94, 110, 306
Campbell clan, 73
Campion, Edmund, 82–83
canon 72, 90
canons, 54, 90, 104

Canterbury, archbishopric and archbishops of, 21, 30, 43, *45*, 47, 50, 52, 55, 87, 103, 116, 143, 178
Cape Ann, 129, 163
Cape Breton, 27, 126, 154–55
Cape Cod, 131
Caribbee Islands, 145–46, 181, 257
Caribs. *See* Kalinago
Carisbrooke Castle, 252
Carliola, 257
Carlisle, Earl of, 145–48, 153, 181, 185, 256–57, 278. *See also* Hay, James
Carolana, 148, 190, 209–10, 213, 233, 241, 253, 298
Carolinism, 147. *See also* Laudianism
Carter, Edward C., 350n16
Cartwright, John, 122
Cartwright, Thomas, 86, 89
Cary, Henry, 28–29, 183
Castell, William, 212–13
Castle Island, 171
Catherina of Aragon, 296
Catholic Confederates, 235
Catholicism: in the colonies, 33–34, 63, 133–35, 148–50, 158–59, 180–81, 189–90, 197, 210, 254, 258–59, 282; and colonization, 20, 94, 105, 114, 156, 188, 207, 295; and conversion, 29, 182–83, 208; displays of, 79, 178; in England, 17–18, 285; hegemony of, 23; in Ireland, 151; and Laudianism, 57; and loyalty to the pope, 107; and the monarchy, 74, 78, 117, 180–81; opposition to, 42, 79–82, 87, 106, 112, 119, 145, 159, 300–302, 308; perceptions of, 40–41, 46, 51, 211, 214; and priest trainings, 80; and Protestantism, 8, 25, 40–43, 67–69, 106, 115–16, 143, 154, 157, 196, 214, 221, 274; and puritans, 85; restoration of, 48, 73, 80, 88, 184, 186, 330n10; scholarship on, 5–6; tolerance of, 136, 268, 299–300. *See also* anti-Catholicism; papacy; recusancy
Cavalier Parliament, 304
Cecil, Robert, 25–26, 54, 57, 102, 105–6, 127, 190
Cecil, William, 26, 50–54, 88, 102, 106
censorship, 224, 244
Channel Islands, 64, 89
Charles, Prince of Wales, 25, 118–20, 123, 135
Charles I (king): and the Civil War, 215, 225, 235–36, 248, 252; and the colonies, 150, 156, 158–59, 182–83, 186–87, 216, 223, 282; loyalty to, 112, 142, 148, 194; and the Personal Rule, 172–73, 180, 211–12; religious policies of, 135, 143–44, 151–54, 172–73, 201, 205–8, 307; trial and execution of, 242–44, 254, 270, 275. *See also* English Civil War; Personal Rule
Charles II (king), 265, 268–70, 297–301, 304, 307
Chesapeake, *121*
Cheshire lordship (England), 65
Child, Robert, 240
Chile, 142
Christianity. *See specific denominations*
Christmas, 72, 75, 129, 132, 272. *See also* holidays
church attendance, 43, 46–47, 67, 167, 248–49, 272, 276–77, 306
church buildings, 54–56, 166
Church of England: and anti-Catholicism, 247; and Calvinism, 111; and the colonies, 127, 129, 159, 195, 198; and the Congregationalists, 110; doctrine of, 12, 51, 54, 57, 72, 91, 227, 307; dominance of, 10, 38, 58, 133, 155, 161, 257; opposition to, 132, 167, 202, 241, 265; restoration of, 305. *See also* Reformation; Restoration
Church of Ireland, 144, 151–52, 305. *See also* Ireland
Church of Scotland, 53, 71–73, 76, 126–27, 206, 212, 305. *See also* Scotland
Church Papists, 78, 101

Claiborne, William, 189, 234
Clarendon, Earl of, 308
Clarendon Code, 308
Clarke, John, 267
Clarkson, Laurence, 271
classis movement, 86, 89, 110
Coddington, William, 203
Coffey, John, 355n13
Collins, William, 147
colonial charters, 107, 118, 122–27, 131–34, 148, 158–59, 173, 187, 202, 221–24, 298
colonies: and the English Civil War, 216–17, 243, 247, 265; perceptions of, 9; as punishment, 70, 251; religious climate of, 220, 232, 239; and trade, 18, 144, 279. *See also specific colonies*
colonization: Caroline pattern of, 160; contexts of, 141; enthusiasm for, 83, 96; goals of, 17–18, 21, 23, 29, 32, 93, 131, 182; processes of, 9, 189; religious motivations of, 17–23, 27, 38, 79, 88, 92–94, 105, 114, 120, 160–63, 203, 207, 295, 309
Colt, Sir Henry, 193
Columbus, Christopher, 27
Commissioners for Foreign Plantations, 235
Commission for Regulating Plantations, 172–73
Commission on Foreign Plantations, 254
Common Sense (Paine), 1
Commonwealth era, 278
Comoros islands, 238
Con, George, 207–8
Conant, Roger, 163
concordia, 7, 108, 250
Confederation of New England, 240
Confession of Faith, 246
conformity: and censorship, 145–46; and Church of England, 58; in colonies, 38–39, 83, 129, 148, 163, 176, 345n25; definitions of, 12, 51; displays of, 47, 59, 62, 99, 109, 141; effectiveness of, 39–40, 76, 100, 198; under King James VI, 54; and law, 39, 41, 46–47, 61, 90, 122; and loyalty, 78, 119, 148; as a norm, 116; opposition to, 52, 78, 164–65, 171; support for, 10, 46, 62, 95, 103–5, 112, 172, 259. *See also* diversity; pluralism; religion; tolerance; unity
Congregatio de Propaganda Fide, 151
Congregationalism: consolidation of, 202, 243, 246; doctrine of, 166, 225; formation of, 12, 108–10, 162, 164, 337n28; and Independents, 267; opposition to, 165, 232, 244; and Presbyterians, 286, 321–22; spread of, 166–67, 178, 205, 220–22, 227, 231, 239–40, 251, 261, 266, 282, 293, 301
Connecticut, 149, 156, 169, 222, 227, 266
conscience, 46, 286, 330n10
Constantine, Emperor, 41
Convention Parliament, 301
conversion: to Catholicism, 82, 159, 182–83, 195, 208; by coercion, 20, 31–32, 39, 74–75, 250; of non-Christians, 17–18, 26, 31, 35, 111; by persuasion, 54–55, 65, 280. *See also* religion
Copland, Patrick, 174, 231, 251
Copley, Margaret, 294
Corporation Act of 1661, 308
Cosmographia (Münster), 21
Cotton, John, 52, 110, 161, 170, 231
Council for New England, 106, 127, 129–31, 156, 173, 207, 209
Council of State, 279, 297
Counter-Reformation Catholicism, 184
Courteen, Sir William, 208
Courteen, William, Jr., 237
Courteen Association, 237
Court of High Commission, 43, 177, 212
Court of Star Chamber, 70–71, 212

Covenanters, 207
Crab Island (Vieques), 259
Cradock, Matthew, 164–65, 168
Cranmer, Thomas, 47–48
Crèvecoeur, J. Hector St. John de, 311
Croft, Pauline, 57
Cromwell, Henry, 274, 287
Cromwell, Oliver, 176, 223, 227, 234–35, 239, 246–48, 253, 259–60, 270–74, 279–82, 285–87, 290–303. *See also* English Civil War
Cromwell, Richard, 301
Crosby, Sir Pierce, 181–82
Crown of Ireland Act of 1542, 68
Curtyn, Anne, 296–97
Cushman, Robert, 133

Dare, Virginia, 22–23
Davenant, William, 208
Davenport, John, 163, 169, 289
Decades of the newe worlde or West India (Eden), 21
Declaration of Faith, 301
Dee, John, 83–84, 134
Dee River colony, 84
Defense of the seven sacraments (King Henry VIII), 41
Devereux, Robert, 102. *See also* Essex, Earl of
Devonshire, Earl of, 105
Directory for Public Worship, 225, 232, 253, 266. See also *Book of Common Prayer*
Discovery of Witches, The (Hopkins), 245
dissent, 10, 41, 79, 108, 162, 271, 306
Dissenters, 4, 13, 308
Dissenting Brethren, 228, 248
dissidents, 203, 205, 358–59n31
diversity, 5, 8, 13, 23, 223, 273. *See also* conformity; pluralism; religion; tolerance; unity
Divers Voyages touching the Discovery of America (Hakluyt), 23
Doctrine of Passive Obedience, 308
Donne, John, 29
Dorchester Company, 129, 163
Doughty, Francis, 306
Dover, New Hampshire, 204
Downing, Emmanuel, Sr., 32, 36
Dublin, 214
Dudley, Robert, 84. *See also* Leicester, Earl of
Dunkirk, 285, 293, 298–300, 302
Durham, 55, 65, 211
Durham House, 55
Dury, John, 239
Dutch Anabaptists, 90
Dutch Reformed Church, 204
Dutch Republic, 86, 279
Dutch Revolt, 194
Dyck, Anthony van, 208–9

East Anglia, 91, 245
East India Company, 21–22, 61, 93, 106, 123, 134, 208, 210, 220, 229, 238
Eaton, Theophilus, 60
Eden, Richard, 21, 25–26
Edgehill, Battle of, 216
Edict of Nantes, 68
Edwardian Reformation, 47–48
Edwards, Thomas, 229–30
Edward VI (King), 42, 47–48, 62, 78
El Dorado, 23–25
Eleutheria, 242–43, 249–51, 275, 310, 312
Eliot, John, 31
Elizabethan policies, 13, 49, 84, 95, 105, 116
Elizabeth I (queen): advisors to, 57, 83, 100, 190; and colonization, 38, 78–79; empire under, 21–22, 151; excommunication of, 80, 107; religious attitudes of, 49–50, 52–53, 72, 85, 305, 331n17
Encouragements (Gordon), 27–28
encouragement to colonies, An (Alexander), 27, 126
Endecott, John, 164–65, 171
Engagers, 270
English American, The (Gage), 294
English Civil War, 206–9, 213–16, 221–

25, 233–36, 240–43, 246, 252–53, 260, 265, 270, 278, 294, 304. *See also* Cromwell, Oliver; English revolution; Parliament
English College, 80
English Empire, 4–6, 8–10, 21–24, 36, 44, 69, 99, 211, 226, 269, 285, 302, 310. *See also* British Empire
English Protestant Seekers, 203
English Revolution, 11, 260. *See also* English Civil War
English world, 4–7
episcopalianism, 43, 237. *See also* Laudianism
Erasmus of Rotterdam, 20–21, 65, 88
Erastian system, 228, 282
Essex, Earl of, 102–5, 127. *See also* Devereux, Robert
Everard, Clement, 258–59
excommunication, 79–80, 105, 107. *See also* papacy
executions, 41–42, 48–49, 83, 91, 119, 330n10
exorcisms, 90

Fairfax, Sir Thomas, 248, 253
Falkland, Viscount, 150, 183, 344–45n19
familism, 201
Family of Love, 91. *See also* Niclaes, Hendrik
Fawkes, Guy, 106. *See also* Gunpowder Plot
Featley, Daniel, 145–46
Featley, John, 141, 145–47, 224, 258, 304
Fell, Henry, 284–85, 291–93
feoffees of impropriations, 163
Ferrar, John, 58
Ferrar, Nicholas, 58, 124
Ferrar, William, 58, 176–77
Ferryland, 134, 156–58, 177–78
Fifth Monarchists, 305
Fleetwood, Charles, 274
Fonseca, 148
Forbes, Andrew, 299
"Forme of Polisie to Plante and Governe Many Families in Virginea" (Bargrave), 123
Fort Saint George, 210
Forty-Two Articles of Faith, 48
Foxe, Richard, 41
France, 47, 259
Frederick V (Elector of the Palatinate), 118, 208
French Wars of Religion, 68–69
Frith, John, 337n36
Frobisher, Martin, 22, 24, 63
Fuller, Samuel, 164

Gage, Sir Henry, 294
Gage, Thomas, 294–95
Gauden, John, 287, 292
Gayner, William, 186
gender, 32–33, 58, 288
General Assembly of the national church, 72–74
General Council of the Army, 248
General Venables, 295
Gerard, Sir Thomas, 83
Gerbier, Balthazar, 253
Gibbons, Edward, 218
Gilbert, Adrian, 84
Gilbert, Sir Humphrey, 38–39, 83–84, 93–94, 102, 134
Glasgow University, 69
Glastonbury, 134–35
Goa, 238
Golding, William, 231, 240
Goodwin, Thomas, 228
Gookin, Daniel, 168
Gookin, Sir Vincent, 70, 183–84
Gordon, John, 205
Gordon, Sir Robert, 27–28, 126, 148
Gorges, Sir Ferdinando, 106, 127, 131, 173
Gorges, Sir Robert, 129–30
Gorges, Thomas, 33, 205
Gorton, Samuel, 203, 219. *See also* Gortonists
Gortonists, 219, 224, 283. *See also* Gorton, Samuel
Gosnold, Bartholomew, 92

Goulding, William, 232
Graces, the, 151–52, 183–85, 213
"Grand Remonstrance" (Pym), 215
Greek Orthodoxy, 57, 122
Greenwood, John, 92
Grey, Lady Jane, 48
Grindal, Edmund, 85, 87
Guadeloupe, 259
Guernsey, 65
Guiana, 24, 112, 117–18, 130, 145, 148, 185–86, 207
Guiana Company, 207
Guinea, 25–26, 63
Gunpowder Plot, 106–8, 111, 114, 159, 339n15. *See also* Fawkes, Guy
Gustavus Adolphus, 182

Hackett, Richard, 214–15
Hakluyt, Richard, 23, 46, 61
Hakluytus Posthumus (Purchas), 23
Hampton Court, 54, 104
Hapsburg Empire, 208
Harcourt, Robert, 24–26
Harington, Sir John, 100
Hartlib, Samuel, 239
Hartlib circle, 239
Harvey, Sir John, 176–77, 194
Hatfield Chase, 286
Hatfield House, 58
Hawkins, William, 20
Hay, James, 148. *See also* Carlisle, Earl of
Haydon, John, 177
Hayes, Edward, 23
Hayman, Robert, 26, 111–12, 150
Heads of the Proposals, 248
Heath, Sir Robert, 148, 153–54, 209–10
Helwys, Thomas, 109
Henderson, Alexander, 212
Henrician church, 47, 49
Henrician Reformation, 20, 40–43
Henrico, 123
Henry Frederick, Prince of Wales, 106, 117
Henry II (king), 82
Henry IV (king), 114
Henry VII (king), 17, 19, 296
Henry VIII (king), 21, 41–42, 47, 134
Herbert, Philip, 148. *See also* Montgomery, Earl of
Herbert, William, 148. *See also* Pembroke, Earl of
heresy, 41, 46, 48, 91, 119, 244, 252
High Commission Court, 43, 177, 212, 305
Hilton, Anthony, 185
Hispanophobia, 40, 89, 141–42
historiography, 2–3, 5–6, 9, 17, 181, 310
holidays, 72, 75, 132, 163–64, 177, 306. *See also* Christmas
Holland, 91–92, 105, 108–9, 167, 173, 178
Holy Fairs, 205
Holy Roman Empire, 47, 82, 93–94, 152, 208, 310
Honduras, 175
Hooker, Richard, 52
Hooker, Thomas, 169
Hopkins, Matthew, 245
horizontal tolerance, 7, 108
Howard, Henry Frederick, 209
Howard, Thomas, 26, 207, *209*. *See also* Berkshire, Earl of
Hughes, Lewis, 113, 124, 174
Huguenots, 27, 78, 154, 210, 239, 253, 298, 308. *See also* Nicodemites
Hunt, Robert, 46, 50, 61, 110–11
Huntly, Earl of, 126
Hutchinson, Anne, 147, 202–4, 220

Iberian Catholics, 297
Independents, 223, 226–27, 239, 242–43, 252, 266, 302
India, 4, 267
Indigenous people: cooperation with, 24–26, 94, 142, 171, 186, 237; fears of, 144–45, 161, 176; religious beliefs of, 8, 31–35, 244, 302; resistance by, 36; as targets of conversion, 22–23, 111, 135, 167, 187, 196, 208, 296–97. *See also specific groups*
Ingle, Richard, 234
Instrument of Government, 280

Insula Caroli, 148
Interregnum, 307
Ireland, 11, 24–25, 67–68, 91–92, 95, 103, 151, 182–83, 186, 214–15, 268. *See also* Church of Ireland
Ireton, Henry, 248, 268, 274
Irish Catholic Confederate army, 246
Irish colonists, 24–26, 74, 82, 87–88, 93, 111, 115, 187, 196, 234, 258–59
Irish uprising of October 1641, 213–14
Islam, 30, 122
Isle of Man, 66
Isle of Wight, 120

Jacob, Henry, 109, 121, 166, 279
Jacobs, Henry, 167
Jamaica, 285, 293, 295, 301–2
James I (king): accession of, 30, 92–93; colonial policies of, 26, 70–71, 107, 126, 132–33, 136, 144–47, 339n15; loyalty to, 69, 115, 187; religious policies of, 30, 54, 57, 73–76, 90, 99, 101–8, 113–20, 205, 331n24
Jamestown, Virginia, 10, 46, 63, 118, 218
Jermyn, Henry, 208
Jersey, 64–65
Jesuits, 12, 31, 74, 82, 87–88, 93, 111, 115, 187, 196, 234, 258–59
Jews, 256, 272, 296–98. *See also* Judaism
Johnson, Francis, 110, 120
Judaism, 41, 122, 272, 285, 290, 293, 296–98, 302–3, 364n29–364n30. *See also* anti-Semitism; Jews
jurisdiction, 10, 43, 46, 61, 203

Kalinago, 24, 145, 176, 185, 216
Kaynell, Christopher, 176, 260
Keith, George, 113
Kildare, 67
Kilkenny, 214
King James Bible, 54. *See also* Scripture
Kirbie, Thomas, 272
Kirk. *See* Church of Scotland
Kirke, Sir David, 154, 156, 177, 275
Kirk Party, 270
Knolles, Richard, 122
Knox, John, 155
Kupperman, Karen, 169

Lake, Peter, 12
Lambe, John, 152–53
Lambeth Articles, 52–53, 110
L'Amy, Hugh, 154
Lancashire, 65
Lane, Ralph, 89
La Rochelle, France, 152–53
Laud, William, 55–56, 119–20, 142–47, 161–63, 170–73, 178, 184–85, 201, 212, 228–30, 236–37, 250. *See also* Laudianism
Laudianism: doctrine of, 55–56, 141–46, 176–78, 203, 250, 331–32n28; opposition to, 168, 198, 211, 236, 286, 307; spread of, 58–59, 160–63, 184–85, 218, 258. *See also* Carolinism; Laud, William
Leeward Islands, 144, 175, 178, 181, 185, 193, 256–57, 260, 275
Leicester, Earl of, 84. *See also* Dudley, Robert
Leiden Separatists, 130–36, 166. *See also* Mayflower Compact; Pilgrims
Leigh, Charles, 24–25
Leigh, Sir Oliph, 24
Lennox, Duke of, 127
Levant Company, 21–22, 122
Levellers, 251
Leverton, Nicholas, 175, 216–17, 293
Levett, Christopher, 129
Lewis, Clifford, 350n16
Lewis, William, 196
Ley, John, 24, 257
liberty, 202–4, 220–21, 229–30, 251, 254, 261, 272, 286
Limerick, Ireland, 69
Lincolnshire, England, 108, 286
Little Gidding, England, 58

liturgy, 47–48, 75, 81, 85, 172. See also *adiaphora*
Lockhart, Sir William, 299–300
Lollards, 40–41
London, 44–45, 81, 91, 108, 216, 272
Long Island, 156, 188
Long Parliament, 224–25, 230, 252, 271. *See also* Rump Parliament; Short Parliament
lords of the congregation, 71
Louis XIII (king), 143, 152–53, 190
Louis XIV (king), 299
Low Countries, 84, 90, 94–95, 300
loyalty, 50, 69, 80, 99, 108, 113–15, 142, 148, 158, 181, 194, 221, 257, 304
Luddington, Thomas, 326n11
Luther, Martin, 41, 46, 51
Lutheranism, 41, 47
Lyford, John, 132, 163, 177

MacDonnell, Randal, 69. *See also* Antrim, Earl of
MacDonnell clan, 69
Madagascar, 207–8, 221, 237–38, 241, 350n14, 357n36
Madagascar Portrait of Thomas Howard and his wife Aletheia Talbot (Van Dyck), *209*
Madoc (prince), 25
Madras, India, 210, 220, 302
Magdalen Islands, 92, 108
Maine, 22, 94, 107–8, 129–30, 156, 180, 205, 266
Maltravers, Lord, 209–10
Manhattan island, 187
Manteo, 22–23
Maria, Henrietta, 21, 48–49, 62, 67–68, 71, 79, 83, 143, 152, 207–9, 267
marriage, 50, 117
Marston Moor, 233, 235
Martin Marprelate tracts, 89
Mary, Queen. *See* Maria, Henrietta
Maryland: and Baptists, 3, 267; and Catholicism, 29–31, 142, 180–81, 197, 269–70, 282; colonial charter for, 158–60, 210, 235; and England, 148, 195, 198, 254, 275, 312; religious climate of, 36, 189–91, 193, 220–21, 234, 289, 310, 268–312. *See also* Act concerning Religion of 1649; Catholicism
Maryland Act of Toleration, 268
Maryland loyalty oath, 207
Mason, John, 125–26, 129–30
Massachusett (Indigenous nation), 31–32
Massachusetts: and England, 172, 234; formation of, 18, 129–31; and other colonies, 201–3, 219–23, 260–61; religious climate of, 31, 165–69, 204, 227, 231, 239–41, 243–46, 266–67, 288–89, 301
Massachusetts Bay Company, 149, 163–66, 173
Massachusetts General Court, 240, 245–46
Mather, Cotton, 161–62
Mather, Richard, 161
Matthew, Toby, 187
Maverick, Samuel, 129, 240
May Day 1627, 163–64
Mayflower Compact, 131. *See also* Leiden Separatists; Pilgrims
Mayne, Cuthbert, 81–82
McClain, Lisa, 157
McDonald clan, 69, 73
Mediterranean Sea, 123
Melville, Andrew, 74
Merchant Adventurers, 89, 109, 132–33
Merrymount, 163
Middlesex sessions, 272
Militia Ordinance, 216
millenary petition, 54, 109
Milton, John, 230
moderate rhetoric, 99–100
Moghul Empire, 229
Montgomery, Earl of, 148, 216. *See also* Herbert, Philip
Montserrat, 181, 185, 198, 257, 259
Moore, Richard, 113
Moors, 30, 32
More, Sir Thomas, 20–21, 27, 42, 65, 88

Morrell, William, 129
Morton, Thomas, 163–64, 173
Mount Dagon, 164. *See also* Mount Wollaston
Mountjoy, Baron Charles Blount, 68–69, 105
Mount Wollaston, 164. *See also* Mount Dagon
Mughal Empire, 125
Mughals, 118
Munster, 67–68, 70, 184, 213, 274
Münster, Sebastien, 21, 68, 70
Muscovy Company, 62
Muslims, 30, 122

Nansemond, 120
Narragansett Bay, 83, 202
Narragansetts, 31–32, 202, 219
Narration (Goodwin et al.), 355n14
Natick, Massachusetts, 31
Naumkeag. *See* Salem
Naunton, Sir Robert, 130, 133
Navigation Act of 1651, 279
Nayler, James, 280, 286
Negative Confession, 72–74
Neile, Richard, 54–55, 57, 59, 172
Nevis, 144, 175, 185, 257, 260, 267, 298
New Albion, 187–89, 197, 310, 312, 350n16
New England: colonization of, 22, 93, 129–31, 161, 167; and England, 147, 164, 170, 181, 206; and presbyterianism, 240; and puritanism, 13, 17, 127, 178; and Quakerism, 288; religious climate of, 13, 130, 171–73, 201–4, 276, 285, 306, 311–12. *See also* North Virginia
New England Company, 163–64, 205
New England Way, 227, 231, 241, 266
Newfoundland, 18, 28–29, 31, 38, 60, 84, 92, 111–12, 116, 125–26, 134, 177–78; colonization of, 28–29, 31, 38, 60; and England, 256; religious climate of, 18, 111–12, 116, 177–78, 275, 344–45n19; resources in, 92, 134
Newfoundland Company, 22, 107–8
New Galloway, 27, 126–27, 148, 205
New Hampshire, 129–30, 204, 219, 266
New Haven, 60, 169, 180, 222, 227, 266, 285
New Jersey, 131
New Model Army, 235, 242–43, 246–48, 251, 268, 270, 273
New Netherland, 131, 204, 220, 280, 288–89
New Plymouth, 130, 132–33, 173, 222, 289. *See also* Plymouth, colony of
Newport News, 70
New Scotland, *128*
News from Spayne (Scott), 125
New Sweden, 188
Niclaes, Hendrik, 91. *See also* Family of Love
Nicodemites, 78. *See also* Huguenots
Nine Years' War, 68, 93, 95, 184
"No Bishop, No King," 73–74, 144
Nominated Parliament, 279–80
North African Muslims, 33
Northern Rebellion, 79
Northern Rising of 1569, 65
Northumberland, 211
North Virginia, 107–8, 127. *See also* New England
Northwest Passage, 22, 84, 93
Norton, Humphrey, 289
Nova Scotia, 27, 126, 142, 154–56, 160, 168, 182, 281, 302
Nye, Philip, 228

oaths, 114, 124, 134–35, 162, 193, 207, 249, 267, 299, 308
Obedience and Submission (Featley), 146–47
Ochiltree, Lord, 155
October 1645 Act "for the establishment of freedom of worship," 232
Of the Lawes of Ecclesiastical Politie (Hooker), 52
Ogilvie, John, 75
"On the New Forcers of Conscience under the Long Parliament" (Milton), 230

Ordinance of 1639, 195
Ormond, Duke of, 214
Osborne, Roger, 185, 259–60
Ottoman Empire, 21–22, 93, 118, 122–23, 125, 171
Oxenbridge, John, 231, 293
Oxford College of Corpus Christi, 41
Oxford University, 52, 55, 80, 109, 133, 142, 146, 172, 306

Pacification of Berwick, 207
Paine, Thomas, 1, 4
Palatinate, 208
Pale, 68
papacy, 47–48, 57, 66, 79–81, 105, 107, 114. *See also* Catholicism; excommunication
Parker, Matthew, 50, 85
Parliament, 161, 180, 187, 211, 215, 223, 232, 275. *See also* English Civil War
Parliamentarians, 101, 222, 234
Parsons, Robert, 82, 93–95
patriotism, 89, 106, 135, 148, 182
Pawtuxet, 219
Peckham, Sir George, 83–84
Pembroke, Earl of, 148, 216. *See also* Herbert, William
Penn, William, 275, 294
Penobscot River, 129
Penry, John, 89
Pequots, 32
Personal Rule, 160, 162–63, 180–81, 183, 197, 201, 205, 211–13. *See also* Charles I (king)
Pestana, Carla, 3
Peter, Hugh, 167
Peters, Hugh, 237, 247
Petition of Right, 160
Philip II (king), 21
Philip IV (king), 186
Philo-Semitism, 296
Pilgrimage of Grace of 1536, 49, 65
Pilgrims, 131, 136. *See also* Leiden Separatists; Mayflower Compact
Piscataways, 31
Plowden, Sir Edmund, 187–88
Plowden Island, 188
Plumbers' Hall, 85
plundering time, 234
pluralism: debates over, 8, 78; and diversity, 13; emergence of, 6, 36, 62, 82, 116, 118, 136, 198, 221, 241, 285, 309–12; opposition to, 20, 27, 253; utility of, 2–3, 8, 27, 32, 76, 202. *See also* conformity; diversity; religion; tolerance; unity
Plymouth, colony of, 31, 70, 105, 108, 127, 132–33, 151, 164, 166, 177–78, 201, 233, 246, 266. *See also* New Plymouth
Plymouth Company, 106, 127
Plymouth General Court, 246
Plymouth-Massachusetts model, 347n16
Pocahontas, 110
Pole, Reginald, 21
Poole, William, 158
Pope Gregory I, 30
popery, 87, 143, 160, 205–6, 226, 280. *See also* anti-Popery
Popham, George, 107–8
Popham, Sir John, 107–8
Popham's Colony, 107–8
Porter, Endymion, 208
Porter, Olive, 208
Port Royal, 155, 281
Portsmouth, 204
Portugal, 26
poverty, 66, 70
Powell, Hunter, 355n14
Powhatan country, 136
Powhatan Uprising of 1622, 36, 123
Powhatan War, 31, 70, 124
Prayer Book, the. See *Book of Common Prayer*
Prayer Book Rebellion of 1559, 49
predestination, 161
Presbyterianism: in the colonies, 89, 165, 204–5, 249, 302, 306; and Congregationalists, 167, 232, 286; and the monarchy, 74, 248; and

Scotland, 69, 102, 206, 212, 220; spread of, 12, 86, 214, 226, 236, 246, 270, 282, 321
Price, John, 259
Price, Rupert, 208
Pride, Thomas, 253
Pride's Purge, 253
private religion, 91, 157
Privy Council, 54, 71, 130, 133, 135, 158, 172–74, 190, 197, 342n23
Proprietary party, 289
Protectorate Parliament, 287
Protestantism: and Catholicism, 8, 25, 40, 42–43, 67, 69, 106, 115–16, 143, 154, 157, 196, 214, 221, 274; in the colonies, 18, 21, 23, 35, 38–40, 60, 95, 108, 121, 142, 168, 190, 300; dominance of, 2, 42, 53–54; opposition to, 42, 48–49, 78–79, 308; priorities of, 203–4. *See also* Reformed Protestantism
Protestant revolt of 1644, 31
Providence Island, 32–33, 163, 169, 175, 293
Providence Island Company, 150, 175
Providence Plantations, 203
Prynne, William, 232
public acts of religions, 43
Purcell, Philip, 24–25
Purchas, Samuel, 23
puritanism: and Catholicism, 85; and the Church of England, 12, 52–54, 100, 113; in the colonies, 12–13, 17, 88–89, 110, 120, 125–26, 130, 147–50, 162–63, 169, 176–78, 260, 267, 295; emergence of, 85–86, 321, 337n28; and the English Civil War, 206; and migration, 141, 160, 162, 180, 197, 204; and the monarchy, 101, 160, 201, 212; opposition to, 55, 112, 143, 175, 304; and pluralism, 78; and Separatists, 167; sympathy for, 87, 145, 148, 175. *See also* antipuritanism
Pym, John, 117, 175, 211, 215, 223
Quakerism, 12, 65, 273, 280, 283–86, 288–92, 302, 306, 308
Quebec, 154, 156
Quinn, David Beers, 326n11

Ralegh, Sir Walter, 22–27, 102, 207. *See also* Roanoke
Raleigh, Sir Walter. *See* Ralegh, Sir Walter
Ranters, 272, 291
recusancy, 81, 143, 244, 304. *See also* Catholicism
Reformation, 20, 40–41, 43, 61, 65, 71, 79, 144
Reformed Protestantism, 13, 43, 47, 49, 102, 204, 225, 257, 282, 285, 287. *See also* Protestantism
Regnans in excelsis, 79–80, 107
Relation of the State of Religion (Sandys), 122
Relation of the successful beginnings, A (White), 192
religion: ambiguity of, 49–50, 103; and authority, 12, 39, 43, 60, 83, 90, 110, 113, 127, 165, 171, 201–5; displays of, 43, 205–6; and emigration, 29; and holidays, 72, 75, 132, 163–64, 177, 306; and jurisdiction, 10, 43, 46, 61, 203; and the law, 8, 271; as a marker of difference, 37, 191; and slavery, 35–36; and the state, 41, 77, 146, 203, 228, 271; symbols of, 17, 50, 54, 63, 171, 174, 178, 215 (see also *adiaphora*). *See also* conformity; conversion; diversity; pluralism; tolerance; unity
religious executions, 41–42, 48–49, 83, 91, 119, 330n10
religious liberty, 202–4, 220–21, 229–30, 251, 254, 261, 272, 286
Remonstrance of the Army of 1648, 253
Renaissance English religious history, 10
Renaissance humanist thought, 17
republicanism, 17

Resolutioners, 273
Restoration, 236, 287, 297, 301, 304
Restoration Church, 237
revolutionary Parliament, 252–53
Rhode Island, 32, 77, 83, 201–3, 219–24, 227, 240–41, 254, 267, 285, 290, 301, 310–12
Rich, Robert, 149, 223. *See also* Warwick, Earl of
Ridolfi Plot of 1571, 80
Ridouet, Antoine de, 154
Roanoke, 22–23, 89, 92. *See also* Raleigh, Sir Walter
Robins, John, 272
Robinson, John, 109, 132–33
Roborough, Henry, 110
Roe, Sir Thomas, 25, 117, 186
Roman Catholic Church, 17
Root and Branch Petition, 212
Rosier, James, 94
Royalist Parliament at Oxford, 216
Royalists, 226, 243, 247, 260, 265, 268
Rudolf II (emperor), 94
Rump Parliament, 253, 271–72, 279, 282, 301. *See also* Long Parliament
Russell, Sir Francis, 287
Rutherford, Samuel, 205

Sabbatarianism, 271
Sagadahoc colony, 107–8
Saint Albans declaration, 248
Saint Andrews, 30, 71
Saint Christopher, 141–42, 147, 153, 175, 185, 193–94, 214, 224, 241, 257–59, 277, 304, 358–59n31
Saint Croix, 175
Saint David, 30, 142
Saint Helena, 207–8
Saint John's College, 55
Saint Kitts. *See* Saint Christopher
Saint Lawrence River, 92
Saint Lucia, 24
Saint Mary, 195
Saint Patrick, 30
Saint Paul's Cross, 40–41, 229
Saint-Thomé, 210
Salem, 163–66, 202
Salisbury Cathedral, 278–79
Salman, Joseph, 291
Saltonstall, Charles, 147
Sandys, George, 123
Sandys, Sir Edwin, 117, 122–23, 130–31, 136
Santa Cruz, 175, 257
Santo Domingo, 214, 293–94
Savoy Assembly, 225
Savoy Conference, 305
Saybrook colony, 169
Saybrook Company, 148–49
Saye, Viscount, 148–49, 169, 223, 281
Sayle, William, 231, 240, 249, 251
schismatics, 91
Schnepper, Rachel, 233
Scilly Isles, 286
Scotland: colonists from, 126; and England, 211, 225, 270; and heresy executions, 42; Highlands of, 69, 73; Lowlands of, 71; Presbyterianism in, 86. *See also* Church of Scotland
Scott, Thomas, 125
Scottish National Covenant, 206
Scottish Privy Council, 206
Scripture, 53–54, 90, 228. *See also* Bible; King James Bible
Searle, Daniel, 290–93
Sedgwick, Robert, 280, 295
Sele, Viscount, 169, 223
Separatism, 77, 91–92, 105, 108–10, 120, 131–33, 145, 164–67, 337n28. *See also* Barrowists; Brownists
sermons, 50, 55, 72, 81, 146, 196, 229, 287
Shagan, Ethan, 355n14
Shawomet, 203, 219, 224
Sheehan, Jaspar, 186
Sherrard, Hope, 175
Short Parliament, 211. *See also* Long Parliament
Simpson, Sidrach, 228
Six Bookes of a Commonweale (Bodin, trans. Knolles), 122

Skippon, Philip, 260
slavery, 32–36, 63, 144–45, 175–76
Smith, Henry, 196
Smith, John, 50, 144–45, 171
Smith, Ralph, 166
Smyth, John, 109
Society for the Propagation of the Gospel in New England, 31
Society of Friends. *See* Quakerism
Solemn League and Covenant, 225–27, 249, 270, 308
Somers, Sir George, 112
Somers Isles. *See* Bermuda
Somers Isles Company, 106, 112, 124, 149, 175, 239–40
Southampton, Earl of, 106, 122–23. *See also* Wriothesley, Henry
South Carolina, 34
South Falkland, 28–29
Southwell, Robert, 294
Spain, 21, 23, 26, 92–93, 133, 141–42
Spanish Armada, 88
Spanish Match, 118, 125, 133–36, 158, 187, 207
Spanish Netherlands, 80, 88, 94, 209
Standish, Miles, 164
Star Chamber Court, 70–71, 212
Steward, Sir James, 155
Stiles, Ezra, 1–2
Stirk, George, 174
Stirling, Earl of, 156. *See also* Alexander, Sir William
Stock, Simon, 151
Stokes, Luke, 175, 295
Stone, William, 254, 268
Stourton, Erasmus, 150, 157–58, 346n36
Strachey, William, 30
Strafford, Earl of, 211. *See also* Wentworth, Sir Thomas
Strawberry Bank, 204
Stuart dynasty, 40, 53, 159–60, 205
Stuert, Adam, 229
Suffolk, Earl of, 26
Supremacy Act. *See* Act of Supremacy
Surat, 238
Surinam, 34, 278, 284–85, 292, 298
surplice, 49, 111
Sutherland, Earl of, 126
Switzerland, 43, 47, 86
symbols, 17, 50, 54, 63, 171, 174, 178, 215. See also *adiaphora*
Synod of Dort (1618–19), 119
Syon, 187

Talbot, Aletheia, 207, 208, *209*
Talbot, Sir Robert, 150
Taylor, Jeremy, 250
Temple, Sir Thomas, 281
Terry, Edward, 229
Thirty-Nine Articles, 49, 67, 227, 307–8
Thirty Years' War, 116, 118, 126, 206–7
Thompson, Maurice, 145, 147
Thomson, David, 129–30
Throckmorton Plot, 80, 84
tobacco, 24–25, 29, 144, 175–76, 185
Tobago, 148
tolerance: debate over, 68, 117, 221, 224, 233, 249, 354n1, 355n13; experiments in, 282; horizontal or ecclesiastical, 108; informal forms of, 120–21, 191; in Ireland, 151; in Madagascar, 238; in Maryland, 289; of non-Christians, 36; official forms of, 83, 105, 116, 122, 136, 143, 150, 181, 186, 189, 218, 268, 297; opposition to, 106, 183, 228–31, 309; support for, 77, 82, 88, 95, 101–3, 109, 221–22, 224; utility of, 1, 32, 62, 122, 243. *See also* conformity; diversity; pluralism; religion; unity
Tortuga, 175–76
Tower of London, 25
trade, 18, 22, 24, 70
treason, 41, 78, 81–82
Treaty of Breda, 282
Treaty of Ripon, 211
Treaty of Saint-Germain-en-Laye, 156
Treaty of Susa, 156
Treatyse of the Newe India (Eden), 21
Trinidad, 148
Trinity College, 67, 168

True Law of Free Monarchies (King James), 74
Tuchin, Samuel, 70
Tucker, Daniel, 114
Tudor dynasty, 40, 47, 76–77, 95, 99–100
Tudor Reformation, 79
Tunstall, Cuthbert, 65
Turner, Thomas, 239–40, 249
Tuscany, Grand Duke of, 288
Twelve Articles of Faith, 67
Tyrone, Earl of, 69

Ulster, 68–70, 83, 95, 126, 184, 214
Uniformity Act. *See* Act of Uniformity
United Colonies of New England, 222
United States of America, 1–6, 9, 310. *See also* America
unity, 6–11, 20, 27, 40, 88, 171, 201, 238–39, 302, 309. *See also* conformity; diversity; pluralism; religion; tolerance
University of Douai, 80
Upper Norfolk, 120
Usher, Mary, 272
Ussher, James, 67, 287
Utopia (More), 20–21
Utopus, 32

Vane, Sir Henry, 227
Vassall, Samuel, 210, 233
Vassall, William, 233
Vaughan, Sir William, 112
Venables, Robert, 294
Vieques, 259
Villiers, Christopher, 158
Villiers, George, 130
Virginia: colonization of, 54, 103; and the English Civil War, 256, 268, 275; Irish in, 70, 95; land policies in, 118; and Laudianism, 176–79, 198; and other colonies, 194–96, 234; population of, 180; and puritans, 110, 177; religious climate of, 23, 39, 46, 99, 110–11, 116, 121–23, 130–31, 197, 241, 301, 305–6; as a royal colony, 124, 133, 181, 221, 276; survival of, 120; and tobacco, 24, 29, 185
Virginia Act of Uniformity, 177
Virginia Company, 23, 25, 30, 58, 61, 96, 106–7, 117, 120, 122–24, 130, 134–36, 188, 190
Virginia General Assembly, 39, 177, 218, 306
Virginia 1660 act regulating servitude, 35
Virgin Mary, 159
Virgo Triumphans, 276
Vox populi (Scott), 125

Wales, 25, 66
Walsingham, Sir Francis, 83
Walwyn, William, 230
Wampanoag, 131
Ward, Harry, 223
Ward, Nathaniel, 221
Wardour, Baron of, 159. *See also* Arundell, Sir Thomas
Warner, Sir Thomas, 153, 258
Warner, Thomas, 144–45, 147, 193, 259
Wars of the Three Kingdoms. *See* English Civil War
Warwick, Earl of, 26, 131, 149–50, 174–75, 216–17, 223, 232, 235, 240, 254, 256. *See also* Rich, Robert
Wentworth, Sir Thomas, 158, 172–73, 184, 187, 211–13. *See also* Strafford, Earl of
Wessagusset, 129
West Africa, 63
West Country, 235
Western Design, 293, 295, 298
West India Company, 142, 149, 209
West Indies, 182
Westminster Assembly, 224, 226–27, 236, 246, 248, 252, 280
Westminster Confession of Faith, 225
Weston, Thomas, 129
Wexford, 70
Weymouth, George, 93–94, 106, 122
Wheelwright, John, 202–5, 219

Whistler, Henry, 256
Whitaker, Alexander, 110–11, 123
Whitaker, Jabez, 111
Whitaker, William, 52, 55, 110. See also *adiaphora*
White, Andrew, 191–93, 195
White, John, 163
White, Nathaniel, 231–32
Whitgift, John, 52–53, 87, 89, 103
Wiapoco River, 24
Wightman, Edward, 203
Willet, Andrew, 104
Willet, Thomas, 104–5
Williams, Roger, 31–32, 58, 77, 171, 202–3, 219, 221–23, 229, 231, 267, 282–83, 312, 337n36
Willoughby, Francis Lord, 278, 292–93
Winship, Michael, 347n16
Winslade, Tristram, 93–94, 106
Winslow, Edward, 31, 173, 233, 240, 249, 295, 342n23
Winthrop, Henry, 35
Winthrop, John, 32, 52, 110, 149, 166, 168, 170–71, 176, 181, 218, 242, 245, 260
Winthrop, John, Jr., 168
Winthrop, Samuel, 176, 260, 288
witchcraft, 75, 90, 245–46
Wolfall, Robert, 22
Wood, Roger, 174
Wren, Matthew, 236–37
Wriothesley, Henry, 106, 122–23. *See also* Southampton, Earl of
writ of *quo warranto*, 173
Wyatt, Sir Francis, 39, 123, 197
Wycliffe, John, 40–41
Wyndham, Thomas, 62

York: archbishopric and archbishops of, 43, *45*, 54, 172; and colonization, 129; and imprisoned Catholics, 78; siege of, 233
York, Duke of, 299
Yorkshire, 106, 133, 158

Zouche, Sir John, 94
Zwingli, Ulrich, 46–47

ALSO IN THE SERIES:

Liberty Power: Antislavery Third Parties and the Transformation of American Politics
BY COREY M. BROOKS

The Making of Tocqueville's America: Law and Association in the Early United States
BY KEVIN BUTTERFIELD

Planters, Merchants, and Slaves: Plantation Societies in British America, 1650–1820
BY TREVOR BURNARD

Riotous Flesh: Women, Physiology, and the Solitary Vice in Nineteenth-Century America
BY APRIL R. HAYNES

Holy Nation: The Transatlantic Quaker Ministry in an Age of Revolution
BY SARAH CRABTREE

A Hercules in the Cradle: War, Money, and the American State, 1783–1867
BY MAX M. EDLING

Frontier Seaport: Detroit's Transformation into an Atlantic Entrepôt
BY CATHERINE CANGANY

Beyond Redemption: Race, Violence, and the American South after the Civil War
BY CAROLE EMBERTON

The Republic Afloat: Law, Honor, and Citizenship in Maritime America
BY MATTHEW TAYLOR RAFFETY

Conceived in Doubt: Religion and Politics in the New American Nation
BY AMANDA PORTERFIELD